Modernization, Urbanization and Development in Latin America, 1900s–2000s

In this book, Arturo Almandoz places the major episodes of Latin America's twentieth and early twenty-first century urban history within the changing relationship between industrialization and urbanization, modernization and development. This relationship began in the early twentieth century, when industrialization and urbanization became significant in the region, and ends at the beginning of the twenty-first century, when new tensions between liberal globalization and populist nationalism challenge development in the subcontinent, much of which is still poverty-stricken

Latin America's twentieth-century modernization and development are closely related to nineteenth-century ideals of progress and civilization, and for this reason Almandoz opens with a brief review of that legacy for the different countries that are the focus of his book – Mexico, Chile, Brazil, Argentina and Venezuela – but with references to others.

He then explores the regional distortions, which resulted from the interaction between industrialization and urbanization, and how the imbalance between urbanization and the productive system helps to explain why 'take-off' was not followed by the 'drive to maturity' in Latin American countries. He suggests that the close yet troublesome relationship with the United States, the recurrence of dictatorships and autocratic regimes, and Marxist influences in many domains, are all factors that explain Latin America's stagnation and underdevelopment up to the so-called 'lost decade' of the 1980s.

He shows how Latin America's fate changed in the late twentieth and early twenty-first centuries, when neoliberal programmes, political compromise and constitutional reform dismantled the traditional model of the corporate state and centralized planning. He reveals how economic growth and social improvements have been attained by politically left-wing yet economically open-market countries while others have resumed populism and state intervention. All these trends make up the complex scenario for the new century – especially when considered against the background of vibrant metropolises that are the main actors in the book.

Arturo Almandoz is Professor at Simón Bolívar University, Caracas, Venezuela, and Professor Adjunct in Santiago's Catholic University of Chile. He has published extensively on Latin America and has taught at other universities across the region.

Planning, History and Environment Series

Editor:
Ann Rudkin, Alexandrine Press, Marcham, UK

Editorial Board:
Professor Arturo Almandoz, Universidad Simón Bolivar, Caracas, Venezuela and Pontificia Universidad Católica de Chile, Santiago, Chile
Professor Nezar AlSayyad, University of California, Berkeley, USA
Professor Scott A. Bollens, University of California, Irvine, USA
Professor Robert Bruegmann, University of Illinois at Chicago, USA
Professor Meredith Clausen, University of Washington, Seattle, USA
Professor Yasser Elsheshtawy, UAE University, Al Ain, UAE
Professor Robert Freestone, University of New South Wales, Sydney, Australia
Professor John R. Gold, Oxford Brookes University, Oxford, UK
Professor Sir Peter Hall, University College London, UK
Professor Michael Hebbert, University College London, UK

Selection of published titles

Planning Europe's Capital Cities: Aspects of nineteenth century development by Thomas Hall

Selling Places: The marketing and promotion of towns and cities, 1850–2000 by Stephen V. Ward

The Australian Metropolis: A planning history edited by Stephen Hamnett and Robert Freestone

Utopian England: Community experiments 1900–1945 by Dennis Hardy

Urban Planning in a Changing World: The twentieth century experience edited by Robert Freestone

Twentieth-Century Suburbs: A morphological approach by J.W.R. Whitehand and C.M.H. Carr

Council Housing and Culture: The history of a social experiment by Alison Ravetz

Planning Latin America's Capital Cities, 1850–1950 edited by Arturo Almandoz

Exporting American Architecture, 1870–2000 by Jeffrey W. Cody

The Making and Selling of Post-Mao Beijing by Anne-Marie Broudehoux

Planning Middle Eastern Cities: An urban kaleidoscope in a globalizing world edited by Yasser Elsheshtawy

Globalizing Taipei: The political economy of spatial development edited by Reginald Yin-Wang Kwok

New Urbanism and American Planning: The conflict of cultures by Emily Talen

Remaking Chinese Urban Form: Modernity, scarcity and space, 1949–2005 by Duanfang Lu

Planning Twentieth Century Capital Cities edited by David L.A. Gordon

Planning the Megacity: Jakarta in the twentieth century by Christopher Silver

Designing Australia's Cities: Culture, commerce and the city beautiful, 1900–1930 by Robert Freestone

Ordinary Places, Extraordinary Events: Citizenship, democracy and urban space in Latin America edited by Clara Irazábal

The Evolving Arab City: Tradition, modernity and urban development edited by Yasser Elsheshtawy

Stockholm: The making of a metropolis by Thomas Hall

Dubai: Behind an urban spectacle by Yasser Elsheshtawy **(paperback 2013)**

Capital Cities in the Aftermath of Empires: Planning in central and southeastern Europe edited by Emily Gunzburger Makaš and Tanja Damljanović Conley

Lessons in Post-War Reconstruction: Case studies from Lebanon in the aftermath of the 2006 war edited by Howayda Al-Harithy

Orienting Istanbul: Cultural capital of Europe? edited by Deniz Göktürk, Levent Soysal and İpek Türeli

Olympic Cities: City agendas, planning and the world's games 1896–2016, 2nd edition edited by John R. Gold and Margaret M. Gold

The Making of Hong Kong: From vertical to volumetric by Barrie Shelton, Justyna Karakiewicz and Thomas Kvan **(paperback 2014)**

Urban Coding and Planning edited by Stephen Marshall

Planning Asian Cities: Risks and resilience edited by Stephen Hamnett and Dean Forbes **(paperback 2013)**

Staging the New Berlin: Place marketing and the politics of reinvention post-1989 by Claire Colomb

City and Soul in Divided Societies by Scott A. Bollens

Learning from the Japan City: Looking East in urban design, 2nd edition by Barrie Shelton

The Urban Wisdom of Jane Jacobs edited by Sonia Hirt with Diane Zahm **(paperback 2014)**

Of Planting and Planning: The making of British colonial cities, 2nd edition by Robert Home

Healthy City Planning: Global health equity from neighbourhood to nation by Jason Corburn

Good Cities, Better Lives: How Europe discovered the lost art of urbanism by Peter Hall

The Planning Imagination: Peter Hall and the study of urban and regional planning edited by Mark Tewdwr-Jones, Nicholas Phelps and Robert Freestone

Garden Cities of Tomorrow? A new future for cottage estates by Martin Crookston

Sociable Cities: The 21st-century reinvention of the Garden City by Peter Hall and Colin Ward

Modernization, Urbanization and Development in Latin America, 1900s–2000s by Arturo Almandoz

Modernization, Urbanization and Development in Latin America, 1900s–2000s

Arturo Almandoz

LONDON AND NEW YORK

First published 2015
by Routledge
2 Park Square, Milton Park, Abingdon, Oxon OX14 4RN

and by Routledge
711 Third Avenue, New York, NY 10017

First issued in paperback 2017

Routledge is an imprint of the Taylor & Francis Group, an informa business

© 2015 Arturo Almandoz

This book was commissioned and edited by Alexandrine Press, Marcham, Oxfordshire

The right of the authors has been asserted in accordance with sections 77 and 78 of the Copyright, Designs and Patents Act 1988.

All rights reserved. No part of this book may be reprinted or reproduced or utilized in any form or by any electronic, mechanical or other means, now known or hereafter invented, including photocopying and recording, or in any information storage or retrieval system, without permission in writing from the publishers.

The publisher makes no representation, express or implied, with regard to the accuracy of the information contained in this book and cannot accept any legal responsibility or liability for any errors or omissions that may be made.

Trademark notice: Product or corporate names may be trademarks or registered trademarks, and are used only for identification and explanation without intent to infringe.

British Library Cataloguing in Publication Data
A catalogue record of this book is available from the British Library

Library of Congress Cataloging in Publication Data
　Almandoz Marte, Arturo, 1960– author.
　　Modernization, urbanization and development in Latin America, 1900s-2000s / Arturo Almandoz.
　　　pages cm. — (Planning, history and environment series)
　　Includes bibliographical references and index.
　　　1. Economic development — Latin America — History — 20th century. 2. Urbanization — Latin America — History — 20th century. 3. Diffusion of innovations — Latin America — History — 20th century. I. Title.
　HD78.A46 2014
　338.98—dc23
　　　　　　　　　　　　　　　　　　　　　　　　　　　　　　　　　　　　　2014016225

ISBN 13: 978-1-138-49050-5 (pbk)
ISBN 13: 978-0-415-52152-9 (hbk)

Typeset in Aldine and Swiss by PNR Design, Didcot

Contents

Prologue	vii
Preface	xi
Acknowledgements	xv

1 Introduction — 1
  Industrialization and Urbanization, Modernization and Development — 1
  On Urban Cultural History and Latin America's Overviews — 4
  Approach and Structure of the Book — 8

2 Nineteenth-Century Antecedents — 14
  Postcolonial Changes — 14
  Civilization and Barbarism — 17
  European Godfathers — 21
  Conservatives and Liberals, Oligarchies and Bourgeoisies — 24
  From Postcolonial to Bourgeois Cities — 34

3 From *Arielismo* to World War I — 39
  Overshadowed by the Colossus — 39
  Arielismo, Modernism and Belle Époque — 42
  From Dictatorial *Pax* to Democracy — 47
  The Centenary's Urban Agenda — 53

4 Good Neighbourhood, *Masificación* and Urbanism — 63
  From Caliban to Prospero — 63
  Towards Welfare States, Corporatism and Citizenship — 66
  Mass Metropolises — 70
  Between Vanguards and Social Sciences — 74
  Urban Reforms and the Emergence of *Urbanismo* — 78

5	**Developmentalism, Modernism and Planning**	87
	Industrialization, Urbanization and Development	87
	Fifty Years in Five	90
	Asynchronies in Urbanization and Modernization	96
	From Academicism to Functional Modernism	99
	Between *Urbanismo* and Planning, City and Region	106
6	**Between Cold War and Third World**	110
	Revolution and Alliance in the Backyard	110
	AFP, Coup and Communism	113
	Guerrillas, Anti-Imperialism and Revolution	118
	The Failure of Industrialization and the Distortions of Urbanization	123
	From *Vecindades* to Shantytowns	127
	Central Planning and Regional Development	132
7	**Dismantling a Model**	138
	From the Oil Crisis to the Lost Decade	138
	Between New Right and Neoliberalism	144
	National Packages and Prescriptions	147
	The Completion of Urbanization: From Demography to Globalization	155
8	**New Century and Old Demons**	163
	Post-Liberalism and Neo-Populism	163
	Incomplete Reforms	166
	Poverty Alleviation and Fragmented Metropolises	172
	Trends of the 2000s	179

Appendices	189
Initials and Acronyms	189
Dramatis Personae	191
Table 1: Urban and rural population of Latin American countries, 1955–2010 in thousands	204
Table 2: Urbanization, growth and level of transition, 1950–2010	207
Table 3: Human Development Index (HDI), 1980–2011	208
References	209
Index	234

Prologue

... much of yesterday is still with us. That's another reason for wanting to understand the yesterday's world.

Jared Diamond, *The World Until Yesterday* (2012)

Arturo Almandoz has transformed his personal journey through the urban cultural history of Latin America into a comprehensive narration of the transformation of nations and their major cities. This sometimes intimate approach turns an account of macro-structured processes into a sum of subtly highlighted details.

The author moves us towards a reading of urban modernization and how it has been shaped by his experience in research and teaching. His route through various Latin American classrooms delivers this respectful and authentic essence of each country and society's processes.

One can imagine Arturo Almandoz wandering through Latin American history with the pleasure of a *flâneur*, the rigour of a *new historian* and the eye of an *urbanista* – a history where the political, economic and social confluences that articulated the basis of regional societies can be recognized in their diversity.

In a region that has always been in search of its identity and that has been the result of interactive influences, this panoramic view recognizes the most structured transformations. These are not necessarily linear or continuous processes, but are identified as the transforming logics of the metamorphosis in towns, cities and metropolises.

Modernizing changes driven by the ideals of development and globalization are identified both in their similarities and differences. The common pursuit of progress has been strongly linked to technological advances and wealth, first following European and later American patterns.

From their Hispanic foundation, cities and societies were sensitive to foreign models, constructing their environment with imported elements and models. The force of transformation and the ambition to strengthen the republics influenced the configuration of cities that we know today. The centennial celebration resulted in the common pursuit of constructing republican identity through symbols, buildings and monuments.

The elitist societies of centenary republics were manifest in urban projects that reflected an exclusivity, which is now part of our cultural capital. However, the recent bicentennial commemorations have seen a wide spectrum of proposals and expectations at various scales with a more democratic approach. This time the focus has been placed not on the monumental, but on public works of high appeal and value at a local level.

This recognition is very important when considering how globalization has helped to produce homogeneous urban spaces with global artefacts as new symbols of economic development and individual aspiration. While the basis of today's unequal societies was established by the convergence of economic and political power of elites, the emergence of the bourgeoisie and middle class, notwithstanding the relegation of the poorest in many cases, has created a new scenario for transformation.

The evolution of economic models and the role of the State are common factors in the various cases presented. These conditions are today being challenged where citizens' movements around the world, and particularly in the Latin American region, are questioning the predominance of the current models. The nature of these societies, mostly configured after neoliberal models – the Consensus of Washington – are reflected in the cities and the quality of life of their inhabitants. Presently there is discussion about the role of the State and its responsibility in safeguarding guarantees for quality of life and development opportunities.

Citizens seem more aware that their futures are conditioned by the type of urbanization in which they live. There is increased discontent due to the spatial inequities that reflect the socioeconomic inequalities which have existed since the beginning of the republics, but which have increased in recent decades.

With the understanding that Latin America is the most urbanized continent of the Third World, it is important to recognize and study the various urban phenomena that are occurring. This recognition can be a contribution to the construction of her own identity, as it can be for regions and nations that are beginning to face more accelerated urbanization processes.

This journey through history will appeal to all lovers of cities and the political and social evolutions that have determined them, to those interested in regional and collective construction of knowledge, but especially to *urbanistas* and urban planners. Almandoz's historical review, along with opening up a rethinking the past, gives us some clues that were present at the birth and development of the discipline of *urbanismo* and urban planning.

Established on traditional knowledge of Anglo-Saxon schools, *urbanismo* and town planning have had particular developments in the region. As can be seen in this text, the foundations of urban planning as State action was confirmed in the first quarter of the twentieth century. These initiatives were affected by the rotation after the First World War and especially after the Second World War, when the American way of life had a profound influence.

Thus, this multidimensional window that Almandoz presents can be seen as a platform for the discussion of this discipline. Where current urban situations have their conceptual foundations underpinned decades ago, requiring an innovative approach, but one that is conscious and informed. We can admit that one of the main lessons from this book is that watching the transformation of cities may help us to understand the overall context in which we live.

Roberto Moris
Instituto de Estudios Urbanos y Territoriales
Pontificia Universidad Católica de Chile

Preface

To Anthony Sutcliffe (1942–2011),
who encouraged me to face panoramic and comparative work

Every book has a personal story that is often, I believe, the best way to start presenting it to the reader and introducing its genesis. During my years at London's Architectural Association, from 1993 to 1996, a first approach to the subject of modernization and urbanization was shaped in my doctoral research on the transfer of town planning models and urban culture to Caracas. Intertwining the processes of national modernization, urban growth and city sprawl with the emergence of *urbanismo* or town planning as a discipline, the thesis ranged from Antonio Guzmán Blanco's liberal reforms during the so-called *guzmanato* (1870–1888) to the Venezuelan capital's first urban plan or 'plan Rotival' (1939), named after the French engineer who was invited by the city government to coordinate it.[1] The progress of Caracas and Venezuela was relatively sluggish and insignificant by comparison with fascinating enterprises of national modernization and urban surgery undertaken by other Latin American states during the same period. However, setting the former in perspective against the continental background was the first opportunity for me to realize that the historical agenda of modernization, urbanization and planning configured a vast canvas waiting for comparative and panoramic elaboration.

An opportunity for that enlargement came with the invitation from Professor Anthony Sutcliffe – former Editor of Routledge's Planning, History and Environment series – to produce a volume on the subject of the book about Caracas, but on a continental scale. The result was the review of nine cases in *Planning Latin America's Capital Cities, 1850–1950* (2002, 2010), where two introductory chapters allowed me to sketch the transformation of post-colonial towns into bourgeois cities and, later on, into large metropolises. Urban growth and sprawl is traced there in parallel with the emergence of a territorial agenda of renewal, sanitation and communication that, by the 1920s and 1930s, matured as an academic and professional *urbanismo*, on the eve of the arrival of CIAM-inspired functionalism by the end of World War II (Almandoz, 2010*a*). Although the book focuses on city projects and the emergence of planning as a discipline in Latin American capitals, it was another opportunity to trace the conversion of positivistic ideals, such as order, progress and civilization, into twentieth-century conceptions of industrialization, urbanization, modernization and, eventually, development. It was a period of fascinating metamorphosis when European powers, which were still predominant in most of the young republics until World War I, were replaced by the United States as a political gendarme and as both an economic and technological hub for Latin America as a whole.

At this time – as I participated more often in international events, presenting papers dealing with comparative episodes, and also teaching graduate courses at universities in Venezuela, Brazil, Chile, Argentina and Ecuador – my original approach to the subject was enriched by the political, economic and intellectual contextualization of Latin America and the main cases considered in my research – Argentina, Brazil, Chile, Mexico and Venezuela – although other countries and their cities are also included.[2] Conceived with an approach of *urban cultural history* – more than planning history – the teaching material resulting from those experiences has been published in Spanish by Chile's Catholic University as a volume that ranges again from the early republican period through the mid-twentieth century (Almandoz, 2013a).[3]

As the time span covered in my research[4] and courses extended and aspects beyond the transformation of cities and the consolidation of town and regional planning were incorporated, I recognized the need to set in perspective Latin America's entire process of social, economic and urban change throughout the second half of the twentieth century, when modernization gave way to other ideals of development and globalization.

Thus, on the basis of more than two decades working on related subjects, I have written this panoramic study prompted by the scarcity of up-to-date, general or comparative reviews of Latin America's modernization and development in the twentieth and early twenty-first centuries. Further, as a result of teaching students with diverse backgrounds, I am aware of the need to integrate Latin America's urban modernization within broader processes of economic, political and cultural change, as I have attempted to do in previous writings (Almandoz, 2004a; 2008a; 2009; 2013a; 2013b; 2013c). And I apologise in advance to the reader for any oversights and omissions in the following narrative which are the pitfalls faced by any author of a panoramic book.

Arturo Almandoz
Caracas–Santiago, Summer 2014

Notes

1. Supervised by Dr. Nicholas Bullock, King's College, Cambridge, the original thesis was submitted as 'European Urbanism in Caracas (1870s–1930s)', London: Architectural Association School of Architecture, Open University, 1996; it was initially published in Spanish in 1997, but the second edition is the one referred to here (Almandoz, 2006a).
2. Since the late 1990s, the conferences in which I have participated with papers and lectures drawn from this research line are countless; however, particular episodes that are directly related to a specific event are to be identified in a footnote at the beginning of the respective section. The

graduate courses were mainly designed for students of architecture, town planning, literature and history of the following universities, which I hereby thank for the opportunities: Universidad Central de Venezuela (UCV, Caracas, 1998–1999); Universidad Simón Bolívar (USB, Caracas, 2002–2005); Universidad de Los Andes (ULA, Mérida, 2003); Renvall Institute, University of Helsinki (2004); Universidad del Zulia (LUZ, Maracaibo, 2007); Universidad Federal de Bahía (UFBa, Salvador, Brazil, 2009); Pontificia Universidad Católica de Chile (PUC, Santiago, 2010–2013); Universidad Nacional del Litoral (Santa Fe, Argentina, 2011); Instituto de Altos Estudios Nacionales (IAEN, Quito, 2013).

3. As it will be indicated in footnotes, some sections of the initial chapters of this book will rely on the material produced for that related volume in Spanish (Almandoz, 2013). I am indebted to the Instituto de Estudios Urbanos Territoriales (IEUT) and Chile's Pontificia Universidad Católica (PUC) for letting me use the material published.

4. Sponsored by the Decanato de Investigación y Desarrollo (DID), Universidad Simón Bolívar (USB), Caracas, from 2011 through 2014.

Acknowledgements

In addition to countless students and colleagues from universities, especially in Latin America and Europe, who inspired me during courses and events that are mentioned in some of the book's footnotes, I would like to thank the following institutions and persons. Starting with the text, I must first recognize Santiago's Instituto de Estudios Urbanos y Territoriales (IEUT), Pontificia Universidad Católica (PUC) de Chile, for allowing me to rely on part of my recent book mentioned in the Preface; also other publications that I have referred to in the footnotes of several chapters of this book. Secondly, I want to express recognition to the Decanato de Investigación y Desarrollo (DID), Universidad Simón Bolívar (USB), Caracas, for sponsoring in technical terms the research line on Latin America's historiography and modernization from which this book is derived.

I am personally indebted to Ann Rudkin, editor of Routledge's series, Planning, History and Environment, who welcomed the idea of this book and helped me along the lengthy process of materializing it. As in previous experiences, Ann's publishing expertise has been extremely helpful in synthesizing and articulating the vast material, not to mention her invaluable dedication to making it understandable. I am also grateful to Angela Herrera – former student and now a colleague graduated as urbanist at Simon Bolívar University, Caracas – who was very competent in reviewing the bibliography and framing the tables that are included in the book's appendices. Last but not least, thanks to Macarena Ibarra, IEUT, PUC, and David Ashurst, Durham University, for their academic and personal support throughout the elaboration of the project and the manuscript.

For the graphic material included in the book, I would like to thank especially the following:

Archivo Audiovisual de Venezuela, Biblioteca Nacional, Caracas;
Archivo de Originales Sergio Larraín García Moreno (SLGM), Facultad de Arquitectura, Diseño y estudios Urbanos (FADEU), Pontificia Universidad Católica (PUC) de Chile, Santiago, especially to Paloma Parrini;
Arquivo Nacional, Rio de Janeiro;
Centro de Documentación de Arquitectura Latinoamericana (CEDODAL), Buenos Aires;

Roberto Segre's Archive, Rio de Janeiro;
El Nacional Archive, Caracas;
Andrea Rojas, Andrés Téllez, Carmen Gloria Troncoso, Juan Camilo Pardo and Ximena Arizaga, PUC, Santiago; Marco Aurelio Gómes and José Carlos Huapaya, Universidade Federal da Bahía (UFBa), Salvador, Brazil.

Arturo Almandoz
Caracas-Santiago, Summer 2014

Chapter 1

Introduction

A 'fictitious' appraisal of capital dominates this new moment that features 'market' and 'globalization' as guidelines. This is perhaps the contemporary nickname of the old colonial curse: to build the country and then to globalize it, as it was to civilize and modernize it in the past.
Antonio Carlos Robert Moraes, Território e história no Brasil (2004)

Industrialization and Urbanization, Modernization and Development

The Urban Scale

Partly as a result of my background as urbanist – and partly as a precaution against becoming entangled in a notion that has been addressed from so many perspectives – this chapter departs from the mid-twentieth-century conception, based on functionalist sociology, according to which *modernization* is closely linked to industrialization and urbanization. In one of the classic formulations of the theory, in the 1950s Gideon Sjoberg established that, after the 'folk' or popular stage, followed by the 'feudal' or urban, the 'modern industrial city is associated with a third level of complexity in human organization, a level characterized by mass literacy, a fluid class system and, most importantly, the tremendous technological breakthrough to new sources of inanimate energy that produced and still sustains the industrial revolution' (Sjoberg, 1973, p. 19).[1] On an urban scale, industrial modernity was characterized by an expansion of the clearly-defined and community-based structure of traditional cities, greater territorial mobility made possible by mechanical means of communication, along with a more fluent social mobility facilitated by functional specialization of production, mass education and far-reaching media.

Sjoberg's characterization thus coincided, to a large extent, with previous approaches to social change and modernization in the industrial era – from Ferdinand Tönnies's *Gemeinschaft* and *Gesselschaft* antinomy to the Chicago School's analysis of the spatial, functional and cultural segregation of the industrial metropolis.[2] Going beyond the urban domain, and into the 1950s and 1960s, the connection between industrialization, urbanization and modernization was also assumed, following an almost causal derivation, by Kingsley Davis and Leonard Reissman (1921–1975). Their approaches were from the standpoints of patterns associated with demographic transition and way of life, respectively, and relied on the examples of the North Atlantic countries that had industrialized in the nineteenth century (Davis, 1973; Reissman, 1964). The direct relationship between the three processes was maintained by countless others whose writings proliferated in different contexts and disciplines, following a reasoning that has been summarized by Savage and Warde in the following terms:

> Modernisation theory maintained that places became more alike as industrialisation and urbanisation developed. Ways of life, culture and politics would become more homogeneous with a more developed division of labour, centralisation of state functions and the growth of the mass media. As a consequence, political cleavages typical of early modern and pre-industrial societies, those based on religion, region, clan or ethnic group, would subside and industrial divisions, essentially of class, would replace them. (Savage and Warde, 1993, p. 175)

Apart from the demographic transition identified by Davis – according to which industrial countries tended to stabilize their urbanization at 75–80 per cent, following an S-shaped curve developed over more than a century – the direct relationship of urbanization with modernization, and later with development, came through an assumption more or less explicit in different approaches, namely that 'urban areas and the transport corridors between them are the focus of dynamic change'. As it has been pointed out by Potter and Lloyd-Evans, here lies another key for conceiving modernization, and eventually development, as a 'temporal-spatial process' by which modernity – assumed as a *stage* and not a process – is spread throughout space and territory. The way this modernity or development is diffused has been subject to different interpretations, but most of them coincide around the 'top-down paradigm' according to which major cities are the engines of that dissemination within a national territory and society (Potter and Lloyd-Evans, 1998, pp. 37–38).

From National to International Challenges

The approach of Walt Whitman Rostow in *The Stages of Economic Growth. A Non-communist Manifesto* (1960) – to be discussed later (see Chapter 5) – was perhaps the best known formulation, on a national scale, of that process of industry-driven and city-based modernization. In Rostow's work the capitalist system is also assumed to be the expression of modernity or, more precisely, of the economic development that was the dominant paradigm after World War II, when the theory of modernization achieved its greatest influence (Weiner, 1966), including in Latin America, as we shall see. But not everybody was so elated with the prospect: in the midst of the developmental euphoria of post-war decades, the cautious view of the Swedish economist Gunnar Myrdal maintained that 'capitalist development is inevitably marked by deepening regional and personal income and welfare inequalities', which produced 'backwash effects' on the distribution of benefits supposedly spread by capitalist modernization (Potter and Lloyd-Evans, 1998, p. 38; see also Myrdal, 1957).

Part of Myrdal's pessimistic interpretation was applicable to Latin America in spite of the subcontinent's progressive image during the mid-twentieth century. Indeed, favoured by Franklin D. Roosevelt's 'Good Neighbour' policy towards the region in the early 1940s, and especially after World War II, most of Latin America became the experimental land of Import Substitution Industrialization (ISI) and economic *desarrollismo*, boosted by political nationalism and artistic *modernismos* (see Chapter 4). Regarded as promising examples of *developing* countries – a category that seemed to have great resonance until the 1960s – most of Latin America's industrializing societies were supposed to be exponents of the theory of modernization, as it was explained by developmental economics and functionalist sociology. This was at the same time as the agenda of social and historical studies about Latin America's urbanization and cities was shaped with the sponsorship of the United States. It comprised a literature imbued with those theories of industrialization and urbanization, modernization and development, from Gino Germani (1969) to Philip Hauser (1967), among others. This literature seemed to show that Latin America's developing nations were on the route to urbanization and industrialization, but at the same time warned that they were actually suffering from profound distortions when compared with the successful experiences of modernization in Europe, North America and other parts of the world. As we shall see in Chapter 6, the failure of capitalist-inspired modernity as a paradigm would give way to Marxist-oriented studies of urbanization and underdevelopment that put aside ideas of modernization and focused instead on reviewing the centre-periphery antinomy and *dependence* as key factors to explain Latin America's sluggish inclusion within international circuits (Palma, 1978; Almandoz, 2008a, pp. 163–168). As the founder of Latin America's very influential Theory of Dependence, in *Capitalism and Underdevelopment in Latin America* (1967) André Gunder Frank arrived at a thesis that could be said to be the opposite to Rostow's: developed countries became so at the expense of other nations' underdevelopment (Frank, 1967, 1982).

Third World Urbanization and Globalization

Although it was not sufficiently stressed at the time by Manuel Castells, Aníbal Quijano and other analysts of the so-called 'dependent urbanization' in the region, much of the hindrance to Latin America's path towards development was caused by urbanization patterns associated with what came to be known as the Third World syndrome (Castells, 1973; Quijano, 1977). Instead of the process for early-industrialized countries, which Davis characterized as an S-shaped curve extending over more than a century, the urbanization of developing nations was typified by a sudden and steady increase from the 1930s, and especially after 1945, mainly caused by rural-urban migrations (Drakakis-Smith, 1990, pp. 1–10). It was not accompanied by an industrial revolution – that had historically exerted a 'pull' effect on cities – but rather by an abandonment of the countryside that could be seen as a 'push' force. In addition to the fact that absolute numbers involved in Third World urbanization are larger than those of industrialized societies, the relative improvements in infrastructure, services and welfare standards in urban areas explain that, in relation to demographic transition, 'Third World cities exemplify *par excellence* the combination of pre-industrial fertility with post-industrial mortality' (Potter and Lloyd-Evans, 1998, p. 12; see also Drakakis-Smith, 1990, pp. 1–10).

Instead of continuing here with a series of problems that will be addressed in later chapters, what is important in this introduction is to show that the way countries industrialized and urbanized is at the core of their modernization and, especially after the 1960s, their development. The past relationship between industrialization and urbanization is therefore related to today's configuration of the First and Third Worlds, though these domains have been questioned, especially after the disintegration of the Soviet Union and the Iron Curtain that originally informed the Second World.[3] At the same time, it is necessary to understand that the processes of industrialization and urbanization, modernization and development are closely linked in *historical* terms – a perspective that is often missed in studies that have tended to be 'static', as it has been pointed out in the literature (Savage and Warde, 1993, p. 41; Potter and Lloyd-Evans, 1998, p. 28).

This is the case with the few existing studies of globalization in Latin America, with the notable exception of Carlos de Mattos (2010) who will provide input to several of the chapters which follow. For the most part, case studies have been based on short-term comparisons between cities, relegating the continental and historical background that is essential for a better understanding of today's metropolitan hierarchy and rationale (see, for example, Borja, 2007; Sassen, 2007). As a key to that pending exploration, the historical continuity of globalization in terms of the consideration of foreign capital as a fetish has been summarized by the Brazilian geographer Antonio Carlos Robert Moraes: 'A "fictitious" appraisal of capital dominates this new moment that features "market" and "globalization" as guidelines. This is perhaps the contemporary nickname of the old colonial curse: to build the country and then to globalize it, as it was to civilize and modernize it in the past' (Moraes, 2004, p. 142).[4]

So – aided by an urban historiography panorama that I intended to survey during my postdoctoral research – this book assumes a general and comparative standpoint, both in historical and territorial terms, which should enable us to trace a long-term vision of Latin America's processes of urbanization and development throughout the twentieth century (Almandoz, 2008*b*, pp. 145–181).[5] And such an attempt will require the incorporation of political, social and cultural variables that allow us to understand Latin America's eventful and unique path towards development, most of it occurring within a Third World reality, but with promising changes as we move into the twenty-first century.

On Urban Cultural History and Latin America's Overviews

The conception of modernization involves different *dimensions* of urbanization as a process, including not only the demographic transition referred to above, but also the territorial distribution of population and provision of services and equipment, together with the cultural changes associated with urbanization and civilization (Caves, 2005, pp. 503–505). The last is especially relevant for this book's approach, though it does not imply that other aspects of modernization are to be neglected.

Micro-History and Panoramic Approaches

Since the 1980s, the dimensions of modernization and urbanization, with special reference to social change, cultural manifestations and forms of representation, have been combined in countless studies of the urban history of individual Latin American cities. This trend has been boosted by the diversity of sources and discourses assembled for re-creating, usually through a micro-historical approach, the social and cultural roles of different actors in a city, as well as their imaginaries and forms of expression (Sutcliffe, 1984; Burke, 2001). In fact, the incorporation of literary genres and non-specialized discourses – essay, narrative, poetry, travel chronicle, pictorial and cinematographic representation, among others – to the catalogue of traditional primary sources of urban and planning history – mainly comprised of technical and legal literature – has enhanced the documentary corpus of a new field that can be called *urban cultural history*.[6]

Besides mirroring a worldwide tendency to favour case studies of individual cities rather than addressing national or international contexts, today's abundant collection of urban and planning histories in Latin America is a tributary of a mainstream of greater scope and depth in terms of both theory and historiography. As it has been summarized by Nancy Stieber in an article on the micro-history of the modern city, cultural and social history has often put aside both the 'great narratives' and the systemic approaches, derived from Marxist structuralism or from the Annales School's *longue durée*, in order to develop more focused and micro-historical studies, in which the contingency and autonomy of cultural manifestations can be captured and stressed.

> Despite their ideological, methodological, or philosophical differences, what is apparent from the recent reformulations of the relationship between society and culture is the movement from larger totalizing systems applied at large scales of time and geography to smaller-scale investigations of the social interactions through which culture is produced. There is a preference for the concrete over the schematic, an openness to observation, and a distrust of any theoretical construction that might prove constraining. Instead of framing historical problems with long-range developmental trajectories, historians read minute, empirically observable particularities to reveal the codes, forces, and processes at work in shaping cultural forms. There is a rejection of abstraction, the general scheme or concepts through which to interpret expression, in favor of the mapping of material practices, exposing the making of culture as active agent rather than passive reflection… (Stieber, 1999, p. 383)

Diverse theoretical influences, including those referring to the New History, both in its English and French versions characterized by Peter Burke, have contributed to this apparent dispersion of urban cultural history during the final decades of the twentieth century (Burke, 2001). Further, there is the influence of Michel de Certeau's understanding of the 'operation' of historiography as one that combines 'a *place* (a recruitment, a milieu, a craft, etc.), *procedures* of analysis (a discipline) and the construction of a *text* (a literature)' (de Certeau, 1975, 2002, p. 64). Also, the work of David Harvey is especially pertinent for understanding the insertion of cultural forms and urban representation into post-modernity, since he pointed out that one of the 'shifts' after historical materialism was a 'recognition' of the importance of time and space as dimensions, manifested through the 'geographies of social action'. Vital for the 'geopolitics of capitalism', these 'organizing forces' are capable of being materialized and spatialized through the 'innumerable differences and otherness' of social and cultural forms, including cities par excellence (Harvey, 1990, p. 355).

Notwithstanding the epistemological fragmentation of urban history, after more than two decades of historical development of the field, Stieber is optimistic about superseding and synthesizing the myriad of micro-history case studies: 'We have reached the stage where we can expect an increasing harvest from the cross-fertilization that has already taken place and can perhaps even anticipate a future in which comparative studies bring into focus generalizing conceptual tools so that we can talk of the history of urbanism on the large scale again' (Stieber, 1999, p. 384). And although this book is not intended to be a history of urbanism as such, I too believe that approaches somehow panoramic and comparative are necessary in Latin America's urban cultural history, as a dialectic confirmation of the fertility and relative maturity of the field.

Jorge Hardoy, the ICAs and Beyond

Contemplating Latin American urban historiography over five decades, there are not many antecedents that stand out in terms of overviews, most of which date back to the early stages of the field in the region, and prior to the proliferation of case studies from the 1980s. As was already anticipated in relation to the academic agenda encouraged by the *desarrollismo*, Latin America's urban studies began, in the 1960s, to analyze systematically the historical, economic and sociological relationships between industrialization, urbanization and modernization, portrayed by then as a sort of 'epochal equation' (Almandoz, 2008b, pp. 157–159). Coming from developmental theories, as we have seen, the vision of the city as a catalyst of social change was present in *La urbanización en América Latina* (1962) edited by Philip M. Hauser (1967), a book resulting from an international conference held in Santiago de Chile in July 1959, under the patronage of UNESCO and the Economic Commission for Latin America and the Caribbean (ECLAC) (see Chapter 5). Without including much historical review, that book's rather sociological interpretation would be influential not only for later publications that adopted its functionalist approach – such as Walter D. Harris's *The Growth of Latin American Cities* (1971) – but also in terms of the critical reaction it prompted, which would be led by the Argentine architect Jorge E. Hardoy.

Jointly with Americans Richard Schaedel and Richard Morse,[7] among others, Hardoy organized symposia on regional urbanization in the context of the International Congresses of Americanists (ICA): Mar del Plata (1966), Stuttgart (1968), Lima (1970), Rome (1972), Mexico City (1974) and Paris (1976). The early ones dealt with Latin

America's urbanization in general and throughout different historical periods, seeking 'to facilitate a wide exchange of ideas among archaeologists, architects, anthropologists, social and art historians, as well as town planners' (Hardoy and Schaedel, 1975, p. 16). But after Lima's ICA, a central theme was set for each meeting, which reviewed the subject from pre-Columbian to contemporary times. The all-embracing perspective of colonial and republican periods was consolidated by the 1960s and 1970s in several compilations about Latin America's urbanization, some of them resulting from those events. They were completed by further editions in Spanish by Hardoy and Carlos Tobar (1969), as well as by Francisco de Solano (1978), while Hardoy (1975a), Morse (1971; 1973) and Bryan Roberts (1978), among others, published in English. As parts of those collective volumes – excepting Robert's single-authored work – some chapters of these books – usually edited by Hardoy – explored the relationship between urbanization and industrialization, modernization and development from a historical perspective, while posing issues for the contemporary interaction between those processes and how they could be addressed by Latin America's emerging historiography and urban studies (see, for example, Hardoy, 1975b).

Led by Hardoy, that body of work provided the broadest perspective regarding the historical relationship between industrialization, urbanization and modernization. Very few studies since have had such extensive scope, while the modernizing component of the equation has been replaced first by development and later by neoliberalism (Portes and Roberts, 2008) and globablization (de Mattos, 2010). Indeed it was Jorge Hardoy and David Satterthwaite who shifted this agenda towards regional development and urban centres, while Nora Clichevsky updated the demographic and economic panorama after the so-called 'lost decade' of the 1980s (Hardoy and Satterthwaite, 1986; Hardoy et al., 1981; Clichevsky, 1990) (see Chapter 7). The replacement of modernization by development, so to speak, made Latin America's approaches to urbanization more economy-oriented overall, a trend that had been favoured by the above-mentioned School of Dependence.

José Luis Romero's Cultural Forms

The monumental work of Argentine historian José Luis Romero swam against the economic tide and pioneered a culturally oriented approach to Latin American history from early colonial times. Here secular modernization resurfaced linked to its nineteenth-century antecedents, such as progress and civilization, while it was mapped and given coordinates within Western culture.[8] Stepping aside from the materialism of the School of Dependence, in *Latinoamérica, las ciudades y las ideas* (1976, 1984, Latin, the Cities and the Ideas) Romero proposed a reappraisal of the cultural dimension of urban societies, which had been disregarded by the economic determinism of Dependence-focused studies, while seeking to demonstrate the autonomy and uniqueness of cultural forms among the Europeanized cities of Latin America (Almandoz, 2013c). As it was summarized by Romero in the introduction to his classic work:

A meticulous investigation of the shaping of urban societies and their changes, of the urban cultures – different for each period in each city, and different within the latter according to social groups in epochs of intense change – has led to the results presented in this book. In the bottom, it aims at clarifying how the heteronomous development of cities plays with the autonomous one, assuming that in that game are elaborated not only the urban cultures and subcultures, but also the relationships between the rural and urban worlds. It is the latter where the ideologies become more vigorous and resurface more clearly, making evident their clash – dialectic game – with real structures. (Romero, 1976, 1984, p. 20)

Without dismissing the centre–periphery relationship that had conditioned ECLAC's and the *dependentista* interpretations, Romero thus adjusted, so to speak, the vectors among hegemony, heteronomy and autonomy, while highlighting the value of 'ideologies' that nowadays might be called 'imaginaries'. At the same time, as a counterbalance to the growing specialization of Latin America's urban historiography – much as Lewis Mumford (1961) did for North America's academia – Romero's classic innovated by incorporating cultural change into a research agenda which until then had focused on either the Dependence's economic and social processes, or changes of urban forms derived from architectural periods and categories.

Echoing Romero's approach,[9] Latin America's major metropolises – São Paulo, Mexico City, Buenos Aires – have been regarded by Argentine-Mexican Néstor García Canclini as transnational stages of a globalization that is descended from modernization. As it was recognized in *Culturas híbridas* (1990) by García Canclini, the 'multiculturalism' and 'constitutive hybridity' of modern republics is not new to Latin American intelligentsia, who had articulated it since the so-called *arielista* 1900s debate against North-American expansionism (see Chapter 3); but it was not until the 'transnationalism of the media and massive migrations' (García Canclini, 1990, pp. 11–12) that Latin America's cultural globalization was framed – and in fact consolidated more than the economic one. But the historical grounds of that regional globalization are still a pending issue in Latin American studies, as is its relation to urbanization on a panoramic scale.[10]

Approach and Structure of the Book

They are neither exclusively Iberian nor definitively Latin. By saying that they are Latin they are being opposed in bloc to the great Saxon nation, thereby indicating that in their spiritual formation not only Spain but also France, and ancient moral forces that Spain and France drew from Rome – legislation and Catholicism – have intervened…

Francisco García Calderón, *La creación de un continente* (1913)

The Notion of Latin America

There is a pending consideration that the reader may have been surprised at not finding so far, regarding the very notion of Latin America that this introduction seems to take for granted. To some extent it is so, in the sense that most of the histories of republican or contemporary Latin America referred to in this text – from those of the French Gustavo and Hélène Beyhaut and the Argentine Tulio Halperin Donghi, originally published in the 1960s, to that of the British Edwin Williamson in the early 1990s and the Montreal-based Chilean José del Pozo's in 2002 (Beyhaut and Beyhaut, 1985, pp. 1–6; Halperín, 1967, 2005, pp. 10–11; Williamson, 1992, pp. vii–viii; del Pozo, 2002, pp. 5–9) – make use of that notion without any preamble, apart from the recognition of the diverse nationalities that are being put together. However, it is important to précis our understanding of what constitutes Latin America, particularly given the book's cultural approach to urban history.

The notion relies, firstly, on the geographical determination of Latin American as the territory south of the Grande or Bravo River, on the frontier between the USA and Mexico, extending down to the Southern Cone. From an historical perspective, this book's understanding of the region also relies on the aggregation of the former Hispanic and Portuguese colonies after their independence in the first decades of the nineteenth century, as will be summarized in the section on postcolonial changes in Chapter 2.

If one pursues that historical conception, and also considers their analogous colonial past, the eventual integration of the former dominions of Spain and Portugal into one republican bloc with convergent economic, political and cultural interests, different from the USA and Canada, might lead to the possible denomination of *Iberian* America. This was in fact the case by the late nineteenth century, when the issue was catalysed by the Pan American conferences organized since 1889, while the term was allegedly introduced by the French academic L.M. Tisserand in 1861 (García Calderón, 1979, pp. 242–243).[11] However, the reasons for putting aside this Iberian denomination of the colonies were spelt out in the early twentieth century by, among others, Peruvian diplomat and man of letters Francisco García Calderón in his *La creación de un continente* (1913, The Creation of a Continent). He participated in such political and intellectual debates at the time when *Latin America* began to prevail as a continental designation worldwide:

> They are neither exclusively Iberian nor definitively Latin. By saying that they are Latin they are being opposed in bloc to the great Saxon nation, thereby indicating that in their spiritual formation not only Spain but also France, and ancient moral forces that Spain and France drew from Rome – legislation and Catholicism – have intervened. America's Latinism is not a direct importation from classical influences. Spain and Portugal stamped it with the national hallmark and weakened its ancient virtue. (García Calderón, 1979, p. 244)

Shared by many writers of the 1900s *arielismo* and *modernismo*, as we shall see in Chapters 2 and 3, García Calderón's interpretation of the subcontinent's Latin roots is especially significant because of its acknowledgement of France's influence in thinking and arts, along with Italy's, through immigration and customs. Since those times when the US established the name of the continent for itself – after the original appropriation of its independence – the scene has, of course, changed politically and economically.

On the one hand, from within the US, the resonance of *Latin* America is nowadays strongly associated with the expanding Latino culture, especially in contrast to the Anglo-Saxon one that originally informed that country. On the other hand, partly as a legacy of that historical dispute with the US over the American denomination, later fuelled by political and economic conflicts, the Latin adjective has often been invoked, south of the Rio Grande, in the recurrent confrontation with the Anglo-Saxon Caliban looming in the North, whose faces, meanings and names have changed throughout the period encompassed in this book (see Chapters 4 and 8, for instance).

Geographical and Cultural Scope

It is a reality anyway that the denomination of Latin America has definitely been accepted since the early twentieth century, and remains fundamental to understanding this book's approach regarding the cultural heritage and presence in the New World of countries like France and Italy, in addition to the historic legacy of the former Iberian metropolises. Such recognition of the Latin descent will not imply, however, a special linguistic or cultural consideration of the French Caribbean colonies of Guadalupe and Martinique – a criterion that might lead us to also include Canada's French-speaking Quebec – nor will it exclude occasional references to Trinidad, Guyana or Surinam in demographic terms.

I am aware that there are discussions about this Latin definition in the Caribbean basin, but following the majority of the sources consulted, this book, in spite of claiming to have a cultural historical approach, does not consider literature of the Caribbean. In this respect, the book is only a panoramic history of Latin America – and not of the Caribbean, though Cuba and Puerto Rico, as former Spanish colonies, will have an occasional presence. And in addition to countless case studies, there are some cultural and historical studies that the reader may consult in (see, for example, Knight, 1990; Gerard, 1981). Besides such cultural considerations about the Caribbean, as Silva Aristiguieta points out in the introduction to his *Breve historia de América Latina* (2001, p. 18), the linguistic approach is a very complicated and slippery one, given that, in addition to major European languages alive in Latin America, there is also a great variety of native languages and dialects that were historically present and are still spoken.

Last but not least in relation to my approach to Latin America, it is important to remind the reader that most of the book's narrative is to refer to general or panoramic changes, treated from a comparative perspective. Such a standpoint will mainly address the cases of Argentina, Brazil, Chile, Mexico and Venezuela, with references to Colombia, Cuba and Peru in some episodes, while other countries of the region will remain in the background.

Episodes and Chapters

This book places the major episodes of Latin America's urban history within the changing relationship between industrialization and urbanization, modernization and development. This relationship began in the early twentieth century, when the momentum among the first two processes became significant in countries of the Southern Cone, and ends at the beginning of the twenty-first century, when a new tension between liberal globalization and populist nationalism challenges the whole notion of development in the subcontinent, much of which is still poverty stricken. Even though the book relies on demographic and economic changes that have been previously considered in the national and urban analyses referred to in this introduction, it frames that agenda of secular modernization and development within political, intellectual and literary discourses that accompanied those processes – an orientation that is indebted to pioneers of Latin America's urban cultural history in different disciplines, from Jean Franco (1967) and Ángel Rama (1984) in cultural studies, to Richard Morse (1973; 1982) and the above-mentioned Hardoy and Romero in urban history.

As has already been pointed out, Latin America's twentieth-century modernization and development are – perhaps more strongly than in other parts of today's Third World – closely related to nineteenth-century ideals of progress and civilization, which most of the young republics embraced amidst liberal reforms and positivistic renewal. This is why the book opens with a brief review of that legacy for the different countries that provide exemplars – Mexico, Chile, Brazil, Argentina and Venezuela – with incidental references to others. After the 1860s it was also in those countries that the transformation of the so-called 'bourgeois cities' took place – a category borrowed from Romero that will allow us to connect and contrast with urban changes prior to the *masificación* that followed World War I and the rural-urban migration (Romero, 1984, pp. 247–318, 319–389; Amandoz, 2013d) (see Chapter 4).

In accordance with what actually happened in Latin America during most of the twentieth century, and especially after World War II, a central part of the book explores the regional distortions of the theoretical conception, drawn from functionalist sociology, according to which modernization resulted from the interaction between industrialization and urbanization, as had occurred in Western Europe and North America from the nineteenth century. In terms of W.W. Rostow's famous stages of development – which inspired the Kennedy administration's Alliance for Progress in the early 1960s and was very popular among Latin America's academic and political elites until the 1970s – the book aims to illustrate how the imbalance between urbanization and the productive system helps to explain the fact that major Latin American countries' 'take-off' was not followed by the 'drive to maturity' (Rostow, 1960, 1990) (see Chapter 5).

Along with the close yet troublesome relationship with the United States, beginning with the 1900s *arielismo* of Latin politicians and intellectuals against the Colossus's expansionism, the recurrence of dictatorships and autocratic regimes, as well as Marxist influences in many domains, especially after Cuba's 1959 Revolution – which fuelled urban and rural guerrilla movements, social sciences and populism – hyper-urbanization and the failure of mid-century modernization are all factors put forward to explain Latin America's stagnation and underdevelopment up to the so-called 'lost decade' of the 1980s (see Chapters 6 and 7).

This negative picture should not detract from the fact that, in spite of its shortcomings, Latin America's modernization project witnessed the education of much of the middle and working classes, and a rebalancing of gender relations in societies which were strongly patriarchal until the mid-twentieth century. Among other achievements that cannot be disregarded, the book highlights the constitutional reforms and administrative decentralization that, from the late 1980s, gave greater autonomy to local governments in countries like Brazil, Venezuela and Colombia, and how with stronger local powers, municipal governments have assumed new roles in national politics, though their financial restrictions remain a chronic problem (see Chapters 7 and 8).

As the book's last part shows, Latin America's fate started to change in the late twentieth century and early twenty-first, when neoliberal programmes – first introduced in Pinochet's Chile and then in other countries from the 1990s, under the so-called Washington Consensus – and processes of political compromise and constitutional reform dismantled the traditional model of the corporate state and centralized planning. Economic growth and social improvements have also been attained by politically Left-wing yet economically open-market countries led by Brazil, whereas others, epitomized by Bolivarian Venezuela, seconded by Argentina, resume populism, state intervention and other practices deeply rooted in the region. In spite of their different paths, some progress seems to have been attained regarding most of the countries' reduction of poverty and the increase in literacy, but urban criminality and deficient services remain all too common. All these trends make up the complex scenario for the new century – especially when considered against the background of vibrant metropolises that are to be the main actors in the diverse processes intertwined in the book.

Notes

1. The historical review of the first stages according to different aspects and institutions is in Sjoberg (1965).
2. Among many examples that cannot be referred to here, see the classic examples of Tönnies (1887, 1965) and Park and Burgess (1925, 1984).
3. As has been stressed by Potter and Lloyd-Evans (1998, pp. 9–12)
4. Unless otherwise indicated, all translations are mine.
5. An English version of that historical background in relation to the discipline of urbanism can be found in Almandoz (2006b). These publications were drawn from the author's postdoctoral research on the emergence of Latin America's urban historiography, developed between 2003 and 2004, at the Centro de Investigaciones Posdoctorales (CIPOST), Facultad de Ciencias Sociales y Humanidades (FACES), Universidad Central de Venezuela (UCV).
6. I have tried to characterize and give examples of this field in Almandoz (2008c); see also Almandoz (2008b, pp. 182–235).
7. Trained as an architect in Argentina, Hardoy received a PhD in city and regional planning from Harvard University, which made him familiar with the North American academia and professional milieu. By the time of these events and collective publications, Richard Morse was Professor at the Department of History, Yale University; Richard Schaedel was Professor at the Department of Anthropology, University of Texas, Austin.
8. This attempt dates back to the author's early works; see for instance Romero (1953, 2004).

9. A review of Romero's legacy and influence in Latin America's urban historiography can be seen in Burucúa *et al.* (2013).
10. Beyond the countless case studies that cannot be identified here, cultural expressions of globalization from a comparative perspective have been elaborated by, for instance, Téllez (1993); Martín-Barbero (2010); García Canclini (2010).
11. As to the coinage of the denomination, see for instance Silva Aristiguieta (2001, p. 17).

Chapter 2

Nineteenth-Century Antecedents[1]

Postcolonial Changes

By the 1820s most Hispanic American nations had achieved independence and 1830 saw the disintegration of Gran Colombia and the birth of Ecuador, Nueva Granada and Venezuela as independent states. This was followed in 1838 by the separation of Central American republics, which completed a map that reproduced, to a large extent, the boundaries established by the Bourbon reforms of the late eighteenth century. Although it did not suffer Hispanic America's Balkanization, Brazil was influenced by the internal weaknesses inherent in the vast territory and Portugal's unarticulated yet controlled colonization. After hosting the Lusitanian court during the Napoleonic wars, it emerged as a relatively integrated political and economic bloc. These developments underpinned the country's comparatively smooth transition from Monarchy (1822–1831) and Empire (1831–1889) to Republic.

Critical of Brazil's colonization by Portugal, which he saw as scarred by a greedy exploitation of natural resources, Paulo Prado, in his classic and controversial essay, *Retrato do Brasil. Ensaio sobre a tristeza brasileira* (Portrayal of Brazil. An Essay about Brazilian Sadness) (1928), bemoaned the colonial era which ended in 1822, arguing that:

> Three centuries had brought the country into that pitiful situation. A century after its independence, the colony was a shapeless body of mere vegetative life, barely maintained by the tenuous bonds of language and worship. (Prado, 1928, 2000, p. 75)

Despite this gloomy view, following the political and economic upheavals of the mid-nineteenth century, Latin America saw the development of diverse exporting economies, except – as Prado (1928, 2000, p. 92) pointed out – in the countries led to independence by Simón Bolívar. Cattle rearing in Argentina and Uruguay, mining in Chile and Mexico, and coffee growing in Brazil allowed the new states to benefit from the competitiveness of their products in international markets, no longer fettered by colonial ties, while Cuba's sugar production soared as colonial bonds to Spain weakened.[2] Boosted by European capital investment and immigration from the 1860s onwards, commercial prosperity in some republics brought about regional differences in development across the continent: on the one hand, the non-tropical Atlantic shore and Chile became the leaders of the 'era of economic expansion' that lasted until World War I; on the other hand, the remaining Andean countries were of little interest to international capitalistic blocs, especially Britain, whose investments in that region were 'minimal' until the end of the nineteenth century (Rippy, 1959, pp. 12, 116; Griffin, 1961, pp. 25, 88–89, 126).

The relative prosperity of the countries on the Atlantic seaboard was already evident to the Argentine Miguel Cané during his journey across South America in the early 1880s; to him they seemed 'to have felt more rapidly and intensely' the influence of Europe, 'undoubted source of all material progress', so that they could 'get rid of the colonial hindrance' (Cané, 1883, 1942, p. 11). By contrast, on the other side of the continent, M.G. Mulhall, the author of *The English in South America* (1878), summarized a pessimistic prospect for the small British capital investment in Venezuela, Bolivia, Nueva Granada and Ecuador: 'The amount of British capital in these 4 republics is trifling and consists almost wholly of loans raised in England, a great portion of which may be considered as so much money lost' (Mulhall, 1878, p. 530).

Ruralization and Recuperation

Despite economic diversification and political independence, there were no major changes in the urban geography of Latin America until the second half of the nineteenth century. Since the 1750s, there had been an obscure period of urban stagnation, whose gloomiest phase coincided with the peak of civil wars that devastated some new republics in the early years of independence. Among other effects, the volatile political climate brought about a process of decentralization and 'ruralization' of the backward societies, which caused further stagnation, accentuated by the disarticulation of infrastructure and interurban networks (Morse, 1975, pp. 266–268).

From the 1860s onwards, demographic urban changes started to be noticeable both in the structure of new centres and the traditional capitals. In relation to the former, as Hardoy summarized, 'the building of railroads and the opening up of new lands, the exploitation of coal and mineral resources, and the administrative need of new political subdivisions motivated the construction of thousands of new cities and towns'. Brazil's Belo Horizonte and Argentina's La Plata became the emblematic examples of Frenchified design applied to the imposing layout of new provincial capitals. But these were exceptional new settlements: 'The majority of new cities founded, however, were simple service centres and transportation hubs for shipment of agricultural products to the ports' (Hardoy, 1975*b*, p. 50).

With a total population of 30 million by 1850, the density of Latin America barely reached 1.5 inhabitants per square kilometre, while the capitals' populations were only 3.5 per cent of the rural ones. However, the national capitals' 'primacy dip' – which had plunged their growth rates below national growth during the previous decades – had ended by the middle of the century. The degree of primacy in the different

Latin American countries was related 'to the extent of their connection with the world economy'. Foreign investments in general, and British in particular, 'were deployed in a way likely to increase primacy by helping to provide the administrative and economic infrastructure for exports; this infrastructure was concentrated in the major city through which exports were channelled' (Roberts, 1978, pp. 47–48).

Latin capitals pulled ahead of the national growth rate in the following order: Havana (1840s), Rio (1850s), Lima and Buenos Aires (1860s), Bogotá (1870s), Caracas and Santiago (1880s), and Mexico City at the turn of the century. The domestic importance of the capitals must be set in perspective with the absolute differences of magnitude among countries (Geisse, 1987). Generally speaking the former vice-regal metropolises such as Mexico City and Lima forfeited their attractiveness to cities of the new expanding economies – a trend confirmed by the respective population growth of the cities. Buenos Aires was about 90,000 by the 1850s and jumped to 178,000 by 1869; Rio already had 186,000 by 1854 and increased to 267,000 by 1872; Santiago was 115,000 in 1865 and jumped to 150,000 by the mid-1870s; Havana, which already had 130,000 by 1847, grew to 197,000 by 1861; mostly due to its former colonial splendour, Mexico City already had 200,000 by 1855, but only increased to 210,000 by 1862, whereas Lima had only 89,000 by 1862, and Bogotá kept its moderate 40,000 from the mid-1820s up to 1870. Meanwhile, Caracas had 47,013 by 1869 and rose only to 48,897 by 1873 (Morse, 1971, pp. 5–6).

The Contrast with the USA

According to the Dependency theory, the assumption by Latin America of its role as raw material producer within the nineteenth-century international division of labour implied a reinforcement of the 'outward-oriented model of growth' inherited from colonial times. A dramatic demonstration of that economic distortion was the dependent nature of urbanization in most Latin American countries, whose urban networks, weak since colonial times, showed little expansion during the early republican era, only responding to the requirements of foreign capital (Castells, 1973; 1976, pp. 54–61; Rofman, 1977). From the nineteenth century on, this outward-oriented economy also brought about the local elites' association of 'modern' with all that had to do with the export sector and everything foreign in general, whereas 'traditional' remained associated with activities linked to domestic production and consumption (Cardoso and Faletto, 1969, pp. 42–48).

It is instructive to contrast that process in Latin America with the industrialization and urbanization of the United States, which spread from the compact strip of New England and early states of the Union, and was eventually expanded by the piecemeal incorporation of southern and western territories of North America. In that respect, it has often – and plausibly – been argued that, putting aside the political implications of expansionism, to a large extent the USA's path to power was cleared by acquiring or annexing territories that had been colonized, for example French Louisiana in 1803, Spanish Florida in 1819, Mexican Texas in 1845 and British Oregon the following year. But it is harder to explain the so-called 'Great Turnabout' of 1830: the point when the former colonies of New England ceased to be dependent on the commodity-based model of exportation on which the Latin American republics would continue to rely for the rest of the nineteenth century.

Indeed, from the 1830s, US industrialization centred on Chicago, and ran parallel to the occupation and urbanization of the Midwest. That vast territory and its concentration of population provided new markets so reducing dependence on the exportation of raw materials and produce to former European metropolises that demanded them for industrialization (Morse, 1975). And access to those new markets was greatly enhanced by construction of the railways: from the east, the Union Pacific Railroad headed westwards relying on the cities of Iowa and nearby states; from California's Sacramento, meanwhile, the Central Pacific advanced eastwards, creating and boosting the so-called 'railway cities', the most conspicuous of which was San Francisco's terminal. Meeting in May 1869 at Promontory Point, Utah, the lines created a rail link coast to coast (Glaab and Brown, 1967, pp. 107–132; McLaughlin, 1968, pp. 91–96).

Such giant steps towards the west led Frederick Jackson Turner to conceive North American history as a continuous overcoming of frontiers between the settlements' civilization and the wilderness's barbarism. US expansion increasingly focused on territories of the northwest, however a 1787 ordinance had established that territories had to reach 60,000 free citizens and an economic base in order to be incorporated as federal states. Following the same rationale, the 1862 Homestead Act encouraged the occupation of 160-acre ranches by cowboys who were residents for more than five years, including the future President Theodore Roosevelt. During the following decades, this policy of colonization gave rise to the Wild West myth, and made possible the occupation of the previously unproductive land of Colorado, Dakota, Wyoming and Montana (*Reseña...*, n/d, pp. 119–120; Remini, 2008, pp. 145–146).

Successive generations of anti-Yankee intelligentsia, from the *arielistas* to the social scientists of the Dependency school (see Chapters 3 and 6), found it difficult to come to terms with the USA's nineteenth-century exploits which they saw as tarnished by territorial plundering and political and economic expansionism. However, the contrast with Latin America's fragmentation and sluggishness in the post-colonial era is all too apparent – even unified Brazil, which became a Republic in 1889, dragged some of the baggage of its colonial heritage into the twentieth century, as did its Hispanic neighbours.

Civilization and Barbarism

There is no progress without association or rather the latter is the prerequisite of all progress and civilization... To work to diffuse and spread among all classes the spirit of association will be to grasp the huge task of the progress and civilization of our homeland.

Esteban Echeverría, *El Dogma socialista* (1839, 1977), I

Buenos Aires is supposed to be, someday, the most gigantic city of both Americas... In the midst of the vastness of Argentina, she alone is in contact with European nations; she alone exploits the advantages of foreign trade; she alone has the power and income. The provinces have asked her in vain to let them receive a bit of civilization, of industry and European population: a stupid and colonial policy was deaf to these clamours. But the provinces took revenge by sending, through Rosas, much of the barbarism that they had in excess.

Domingo Faustino Sarmiento, *Facundo, o civilización y barbarie* (1845, 1991)

More dramatically than in US history, civilization and barbarism were a contradiction that spanned Latin America's nineteenth century, and continued into the early twentieth; it intertwined the conflicts of unionism and federalism, conservatism and liberalism, along with tensions between the capital cities and provinces of the fledgling nations. Such was the case of the Argentine intelligentsia who closed ranks against Juan Manuel de Rosas – an early incarnation of Hispanic America's endemic *caudillismo*.

Argentina's 1837 Generation

As a reaction to Rosas's dictatorship (1835–1852), the so-called 1837 Generation was epitomized by the Asociación de la Joven Argentina (Young Argentina Association or Joven Generación Argentina, as it was also known), comprising among others Esteban Echeverría, Juan Bautista Alberdi, Domingo Faustino Sarmiento, José Mármol, Bartolomé Mitre and Miguel Cané. Inspired by *La Giovine Italia* (Young Italy) founded by Giuseppe Mazzini in 1831, and influenced by Claude Henri Saint Simon's utopian socialism, the Joven Generación Argentina proclaimed themselves '*builders* of the *sacred mission* of defining their *nations*'. Their manifesto was the *Dogma socialista de la Asociación de Mayo* (Socialist Dogma of the May Association), originally published in 1839, with a second edition by Echeverría published in 1846 in Montevideo.

Curiously, *civilización* is not singled out as one of the 'symbolic words' of the *Dogma socialista*, but it is obviously intertwined with the most fundamental ones, such as 'association' and 'progress'; for example: 'Without association there is no progress, or rather the former is the necessary condition of all *civilization* and progress. To work to make known and spread the spirit of association among all classes will be the same as grasping the great task of progress and civilization in our homeland' (Echeverría, 1839, 1977, p. 92, emphasis added). Those secular categories permeate the presentation of the Young Argentine Generation's manifesto, which aimed to transcend the republican values of the French Revolution and American Independence. These movements may have inspired Hispanic America's libertarian epic, but they were not strong enough to achieve the momentum required by the national project, so the *Dogma* proclaimed in that respect:

> The association of the Young Argentine Generation represents, in its provisional organization, the future of the Argentine nation: its mission is essentially organic. It will try to extend its spirit and doctrine – to extend the circle of its progressive trends – to attract the spirits to the big association, unifying opinions and focusing them on the homeland and the principles of equality, freedom and fraternity amongst all men. (Echeverría, 1839, 1977, p. 95)

Capital versus Province

Beyond its founding manifesto, the literary imagery of the 1837 Generation recreated, to a great extent, the tensions that fractured the Argentine territory, and other Latin American republics struggling to hold firm in the midst of internal upheaval. The civilization-barbarism 'conflict' is epitomized by Domingo Sarmiento's *Facundo* (1845), in which the antagonism between the terms is reflected in a series of dichotomies – capital and province; progress and backwardness; federalism and unionism – as the future Argentine president summarized in the following excerpt:

> Buenos Aires is supposed to be, one day, the most gigantic city of both Americas… In the midst of the vast area of Argentina, she alone is in contact with European nations; she alone exploits the advantages of foreign trade; she alone has the power and wealth. The provinces have vainly asked her to let them receive a bit of civilization, of industry and European population: a stupid and colonial policy was deaf to these clamours. But the provinces took revenge by sending, through Rosas, much of the barbarism that they had in excess. (Sarmiento, 1845, 1985, p. 25)

Even though Sarmiento had not visited Buenos Aires when he wrote his book, he seemed to blame the city for its lack of openness towards the provinces, just as José Mármol suggested in his classic novel *Amalia* (1851–1855). *Amalia* is a critique of Buenos Aires's closed capital-based society; this is epitomized by the posh lady who during a ball in 1840 complains about the lack of 'good taste' in Rosas's court, and fails to recognize the novel's protagonist as a 'fellow countrywoman' because she comes from the provinces (Mármol, 1851–1855, 2000, pp. 305–306). In addition to numerous tableaux representing the postcolonial city, Mármol's *Amalia* contains barbaric images of the *mazorca* or Rosas's police – antecedent of partisan groups that Latin America's autocratic regimes still have today – while vividly depicting private scenes of the caudillo and his entourage.

For the 1837 Generation, *civilización* had fundamental and formative dimensions beyond its portrayal in novels and essays; thus for instance, in contrast to the conflict that tore asunder his own nation, from his arrival in Montevideo, *Amalia*'s narrator portrays it as a 'new Tyre', where '… the man is not asked where he is from, but what he knows, and the man from any place in the world arrives there to be protected by institutions, while the commerce and industry at once open to him their generous channels; and so that is how [Uruguayans] have made themselves strong and rich' (Mármol, 1851–1855, 2000, p. 367).

Staged in a Tyre of more industrious than materialistic connotations, Mármol perhaps idealized a Uruguayan milieu that was certainly more prosperous than the Argentine in 1840, when *Amalia* was written; but there is in the novel a valid appeal in favour of the institutionalism and progress of advanced nations. Also in that sense, Sarmiento, in exile in Chile, told of his memories and ancestors from San Juan in *Recuerdos de provincia* (1850, Memories of Province); in this book he blames insular and narrow-minded Argentina for its lack of example and openness towards industrial progress, in contrast to the USA and Europe which he had visited:

The modern nations' richness is the daughter of cultivated intelligence. It is encouraged by railways, steamships and machines that are the fruit of science; they give life and liberty to everybody, freedom of movement, the post, telegraph, journals and discussion anyway. Barbarians! You are committing suicide; in ten years' time, your children will be scoundrels or beggars on the street. Look at England, France, the United States, where there is neither the *Restorer of the laws* nor the stupid *Hero of the desert*, armed with a whip, a dagger and a gang of wretches shouting *death to the savage Unitarians*, namely those who no longer exist and among whom many illustricus Argentineans can be counted. (Sarmiento, 1850, 1991, p. 47)

Federation versus Unitarianism

At odds with the institutionalism required by Progress and Civilization – the duo of nineteenth-century ideals that prefigured Latin America's transition from independentist Enlightenment into republican Positivism (Crawford, 1944, 1961) – Mármol opposed, as did Sarmiento, Argentina's Napoleonic drama, whose people 'kicked down the civilization and justice'. Rosas, however, 'understood it, and, without the golden crown on his head, put his caudillo persona where the monarch was lacking, and an imaginary idol called "Federation" in the place of the preacher and the Franciscan' (Mármol, 1851–1855, 2000, pp. 141–142). *Amalia*'s author thus characterizes not only that 'bloody Messiah' as a Napoleonic relative of the king, but also, amid the faithless devastation that followed Independence, vests the handy Federation with the sectarian and religious connotations that the word – *federación* – would continue to have in other parts of Latin America until the end of the century.

An allegory of that self-proclaimed Federation as a bloody machinery of a barbarism which decimated and suffocated the fledgling republic is to be found in Echeverría's poem *La cautiva* (1841, 1999, The Captive), and again, more vividly, in his posthumous work *El matadero* (1871, The Slaughterhouse). Here the metaphors are made explicit, from the feudalism of governmental taxes to the carnage as an expression of caudillismo, from the slaughterhouse as a tiny republic to the Restorer's nepotism (Echeverría, 1841, 1999). All these ingredients made *El matadero* an especially strong image for the Argentine historian José Luis Romero, because it represented 'the perpetuation of some forms of life and country habits mingled with the belligerent hostility towards urban expressions that [the society] formally shared' (Romero, 1946, 2008, p. 143).

But there is also in Echeverría's *El matadero* the diatribe (delivered in the words of the narrator) against the *mazorca*, the Rosas-loyal police whose abuses tormented the lives of Argentines opposed to the ominous regime: 'The slaughterhouse was the training ground, the cradle and school of those knife-armed gendarmes who spread fear and despair to all the places reached by the irresponsible governor's influence' (Echeverría, 1841, 1999, p. 146). That carnage of the slaughterhouse is analogous to Mármol's obscure images of the regional caudillos who paved the way to the great butcher by brandishing the machetes of the self-proclaimed Federation; because, as *Amalia*'s author accused him, Rosas made the citizens 'take their public baptism in that pool of blood that is called Federation of the republic' (Mármol, 1851–1855, 2000, pp. 555).

Destructive of the young Argentina's primeval Unitarianism – which was vested by the 1837 Generation with an idealized Civilization – the barbarism of Mármol's regional Attilas is reinforced by Echeverría with the federalist butchers, as portrayed at the end of his manifesto:

> At that time, the slashing butchers of the Slaughterhouse were the apostles that propagated Rosas's federation, with rod and dagger, and it is not hard to imagine which federation would stem from their heads and knives. Following the jargon invented by the Restorer, patron of the brotherhood, they called savage Unitarian everyone who was not a slitter, butcher, savage or thief; every decent and good-natured man, every illustrious patriot, friend of light and freedom; and judging by the event referred to, it can be clearly seen that the Federation's focus was in the Slaughterhouse. (Echeverría, 1999, p. 173)

Like the Young Argentine Generation that he led, Mármol thus unmasked Rosas's mendacious story that subverted and downgraded the federation, finally debasing it to a caudillo-like password for the outrage and abuses against any form of dissidence. With its harsh and obscure metaphors of the slaughterhouse and the desert, rape and the *marzorca*, contrasted against the shining horizons of the republican city and unity, the 1837 Generation articulated a debate where not only barbarism and civilization were antagonized, but also the tensions between province and capital, federalism and unity in the evolution of the republic. Later generations would reach a more considered view, recognizing Rosas's unifying contribution, in spite of his initial excesses (see Luna, 1993, 2005, for instance).

Such a debate summarizes the tensions that Argentina went through earlier and more dramatically than other republics of the continent, even the USA. But the tensions between federation and unity, as they played out during Rosas's dictatorship, would persist with other such juxtapositions in Latin American geography. Thus imagery of barbarism and civilization would survive beyond the 1837 Generation in other literary trends and movements that would appear as reactions against foreign-oriented projects of liberalism.[3]

European Godfathers[4]

… In the charming life, in fashion and art, French spirit prevails; in letters and sciences, French with German and Italian; and in industrial and mercantile life, English…
  José Gil Fortoul, *El hombre y la historia. Ensayo de sociología venezolana* (1896)

The republican programme drafted in the Young Argentine Generation's *Dogma* made explicit that *progress* relied on political and cultural independence from Spain and rapprochement with non-Iberian Europe.

> Revolution is for us progress. Having believed that its condition would improve, America emancipated from 'Spanish colonial rule', entering from then on the path to progress. To progress is to civilize, or to channel the action of strengths to achieving welfare, in other words, to realize the rights of the individual.

Europe is the centre of centuries of civilization and human progress. (Echeverría, 1977, p. 96)

Latin America's bonds with that progressive Europe dated back to 1739 at least, when Britain had declared war on Spain over the latter's monopoly beyond the Atlantic. With the entrance of France – whose quarrels with Britain included disputed possessions in Louisiana – the Bourbon conflict turned into the Seven Years War (1756–1763), which also involved the Prussians. Hostilities ended with the Treaty of Paris (1763), which gave advantage in the New World to the British. The latter then abolished slavery in their possessions by the 1807 Abolition of the Slave Trade Act and tried to do the same in the Iberian colonies. At the same time, the weakened position of Spain and Portugal in a continent disputed by Britain and France on the eve of Napoleonic invasions, on the one hand, along with the economic and political pressure exerted by Creole elites on the other, enabled Latin American dominions to get some commercial concessions that relaxed metropolitan hegemony (Woodward, 1962, 1984, pp. 166–167). While by the 1810s these factors had paved the way for the beginning of Hispanic America's independent movements, from then on the British Empire was, so to speak, the economic and technical godfather of the nascent republics, and France was confirmed as cultural godmother.

Liberal and Mighty Britain

With its leadership in post-Napoleonic Europe consolidated, Britain began to harvest the fruits of more than a century of sustained presence in Latin America. More apparently than in the Spanish dominions, the political alliance with England had almost converted into 'an axiom of Portuguese diplomacy' during the eighteenth century, especially as a legacy of the first tenure of the Portuguese Prime Minister, the Marquis of Pombal (1750–1777). He aimed at reducing Britain's economic advantages, but keeping British protection (Novais, 1979, pp. 30–31). By the 1810s, Britain had become the main customer for the traditional staples produced by the new republics, which not only supplied raw materials for British industry but also relied on British trade and loans for their incipient economies. In terms of the capital investment and the supply of technology, the predominance of Britain was more evident from the 1850s to the 1900s, including two marked booms during the 1880s and in the decade following 1902. After that, the US was to have an increasing presence which would overtake that of Britain from World War I (Rippy, 1959, pp. 11, 36).

Although they were not numerous, the British possessed an economic supremacy which was what most struck and pleased Michael G. Mulhall in his report *The English in South America* (1878):

> It may appear surprising that in a continent twice the size of Europe, where the total number of English residents is hardly equal to the population of Chester or Carlisle, and does not reach one in 800 of the inhabitants, the English element has in a few years been able to make its impress felt in a greater degree than any other foreign nationality. This appears mainly owing to the influence of British capital and trade. (Mulhall, 1878, p. 599)

He certainly had reasons to be proud. 'His fellow countrymen' brought to Latin America technological devices and manufactures which gave the ex-colonies a sample of the coming industrial era. Mining machinery, steam engines and railways were among the technologies introduced in the new republics by British companies and citizens, who with Americans and Germans provided most of the tools of the industrial era until the beginning of the new century (Rippy, 1944, pp. 19, 189).

For these reasons, the relationship between nineteenth-century Latin America and the British Empire cannot be reduced to a mere 'commercial domination', as the Dependence theorists have sometimes tried to do. On the one hand, British trade interests in the new republics certainly broke the brief dream of independence, reproducing neo-colonial bonds that reinforced Britain's 'informal imperialism' in the region (Stein and Stein, 1970, pp. 137, 154–155). On the other hand, it is also true that thanks to the technological and commercial benefits received from Britain, Latin American republics realized the meanings of progress, industrialization and innovation. At the same time, the former colonies were allowed a stable *modus vivendi* with liberal Britain, which thereafter tutored the new republics in 'the arts of peace' (Griffin, 1961). As Mulhall suggested: 'Whatever may be the fortunes of South America during the next fifty years, one thing seems certain, that its development in the arts of peace will be in a great manner identified with the growth of its relations with Britain' (Mulhall, 1878, p. 600). And – as we shall see – he was right.

Civilized France

Even though France played a part in Latin American economies during the eighteenth century, her predominant role was social and cultural. Taking the lead in bringing the European Enlightenment to the New World, French philosophers had inspired the Creole intelligentsia which championed the crusade for Independence and early republicanism. France was not only revered as a philosophical and artistic power but also as the main recipient and translator of modern European humanism for the Latin world (Crawford, 1944, 1961; Pagden, 1995, pp. 178–200).

Sarmiento pointed out in his *Facundo* that 'the Europeanization' of Argentina's urban society was already evident in early republican times: Europeans arriving in Buenos Aires believed that they were in Parisian salons – not even the characteristic French petulance was lacking (Sarmiento, 1845, 1985, pp. 109–110). In another metaphor provided by Sarmiento's *Recuerdos de provincia*, the capital's seeming Europeanization was mirrored in the 'winding and narrow streets of Vauxhall', an 'English garden' visited by 'Buenos Aires families pretending to be civilized', while deceiving themselves 'in that oasis of civilization that took long in spreading its benefits over the pampas' uncultivated land' (Sarmiento, 1850, 1991, p. 133).

So through his image of Buenos Aires, he anticipated the French-oriented culture which spread across the continent for more than a century. This is what Manuel Ugarte, another Argentine man of letters and Ambassador to France, would call 'the second conquest', paralleling the fifteenth-century occupation of the vast land by the Spanish and Portuguese with the nineteenth-century subjugation of its people by French thought (Ugarte, 1911, p. 77). Even though that supremacy would not be so absolute by the beginning of the twentieth century, the Peruvian writer Francisco García Calderón still proclaimed on the eve of World War I, 'France has been the teacher of social life and letters to the American democracies' – a tutelage that he praised gratefully as one of the main traits of the 'Latin spirit' (García Calderón, 1913, p. 287).

As well as being the herald of social change and philosophical thought, France showed the way in fine arts and civilization, refinement and urbanity for the young republics. Though recognizing the German and Italian influences on the writing and sciences of post-colonial Latin America, the Venezuelan sociologist José Gil Fortoul identified, as quoted in the epigraph to this section, the French predominance in 'the elegant life, the fashion and the art' as a feature of the 'social race' of the new republics (Gil, 1896, pp. 29–30). In a similar way, when mapping the influence of Southern-European immigration on this Latin American 'race', Ugarte accurately highlighted that spiritual yet powerful influence of France in 'embellishing the life' in the continent (Ugarte, 1911, p. 62).

From the second half of the nineteenth century, the emergent bourgeoisie, benefiting from the export boom, adopted a so-called 'French style' in domestic and public life. Second-Empire Paris became the archetype of urban modernity and refinement for Latin American elites until the 1910s Bella Época (Griffin, 1961, pp. 83–84; Rama, 1984, p. 116) (see Chapter 3). The supremacy of Second Empire France as the quintessence of civilization did not exclude some ideas borrowed from Victorian England; in fact, the two appeared as a cultural duo in nineteenth-century Latin America, as, for example, in the case of the theories on social change. In this respect, the philosophical evolutionism underlying English industrialism provided the clue for the vernacular adaptation of some French philosophers' avant-garde theories, which sometimes were premature for the Latin American context. This was so in the case of Comte's positivism, which stressed collective harmony more than individual liberty – an ideal far from being reached in Creole societies. Instead, Herbert Spencer's social Darwinism turned out to be more appropriate and realistic.[5] Social harmony thereby became more feasible in the long term, thus representing an achievable alternative to oligarchic Latin America (Bradford, 1979, pp. 15–16; Griffin, 1961, p. 117; Romero, 1984, p. 284). In addition to social Darwinism, urban protocol and moral decorum were among the Victorian ingredients which Latin elites and rulers added to their French-inspired projects throughout the nineteenth century. The progressive godfather and the civilized godmother thus performed more than one *pas de deux* in the modernization of the novice republics, with dazzling effects on their political and urban stages.

Conservatives and Liberals, Oligarchies and Bourgeoisies

Our contracts or constitutional pacts in South America have to be a sort of mercantile contract of collective societies, especially formed to provide settlers for these deserts that we christened with pompous

names of Republics; to shape railroads that suppress distances that make possible that indivisible unit in political action...
        Juan Bautista Alberdi, *Bases y puntos de partida para la organización política de la República Argentina* (1852)

The rapid increase and improvement of our population will only be reached with these and other measures of the same nature, with the consolidation of the public peace, with the arrangement of justice administration, with freedom of worship and with the facilities that at the same time must be provided by the Government for moving emigrants to our ports...
        Benito Juárez et al., 'Justificación de las Leyes de Reforma' (1859, 2007)

In spite of the above-mentioned differentiation between the Atlantic and the Andean blocs, it can be said that, as the second half of the nineteenth century went by, the diversification in the export of raw materials benefited Latin America overall, amid a growing international demand for industrialization; by then, copper and wheat were Chile's main staples, wool was Argentina's and the guano was Peru's; coffee expanded in Brazil, Venezuela, Nueva Granada and Central America, while sugar thrived in the Antilles, Mexico and Peru (Halperin, 1967, 2005, p. 230–231). The development map is further nuanced when investments and improvements in infrastructure and services are incorporated: by 1878, Argentina led the continent, with 2,200 kilometres of railways and more than 7,000 of telegraph lines; in relative terms, Chile followed with 1,500 and more than 4,000 respectively. Even though it had more than the latter with over 2,000 kilometres of railways and nearly 7,000 of telegraph lines, Brazil – given its immensity – can be said to have been lagging in third place, while Mexico was in fourth, with 600 kilometres of railroads and a bit over 1,100 of telegraphic lines; finally, countries like Nueva Granada and Venezuela were even more backward, with only 100 kilometres of railways and above 2,000 of telegraph lines (Rippy, 1944, p. 30).

The economic and social development of the countries of Latin America was influenced by factors such as their competitiveness in exporting staples to meet the demands of industrializing powers, investments that the latter would make in improving infrastructure and services, along with immigration policies; in the institutional domain, constitutional frameworks interacted with political vicissitudes preserving, renewing or dislocating the new societies. As Marcelo Carmagnani has pointed out, from the last third of the nineteenth century, all that was possible on the basis of increasing 'public investments in the process of economic modernization, even by subsidies to the private enterprise', and reduced expenditure in other sectors, such as the military one (Carmagnani, 2004, p. 227).

An early evaluation of how those modernizing factors informed Latin America's mid-nineteenth-century constitutional debate can be found in the aforementioned *Bases* – a sort of Decalogue written by Juan Bautista Alberdi from Valparaíso as a guide to the reconstruction of his country after Rosas's defeat in the battle of Monte Caseros. As is clear in the first epigraph to this section, Alberdi's *Bases* invoked the means for shifting from colonial-rooted conservatism to the competitive liberalism required by the republican project of the second half of the nineteenth century. Different states conceived and applied such economic and political conservatism and liberalism in diverse ways, initiating processes of secularization and modernization that left behind the religious past, while elites changed their profiles and attires from oligarchic into bourgeois. It is impossible to deal with each country individually in this respect, therefore I will sketch some of the economic and political reforms in the cases of Chile, Argentina, Brazil, Mexico and Venezuela.

Portalian Chile

Combining the conservatism of the landowners and the liberalism of the miners, independent Chile came together as a country thanks to the 'progressive authoritarianism' of Bernardo O'Higgins, followed by Diego Portales's 'conservative order' and, towards the mid-nineteenth century, by the 'liberalization' led by Manuel Montt. Having abolished slavery as early as 1823, Chile's national identity was boosted by its victories in the First Pacific War or War of the Confederation (1837–1839), jointly with the Second War (1879–1883) against Peru and Bolivia; such exploits not only consolidated the international image of an 'Iberian American Prussia', but also gave the country control over the deserts of Antofagasta and Tarapacá, as well as the exploitation of saltpetre (Williamson, 1992, p. 258; Halperin, 1967, 2005, pp. 212, 279). In institutional terms, the prevailing model of that period was the 1833 constitution, written by Mariano Egaña as expression of the oligarchic and centralized republicanism of Portales; Portales's ideology was encapsulated in one of his letters, with succinct yet penetrating ideas that Chilean historian Armando de Ramón labelled as 'desktop reflections':

> I am not interested in politics, but, as a good citizen, I can freely comment on and even censor the government's acts. *The democracy so much praised by dreamers is absurd* in American countries, full of vices and where citizens lack all virtue as is required to establish a true republic... Republic is the system that has to be adopted, but do you know how I understand it for these countries? A *strong centralized government*, whose men are real models of virtue and patriotism; citizens would thus follow the straight road of order and virtue. When they learnt morality, a completely free and idealistic government would be welcome, embracing all citizens. This is what I think and every right-minded man shall think the same. (Portales quoted in de Ramón, 2006, pp. 72–73)

Partly due to the Valparaiso merchants' links with British traders, from the mid-nineteenth century Chile's mining sector represented the progressive spirit that contrasted with the landowners' economic conservatism (Halperin, 1967, 2005, pp. 212, 216). Beyond these economic and regional differences, the political institutions of the so-called 'Portales era' (1830–1890) were very sophisticated compared to the rest of Latin America. Alberdi recognized that the Chilean constitution was 'superior in writing to all South America, most wise and profound concerning the composition of the executive power', though it was 'incomplete and backward as to the economic means of progress and the great material needs of Spanish America'; in this he was highlighting the constitutional imposition of Catholicism and the ban on foreigners holding national and municipal posts (Alberdi, 1852, 2008, p. 67).

The economic and territorial legacy of that oligarchic liberalism included the development of Chile's central valley, traditional producer of wheat; the strengthening of the Santiago-Valparaíso axis in terms of trade and railways, as well as between the mining-based Copiapó and the port of Caldera; the pacification of the Araucanía and the occupation of the Magellan region, with the foundation of Fort Bulnes, later called Punta Arenas (de Ramón, 2006, pp. 67, 80–90; Villalobos, 1979, 2010, pp. 124–125, 130–131, 148–151).

Boosted by the gold rush in California and the relative decline of Callao as the main port of the South American Pacific, especially after Peru's defeat in the War of the Confederation, from the mid-nineteenth century Valparaíso became a stronghold of commercial and cosmopolitan liberalism. It not only consolidated its importance in demographic terms – increasing from 41,000 inhabitants in 1840 to 97,000 in 1875 and 162,000 in 1907 – but also disseminated commercial dynamism through the railway connection with Santiago from 1863, all of which was evinced in a strong foreign immigration arriving to the capital since the 1870s (de Ramón, 2000, pp. 132–133, 137; Williamson, 1992, p. 256). Such immigration sped up the modernization of Chilean society after the liberal revolution of 1850–1851; events were prompted by the Sociedad de la Igualdad (Society of Equality), led by intellectuals such as José Victorino Lastarria, Francisco Bilbao and Alberto Blest Gana, who portrayed the revolts in the novel *Martín Rivas* (1862).

The consolidation of the so-called *pipiolo* liberalism that confronted the *pelucona* or old-fashioned oligarchy had to await the arrival of José Manuel Balmaceda's presidency (1886–1891). Balmaceda unleashed the first crisis between the conservative parliamentarianism and the reformist executive. But even so, he ended up guaranteeing the Portales legacy, which, in his own words, sought 'to apply fiscal resources to the construction of high schools, basic schools and all sorts of establishments that improve Chile's intellectual capacity; and this is why I will not stop undertaking the construction of railways, roads, docks and ports that facilitate production, that promote work, that encourage weak individuals and increase the sap along which the nation's economic vitality circulates' (Balmaceda quoted in Villalobos, 1979, 2010, p. 168). According to Chilean historian Jaime Eyzaguirre, Portales's legacy 'became a national tradition and not only the heritage of a group or party'; he suggested that the continuity of Portales's work beyond all the nineteenth-century vicissitudes, made the cardinal difference with other Hispanic American autocracies: 'Neither France, nor Rosas, nor García Moreno, nor Porfirio Díaz had continuators, whereas Portales had them interruptedly over half a century' (Eyzaguirre, 1948, 2004, pp. 126–127).[6]

Imperial Brazil

Boasting an export sector that between 1840 and the 1860s had grown more than 200 per cent, the Empire of Brazil had emerged as another stronghold of Latin America's economic liberalism. In 1808 Brazil became the venue for the Portuguese court, displaced by the Napoleonic invasions of the Iberian Peninsula; such a move consolidated Rio's primacy over Salvador de Bahia, which had been the capital up to 1763. Once the Rio-based court returned to Lisbon, on 7 September 1822, the regent prince, later Dom Pedro I, proclaimed independence from Portugal with the famous 'cry of Ipiranga', and the Brazilian Empire was established on his coronation the following month. On the basis of an absolutist constitution which he issued in 1824, the Empire thrived, especially after Dom Pedro II's rise to power in 1840, whose reign saw the resolution of both national and international conflicts until the declaration of the Republic in 1889.[7]

In *Bases*, Alberdi regretted Brazil's lack of republicanism; however, he hailed the peaceful transition of that 'beautiful example … that knows how to protect civilization', which was 'the common aim of governments' everywhere (Alberdi, 1852, 2008, p. 86). Indeed, under the aegis of illustrious monarchs such as Dom Pedro II, not only was material progress sponsored, but also culture and humanities, through the invitation to the architect Grandjean de Montigny and other European figures to establish academies in the new *carioca* capital; such a development was especially significant in a vast territory that, unlike Hispanic America, had lacked universities and presses during the colonial era.

With its population rising from 186,000 in 1854 to 267,000 in 1872, Rio de Janeiro's improvements were evinced, for instance, in the introduction of telegraph in 1852, as well as in the railways that connected the capital with the Mauá port and São Paulo from the mid-1850s, though the Grand Central station was not inaugurated until 1880 (figure 2.1). Indeed, telegraphic lines expanded nationwide from 200 kilometres in 1864 to 19,000 in 1889. The most spectacular changes were propelled by coffee-exporter São Paulo; the *paulista* state and its capital turned into a receptive and radiating hub of Portuguese and Italian immigration, aimed at replacing the workforce diminished by *manumiso* or liberated slaves. In this respect, it is worth noting that Brazilian coffee jumped from 18 per cent of the world production in the 1820s to more than 50 per

Figure 2.1. Entrance to Rio de Janeiro's Central Railway Station. (*Photo:* Marc Ferrez, 1880. *Source*: Hoffenberg Collection, Archivo Audiovisual de Venezuela, Biblioteca Nacional, Caracas)

cent by the late 1880s, while as a percentage of the country's exports it grew in the same proportion (Schneeberger, 2003, pp. 218, 228).

There remained profound contradictions between Rio's conservative administrations, on the one hand, who favoured the oligarchy based on sugar and cotton plantations, and on the other, the so-called coffee-barons and other industrial groups of São Paulo and Minas Gerais, whose liberalism contrasted with their hidden support for slavery (Williamson, 1992, pp. 251–253). Indeed, notwithstanding the constitution of an urban elite who tried to get rid of their 'rural roots' by abolishing slavery in 1888, Sergio Buarque de Holanda declared the 'impossibility of a bourgeoisie' by the late nineteenth century and early twentieth, due to cultural and territorial factors, such as the 'mentality of *casa grande*' or extensive household, the scarcity of intermediate towns and the 'overwhelming predominance of ruralism' across such a vast territory (Buarque de Holanda, 1936, 2005, pp. 74, 87–88, 92). Buarque's reasoning appealed to Gilberto Freyre's famous thesis in *Casa-grande e senzala* (1933, The Masters and Slaves), where the Pernambuco-born sociologist had established that, as in the 'colonies of owners' of the southern United States, the social structure of colonial Brazil had been underpinned by the institution 'of the slavery-based family; of the *casa-grande*; of the patriarchal family'; in other words, a rural kinship supported by a *latifundio* or large-estate that, unlike that of Spanish colonies, relied mainly on an 'agrarian basis' (Freyre, 1933, 2000, pp. 251–252).

Mexico: Reform, Empire and Porfiriato

From political independence in 1821, which was labelled by Nobel-laureate writer Octavio Paz as an 'agrarian revolution in the making' (Paz, 1950, 1980, p. 111), Mexico had been very close to political liberalism with the so-called Plan of Iguala, whereby Creole *realistas* or monarchists such as Agustín de Iturbide, along with *mestizos* led by Vicente Guerrero, conceived a sort of compromise based on independence, union and religion. It was likewise a way of balancing the complex extension and structure of the nascent republic, where conservatives tended to be centralists, whereas liberals preferred US-like federalism (Williamson, 1992, p. 259). After Mexico's substantial territorial losses inflicted by its expansionist Yankee neighbour, including the states-to-be of Texas, California, Colorado, New Mexico, Arizona and Nevada, a new phase of political liberalism arrived with the 1854 Plan of Ayutla and the ensuing 1857 Constitution; the latter was reinforced by the first Laws of Reform that comprehended, among other aspects of laicization: 'To adopt, as an invariable general rule, the most perfect independence between business of the State and those purely ecclesiastic' (Juárez *et al*, 1972, 2007, p. 89).

With a strong wind of secularization, the 'Justification of the Reform Laws' was summarized in a document published in 1859, signed by Miguel Lerdo de Tejada and Benito Juárez, among others. It was a sort of manifesto and government plan at the same time, where, among many other aspects, the State's secularization was reinforced, along with the nationalization of ecclesiastical property and the establishment of religious freedom. This should be enforced by the Republic 'with all its authority', for it is 'necessary for its prosperity and aggrandizement, while a requirement of current civilization' (Juárez et al, 1972, 2007, p. 90). For the rest, through the 'Justification...' it is possible to visualize the ambitious programme of educational, administrative and infrastructure improvements, jointly with the promotion of immigration and colonization; in order to favour the latter, the document synthesizes the need to coordinate measures that mirror Mexican and continental liberalism, as it is epitomized in this section's second epigraph (Juárez et al., 1972, 2007, p. 106).

But foreigners and colonization arrived at the flimsy republic from the most inconvenient side: mainly due to their attacks against large estates and ecclesiastical privileges, the progressive and secularizing reforms of the late 1850s were not welcomed by the European powers that were Mexico's creditors; facilitated by the lack of attention from the United States, immersed in its own Secession War, the Mexican Reform unleashed the unexpected imposition of Maximilian of Habsburg's short-lived empire (1862–1867). When the Republic was reinstated, Juárez's second wave of liberal reforms was not able to rescue a country torn between urban professionals and *hacendados* or farmers, on the one hand, and the Indian peasantry, on the other (Williamson, 1992, p. 266).

Improvements in economic rather than political liberalism, along with the seeming creation of a Europeanized bourgeoisie, would arrive in the debt-stricken country with the autocracy dominated between 1876 and 1910 by Porfirio Díaz, who had helped Juárez to expel the French invaders. During don Porfirio's 'honest tyranny' – with 'little politics and much administration', according to one of his slogans – the Mexican population increased by more than 50 per cent, reaching 15 million, while the railway network extended from 800 to 24,000 kilometres (Williamson 1992, p. 267; Halperin, 1967, 2005, pp. 247–248; Cosío, 1973, 2005a, p. 113). However, factory, mill and plantation workers, most of whose workplaces belonged to foreign investors, were not entitled to unionize, while peasants demanded land reform; led by a 'new *latifundista* cast' instead of a true entrepreneurial bourgeoisie, the *porfiriato*'s alleged progress only meant, for Paz, the reappearance of 'colonial feudalism' (Paz, 1950, 1980, pp. 116–117).

Argentina: From Confederation to Expansion

In spite of the benefits during the *porfiriato*'s *pax*, the latency of regional *caudillismo*, among other factors, prevented Mexico's constitutional progress from equalling those of Chile and Argentina (Williamson, 1992, p. 268). After the fall of the Rosas regime, the up-to-then 'Confederation of the River Plate' turned into a true federal union, its bases established in the 1853 Constitution; Buenos Aires's reluctance to share with the rest of the country the advantages of being a port city led to brief civil wars in 1859 and 1861, but the underpinnings of the new country, prosperous and cosmopolitan, were already laid. The emerging nation was to be presided over by members of the 1837 Generation (see p. pp. 18–21), notably Bartolomé Mitre (1862–1868) and Domingo Faustino Sarmiento (1868–1874), who instituted US-inspired policies aimed at encouraging immigration, developed public education, and improved infrastructure and the railways (del Pozo, 2002, p. 49). Even by the final years of the Rosas regime, the president-to-be envisaged in his *Facundo* the potential for Argentina to become an attractive and alternative destination for the immigrants that by then headed for North America:

> From Europe currently emigrate half a million men a year, at least, who hold a craft or office and go out looking for fortune and in order to settle where there is land to possess. Until 1840, this immigration mainly headed to North America... There has sometimes been such a fad for migrating that entire settlements from Germany have moved to North America with their mayors, priests, schoolteachers, etc. But it has eventually happened that, in coastal cities, the population's increase has made life as hard as in Europe, so emigrants have found there the discomfort and misery they escaped from... (Sarmiento, 1845, 1985, p. 242)

In contrast to the densification of the North American coast, Sarmiento regarded the temperate cities of the River Plate as the most beneficial destination for those not able to adapt to other latitudes of the New World, as was proved by the 'blossoming and rich city' of Montevideo, which had capitalized on the exodus generated by Rosas's satrapy (Sarmiento, 1845, 1985, p. 242).[8] Once the autocracy was over, Argentine governments grasped the destiny prefigured by Sarmiento in *Facundo* and *De la educación popular* (1849, On Popular Education), as well as in Alberdi's *Bases*, a destiny for which, according to the ideals of the Young Argentine Generation, European immigration was the source of civilization and progress. In this respect, while explaining his most famous aphorism – 'gobernar es poblar' (to govern is to populate) – Alberdi said that such immigration should be understood as a science; it was simply 'the political economics, which considers population as an instrument of wealth and an element of prosperity'; pointing, like Sarmiento, to the formidable US example, Alberdi deemed that such immigration had to be more selective and distributive throughout the territory:

> Northern Europe shall spontaneously go to North America; and since the north in both worlds seems to be the world of freedom and industry, South America must give up the illusion of having immigrations capable of educating in freedom, peace and industry, if they are not attracted artificially.
>
> The sole spontaneous immigration that South America is capable of attracting is those populations that are not needed: these come on their own, as the weed. America can be sure that it will have such population without bringing it, since European civilization expels it as slag.
>
> The secret of populating is given by the art of distributing population in the country. Immigration tends to remain in ports, where its long voyage ends, and where high salary and pleasant life are found. But the country seems to lose all that ports seem to gain. It is necessary to multiply ports for distributing population along the coasts; and in order to populate the hinterland whose livelihood is based on agriculture and rural industry, America needs to take in Europe's rural emigration, not the slag from its shining cities... (Alberdi, 1852, 2008, p. 36)

Epitomizing the principles of that economic, political and demographic liberalism, the Argentina of the second half of the nineteenth century encouraged immigration, urbanization and infrastructure amelioration in order to realize Alberdi's slogan, thereby increasing its population from 800,000 in 1852, to 3 million in 1890, including

1,745,271 newcomers. Urbanization and immigration also enabled territories seized from the indigenous peoples to be secured; the supreme exponent of that thriving and expanding country was General Julio Roca, twice president (1880–1886; 1898–1904), whose desert campaigns against the Pampas' Indians released a 15,000 square kilometre territory used to consolidate the railway network and the spread of foreign capital, mainly British. Because of the reduction of the 'desert' by increasing the 'civilized soil', Roca's campaigns can be deemed 'the real beginning of Alberdi's programme' (Fernández, 2008, p. 24).[9]

For the new Argentina 1880 was a key year. The national army was consolidated after the war against Paraguay and the conquest of the desert. Economic growth was propelled by the exportation of wheat and frozen beef from the 1870s, boosted also by the Nation's Mortgage Bank from 1880. New national ministries, such as those of Public Works and Public Instruction, were created, while the Law of Federal Capital that finally put an end to the old disputes between Buenos Aires and the provinces was passed (figure 2.2) (Luna, 1993, 2005, pp. 127–131, 147). In such a booming State, the increasing presence of foreign immigration catalysed demands from those who, within the Latin American context, are closest to an urban bourgeoisie (Romero, 1946, 2008, p. 171). This bourgeoisie tried to achieve political and electoral reforms; however, given the conservative hindrances of nineteenth-century liberalism, those claims would only be reached by the 1910s (see Chapters 3 and 4).

Guzmanato's Venezuela

For a small and backward country like Venezuela – representative of the North Andean strip which travellers such as Cané and Mulhall had deemed behind their neighbours

Figure 2.2. Calle Florida (Florida Street), Buenos Aires, circa 1870. (*Source*: Archivo del Centro de Documentación de Arquitectura Latinoamericana (CEDODAL), Buenos Aires)

from the Atlantic shore and the Southern Cone – political and economic liberalism arrived later, after the Federal War ended in 1863. However, some concretion of the new trends came during the presidencies of Antonio Guzmán Blanco or *guzmanato*, comprising three tenures: the seven-year *Septenio* (1870–1877), the five-year *Quinquenio* (1879–1884) and the 'Acclamation' or 'Biennium' (1886–1888). The first time that the so-called 'Illustrious American' addressed the Venezuela congress after he came to power, he summarized the previous three decades of radical and bloody opposition between *godos* or conservatives and liberals with these words:

> From 1840 Venezuela has been torn between two parties, one striving for freedom and the other armed with authority; the latter heir of the Colony, the former marching towards future; the second one holding to the past; between the oligarch and the liberal has always existed a distance impossible to be shortened by time or its lessons, or the prestige of popular majority, or its material achievements, or its moral conquests or its magnanimity... (Guzmán, 1876, p. 6)

By so speaking, he officially vested the liberal cause with the values of freedom, republicanism and progressiveness, which were, as we have seen, cornerstones of other liberal constructions in nineteenth-century Latin America. But Guzmán's project brought about an adjustment in the priorities and values of Venezuela's traditional liberalism. If the institutional consolidation of the fragile republic had been of prime political importance for his predecessors, the caudillo considered such strengthening as requisite for more positive achievements, such as progress and civilization. When resources had to be diverted from school building or infrastructure development to quashing revolts in the country, Guzmán repeatedly told congressmen that peace was the starting point for all progress. He compared the untamed republic with 'dry leather': 'if you push it in on one side, it pops out at the other' (Guzmán, 1876, p. 29; 1880, p. 7). But after some order was achieved during the *Septenio*, the positivistic ideals made possible the miracle of Guzmán's liberalism: namely the establishment of progress 'on the ruins of Freedom', together with the transformation of the 'semi-wild' country into a nation of citizens. This was even recognized by opponents of the autocratic Guzmán, such as the Venezuelan Aristiguieta Montero (1879, p. 16) and the Colombian Vargas Vila (1913, pp. 184, 187).

Beyond proclamations, the progressive tenets of Guzmán Blanco's project had to be turned into administrative goals. In a message delivered to congressmen in 1874, he prioritized mass education, immigration and transport infrastructure as necessary conditions to achieve stability and worthwhile future (Guzmán, 1876, p. 823). And indeed, besides improving public education, immigration and railways rapidly became aims of his governments until the Acclamation, framing a liberal agenda that would be maintained, with slight changes, until the end of the nineteenth century (Almandoz, 2006*a*, pp. 59–88).

Despite the chronological gap between Chile's early and Venezuela's rather late progressivism, it can be said, paraphrasing Portales, that the first part of Latin America's modernizing project was led by oligarchies hovering between conservatism and liberalism. They sought to become secularized and Europeanized bourgeoisies, the most ostensible of which was that of Argentina, once the Rosas regime and the Federal War were over. The progressive agenda, comprising immigration and foreign investment, along with improvements to railways and infrastructure in general, was carried on by states that, as in reformist Mexico, reached a high level of secularization, imbued with a Positivism marked by the notions of Order, Progress and Civilization. It was an ambitious programme that seemed to correspond to the questions and guidelines informing Alberdi's *Bases* for the transformation of deserts into republics. However, at the beginning of the twentieth century and on the eve of the first centenary of republican life, such ideals were far from achieved in many Latin American countries, as we shall see in the next chapter.

From Postcolonial to Bourgeois Cities

Liberal reforms in most Latin American countries also shaped a new type of postcolonial city, whose Europeanism was evident in the physical transformations and the cultural ethos sponsored by emerging economic groups, social elites and political leaders. The worship of Second Empire Paris was one of the features of what Romero called the 'bourgeois city' of Latin America, which bloomed in the second half of the nineteenth century in those countries which had been incorporated in the capitalistic circuits (Romero, 1984, pp. 274–299; Almandoz, 2013*d*). Urban renewal was part of a more ambitious package of reforms intended to modernize social landscapes, whereby countries such as Argentina, Chile, Brazil and Mexico decided to improve the image of the then untouched colonial cities, as well as to restructure their regional networks of settlements by introducing railways and other infrastructure.

Haussmannization of the Dameros

The example of the transformation of Paris by Baron Haussmann was invoked by local elites to speed up the physical and cultural transformation of the *gran aldea* (big hamlet) – to use the expression coined by Lucio López's novel, staged in postcolonial Buenos Aires (López, 1882, 1953) – into a bourgeois city. Breaking colonial *dameros* (checkerboards) coming from the Spanish foundation, Haussmann's main contributions to the biggest Latin capitals have been traced to the baroque lines of new neighbourhoods, as well as to the huge public parks and tree-lined avenues. Although the French genealogy of some of these designs has been contested in recent times, the following are traditional examples of Hausmannesque works: the Paseo de la Reforma in Mexico City, said to be the first copy of a Parisian boulevard in the New World (Tenorio, 2000, pp. 68, 71); the Parque de Palermo and the Avenida de Mayo in Buenos Aires; the Paseo del Prado and the Avenida Agraciada in Montevideo; the Parque Forestal and the Santa Lucía hill in Santiago (figure 2.3); and the Guzmán Blanco boulevard and Paseo El Calvario in Caracas (Gutiérrez, 1984, pp. 515–518).

Figure 2.3. Cerro de Santa Lucia (Santa Lucia Hill), Santiago. (*Source*: Hoffenberg Collection, Archivo Audiovisual de Venezuela, Biblioteca Nacional, Caracas)

Even the rulers of some cities were compared to the Prefect of the Seine, so they have been regarded as Creole Haussmanns. Torcuato de Alvear, mayor of Buenos Aires (1883–1886), was portrayed in his own time as the Argentine version of the Baron (Gorelik, 1999, pp. 115–124). Benjamín Vicuña Mackenna, *intendente* or governor of Santiago, had also proposed, in the early 1870s, a transformation plan for the capital, including the embankment of the Mapocho river and the delimitation of a Camino de Cintura or Ring Road; the latter contoured the 'proper city' or civilized core to which Vicuña's administration gave priority, in contrast to the informal suburbs and slums that were for him the expression of barbarism (Vicuña, 1872, pp. 18–19; Pérez and Rosas, 2010, pp. 115–120). From the presidential level, Guzmán Blanco's urban reforms in 1870s and 1880s Caracas were also associated with Napoleon III's *grands travaux*, though the ambitious principles of the Haussmann urbanism were difficult to apply to the tiny capital (Almandoz, 2006a, pp. 89–128). Having studied in Second-Empire Paris and taken part in the design of a planning scheme for Rio de Janeiro in the mid-1870s, Francisco Pereira Passos was also supposedly inspired by the Baron's ideas for inaugurating the Avenida Central (1905) and other projects of the 'Cidade Maravilhosa', when he became Prefect of Rio during the Presidency of Rodrigues Alves (Needell, 1987, pp. 33–51; Pinheiro, 2002, pp. 93–158).

In spite of these formal resemblances, it must be remembered that not all the Baron's principles arrived in nineteenth-century Latin America. From the baroque lines of new avenues and the Bois-de-Boulogne-like pattern of some parks to the 'French style' of architecture, associations have been established on the basis of the physical and symbolic apparatus of Haussmannization (Almandoz, 2010b, pp. 24–28; Pinheiro, 2002, pp. 64–88). However, his hygiene reforms were apparently not included in the first portfolio of ideas that arrived in Latin America; they were to be adopted only at the end of the century, and in a different way. Nor, apparently, did Latin Americans perceive the Baron's own conception of an articulated urban surgery which assembled circulation, services and monuments (Haussmann, 1890-1893, 1979) – this would arrive even later, in the first decades of the twentieth century, when urban planning was maturing in several contexts. Even then, Haussmannesque neo-baroque transformations were adopted for their progressive and civilized symbolism, whereby Latin American capitals not only strove to demonstrate their resemblance to the metropolises of the emerging *Belle Époque*, but also tried to manifest their rejection of the *damero* and architectural vocabulary inherited from colonial times.

Hygiene Concerns

Beyond the peculiarities of the Haussmannization and its related morphological changes, another difference of Latin America's bourgeois capitals from their counterparts elsewhere relates to how the incipient urban agenda was shaped. In this respect, the main difference stems from the fact that, as industrialization was less traumatic than in Europe, sanitary concerns in nineteenth-century Latin America, though prompted by deterioration in living conditions, were followed less closely by housing reforms. The smaller contingents of working class did not, however, prevent the proliferation of *conventillos* (tenements) and *casas chorizo* (sausage houses) in Buenos Aires (figure 2.4)

Figure 2.4. *Conventillo* (tenement) in Buenos Aires, *c.* 1880. (*Source*: Archivo del Centro de Documentación de Arquitectura Latinoamericana (CEDODAL), Buenos Aires)

and *corralones* (half-courtyard houses) in Mexico City, along with *cortiços* and *estalagens* in Río de Janeiro and São Paulo, which fuelled protests, strikes and even the constitution of tenants' unions by the 1900s (Pineo and Baer, 1998*a*, p. 259).

Certainly, Britain's sanitary acts of 1848 and 1875 were studied in some Latin American countries, especially in Argentina, where they inspired the reforms promoted by Guillermo Rawson, along with the Paris-published reports by Emilio Coni, *Progrès de l'hyiène dans la République Argentine* (1887) and Samuel Gache, *Les logements ouvriers de Buenos Aires* (1900) (Gutiérrez, 2010, p. 52). Also setting the Chilean case in perspective with the 'sanitary administration' of countries like France, England and Belgium (Puga, 1891, II, pp. 405–470), in *Elementos de Hijiene* (1891, Elements of Hygiene), Federico Puga Borne captured the bleak scene of Santiago's tenements, raising questions that were applicable to many other contemporary Latin American cities:

> … houses inhabited by the underdogs usually are in narrow streets, deprived from artificial paving, what is the cause of humidity in winter, dust in summer; constructions are scarcely elevated above the ground and their floor is sometimes beneath the street's lowest level; therefore, they are narrow, dark, wet and cold… It is hardly surprising then if either diseases declared in those dwellers acquire an exceptional graveness or epidemics find in them the most suitable terrain for their diffusion. (Puga, 1891, I, p. 265)

By the 1880s, Buenos Aires pioneered, with Montevideo, the creation of institutions specializing in hygiene research, with emphasis on tuberculosis, which were followed by similar ones in Mexico City, Santiago and Lima (Wilson, 1942, 1972, pp. 33–35). Founder of Brazil's National Institute of Serum Therapy in 1900, Oswaldo Cruz was responsible for a campaign to eradicate yellow fever, which had been endemic during the nineteenth century; given that the vaccination was gratis yet compulsory, it brought about the so-called 'Vaccine Revolt', when Rio's police clashed with citizens over four days (Schneeberger, 2003, p. 280). Though Cruz's campaign was successful in the long term, it illustrates that sanitary reforms were not always exempt from popular opposition; besides, neither traditional ordinances nor new hygiene institutions seemed to produce, for the rest of the nineteenth century, a comprehensive and permanent response to the explosive problems of salubriousness and housing looming over the horizon. All in all, a real agenda of hygiene and housing in Latin America, to be shaped and raised from the local into national governments, would have to wait for the Belle Époque reforms and would vary in different contexts (for instance Baer, 1998; Parker, 1998; Ramón, 2010, pp. 178–180; Ramón, 1989, pp. 109–144).

Notes

1. This chapter is based on abridged sections from Almandoz (2012) and passages from Almandoz (2006*b*, pp. 45–49; 2010*b*, pp. 13–16; 2013*a*, pp. 33–89).
2. Partly opposing this traditional thesis, though recognizing at the same time the benefits of commodities, the importance of the export sector within Latin American economies throughout the early republican period has been questioned by Carmagnani (2004, pp. 212–216).
3. See below the section 'Conservatives and liberals, oligarchies and bourgeoisies'. Among these

movements *costumbrismo*, which took traditional customs as aesthetical principle, and *criollismo*, based on motifs of Creole context, stood out. See for instance Almandoz, 2013a, pp. 46–52).
4. I rely on passages from Almandoz (2006a, pp. 35–44; 2010b, pp. 13–16).
5. It was Spencer, in his *The Principles of Biology* (1864–1867) – and not Charles Darwin, as it is usually assumed – who coined the phrase 'survival of the fittest'.
6. José Gaspar Rodríguez de Francia was Paraguay's dictator (1816–1840); Gabriel García Moreno was twice president of Ecuador (1861–1865; 1869–1875).
7. In addition to internal revolts in Maranhão (1841), São Paulo y Minas Gerais (1842), Río Grande do Sul (1845) and Pernambuco (1849), Dom Pedro II's reign had to face conflicts with Argentina over Uruguay during Rosas's government. Likewise, Dom Pedro's Brazil participated, alongside those two countries, in the Triple Alianza War (1864–1870) against Paraguay; the conflict was detonated by the desire of Marechal Francisco Solano López to have access to the Atlantic.
8. The influence that Montevideo, as the Mecca for Argentine exiles, exerted on the 1837 Generation has already been mentioned (see p. 19). The recognition of Uruguayan progress can also be found in Alberdi (1852, 2008, pp. 75–76).
9. In this respect, it is worth noting that Alberdi 'called "desert" the soil to be civilized, as it was usual at the time' (Fernández, 2008, p. 21).

Chapter 3

From *Arielismo* to World War I

Overshadowed by the Colossus[1]

... a war for Cuba ... would be here hugely popular: a blasted port, a looted city, two or three centenaries of merchant ships captured by corsairs, are provocations in the colossus's body; they would only serve to irritate him, without draining or defeating him...

Justo Sierra, En tierra yankee (1895, 2000), in *Viajes*

The Monroe Doctrine and Dollar Diplomacy

By the turn of the century, Latin America's Europeanism was undermined by the growing presence of the United States in political affairs. Prior to Spain's expulsion from its Caribbean dominions in 1898, Washington had decided to revive the golden rule of the so-called Monroe Doctrine – 'America belongs to the Americans', formulated by President James Monroe in 1823 – when dealing with other disputes between some of Hispanic America's flimsy republics and European imperialism. Indeed, by the mid-1890s the US had to mediate in the long-running affair over a strip of Guyana, which had caused the diplomatic split between London and Caracas since 1887. The so-called 'Venezuelan question' then became a point of honour for Latin American nations, which saw in the Victorian claim on the Creole territory as a resurfacing of Europe's imperialism in the New World. William L. Scruggs was then appointed as US Extraordinary Envoy and Plenipotentiary Minister to Venezuela and, following his first visit to the country, he challenged the British claim in the following terms:

> ... if England should finally decide upon this course, and under the flimsy pretext of a boundary dispute, of her own seeking, and which she has hitherto obstinately refused to adjust upon any just and reasonable basis, she should persist in her efforts to extend her colonial system within the territory and jurisdiction of an independent American republic, that factor would be but an additional reason, if any were necessary, why the United States should reaffirm, and maintain at all hazards, the principles of the declaration of 1823. The only alternative would be an explicit and final abandonment of those principles; and that would involve a sacrifice of national honour and prestige as no first-class power is likely ever to make, even for the sake of peace. (Scruggs, 1895, p. 32)

Taking advantage of such an international threat, the new colossus of the Americas was able to consolidate its position. Having been settled through US arbitration during the second administration of President Cleveland (1893–1897), the affair over the 'disputed El Dorado' marked the beginning of the end of the British supremacy in the continent (Whitaker, 1948, pp. 158–160). Later, when Theodore Roosevelt rose to power in 1901, the 'Dollar Diplomacy' in the Caribbean was boosted by the construction of the Panama Canal and what was called 'Roosevelt's Corollary': if the United States wanted to take over from Europe as a continental superpower, the former should help to overcome political upheavals and economic crises in the Caribbean and Latin republics (Munro, 1964, pp. 4–7, 65–66).

While travelling across the United States at the end of the nineteenth century, Justo Sierra heard, in the clubs and theatres of New York, not only the heated polemics about the Venezuelan question before England, but also debates over Cuba's inexorable path to independence. Surrounded by diplomats, businessmen and intellectuals, the Mexican scholar observed that while the Cuban emancipation was almost taken for granted, it was its future that fuelled debate, most of the gringos believing that the Black Pearl should become part of the American federation. Above all, he foresaw the importance that imminent events would have in consolidating the North's position in the Americas:

> ... If his attitude has been up to now reserved and seemingly correct, it is because, here, a preparation for war is slower and more public; but, according to reports that I deem as good, this preparation will be complete during 1898; the friendly warning to Spain will then become a rough intimation, and the colossus will raise its formidable voice to utter an insolent *ultimatum*. And the Spaniards must not fabricate illusions; a war for Cuba, which would start by making of Cuba the praetorian take that secured the war's expenses, would be here hugely popular: a blasted port, a looted city, two or three centenaries of merchant ships captured by corsairs, are provocations in the colossus's body; they would only serve to irritate him, without draining or defeating him... (Sierra, 2000, pp. 74–75)

Sierra's words sounded prophetic, considering the events of February 1898 when, on the pretext that the sinking of the Maine battleship in the Havana's harbour was a provocation to its power, the US lashed out at the old-fashioned fleet sent by Madrid and destroyed it in a brief war that put an end to the Spanish Empire in America and the Pacific. Surrounded by the winds of war, when visiting Washington's Capitol, he felt an awesome admiration, though more moral than aesthetic. Standing on top of Capitol Hill, alternating between resentment and contrition, Sierra asked himself what lessons were to be drawn from the losses that his country had suffered to the United States half a century earlier. Without forgetting the 'iniquities that had been sanctioned there' – from Mexico's invasion to the slavery maintained for so long – Sierra tried to reach the 'proud resignation' that the Mexican nation would have to live with, as others in Latin America, overshadowed by the US to the north of the Bravo river. This is why he concluded, in anticipation of the *modus vivendi* for the forthcoming century:

I admire the people whose centre of political gravity is the Capitol; its greatness overwhelms me, makes me impatient and angry sometimes. But I am not one of those who spend their lives kneeling down before it... I belong to a weak nation that can forgive but must not forget the frightening injustice committed against it half a century ago; like my homeland, I wish to have in relation to the United States – an awesome result of both nature and luck – the proud and dumb resignation that has allowed us to become worthy owners of our destinies. I do not deny my admiration, but search to explain it; my head bows, but does not remain inclined; it then lifts more, to better see. (Sierra, 1895, 2000, pp. 83–84)

Roosevelt's Corollary

As if echoing the lessons learnt by Sierra regarding Latin America's *modus vivendi* with the Colossus of the North, the aforementioned 'Roosevelt's Corollary' in the Caribbean was confirmed by the turn of the century through another US intervention in Venezuelan affairs. During the first years of General Cipriano Castro's presidency (1899–1908), the economic and political crisis led the bankrupt republic to suspend payments of credits and loans with Britain, Germany and Italy. Despite receiving several warnings from 1900 onwards regarding the moratorium issued by Disconto-Gesellschaft's representative in Venezuela, the eccentric president's priority in relation to Europe was to fund magazines edited by fellow countrymen resident in Paris (Castro, 1974, pp. 278–280, 287–288).[2] Even on 6 December 1902, Castro naively considered that Britain and Germany were 'civilized nations that cultivated friendly relationships with Venezuela' (Castro, 1974, pp. 312, 320);[3] but three days later, a fifteen-ship armada blockaded the republic's coasts for the first time since Independence. Then, on the same day and inspired by the eloquence of the Colombian Vargas Vila – a rhetorical archetype for Andean liberals – Castro issued a famous proclamation imbued with patriotic hatred of European aggressors:

> The insolent Foreigner has desecrated the sacred soil of our Homeland! ... The duel is unequal because the attempt has been carried out by the two most powerful nations of Europe, against this country of ours that barely convalesces after long and painful ailments. (Castro, 1902, 1962, II, p. 123)

Unlike the Latin American countries that supported Venezuela, the United States had to be more cautious in relation to the European creditors, without missing the potential of a situation whereby its continental leadership could be strengthened. In spite of initially recognizing the claimants' legitimacy, the Roosevelt administration did not back the blockade and intervened to settle the crisis (Núñez, 1943, 1986). Thanks to the mediation of Herbert Wolcott Bowen, US Minister to Venezuela, an international protocol for resuming payments was signed in February 1903 in Washington, where Bowen acted as representative of Caracas; Castro was absent because – notwithstanding his alleged Pan Americanism – Roosevelt refused to host in the White House that 'unspeakable little monkey' who had almost ruined his 'stick policy' and 'dollar diplomacy' in the Caribbean (Picón Salas, 1953, 1991, pp. 54–55, 259–260).

Having witnessed the Monroe furore in late-nineteenth-century Venezuela, the American traveller Ira Nelson Morris was prone to believe that the United States, 'like its emblem the eagle, which extends its broad wings to protect its young from harms or disturbance, has taken the position of affording its protection to all the young countries of the American continent' (Morris, 1897, p. 153). But the protection by the eagle was perhaps misinterpreted by some Latin American republics, which felt immune to the European capitalism, while miscalculating the imperialism portended in the eagle's claws. From the standpoint of a seasoned diplomat, Scruggs also criticized the fabrications by 'some South American states', according to which the Monroe Doctrine could be 'successfully invoked to prevent a European nation from forcing an international obligation... The absurdity of such a construction is its own sufficient refutation' (Scruggs, 1900, p. 265).

All in all, the revival of the Monroe Doctrine for the sake of helping the weak republics, alongside the dollar diplomacy and stick policy in the Caribbean, paved the way for a new line-up of superpowers in the Americas. Changes mostly affected the supremacy of the British Empire, whose last attempts to control the Latin American republics had been blocked by the United States which, by the end of World War I, completely replaced the political influence of Europe. In the economic domain, the supremacy of English manufactures in Latin markets was no longer safe, being challenged from the early twentieth century by American and German products. Despite relative recuperation in the decade after 1902, British investments in the area were also doomed to decrease gradually up to the late 1920s, by which time a century of financial supremacy was over (Rippy, 1959, pp. 11, 36, 75; Carl, 1980, pp. 139–140). Even with its strong economic presence, Germany would never defy the Monroe Doctrine again, and the possible dream of Latin America as a colonial expansion, if it ever existed, remained as such (Herwig, 1986, pp. 207–208). The supremacy of the United States was to be sealed by World War I, which reduced European trade and investments, gave an impetus to American exports in the region, and left the Colossus unchallenged in the New World (Griffin, 1961, pp. 131–132; Munro, 1964, p. 75).

Arielismo, Modernism and Belle Époque

Caliban and the Tropics

> ... *and in some evenings, I contemplated in the Eiffel Tour's surroundings, with my eyes wide open, panoramas only seen in the mysterious regions of dreams.*
>
> Rubén Darío, *La vida de Rubén Darío escrita por él mismo* (1912)

Before its economic and political consolidation by the time of World War I, the United States' ideological conquest of Latin America had to pass through several cultural battles. At the end of the Spanish-American war in the Caribbean in 1898, Rubén Darío – the Nicaraguan poet and essayist and father of literary modernism in the Spanish-speaking world – had declared his definitive enmity towards the 'Caliban' who defeated and humiliated 'the Daughter of Rome, the Sister of France, the Mother of the America' (Darío, 1989, pp. 161, 166).[4] To a great extent, the animosity was shaped by the international literary crusade undertaken from Hispanic America, which boasted about the potential of Spanish as a language and vehicle of civilization.

The hatred was fuelled by the publication of books which justified the American takeover from Spain in the Caribbean on the basis of the Anglo-Saxons' alleged superiority over tropical races. The thesis was epitomized by Benjamin Kidd's *The Control of the Tropics* (1898) – a manifesto which urged the establishment of Anglo-American protectorates in the former colonies set up by continental Europe. The British sociologist entreated the English-speaking world to define the 'principles' of its relations with pretended 'republics' plagued by 'anarchy and bankruptcy', especially Central and South American states, where unstable conditions attracted German expansionism. Britons and Yankees should assume that 'in dealing with the natural inhabitants of the tropics we are dealing with peoples who represent the same stage in the history of the development of the race that the child does in the history of the development of the individual. The tropics will not, therefore, be developed by the natives themselves.' (Kidd, 1898, p. 41). As an alternative to the old-fashioned policy of colonization carried out by continental Europe, the English-speaking world should thereafter take a grip on its responsibility of 'holding the tropics as a trust for civilization' (Kidd, 1898, p. 58).

Against the Golden Calf

While the expansionism propelled by Presidents William McKinley and Theodore Roosevelt in the Caribbean carried out the Americans' part in such a crusade, Latin intellectuals looked for arguments against Kidd's plea. One of the first answers was to acknowledge that the whole of Latin America was *El continente enfermo* (1899, The Sick Continent), according to the diagnosis given by César Zumeta from New York. Though recognizing the political and economic failure of most Latin republics throughout the nineteenth century, the Venezuelan journalist and diplomat warned fellow citizens about Kidd's doctrine, exhorting them to face proudly the challenge of the new century, threatened by the 'civilizations of the Golden Calf' (Zumeta, 1899, p. 17). Just as it was for the Venezuelan modernist, so the Anglo-Saxons' 'Golden Calf' apparently became a material beast for other intellectuals throughout South America, who fought against the peril by invoking the spiritual tradition inherited from Latin Europe.

In 1900 a manifesto appeared calling on the cultural values of Latin America to face the materialistic dangers of the new century. *Ariel*, by José E. Rodó, featured the Shakespearian character as a personification of the noble spirituality that the young republics of the South should adopt to defend themselves against the utilitarian Caliban lurking in the North. The twentieth-century combat would be highly risky because, the Uruguayan humanist argued, the Yankee conquest had already pervaded the Latin spirit. Relying on the critique of American utilitarianism provided by European thinkers,[5] Rodó not only alerted people to the expansionism of the northern neighbour but also attacked its values. Hinting at metropolitan Buenos Aires, he finally warned about the danger looming over those Latin American cities whose 'material greatness' and 'apparent civilization' ranked them amongst the leading capitals of the world: they could become the modern equivalents of Sidon, Tyre or Carthage. The image was doubly prophetic: Latin capitals should beware not only of the materialism emerging in the markets of Chicago, but also of the dependence on New York as the Rome of the New World (Rodó, 1900, 1912, pp. 66–68, 76).

As we have seen above, the gringos' urban culture had already been reviled by Darío, who abhorred their 'overwhelming cities of iron and stone', where he had spent dark 'hours of vague anguish' (Darío, 1989, p. 161). As he would confess in his memoirs, written for the Argentine magazine *Caras y Caretas* (Faces and Masks), the 'rolls of eagles' – as he disdainfully called the dollar bills received in payments for his literary contributions – were only of use in order to visit the cities of his daydreams, such as Buenos Aires and, above all, Paris (Darío, 1912, 1991, pp. 74–75). Though Rodó never visited the United States, he suggested that it was unlikely that the modern traveller approaching New York harbour and the Statue of Liberty's torch, could feel the same emotion which the ancient Greek sailor arriving in Athens must have felt when seeing Athene's golden spear (Rodó, 1912, pp. 87, 94–95). Some years later, Rodó's irreverence for the Statue of Liberty was transformed into overt heresy by Zumeta: when the American government decided to clean the monument in 1907, the Venezuelan exile proclaimed that the clothes of 'Miss Liberty' would always looked 'bloodstained' to all the descendants of Spain, who had been humiliated by the United States in the Caribbean (Zumeta, 1907, 1983, p. 150).

Unlike the critique of materialism developed by positivist authors like Ernest Renan in his *Caliban* (1878), Rodo's *arielismo* represented, as Jean Franco pointed out, a more hopeful and democratic response to that transition in Latin America; it relied for that purpose on the spiritualism and education, the idealism and culture inherited from Europe (Franco, 1967, p. 62). Beyond these attributes, Rodó would add another value to his *arielismo* when finally visiting the south of the Old World that, despite suffering the misery of World War I, was still the cradle of Latin civilization. In his journey across an Italy whose myriad of cities appeared to him as the most conspicuous manifestation of the local 'patriotism' that was needed to boost the '*magna patria*' of Hispanic America, he recognized that the 'city soul' was one of the idealistic expressions supposed to counterbalance the standardizing effect that democracy and mass society would exert (Rodó, 1994, pp. 17–18).[6]

The Modernistas' Aesthetic Evasion

Although it resulted to a great extent from the political, economic and social crossroads at the turn of the century, the *arielismo* was intertwined with Hispanic American aesthetic trends that sought styles and motifs different from the Spanish legacy (Franco, 1967, pp. 50–51). Besides the *costumbrismo* and *criollismo* – literary genres that reacted to modernizing reforms by recreating traditional customs and characters (Bradford, 1990; Almandoz, 2013a, pp. 89–97, for instance) – the most relevant of those new movements was the *modernismo* (modernism). In poetic terms, it combined Symbolic, Parnassian and Pre-Raphaelite ingredients, all of them acknowledged by Darío, leader of the movement and of the Ateneo group, based in Buenos Aires, where they published the *Revista de América* (Magazine of America) from 1894 (Darío, 1912, 1991, pp. 91–92; Burgos, 1995, pp. 27–103). In the narrative domain, even though the modernism has been linked to Brazil's Joaquim Machado de Assis as an antecedent, the Hispanic American movement went beyond the realism and naturalism with which he was associated. However, a good deal of the thematic catalogue of the modernist novel stemmed, as in Machado, from the conflict between the sophisticated and cosmopolitan imagery of its characters, on the one hand, and the backward and vulgar background from which they came, on the other (Franco, 1967, pp. 50–51; Guerrero, 1978).

In view of that backwardness, the aesthetic evasion of cosmopolitan cities, mainly European ones, can be seen as a feature of Hispanic American modernism, as it is evinced, for instance, in José Asunción Silva's *De sobremesa* (1895, After-lunch Conversation). In this cross between an autobiography and an essay, the Colombian author discusses the *fin-de-siècle* dilemmas of Latin American republics through the eyes of subjects sheltered in salons beyond Latin American shores; salons that are 'microcosms' of the civilized Arcadias epitomized by Paris and London (Giraldo, 2001, pp. 21–26). From the ostracism shared with his partners, who are 'spiritual aristocrats' more than fellow countrymen, José Fernández – the protagonist and Silva's *alter ego* – envisages the Haussmannesque renewal of the Creole city, in a sort of mirage of his republican project (Silva, 1895, 1996, p. 84). *De sobremesa* stages the quintessential conflict between real and ideal cities, the latter usually inspired, according to Rama, by a refined and decadent Europe not only visited by the novels' *dramatis personae*, but also recreated through 'the illustrated magazines and the travellers' fabulous descriptions' (Rama, 1984, pp. 115–116).

Indeed, in addition to travel literature, miscellaneous nineteenth- and early-twentieth-century magazines illustrated the cultural climate of Latin America's Belle Époque in which modernism blossomed. Periodicals such as, in order of appearance, Venezuela's *El Cojo Ilustrado* (1892, The Illustrated Lame Person); the already-mentioned *Revista de América*, founded by Darío in 1894 and Argentina's *Caras y Caretas* (1898); Chile's *Pluma y Lápiz* (1900, Feather and Pencil), *Sucesos* (1902, Events) and *Zig-zag* (1905); and Mexico's *Revista de América* (1909) are only a few examples that catalogued the motifs of the Creole *Bella Época*. As happened in the Caracas-published *El Cojo Ilustrado*, these magazines combined translations of writings by Guy de Maupassant, Alphonse Daudet, Octave Mirbeau, Anatole France, Gabriele D'Annunzio, Oscar Wilde and others; excerpts from the naturalist realism of Spain's Benito Pérez Galdós and Emilia Pardo Bazán, jointly with modernist contributions by Darío and Rodó. Besides correspondents' reports on World Fairs, infrastructure breakthroughs and fashionable changes in advanced metropolises, some of these periodicals featured sections on etiquette and European fashion, including advertising of Paris-based department stores, such as *La Belle Jardinière, Printemps, La Samaritaine* and *Au Bon Marché* (Almandoz, 2006a, pp. 163–165).

Among the works of other modernist writers,[7] the novels *Ídolos rotos* (1901, Broken Idols) and *Sangre patricia* (1902, Patrician Blood), by Venezuelan Manuel Díaz Rodríguez dramatize the uneasiness of the modernist subject amidst the rough context of Caracas, where seeming civilization was undermined by narrow-minded backwardness (Almandoz, 2002–2009, I, pp. 43–54). Having returned to the Venezuelan capital after a long stay in Europe, one of the things most resented by Alberto Soria, the sculptor protagonist of *Ídolos rotos*, was the parochial intrusion in 'the communitarian life of small towns'; this was a contrast with his years in Paris, 'where in any tumultuous boulevard ... the intense and rare voluptuousness of feeling alone, very lonely in the midst of the crowd', assuaged 'the painful roughness of his soul' (Díaz Rodríguez, 1982, p. 48). As Díaz Rodríguez's cosmopolitism is shown in this standpoint of the chronicler and *flâneur*,[8] so the final exile from the hostile milieu of Caracas, the sole way-out against the protagonist's lack of adaptation, is a typically modernist confirmation of Alberto Soria's urban drama.

Metropolitan Fervour

Beside those apathetic and evasive characters of modernism, there was also, in the chronicle at the turn of the century, a new type of urban subject, 'anxious, needing stability and, at the same time, glorifying the whirl and change' (Mattalía, 1995, pp. 525–526). Often by analogy or contrast with the scenes that could be found in cities like Paris, London and New York, such works are written by a *flâneur*-like character who reports the anonymity, mercantilism and cosmopolitism of boulevards and promenades, avenues and arcades. It is what Ramos has labelled 'rhetoric of the walk' in relation to the urban chronicles of Martí's *Cartas de Nueva York o Escenas norteamericanas* (1891–1892, Letters from New York or North American Scenes) (Ramos, 1989).

In contrast to the flat and parochial landscape he came from, the 'love for the great city' is manifest in *El encanto de Buenos Aires* (1914, The Spell of Buenos Aires), by Enrique Gómez Carrillo, as well as in numerous of his Parisian chronicles sent to Hispanic American magazines such as *El Cojo Ilustrado*, while the Guatemalan held diplomatic and journalistic postings. From 'the capital of the Latin civilization' he reported, with metropolitan fervour, the changing scene of the bourgeois bohemia in Belle-Époque Paris (Gómez Carrillo, 1993, pp. 17–24).[9] In the case of Darío, in addition to poems from *Azul* (1888, Blue) or passages from *Peregrinaciones* (1901, Peregrinations), the countless reports during his journalistic and diplomatic sojourns illustrate his celebration of the metropolitan bustle that it was impossible to expect in the villages of his native Nicaragua. Confirmation of the significance of the Parisian stage for his poetic imagery are his dream-like impressions of the 1900 Exhibition, where he was correspondent of the Buenos Aires-based *La Nación*; he later confessed to have contemplated in those days, in the surroundings of the Eiffel Tower, 'panoramas only seen before in the mysterious regions of dreams' (Darío, 1912, 1991, pp. 107–108).

Though not always comparable with Darío's rapture of Paris, the fascination of the bourgeois city – to use again Romero's category – brought about different reactions among Latin America's writers: from the escape from their own obscure and backward reality, to the metropolitan fervour reminiscent of Benjamin's *fin-de-siècle flâneur* (Benjamin, 1986, pp. 146–162). Their reactions would depend, on the one hand, on the urban landscape they came from, which they often contrasted with Europe's Belle Époque cities, idealized by the *arielismo*, modernism and magazines in general. But, on the other, their attitudes would be marked by their belonging to the diverse processes of economic, political and social change that, after a century of republican life, informed Latin American republics in different ways to be catalogued next.

From Dictatorial *Pax* to Democracy

Mexico: From Porfiriato to Revolution

... *he has undertaken, like Augustus, great material works that provide jobs to the masses, while raising sumptuous buildings that satisfy the Mexicans' welfare, pride and vanity.*
Francisco Bulnes, 'Discurso para justificar la sexta reelección del general Díaz' (1903, 1995)

According to a historiography that parallels Latin America's changes with those in other parts of the world, it is assumed that the 1905 revolution of the Russian Duma would have inspired Mexico's 1910 rebellion against the progressive yet dictatorial regime of Porfirio Díaz (1877–1880, 1884–1911). But the Russian revolution became a Marxist movement aimed at overthrowing the Czars' exhausted order, whereas the Mexican revolution gave vent to the nationalism against the foreign penetration during the *porfiriato*, while inciting the indigenous race against the everlasting yoke imposed by the European-descent bourgeoisie (Franco, 1967, p. 66). The essentially 'agrarian' nature of the movement (Suchlicki, 1996, 2008, p. 102) was well summarized by Romero in relation to Pancho Villa, Emiliano Zapata and their heterogeneous armies: 'They defended, with vigorous popular accent and each one in his own way, a rural ideology saturated with class resentments that was also of cast and race' (Romero, 2002, p. 367).

Epitomizing the contrastive benefits of economic liberalism in Latin America, Díaz's 'efficient despotism' had applied a 'swift and brutal' pacification of Mexican territory, especially of rural areas, where he enforced *pan o palo*, another of his slogans: 'Bread for the army and bureaucrats, for the capitalist and the foreigner, even for the Church. The stick for his enemies, for the poor masses, and even for the local caudillos who did not accept his total control' (Suchlicki, 1996, 2008, p. 94). At the same time, with 'little politics and much administration' – another don Porfirio slogan already-mentioned – Mexican population increased by more than 50 per cent, reaching 15 million, while the railway network was extended from 800 to 24,000 kilometres; the latter was mainly due to José Limantour's performance as Minister of the Treasury and Public Credit (Halperin, 1967, 2005, pp. 247–248; Cosío, 1973, 2005a, p. 113). In addition to commerce and manufacturing, American and British companies were allowed to invest heavily in the mining and petroleum sector, which made of Mexico one of the world's largest oil producers by the early twentieth century (Suchlicki, 1996, 2008, pp. 97–98).

In spite of these achievements, in *Ulises criollo* (1935, Creole Ulysses), the contemporary intellectual José Vaconcelos lashed out at the alleged progressivism of the regime with vitriolic images: 'The *porfirismo* believed that progress had been reached because a car arrived to Mexico, yet in the houses of Mexico City cooking was still done with vegetal coal, as in Moctezuma's time' (Vasconcelos, 1935, 2003, p. 363). Indeed, beyond the capital, workers in factories and on plantations, most of which were in foreign hands, still demanded the ever delayed agrarian reform; moreover, Indians were often deprived of their *ejidos* or communal holdings that were passed as concessions to foreign companies, including the subsoil rights that had traditionally belonged to the state, according to the Spanish colonial tradition (Suchlicki, 1996, 2008, p. 95). So, behind seeming progress led by a 'new landowner cast', instead of an entrepreneurial bourgeoisie – as portrayed by the *científicos* (scientists) or intellectuals of the regime, headed by Limantour – for Paz, the *porfiriato* represented only the resurgence of 'colonial feudalism' (Paz, 1950, 1980, pp. 116–117).

The economic and social ambivalence of Mexican liberalism – which was partly shared by unstable countries such as Peru and Venezuela – led *científicos* to exalt the wonders of the Porfirian *pax* in order to justify General Díaz's successive re-elections. As spelt out in 1903 by Francisco Bulnes, congressman and diplomat of the regime, when he compared the welfare of don Porfirio's Mexico with that of Augustus's Rome:

> He has destroyed the caciques' dynasties and dissolved their national guards; he has halted their extortions; he has forbidden tyranny over people and shed streams of civilization in his territories, leaving the former without prestige … he has undertaken, like Augustus, great material works that provide jobs for the masses, while raising sumptuous buildings that satisfy the Mexicans' welfare, pride and vanity. (Bulnes, 1968, 1995, p. 128)

Still on the eve of the revolution, amidst the calm preceding the storm, Justo Sierra –Minister of Public Instruction (1905–1911), respected and admired even by the rebels (see also p. 40–41) – paid tribute to don Porfirio on the inauguration of the National University in 1910, by exalting the *pax* built upon railways, industries and grain:

> You have been the main worker for peace, you have embedded it in our soil with the steel ribbons of rails, you have spread it over our environment with the smoke of our factories and you strive with great effort to transform that into fruits longed for by our rich friends… (Sierra, 1939, 1990, pp. 191–192)[10]

As Vasconcelos pronounced after the revolution was unleashed in 1910, intellectuals like Sierra and Bulnes relied on the positivistic thesis that *mestizos* (people of mixed race) 'cannot aspire to have but a benevolent tyrant' (Vasconcelos, 1935, 2003, p. 303). Indeed, as if reinforcing the arguments over the lack of maturity among nations of

Latin America and other backward regions in the tropics – aimed, as we have seen, at justifying colonialism and dictatorships – Bulnes bolstered his reasoning with premises that seemed to be borrowed from Kidd: 'It is not possible to feel minor and to claim sovereignty' (Bulnes, 1968, 1995, p. 135). When justifying Díaz's sixth re-election in 1903, Bulnes used arguments derived from Mexico's sluggish evolution over a century of republican life: 'kilometres of railways must not be ripped up by the claws of civil war; telegraphic lines must not announce again to the world our barbarism, our laxity, our impotence…' (Bulnes, 1968, 1995, p. 122).[11]

But Díaz's re-election did not occur and telegraphs had to announce that the Porfirian *pax* had been broken when General Francisco Madero, his opponent and defeater in the 1910 contest, had to take refuge in the United States when the regime labelled him a rebel. From San Antonio, Texas, Madero drew up the so-called Plan of San Luis, whose aims were summarized by Vasconcelos – witness of the events and early collaborator of the president-to-be – in terms of not recognizing the Porfirian regime, calling the people to armed rebellion, 're-establishing public liberties according to the Constitution; freedom to the working-class masses in order to organize themselves'; seeking electoral rights and 'popular redemption through labour and culture' (Vasconcelos, 1935, 2003, p. 303).

Some of those early aims prefigured the political, economic, social and cultural programme that the Mexican Revolution would partially carry out, after the so-called 'tragic Decade'; during these years, inflamed by confrontations between political factions and regional movements led by Victoriano Huerta and Venustiano Carranza, and by Villa and Zapata among others, little room was left for positive achievements, the most perdurable of which would be the 1917 Constitution (Cosío, 1973, 2005*a*). It was a cruel and destructive decade recreated in Mariano Azuela's *Los de abajo* (1915, The Underdogs), where the physician of Villa's forces was able to portray the insurgent march coming from the north. Launching an epic of the revolution (Franco, 1967, p. 80; Brushwood, 1975, 1993, pp. 33–34), Azuela's novel describes such villages as Tepic, Jalisco, Aguascalientes, Zacatecas and Juchipila, each of which appears as 'a ruin', mirroring ancestral barbarism and caudillismo. It is not a coincidence that one of Villa's partisans exclaims, with naiveté and poignancy at the same time: 'How nice is the Revolution, even in its own barbarism!' (Azuela, 1915, 1960, pp. 73, 134–135).

With all its vicissitudes and upheavals, coloured by the picturesque mythology of the *charros* (horsemen), the tragic Decade can be regarded, from one side, as that 'fiesta of bullets' referred to by Paz with sadness (Paz, 1950, 1980, p. 134); however, from the other, it would pave the way for a more egalitarian Mexican society, as prefigured in the 1917 Constitution, especially concerning the abolition of the old regime. The economic and territorial recuperation would begin later, with the Bank of Mexico, the National Commission for Roads and the National Commission for Irrigation, and other new institutions (Quiroz, 2008, p. 66). To eliminate the resonance of Díaz's brutal liberalism, the positivistic motto of the nineteenth-century republic – 'Love, Order and Progress' – would be replaced by 'Through my Race Shall the Spirit Speak', adopted in the early 1920s by Vasconcelos, Minister of Education and champion of the revolutionary modernization which was to be a feature of the following decades (Paz, 1950, 1980, pp. 135–138) (see Chapter 4).

Brazil's Old Republic

Although not as resonant as the Mexican Revolution, from the late nineteenth century other Latin American states also ended the liberalism and positivism that the *porfiriato* had tried to maintain into the twentieth. In some countries, internal wars and conflicts mirrored the tensions between the conservative oligarchies based in capital cities and the more dynamic groups of booming provinces. In Brazil, not only was Rio de Janeiro's hegemony challenged by the economic sectors of São Paulo and Minas Gerais, but also by the political claims of foreign immigrants. In São Paulo, for instance, by 1885 the foreign-born population was 20 per cent of the total, and by 1897 there were two Italians for every Brazilian citizen (Frehse, 2002, p. 146). The tension worsened after the abolition of slavery in 1888, which had pitted several groups and freedmen against the imperial regime. Together with a growing republicanism in an army imbued with positivism and masonry, these factors led to the toppling of the monarchy in 1889 (del Pozo, 2002, p. 95; Schneeberger, 2003, pp. 254–259).

The *República Velha* (Old Republic), as it was later known, was launched with a liberal and secularizing reformism that separated official and ecclesiastic powers, while establishing freedom of worship and civil marriage. The drive of social renewal was completed by the decree of 'Grande Naturalização' (Great Naturalization), which enabled foreign residents to acquire Brazilian nationality. Meanwhile, economic modernization was championed by Rui Barbosa from the Treasury, with financial policies aimed at fostering entrepreneurial growth and forming a bourgeoisie, although its industrialism proved to be insufficient. Despite its initial momentum and the passing of the new Constitution in 1891, as a result of the so-called 'policy of the white coffee', the *República Velha* ended up reproducing the economic and political predominance of the São Paulo and Minas Gerais elites, biggest producers of coffee and milk, respectively (Schneeberger, 2003, pp. 264–274).

Gómez's Venezuela

Growing liberalism was also seen in smaller countries. In Ecuador, there were regional confrontations between economic groups where Guayaquil's exporter bourgeoisie promoted changes that led to the Constitution passed from Quito by President Eloy Alfaro (Ayala, 2005, pp. 87–89). In the case of Venezuela, the 1899 revolution headed by Cipriano Castro has usually been interpreted as the military irruption of Andean groups on the Caracas scene, inaugurating a political cycle which lasted until 1945 (Pino, 1988); however, insufficient attention is paid to the fact that the *gochos* – native peoples of the Venezuelan Andes – came from a coffee producing region, and that by the late nineteenth century coffee had replaced cocoa as Venezuela's top export.

A parallel with Mexico's *porfiriato* and its *científicos* can be established through the dictatorship of Juan Vicente Gómez (1908–1935), which was also cemented by the so-called *doctores* (doctors) of the regime. Beyond an ambitious programme of public works, aimed at unifying the territory and suppressing the revolts, objectives that from the late 1920s were facilitated by the oil boom, there was repression and torture which turned the regime into 'the shame of the Americas', according to José Rafael Pocaterra, one of its most ardent opponents (Pocaterra, 1927, 1966, III). The dictatorial machinery relied on the positivistic interpretation of the republic's turbulent history, elaborated by the erudite intellectuals in the service of the illiterate satrap. One of the keystones of that positivistic ideology was provided by Laureano Vallenilla Lanz, whose *Cesarismo democrático* (1919, Democratic Caesarism) not only adopted the arguments of Gil Fortoul in relation to Hispanic Americans' racial weakness (Gil, 1896, pp. 29–30), but also proposed the 'Necessary Gendarme' – drawn from French sociological notions – as the sole political option to overcome the traumas of the fledgling republic (Vallenilla, 1919, 1961). In addition to Díaz in Mexico and Gómez in Venezuela, Vallenilla perhaps had in mind Manuel Estrada Cabrera (1898–1920) in Guatemala and Augusto Leguía in Peru (1908–1912, 1919–1930), whose autocratic regimes also made some economic achievements.

Indeed, Gómez's dictatorship was not very different from contemporary European fascism, according to Pedro Manuel Arcaya in *The Gómez Regime in Venezuela and its Background* (1936). By then Ambassador to Washington, Arcaya refuted the international criticism of the elderly ruler, epitomized in Thomas Rourke's *Tyrant of the Andes* (1936), where the economic achievements of the 'lucky' dictator, beneficiary of the black gold, were tainted by his ominous crimes (Rourke, 1937). As Bulnes had done with Díaz, Arcaya – whose private library held more than 70,000 volumes – had to search among the heroes of Roman Antiquity in order to parallel the exploits of the 'Founder of Peace'; according to Arcaya, when Scipio the African was to be tried before the Roman nation over petty charges, he simply led the citizens to the temple to thank the gods for his conquests.

> Following his example, General Gómez might have said to the Venezuelans, before whom he was accused, 'Let us travel over the Republic by automobile, over the highways which I have opened, and return to the National Pantheon to give thanks to God before the tomb of Bolivar, because civil wars have ceased in our land, which he liberated, and because the debts of the nation have been paid'. (Arcaya, 1936, p. 225)

Unlike Porfirio Díaz, who went into exile in Paris after the Revolution's outbreak, the Venezuelan Scipio died unbeaten in the provincial city of Maracay, in the same year as the publication of Arcaya's panegyric. For a long time, revenge impeded a fair account of Gómez's achievements; but later approaches have established a more balanced evaluation of the controversial era. On the one hand, it is true that, taking advantage of Venezuela's internal conflicts, the *doctores* forced interpretations of European Positivism to justify the relentless dictatorship (Pino, 1993). On the other hand, it must be acknowledged that the costly loan from Comte's school made possible 27 years of 'Union, Peace and

Work', a slogan that proved fundamental for the modernization of Venezuela and the rest of the continent (Lombardi, 1982, p. 207). Even though the officials fabricated the 'golden legend' of Gómez's exploits, for a long time the 'black legend' propagated by his enemies ignored the economic and infrastructure transformation that occurred under the yoke of the 'liberal tyrant' (Caballero, 1994).

Argentina: From the Alluvial Era to Radicalism

Not all Latin America was reduced to dictatorial *pax* and positivistic justification, nor had all changes to come from revolution; some were promoted from clubs and groups where new political parties germinated (Carmagnani, 2004, pp. 261–268). The relative economic prosperity and the resolution of disputes between centralism and federalism, both catalysed by the demands of international immigration from the late nineteenth century, enabled the Southern Cone countries to shift, without major trauma, from political and economic liberalism towards social reform. In this respect, national bourgeoisies, though incipient and weak in terms of their bases being more commercial than industrial, championed constitutional changes that partially responded to challenges posed by populations becoming more urban and heterogeneous.

During Argentina's so-called 'alluvial era' of growth and immigration, the institutionalization and diversification of political parties made it possible to move from the hegemony of the National Autonomist Party (Partido Autonomista Nacional – PAN) – representative of the oligarchic liberalism epitomized by Roca's presidencies (see pp. 31–32) – to the leadership of the Civil Radical Union (UCR), founded in 1891 (Carmagnani, 2004, p. 266; Romero, 1946, 2008). Resulting from the demands of an increasing foreign population and emerging middle class (Luna, 1993, 2005, p. 144; Romero, 2007, p. 293), universal suffrage was reached in 1912 – even earlier than in some European countries – during the presidency of Roque Sáenz Peña (1910–1914). It was the first step towards overcoming recurrent electoral fraud, and heralded the arrival of the UCR to power in 1916 (Halperin, 1967, 2005, pp. 149–150).

That first period of the UCR was led by Hipólito Yrigoyen, whose policy of so-called 'reparation' – or correction of mistakes committed by conservative liberalism in the first part of the alluvial era – gained him, as Romero points out, 'the political feeling prevailing among the masses that informed radicalism' (Romero, 1946, 2008, p. 225). Yrigoyen's popularity was boosted by his government's support for the students' movement that, in the aftermath of the 1917 Russian Revolution, was initiated at the University of Cordoba a year later; the movement prompted a national academic reform that spread across Latin America. In overcoming nineteenth-century *laissez-faire*, Yrigoyen envisioned a corporate and welfare state, with stronger participation in productive enterprises and public services, an approach almost unknown on the continent (Romero, 1946, 2008, p. 227).

Even earlier than in Argentina, some political and social reforms had appeared in neighbouring Uruguay. After rebellions in 1897 and 1904 led by the caudillo of the National or White party, Aparicio Saravia initiated an era of relative democratic stability, whose greatest progress was during the presidencies of José Batlle y Ordóñez (1903–1907, 1911–1915). As leader of the of the Colorado party – traditionally associated with emerging urban sectors, in contrast to the mainly rural ones that informed the White party – Batlle passed Latin America's most advanced social legislation, including 8-hour working days, free public education and divorce law; there was also progress regarding the constitution of unions and universal suffrage, reached in 1919 (del Pozo, 2002, p. 94).

Chile's Social Question

As already mentioned, the so-called 'civil war' that ended José Manuel Balmaceda's presidency (1886–1891) in Chile, was caused to a great extent by a readjustment between the executive and legislative powers, in the midst of a fiscal boom made possible by the exportation of copper and saltpetre. In spite of this bonanza, political setbacks and inflationary pressures disrupted the social climate during the 1900s, with more than 200 strikes which peaked during the Red Week or meat strike in 1905. It all fuelled a so-called 'social question' or demand for reforms by the working classes, which often conflicted with the interests of the growing middle classes (Villalobos, 1979, 2010, pp. 169–170, 175–179). This social variety was mirrored in political terms: to the Radical Party's heterogeneous composition was added the Democrat's since 1897 and the Socialist Worker's since 1912, transformed into an overtly Communist one ten years later. Even though these parties did not rise to power in this period, their social claims, along with the establishment of universal suffrage in 1914, broadened the electoral agenda that made possible Arturo Alessandri's first presidency (1920–1924, 1925), backed by the radicals and democrats who became the majority (Eyzaguirre, 1948, 2004, pp. 165–166) (see pp. 67–68).

While overcoming the nineteenth century conflict between conservative and liberals, the Southern Cone countries enriched electoral life with new parties that, without reaching power in the late Belle Époque, helped to diversify Latin America's political and social agenda. These were attained without the traumas of revolutions as had happened in Mexico, or waiting for the conclusion of cruel dictatorships, as Gómez's in Venezuela. For the rest, these demands were mostly raised by growing foreign populations incorporated into the expanding economies, in the midst of urban environments that turned metropolitan, as we shall see.

The Centenary's Urban Agenda[12]

> … *Caracas is deeply infected; its habitants become slowly poisoned with the air we breathe, with the water we drink and with the food we ingest; infectious diseases like tuberculosis spread freely; the slaughterhouse, market and grocery shops are not hygienically regulated; we do not have potable water, nor sewage nor paving.*
>
> Luis Razetti, *Obras completas*, t. II

The end of Latin America's Belle Époque was epitomized by the transformation of bourgeois cities into incipient metropolises increasingly seduced by urban models and cultural manifestations mainly imported from continental Europe, though some came from British or American contexts abhorred by *arielistas* and *modernistas*. In terms of the way of life in general, the Europeanism of the Belle Époque was overshadowed during the 'Roaring Twenties' and the Americanization that followed World War I, whereas in the domain of the emerging urbanism, the process of transition can be said to have lasted until the end of World War II, as we shall see in the next chapter.

Some of the bourgeois capitals of the expanding economies were to become real metropolises by the 1930s: Buenos Aires jumped from 663,000 people in 1895 to 2,178,000 in 1932 (figure 3.1); Santiago from 333,000 in 1907 to 696,000 in 1930; and Mexico City from 328,000 in 1908 to 1,049,000 in 1933. As a dramatic case comparable to the growth of industrial cities like Manchester and Chicago, São Paulo spiralled from 240,000 inhabitants in 1900 to 579,000 in 1920, and 1,075,000 in 1930 (figure 3.2); while the urban predominance of Rio was diminished, its population increased from only 650,000 in 1895 to 811,433 in 1906. The expansion of the capitals was partly due to a process of industrialization by import substitution, which accelerated urbanization in Argentina, Uruguay, Chile and Cuba, which figured among the world's most urbanized countries in the early 1930s (Hardoy, 1975b). Havana's population jumped from 250,000 inhabitants by the turn of the century to 500,000 in 1925. Fuelled mainly by rural-to-urban migration, other capitals of the Andean countries also underwent significant increase: Bogotá grew from 100,000 people in 1900 to 330,000 in 1930, while

Figure 3.1. Avenida de Mayo (Mayo Avenue), Buenos Aires, 1920s. (*Source*: Archivo del Centro de Documentación de Arquitectura Latinoamericana (CEDODAL), Buenos Aires)

Figure 3.2. Gardens and Light Station, São Paulo, inaugurated in 1908. (*Source*: Arquivo Nacional)

Lima increased from 104,000 in 1891 to 273,000 in 1930. Although Caracas rose only from 72,429 inhabitants in 1891 to 92,212 in 1920, the first effects of the oil boom pushed the population from 135,253 in 1926 to 203,342 in 1936. Although the capital of Central America's most prosperous country, San José de Costa Rica had only 50,580 inhabitants in 1927, though this population represented 11 per cent of the country (Hardoy, 1997).

Mainly staged in those capital and prime cities, official and private responses to the demands of the growingly heterogeneous population shaped the urban agenda of the first centenary of Latin American republics. The most significant responses can be classed as hygiene and housing reforms of historic centres, where colonial *dameros* (checkerboards) also underwent urban reconstruction for embellishing, functional and communication reasons; these processes were accompanied by suburban expansion for a bourgeoisie fleeing old-fashioned centres and seeking new styles and landscapes that mirrored their modernizing cosmopolitism. Flirting, on the one hand, with early samples of International Style and Art Deco functionalism, imported for their luxury villas in posh barrios of Buenos Aires and São Paulo, such a snobbish clientele of newly urbanized landowners and coffee barons still also liked the academic repertoire of Beaux Arts and Art Nouveau. Those were stylistic hesitations also shown by the official sector in their civil and administrative buildings.

Embellishing Central Areas

Following the positivistic trend to reduce progress to public works, the new century's modernization mainly materialized in the embellishment of central areas, with magnificent edifices and parks, boulevards and promenades modelled according to the taste of 1900s elites. At the climax of the eclectic Belle Époque in Porfirian Mexico, the commission for the Legislative Palace (1897) went to Émile Bernard, assistant of Charles Garnier, and Adamo Boari was given the commission for the palaces of the Post and Fine Arts. The Fine Arts building was finished after the Revolution, whereas the cupola of the Post building, curiously, became a symbol of the insurgence. In the late *porfiriato*, the renewal of the Paseo de La Reforma reconstructed Mexican history monumentally with eclectic buildings; they were crowned by Antonio Rivas Mercado's sculpture of the Angel of Independence, symbol of the city to the present day (Tenorio, 2000).

Although Brazil did not celebrate the republican centenary but independence from Portugal, during the first presidency of Francisco Rodrigues Alves (1902–1906), major works were undertaken in Rio for the expansion of the *Cidade Nova* or New City. With some Haussmannesque *percées* (piercings) coordinated by the engineer André Paulo de Frontin, the Central Avenue (figure 3.3) epitomized Brazilian *Bela Época* in the *Cidade Maravilhosa* (Wonderful City) that burgeoned during the municipal administration of Prefect Francisco Pereira Passos (Pereira, 2010, pp. 90–91; Pinheiro, 2002, pp, 125–158). Once the bourgeoisie had moved southwards to Copacabana and Ipanema, during the prefecture of Carlos Sampaio the hygiene debate fuelled the demolition of Castelo Hill in order to facilitate wind circulation and eradicate *cortiços* (slum tenements) from the centre. Sampaio's operation not only vacated valuable ground for celebrating the 1922 International Exhibition, but also expelled a homeless population which would eventually swell incipient *favelas* on the outskirts (Kessel, 2001, pp. 57–62).

Figure 3.3. Avenida Central (Central Avenue), Rio de Janeiro, 1908. (*Photo*: Marc Ferrez, 1880. *Source*: Hoffenberg Collection, Archivo Audiovisual de Venezuela, Biblioteca Nacional, Caracas)

Foreign and local professionals were commissioned for buildings in Santiago to celebrate Chile's centenary. After the arrival of Ignazio Cremonesi, who proposed the renovation of the cathedral, Emilio Doyère was responsible for the Justice Palace, built in partnership with the French-Chilean Émile Jecquier; the latter had also designed the railway stations of Mapocho and Pirque, along with the Fine Arts School, present-day museum, whose references to the Parisian Grand Palais are representative of the centenary's architectural taste (Pérez and Rosas, 2010, pp. 124–125). There were also the 'linear proposals' for the expansion of Santiago, developed from 1909 by the Chilean engineer and architect Carlos Carvajal, on the basis of Arturo Soria's 1890s *Ciudad Lineal* (Linear City) in Madrid (Figueroa, 1995*a*). In the 1910s he initiated a series of so-called 'transformation plans', which included hygiene reforms, renewal of the centre and the civic district, along with railway and road layouts for the capital's metropolitan expansion (Aguirre and Castillo, 2004, pp. 29–32).

Preparing the celebration of the centenary of Argentina's Independence in 1910, the Mayor of Buenos Aires invited Joseph Antoine Bouvard to the city in 1907. The former municipal architect of Paris – where he had organized the 1900 Exhibition – designed a web of diagonals for the transformation of central Buenos Aires, including the project for a new Plaza de Mayo (Berjman, 1998, pp. 175–213). During the same journey to South America – and despite the diagonals for the Argentine capital – Bouvard looked for an alternative to Haussmannesque models in São Paulo, where the invocation of Camillo Sitte's picturesque *Städtebau* was a reaction to the predominance of Paris-like reform during Pereira Passos's prefecture (Segawa, 1995; Pereira, 2010, p. 92). The proposals by the French landscaper were discussed by local professionals but scarcely materialized in the long term, however they stand as the first to be elaborated by a foreign luminary for Latin American cities that thereby sought to internationalize and accelerate the process of urban modernization.

Residential Sprawl

The sprawl of residential areas made up another chapter of the centenary's agenda in the major capitals of Latin America. The image and urban structure of the most populous cities drastically changed from the 1900s onwards: crammed since the late nineteenth century with administrative and commercial activities, the traditional centres were home to rural and foreign immigrants attracted by incipient industrialization. In some cases tram and electricity companies assumed the role of urbanizing enterprises, for example, the Light Company in Rio and São Paulo (figure 3.2), the Electric Drive Company in Santiago and the trams enterprise in Caracas (Pereira, 2010, p. 92; de Ramón, 2000, pp. 156–163; Almandoz, 2006*a*, pp. 179–181). Surrounded by a cult of modernity, the arrival of the car in the 1900s broadened the possibilities and directions of expansion, hitherto restricted in capitals that did not have suburban trains but only trams and those only from the 1890s. This was the situation, for instance, in San José de Costa Rica – the most advanced of Central American capitals – where Amon Fasileau-Duplantier, a French-born landowner and entrepreneur of trams, initiated the bourgeoisie's northeast expansion with the barrio Amón (Quesada, 2001, pp. 45–83; 2007, pp. 71–101). At the other end of Latin America's urban scale, the only underground was launched in 1913 in Buenos Aires, so in most cases the automobile, along with trams and buses, completed the congestion of historic centres where nineteenth-century carts and wagons still circulated.

Fleeing such central bustle, the upper and middle classes had started to look for new residential locations from the late nineteenth century, thus setting the direction of expansion for their capitals (Amato, 1970). The Buenos Aires bourgeoisie had migrated towards northern barrios like Recoleta and Retiro after a yellow fever epidemic in 1871 and the incorporation of Flores and Belgrano as urban municipalities in 1887; the middle classes followed especially after 1910, when the electrification of networks increased the range of urban expansion (Gutiérrez, 2010, pp. 53–54; Liernur and Silvestri, 1993, pp. 26–28). Mexico City's bourgeoisie had moved towards the southwest, establishing *colonias* (suburbs) such as Juárez, Cuauhtémoc, Roma and Condesa, while the middle classes moved westwards into San Rafael and Limantour (Tenorio, 2000, p. 66). Although its late-nineteenth-century growth had taken place in barrios and parishes surrounding the historic centre, such as Egipto and Las Aguas, by 1910 Bogotá was clearly marked by the upper-class expansion towards Chapinero in the north, a direction reinforced by the location of the exposition commemorating the republican centenary (Suárez, 2006, pp. 39–40).

This is the time when the 'garden cities' supposedly arrived in Latin America (Almandoz, 2004*b*). A loose use of the term has sometimes labelled as garden cities such late nineteenth-century examples as the first *colonias* of Porfirian Mexico City, including the 1890s area of Higienópolis in São Paulo, developed by Martin Burchard and Victor Nothmann, through to the *urbanización* El Paraíso in 1900s Caracas. Havana's Vedado (figure 3.4) has also been seen as an expression of the suburban qualities of the garden

Figure 3.4. Panorama of Vedado, Havana, 2010. In the foreground are remnants of the original 'garden city' elements. (*Photo*: CC Escla)

city, mixed with Frederick Law Olmsted's natural ingredients of design and Ildefonso Cerdá's combination of activities within blocks (Segre and Baroni, 1998). Yet Hardoy claimed that Ebenezer Howard's garden city concept 'was never transported to Latin America', which was 'attracted' instead to the ideas of the 'garden suburb' and the dormitory garden suburb for the middle and working classes respectively (Hardoy, 1988, p. 104; Sutcliffe, 1981, p. 168). Late examples of this type include Mexico City's Colonia Balbuena (1933), Rio's Realengo (1942) and Buenos Aires's El Palomar in the 1940s (Almandoz, 2004b, pp. 449–451). The only projects directly related to English garden city principles were some of São Paulo's *bairros*, such as Jardim America (figure 3.5) and Jardim Europa, developed with Barry Parker's collaboration after 1915 (Andrade, 1998; Campos, 2002, pp. 235–242). From then on, São Paulo and other Latin American cities that adopted garden-like patterns were a step closer to their Anglo-Saxon counterparts, in the sense that the bourgeoisie's cosmopolitanism was better mirrored in suburban modernity than in the academic monumentality of Belle Époque centres.

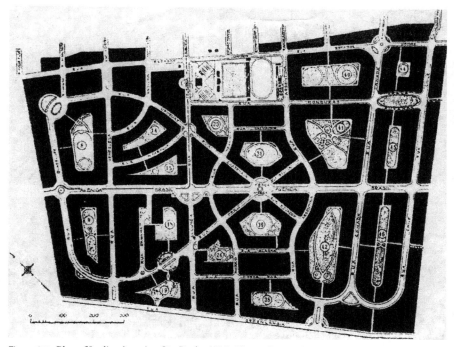

Figure 3.5. Plan of Jardim America, São Paulo, 1915. (*Source*: Prestes Maia, 1930)

Sanitary Reforms

But modernization required other conditions that were less obvious yet more fundamental than embellishing works, design proposals and suburban developments, such as sanitary and housing reforms, which certainly configured another chapter of Latin America's centenary agenda. This happened early in Chile, for instance, on the basis of nineteenth-century advances such as the creation of the Ministry of Industry and Public Works and the passing of the Law of Sanitary Policing (1886). Sewage and drainage networks were boosted during Balmaceda's administration, when another regulation established such services as compulsory for settlements above 5,000 inhabitants (Puga, 1891, II, pp. 446–451). Santiago's early hygiene reforms included the improvement of sewers from 1904 along with the paving of most streets, though 'a minimal part' of them was properly asphalted, according to the detailed report provided by Ricardo Dávila Boza (1910, II, p. 495) – director of the Hygiene Institute – in his paper at the fourth Scientific Congress.

Held in the Chilean capital at the end of 1908, this event was the first of Pan American scope, thus joining a trend to exchange experiences across the Americas in order to diffuse sanitary ideas. This trend can be said to have started in Mexico City with the 1897 and 1902 *Conferencias Interamericanas* (Interamerican Conferences), which discussed the hygiene agenda and encouraged participants to pursue international agreements, some of which were attained in the 1905 *Convención Sanitaria* (Sanitary Convention). Furthermore, the 1898 Congress of Hygiene and Demography, which took place in Madrid, included sections on Urban Hygiene and Urban Engineering and Architecture, and represented a unique opportunity for Spanish-speaking countries to update their sanitary policies. On the basis of those events, by the turn of the century, advanced programmes implemented in Buenos Aires, Montevideo, Rio and Havana inspired hygiene reforms in backward capitals such as Caracas and Lima (*Conferencias...*, 1938; Almandoz, 2013a, pp. 136–146).

Emphasizing that water systems should be improved in order to control plagues and gastrointestinal diseases, the sanitary agenda was analogously addressed in different contexts. Insalubrious conditions in Brazilian cities were alleviated with the improvement of infrastructure networks designed by engineers Saturnino de Brito and Theodoro Sampaio. From the mid-1890s, the former led sanitation projects in about twenty cities, including Minas Gerais, São Paulo and Recife, while Sampaio's work was mainly focused in Salvador de Bahia (Leme, 1999a, p. 22; Leme, 1999b, pp. 451, 454). Mexico was another case of network improvements, where the engineer Roberto Gayol developed projects in 1896 and 1903 for the capital's sanitation office. From the High Council of Salubriousness, the engineer Miguel Ángel Quevedo promoted and chaired the Commission of Embellishment and Improvements of Mexico City; from the same bodies, the task was completed by Eduardo Liceaga, a key figure in Mexican medicine, who participated in the Pan American Sanitary Conferences, the third of which was celebrated in the Aztec capital in 1907 (Sánchez Ruiz, 2008, pp. 242–245; Valenzuela-Aguilera, 2013).

In the case of Caracas, there was a turning point by the late 1910s, not because infrastructure deficiencies denounced since the 1890s by Luis Razetti and other Venezuelan doctors were dealt with, but rather because ordinances that incorporated hygiene rules in construction regulations were issued (Almandoz, 2006a, pp. 196–202). From then on, the hygiene debate can be said to have escalated from the local to the national level, while terms officially used tended to change from *higiene* into *saneamiento*.

Likewise, though demographic and economic differences between countries were considerable, the sanitary question, progressively intertwined with housing reforms, was thereafter taken on by Latin America's central governments, which would introduce new institutions and national regulations that underpinned the welfare states (Pineo and Baer, 1998*b*).

Housing: Between Private Initiatives and Public Regulation

Latin America's housing reform was pioneered by charities promoted by the encyclical *Rerum novarum* – published in 1892, during Leo XIII's papacy (1878–1903). This urged the Catholic Church and Western governments to deal with the industrial proletariat's needs, including their right to form unions. As it was epitomized in Ricardo Larraín Bravo's *La Higiene aplicada en las construcciones* (1909–1910, Hygiene Applied to Constructions), both the sanitary and housing questions were articulated early in Chile, where the 1892 High Council of Public Hygiene would be incorporated into that of Working-Class Dwellings (Larraín, 1909–1910, II) (see also p. 37). The latter was recognized in the *Ley de habitaciones obreras* of 1906, which was catalyzed by the protests of Valparaíso's workers three years earlier (Ferrada and Jiménez, 2007).

In spite of Chile's pioneering institutional framework, 40 per cent of Santiago's population lived in *conventillos* (tenements) during the 1900s in a volatile climate of riots and strikes. This led to the creation of a National Savings Bank in 1910. This *Caja de Ahorros* or Savings Bank was aimed at financing working-class housing and establishing municipal controls on leasing, while more than 193 *cités* or popular ensembles, like the emblematic Huemul settlement, were built in the capital (Aguirre and Castillo, 2004, pp. 69, 73; Ferrada and Jiménez, 2007, p. 40). In spite of these advances in the Chilean case, the *Ley de habitaciones obreras*, in force up to 1924, seemed to prioritize sanitary requirements for habitability over the construction of new dwellings: in Santiago alone more than 1,626 *conventilllos* were demolished without provision of new housing, which created a homeless population of almost 47,000 (Hidalgo, 2007, p. 54).

Also in Argentina, a National Commission of Low-Cost Housing was created in 1915, a decade after the Hogar Obrero (Working-Class Home), promoted by the Socialist Party, initiated its housing production. Fuelled by the restless influx of immigrants from abroad and the countryside – which raised the number of tenement-based families to 150,000, out of 200,000 groups living in inner Buenos Aires by 1919 – a law on rents was finally passed in 1921 (Ballent, 2005, pp. 57–58; Pineo and Baer, 1998*a*, p. 259). Private initiatives for producing inexpensive dwellings had also started in Rio and other Brazilian cities from the 1890s, most of them sponsored by entrepreneurs and companies linked to infrastructure and services (Vaz, 2002, pp. 38–48). However, as most of its Latin American counterparts, the Brazilian state can be said to have remained as a passive and regulatory body instead of an active producer of housing in those decades: control of urban rents was enacted in São Paulo in 1917, while 'tenant strikes' in Mexico City persisted until 1922, when those groups were unionized (Pineo and Baer, 1998*b*, p. 259). Without reaching such magnitude and level of organization, in the case of Caracas, in the late 1910s, Gómez's government passed numerous regulations regarding the crowded *casas de vecindad* (tenement houses) in central parishes (Almandoz, 2006a, pp. 251–252). As happened with Sampaio's demolition of *cortiços* in Rio, such regulations often contributed to the expulsion of low-income population to less-visible districts of Latin America's sprawling cities, which somehow was an original sin of urban marginality in the decades to come.

Notes

1. This chapter is based on abridged sections from Almandoz (2013a, pp. 101–146) and this section on passages from Almandoz (2006a, pp. 139–145; 2010b, pp. 18–21).
2. Letters from 7 March 1900 and 20 June 1900.
3. Letters from 6 December 1902 and 13 December 1902.
4. 'El triunfo de Calibán' (1898, in Darío, 1989).
5. Ranging from social evolutionism to positivism, they included Herbert Spencer, Ernest Renan and Hippolyte Taine; see Dramatis personae.
6. 'Ciudades con alma' (January 1917).
7. Such as the Argentine Leopoldo Lugones and Manuel Gálvez, the Brazilian Alfonso de Lima Barreto and the Venezuelan Rufino Blanco Fombona.
8. This has been extended by Julio Ramos (1989, pp. 126–132) to the Cuban José Martí and other representatives of continental modernism.
9. See for instance E. Gómez Carrillo, 'La bohemia actual' (May 1907).
10. J. Sierra, 'Discurso pronunciado en la inauguración de la Universidad Nacional, el año de 1910'.
11. F. Bulnes, 'Discurso para justificar la sexta reelección del general Díaz'.
12. I rely on passages from Almandoz (2010b, pp. 28–31; 2012; 2013a, pp. 128–165).

Chapter 4

Good Neighbourhood, *Masificación* and Urbanism

From Caliban to Prospero[1]

The world of Rodó and the refined critics of fifty years ago have disappeared; with perplexity, we inquire what is to be born.
    Mariano Picón Salas, *La esfinge en América* (1951, The Sphinx in America)

Traslatio Imperi

The demise of the *Bella Época* came about not only through urban and cultural change, but because Latin America moved to follow the United States and not Europe as its guiding light – a *traslatio imperi* accelerated by World War I. In addition to the enactment of the Monroe Doctrine in the late nineteenth century, and the expansionism boosted by the McKinley and Roosevelt administrations in the Caribbean (see pp. 39–42), the Americans' takeover of Ferdinand de Lesseps's failed project for the Panama Canal, inaugurated in 1914, had cemented the Colossus's dominance in Latin America by the beginning of World War I.

Even in Colombia – which had lost Panama, following the One-Thousand-Day War (1899–1902)[2] – the gringos managed to penetrate and modernize the financial sector. This process reached its peak with the arrival of the Kemmerer Mission in 1921 whose purpose was to create the Central Bank and other institutions. Having received US$25 million in compensation for the loss of Panama, Colombia's reforms prompted the so-called 'Dance of the Millions', a bonanza lasting until the Great Depression, which was fuelled by American investments that rose from US$4 million in 1913 to US$280 million in 1929 (Ocampo, 1994, 2007, pp. 274–275, 279). In the neighbouring countries, meanwhile, the tutelage exerted from Washington, augmented by the canal's commercial operations which began in 1920, was boosted by the influx of loans and the penetration of American enterprises. These were epitomized by the United Fruit Company in Central America, along with the mining companies in several republics and the oil producers in Mexico and Venezuela (Carmagnani, 2004, p. 336).[3]

In the political domain, setbacks in the Caribbean basin led the American government, which was under pressure from public opinion at home, to moderate its expansionism in the region. Thus, for instance, after interventions in the Dominican Republic (1905) and Nicaragua (1912), US forces withdrew from both countries, in the latter repelled by the resistance movement led by Augusto César Sandino (Carmagnani, 2004, pp. 205–206). In Mexico, Woodrow Wilson's diplomatic offensive against Victoriano Huerta's corrupt regime was justified on the basis that some Latin American governments 'subverted the liberties of their people'. However after tensions escalated with revolutionaries, US troops abandoned Mexican territory in 1917, on the eve of their country's entry into World War I (Suchlicki, 1996, 2008, pp. 106, 109).

From then on there was 'a better acquaintance and sincere liking and admiration for American institutions and methods', as summarized by Purl Lord Bell, Washington's commercial secretary to Caracas, in an early 1920s diplomatic report (Bell, 1922, pp. 23–24). And economic data confirm that mutual understanding: in the 1940s, sponsored by Franklin D. Roosevelt's (1933–1945) Good Neighbour Policy, Latin America became the major location for US investment abroad (Roberts, 1978, p. 19).

Old World versus Democratic America

While the United States took on the *traslatio imperi* in the inter-war period, the *arielismo*'s ominous Caliban gave way to a wise and protective Prospero which overshadowed European superpowers in the dusk of Latin America's *Bella Época* (Carmagnani, 2004, pp. 274–275). Maintaining its nineteenth-century role as civilized godmother of the centennial republics, Belle Époque France was signalled by *arielistas* a beacon to oppose twentieth-century materialism, while Paris remained the cultural Mecca for modernist writers (see pp. 44–46). For technical, economic or political reasons, the need to look to France and Europe as the source of Western civilization was still asserted, for instance, in *El porvenir de América Latina* (1911, The Future of Latin America) by the Argentine Manuel Ugarte, as well as in *Las democracias latinas de América* (1912, 1979, America's Latin Democracies) and *La creación de un continente* (1912, 1979, The Creation of a Continent) by the Peruvian Francisco García Calderón.

But the Old World's prestige and seductive powers started to fade for positivistic intellectuals, for example in Venezuela where there was a growing admiration for the gringos' economic and political virtues. In view of the profitable alliance of Gómez's Venezuela with the United States, Vallenilla Lanz, playing again with the Shakespearean characters, asserted that 'Caliban, in the end, is more helpful to us than Prospero', echoing Renan's rejection of the atavistic spirituality inherited from Spain (Vallenilla, 1919, 1961, p. 220). Likewise, before moving to New York during the 1920s, Jesús Semprún reflected the change in attitude of many of Latin America's intelligentsia towards the United States, when he amended his former misconceptions and fears regarding the Northern nation. Blinded by their thoughtless loyalty to a decadent Spain, turn-of-the-century intellectuals had been poisoned against the Yankees because they could not grasp the significance of the independence of Cuba, Puerto Rico and the Philippines. But the nightmare images of Caliban and the 'Golden Calf' had vanished after World War I, when the Latin youth, as a new generation of Ariels, could accept that 'yesterday's masters were mistaken'.

After the war, the United States had thus become the symbol of democracy, modernity, and good citizenship that could be contrasted to the European allies' more practical interests in the recent conflict; these allegedly were, according to Semprún, England's defence of 'its naval power and its dominions', France's preservation of its 'integrity' and Italy's protection of its 'future' as a unified state. Free from fears and suspicions, the Latin American republics could follow Woodrow Wilson's ideals in order to reach 'the peaceful, harmonious and fruitful tree of freedom', concluded Semprún (1918, 1983).[4] This obviously was a biased and incorrect understanding of the causes of World War I, where more complex factors were at stake: Russia, France and Britain had responded to Germany's military escalation and colonial ambitions, boosted by its alliance with the Austro-Hungarian Empire; this juncture had been fuelled by the Balkan states' claims for independence and the European powers' competition for expanding protectorates, including Latin America (Woodward, 1962, 1984, pp. 222–227; Herwig, 1986). But the most significant point for the latter was that, as Semprún and other of Gómez's 'doctors' perceived in Venezuela, the recent conflict had proved to be a golden opportunity for the US to embrace its Manifest Destiny as liberator in the Americas and to negotiate with Europe a 'new world order' (Remini, 2008, pp. 188-–205; Williamson, 1992, pp. 320–321).

Good Neighbours

A 1925 essay by Vasconcelos, *La raza cósmica* (The Cosmic Race) still echoes Rodo's *arielismo* by revisiting the contraposition between Latin and Anglo-Saxon races, now focusing on the US as example of the latter. For this champion of Mexican Revolution the conflict had begun with the defeat of the Invincible Armada and the loss of the Battle of Trafalgar and lasted until Spain's loss of Cuba, Puerto Rico and the Philippines in 1898. However he acknowledged that the animosity caused by the defeat, along with the fragmentation following Hispanic American independence, had led to notions of the supremacy of homeland and republic over race. In contrast, Vasconcelos opposed the idea of the US confederation as a model to be imitated south of Rio Grande (Vasconcelos, 1925, 2007, pp. 7–8).

Over decades in Latin American thought, the sort of political modernism represented by the *arielismo* would resound in Vasconcelos's fellow members of the Athenaeum of the Youth, such as the Dominican Pedro Henríquez Ureña and the Mexican Alfonso Reyes (Franco, 1967, p. 65). Yet, as we have seen, there was also disenchantment with the Old World's miseries among positivistic intellectuals and younger generations born during the Belle-Époque Europeanism, but who had grown up under the aegis of mounting US predominance in all domains, especially after the allies' triumph in World War II.

The victory had been preceded by Franklin D. Roosevelt's Good Neighbour Policy towards Latin America, reasserted by his attendance of the continental conference held in Buenos Aires in 1936. The declaration of principles resulting from the event, also signed by the United States, proclaimed 'their absolute juridical sovereignty, their unqualified respect for these respective sovereignties and the existence of a common democracy throughout America' (Suchlicki, 1996, 2008, p. 122). Amidst that climate of *Buena Vecindad* prevailing across the continent from the 1940s, Mariano Picón Salas returned, in a series of books, to the issue of the reconciliation between the formerly 'disunited Americas' that had been posed by Vasconcelos. From the new perspective of his generation and evoking some mythology used by the political and historical *arielismo* in which he had been educated, he seemed to question both the sphinx – an image used in his book's title quoted in the epigraph – that had abandoned the devastated Europe and the former Caliban converted in Prospero: 'The world of Rodó and the refined critics of fifty years ago have disappeared; with perplexity, we inquire what is to be born' (Picón, 1996, p. 244).

Towards Welfare States, Corporatism and Citizenship

As US influence increased, the exhaustion of European-oriented *arielismo* among Latin American intelligentsia was accompanied by major political and social changes throughout the continent. Although there were still feudalistic dictatorships that overshadowed the inter-war period, such as Gómez's in Venezuela and Manuel Estrada Cabrera's in Guatemala (1898–1920),[5] Latin America can be said to have undergone a significant transition towards socially-oriented, even welfare states from the 1920s to the 1940s. While the state took on greater participation in economic activities and production – the so-called 'corporatism' strongly linked with the political parties' machinery (Williamson, 1992, pp. 346–347) – this transition was not exempt from the reappearance of militarism, even in constitutionally consolidated countries. Yet, in spite of the period's turbulence, some positive progress would be achieved in terms of political rights and citizenship, as we shall see in this section.

The Reformist Phase of the Mexican Revolution

With the passing of the 1917 Constitution, which secularized the state and granted more civil rights to both citizens and peasants, the Mexican Revolution entered a 'reformist phase' leading to positive results after the so-called 'destructive decade' (Cosío, 1973, 2005*b*, p. 139). Relying to some extent on the 1857 Constitution, the new one 'departed drastically from the laissez-faire ideas of the nineteenth century liberals. The new state would actively direct and control the economy; it would be a secular state free of clerical influence' (Suchlicki, 1996, 2008, p. 110). Even though some progress was made during the constitutional governments of Venustiano Carranza (1917–1920), Álvaro Obregón (1920–1923) and Plutarco Elías Calles (1924–1928) – especially in terms of re-establishing the national ownership of land ceded during the *porfiriato* along with improvements in working hours and other labour benefits – the greatest changes would be achieved during the presidency of Lázaro Cárdenas (1933–1940). Purging the corrupt membership of the Partido Nacional Revolucionario (PNR, Revolutionary National Party), founded by Calles in 1928, through the new Partido de la Revolución Mexicana (PRM, Party of the Mexican Revolution), Cárdenas revamped the socially-oriented goals lost during the *callesato*. Adopting the Six-Year plan drawn up by the PNR and influenced by the Soviet system, the new president strengthened Mexico's social breakthroughs and economic 'corporatism' by combining the long-awaited agrarian reform[6] with the industrialization programme and the nationalization of oil and railways (Suchlicki, 1996, 2008, pp. 118–120; Wiliamson, 1992, pp. 390–400).

The Revolution's educational crusade in this period was championed by José Vasoncelos from prominent posts at the National School and the Ministry of Public Instruction and Fine Arts, prior to his appointment as Minister of Public Education. From the latter position he sponsored famous *muralistas* (mural painters) like Diego Rivera, José Clemente Orozco and David Alfaro Siqueiros, while he brought to Mexico leading educators like the Dominican Henríquez Ureña and the Chilean Gabriela Mistral. As we shall see at the end of this chapter, the Revolution's educational renewal was to be completed by modernization of university curricula.

Chile: Around the 1925 Constitution

Even in Latin America's politically most advanced countries, a progressive yet centralist militarism remained threatening, especially when the effects of the Great Depression impacted. As had happened with the presidencies of Batlle y Ordóñez and Sáenz Peña in Uruguay and Argentina respectively, the election of Arturo Alessandri (1920–1924, 1925) in Chile signalled an 'awakening of the masses', backed by the consolidation of the Socialist Party and the enactment of the 1925 Constitution which settled the nineteenth-century dispute between the executive and the parliament. Advocating state secularization and compulsory public education, Alessandri aptly summed up the spirit of the future when he accepted the candidacy in April 1920: 'I want to be a threat for reactionary spirits, for those who resist every fair and necessary reform ... I want to be a threat for those who rise against principles of justice and right; I want to be a threat for those who remain blind, deaf and dumb before the present's historic revolutions...' (Alessandri quoted in de Ramón, 2006, p. 123).

With the military manifesting its discomfort at a social crisis that was not being tackled, Alessandri's reforms were interrupted by the coups led by Luis Altamirano Talavera and Carlos Ibáñez in 1924 and 1925 – heads of the Army and the Cavalry respectively. In an unusual episode in Latin America, the pressure wielded by these officers made possible the enactment of the continent's most progressive social laws, such as those of work contracts, union organization, compulsory insurance for workers and pension funds for private employees (Villalobos, 1979, 2010, pp. 184–185). The successive military and civilian juntas ended up demanding Alessandri's return to power in order to preside over the constitutional reform of 1925, which established the long-awaited separation of Church and State along with the independence between the executive and legislative powers.[7]

The 1925 Constitution did not imply the state's greater participation in economic activities, but this did take place in later governments. Firstly as Minister of Interior and War (1925–1927), and secondly as *de facto* President (1927–1931), Carlos Ibáñez promoted the so-called 'New Chile', including progressive policies in public works along with industrial and agrarian credit, all backed by the creation of the Central Bank and the Republic's National Comptroller (Halperin, 1967, 2005, pp. 404–407). Such a modernizing process was continued during Alessandri's second tenure (1932–1938), with the industrialization policy led by the Corporación Chilena de Fomento (CORFO, Chilean Corporation of Promotion); sanitation and housing came to the fore in this period, as was set out in the 1925 Constitution (Gross, 1991, pp. 130–131). All in all, despite of being the Latin American country most affected by the Great Depression, and the disruptions in its constitutional continuity by military yet progressive governments, by the late 1930s Chile had a strong structure of political parties led by the Frente Popular (Popular Front), as well as an 'urban unionized mass' that bolstered Chilean welfare state and democracy through the early 1970s (de Ramón, 2006, p. 144).

Argentina: the Infamous Decade

Despite Argentina's constitutional and parliamentary progress from the late nineteenth century, a volatile climate of anti-labour and anti-anarchist nationalism pushed the country into social and political unrest.[8] Yrigoyen's second presidency (1928–1930) was plagued by protests. It finally ended with the *coup d'état* headed by José Félix Uriburu in 1930, which unleashed a cycle of constitutional and democratic regression (Williamson, 1992, pp. 459–477; Halperin, 1967, 2005, pp. 288–326). The turmoil had partly stemmed from the complex process of change promoted by the UCR or Civil Radical Union (see pp. 52–53), which allegedly was too moderate to offset the oligarchy's control, as well as unable to respond to the social demands of the urbanized country (Romero, 1946, 2008, p. 230).

Albeit the coup launched the so-called 'Infamous Decade', especially because of its proscription of radicalism and the reappearance of political fraud, Agustín Pedro Justo's presidency (1932–1938) must be credited with achievements in public works and the passing of the *Ley de Vialidad*. This Law on Roads favoured automotive transport over railways originally built by the British – a delicate issue for relations between Buenos Aires and London (Luna, 1993, 2005, pp. 187–190). In the midst of the Great Depression, the Roca-Runciman Treaty (1933) tried to settle the historic dispute by establishing that Britain would buy frozen beef from Argentina, while the latter would treat British investments favourably, including the railroad network. The crisis also brought about more permanent measures that underpinned the corporate state, such as the creation of the Central Bank, chaired by Raúl Prebisch (1935–1943), along with regulatory boards for different staples. Given the import restrictions and growing urban market, fuelled by rural and foreign immigration, the state's intervention encouraged

Argentine industrialization which reached a peak by the 1940s (Luna, 1993, 2005, pp. 192–200).

Getúlio Vargas's Brazil

In Brazil, the political and economic renewal launched during the *República Velha* by the São Paulo and Minas Gerais bourgeoisies had stalled by the 1910s; a new urban, industrial and communist republicanism emerged with the *tenentes* (lieutenants) led by Luis Carlos Prestes, who campaigned throughout Brazil's vast province from 1925. However, the 'white coffee' policy (see p. 50) favoured the candidacy and eventual presidency of Washington Luis Pereira de Sousa (1926–1930). His tenure was characterized by inflation control after the Great Depression, partly tackled through policies inspired by the slogan 'to govern is to build roads' (Schneeberger, 2003, pp. 290–291). Frictions and disagreements between São Paulo and Minas Gerais politicians paved the way for the rise of Getúlio Vargas as leader of the Liberal Alliance, which had configured an alternative to the Old Republic's stale electoral pact.

Former Minister of the Treasury (1926–1927) and Governor of the Rio Grande do Sul state (1928–1929), Vargas had emerged not only as representative of the new entrepreneurs that flourished after World War I, but also as a leader who fractured the presidential hegemony of São Paulo and Minas Gerais. Following the political diversification of the 1920s,[9] Vargas's revolution suspended the constitution in 1930 and declared the Second Republic with a new charter in 1934; the latter enacted the direct and secret vote, even for women, jointly with an advanced labour legislation. Notwithstanding this constitutional and social progress, the autocratic nature of Vargas's first government (1934–1937) fuelled the left-wing Liberator National Alliance (ANL) under the guidance of Prestes, champion of the above-mentioned *tenentismo* of the Old Republic. The alleged 'communist danger' represented by this movement, amidst the stormy climate prior to World War II, paved the way for Vargas's 1937 *coup d'état*. Although the ensuing *Estado Novo* (New State, 1937–1945) set up by Vargas became conservative, centralized and authoritarian, its beginning represented, with hindsight, a break with the Southern oligarchy's control of the *República Velha* along with the foundation of the corporate and socially-oriented state (del Pozo, 2002, p. 96; Schneeberger, 2003, pp. 300–310).

Venezuela's Short-Lived Democracy

In highly autocratic or even dictatorial regimes, such as Augusto Leguía's in Peru (1919–1930), Gerardo Machado's (1925–1933) in Cuba and Juan V. Gómez's in Venezuela, from the 1920s economic liberalism that favoured foreign investment was balanced by modernization of sanitary, communication and urban infrastructure. There were also pressures towards political pluralism, though it sometimes occurred through parties promoted by leaders in exile. Thus it was with Peru's Alianza Popular Revolucionaria Americana (APRA, American Popular Revolutionary Alliance), founded in 1924 by

Víctor Haya de la Torre, who worked in Mexico as Vasconcelos's secretary (Franco, 1967, pp. 96–97).[10]

After the 1928 student revolts against Gómez's regime, Rómulo Betancourt and other young politicians and intellectuals organized clandestine opposition while in exile. With the death of the dictator in 1935, some political openness started during the presidency of Eleazar López Contreras (1936–1941). Another Andean with a military background[11] and appointed by his predecessor, López attempted a more technocratic and socially-oriented progressivism. Renowned writers in exile, such as Rómulo Gallegos and José Rafael Pocaterra, were invited to join the pluralist government, along with younger intellectuals like Mariano Picón Salas and Arturo Uslar Pietri (Chiossone, 1989). Concerned by the civil rights of the migrants, who started to swell the cities and camps of oil-producing Venezuela, Picón warned that 1936 was the decisive moment for including in 'the nation's legal and moral life' those 'Juan Bimbas' (Joe Bloggs) 'without history' that 'informed a peasant and proletarian mass' (Picón, 1988, p. 86).[12]

A decade after Gómez's death, the government of Isaías Medina Angarita (1941–1945) was deposed by a coup led by military and civilians, including Betancourt, who advocated universal and direct suffrage and the end of the Andeans' predominance in government. Reflecting on Venezuelan short-lived democracy, Picón reminded the state of the political urgency of educating those Juan Bimbas of Venezuela's urban mass and providing them with true citizenship (Picón, 1988, pp. 70–71;[13] Almandoz, 2002–2009, II, pp. 168–169).

In 1947, Venezuela finally enacted the constitution that established universal suffrage – almost four decades after Batlle's electoral reforms in Uruguay and Sáenz's in Argentina, and more than two decades later than new charters in Mexico and Chile. That process made possible Rómulo Gallegos's presidency in 1948. However, despite the political renewal of those years when the grassroots reached constitutional representation, after Gómez's death the fledgling democracy was interrupted yet again by a military junta presided over by Carlos Delgado Chalbaud. So even in booming economies like Venezuela, the menace of militarism and autocracy was looming – as it was in other Latin American countries whose seeming stability was to be disrupted in the decades to come (see Chapter 6).

Mass Metropolises

Demographic Changes

The emergence of the welfare state and a new citizenship in larger Latin American countries went hand in hand with urban growth and *masificación* that had begun in the early twentieth century (Romero, 1984).[14] This was evident in the centenary celebrations in major capitals (see pp. 53–57), but later spread to many other cities, especially after the Great Depression and the decline in agriculture. Between 1900 and 1940, Latin America's population rose from 63 to 130 million, reaching a 20 per cent increase in the 1920s (Harris, 1971, pp. 31, 64). The population concentrated in settlements of more than 20,000 grew from 14.4 per cent in 1920 to 19.6 per cent in 1940, making Latin America the least rural among the world's less developed major areas, followed by East Asia (Roberts, 1978, pp. 6–7).[15]

By the beginning of the 1930s, concentration in major centres became another feature of regional urbanization. On the basis of a 3.3 per cent annual growth, Buenos Aires had a population of 2,178,000; the growth of Argentina's capital was surpassed by industrially-based Rosario, where the population rose from 92,000 in 1895 to 481,000 by 1932. As in Buenos Aires, the agglomerations of Havana, Santiago and Panama City represented 15 per cent of their countries' total, while it was 10 per cent in Costa Rica's San José and Paraguay's Asunción (Hardoy, 1997, p. 267). Although in absolute size the populations of Asunción, Managua, Port-au-Prince, San José, San Salvador and Panama City were below 100,000 inhabitants,[16] the process of *masificación* was to be found everywhere, partly as a consequence of widespread rural–urban migration.

Along with other waves of European immigration during the Spanish Civil War and World War II, rural–urban migration became a significant factor in demographic growth in those decades, especially after the abandonment of primary activities, whereas city-based industry was sought as a source of employment (Clichevsky, 1990, p. 47). As had happened earlier in Argentina and Uruguay, from 1930 the proportion of population engaged in agriculture began to decline elsewhere; Chile and Venezuela headed this trend, going from 35 and 50 per cent in the 1930s respectively, to 28 and 32 per cent after 1945.

While this transition partly resulted from expectations of higher income and better conditions in the city, the 'push factor' caused by 'rural poverty' was the predominant force in population movements from the 1930s (Harris, 1971, pp. 74, 84). Although some migrants moved to medium-sized centres, the target for the majority was Latin America's sprawling metropolises. Partly as a result of their past colonial importance, between 1932 and 1950 Buenos Aires grew from 2,178,000 inhabitants to 4,603,000, Mexico City from 1,049,000 to 2,223,000, Santiago from 696,000 to more than a million, and Bogotá from 330,000 to 525,000 (Hardoy, 1997, p. 269). But other cities of lower hierarchy during the colonial period, which had not reached 200,000 by 1930, grew more rapidly than larger metropolises, such as Caracas, Maracaibo and Valencia in Venezuela, Guadalajara and Puebla in Mexico and Medellín in Colombia (Negrón, 2001, pp. 98–100; Quiroz, 2008, pp. 69–70).

New Skylines and Social Segregation

Following the elites' move away from central districts by the late nineteenth century (see p. 58–59), the traditional layout and land use of many Latin American cities still gravitated around colonial plazas and *dameros*, but this changed radically from the 1920s. In terms of circulation, there was the construction or prolongation of wide avenues such as the 9 de Julio in Buenos Aires (figure 4.1), the Revolución and Insurgentes in Mexico City, the Tacna in Lima and the Bolívar in Caracas. Parkways were also created, such as the General Paz in Buenos Aires (Gutiérrez, 2010, pp. 68–71); other major

Figure 4.1. 9 de Julio Avenue, Buenos Aires, aerial view circa 1940. (*Source*: Archivo de Originales SLGM. FADEU. Pontificia Universidad Católica de Chile)

roads were more aggressive and crossed city centres, as happened in Caracas and other Venezuelan cities influenced by North American models (González, 1996).

Urban renewal projects accentuated the administrative function of the centres, while introducing new schemes of mass housing, as in Santiago's Barrio Cívico (Civic District, figure 4.2), masterminded by Karl Brunner (Pérez and Rosas, 2010, pp. 130–132), and in the famous residential blocks of Carlos Raúl Villanueva's El Silencio.

Figure 4.2. Barrio Cívico (Civic District), Santiago, 1940. (*Source*: Archivo de Originales SLGM. FADEU. Pontificia Universidad Católica de Chile)

Figure 4.3. Centro Simón Bolívar from El Silencio, central Caracas, postcard by RIFRA, 1950s. (*Source*: Arturo Almandoz Archive)

Accordingly with the governments' growing economic presence, some of these interventions reinforced the symbolism of the public sector in the capitals' centres, epitomized by the Ministry of Education and Health, designed by Lúcio Costa in Rio de Janeiro, and Cipriano Domínguez's Centro Simón Bolívar in Caracas (figure 4.3); the latter was conceived as a sort of Rockefeller Centre that became a symbol of the capital for decades to come (Fraser, 2000, pp. 110–113, 150–164).

Despite their impact on the urban skyline and landscape, these modern icons could not hide the emergence of squatter settlements, especially on the periphery and on the steep slopes surrounding cities. Prime examples were Rio de Janeiro and Caracas, where *casebres*, *favelas* and *barrios de ranchos* were home to 17 per cent of Rio's population by 1947 and 45.8 per cent of Caracas's by 1950 (Harris, 1971, p. 212; Vaz, 2002, pp. 54–57). They prefigured the imbalances between economic growth and urbanization that, as we shall see (see pp. 96–99, 128–133), were to characterize the dual structure of many cities across the continent.

From the proliferation of cinemas to early department stores, Latin America's mass metropolises of this period also show the social differentiation between the bourgeoisie and upper middle classes in process of US-oriented modernization. They also demonstrate functional, social and spatial segregation marked by the transition of traditional communities that were being displaced and transformed by the urban way of life. Characterized by the Chicago School after the German sociologists (Park and Burgess, 1925, 1984; Wirth, 1938, 1969; Tönnies, 1887, 1965; Simmel, 1903, 1969; Spengler, 1969), that transition was to be influential in Latin American social sciences, as we shall see in the next section. In particular Park's notion of 'neighbourhood' turns into Latin America's *barrio* as the territorial unit of community and cultural identity within the metropolitan structure (Park, 1916, 1984).[17]

Between Vanguards and Social Sciences[18]

As pointed out by Angel Rama, the changes towards the 'revolutionized city' in Latin America – which somewhat overlaps with Romero's mass metropolis – not only occurred through the incorporation of non-traditional groups in the bourgeois and 'lettered' city; it was also a more critical stance by the emerging intelligentsia towards the old-fashioned cliques of literary modernism and political *arielismo* (Rama, 1984, pp. 143–147). It is not possible to summarize here the wide range of artistic and literary trends that shaped this new revolutionized city; however, we can highlight some urban motifs and movements that marked the intellectual climate from which urbanism emerged as a discipline in Latin America.

Literary Newcomers

In concert with the political changes oriented towards welfare states and citizenship, a key motif developed in contemporary literature was that of the newcomers to the cities who were part of the *masificación*. In the case of Venezuela, for instance, there was the aforementioned Joe Bloggs or Juan Bimba, the peasant character profiled in Mariano Medina Febres's cartoons in newspapers such as *Ahora* (Medina, 1991).[19] Illiterate and dressed in ragged traditional clothes (figure 4.4), Juan Bimba was rapidly recognized by the post-Gomez intelligentsia as a symbol of Venezuela's rural and migrant population (Almandoz, 2002–2009, II, pp. 167–169).

Juan Bimba was not an isolated character in Venezuelan literature. In the midst of the *masificación* taking place in the undeveloped yet already-crowded centre of Caracas, students arriving from the provinces to the boarding houses of Gómez's capital were portrayed in the novel *Fiebre* (1939, Fever), by Miguel Otero Silva, in which he recreated the 1928 revolts against the regime. There were also the underdogs from the port of La Guaira seeking petty jobs in the capital's building sector, or sudden stardom in the new sports of the mass society, like baseball and boxing, as described in Guillermo Meneses's *Campeones* (1939, Champions) (Almandoz, 2002–2009, I, pp. 130–134).

In differing contexts and with a variety of characters, newcomers to the emerging metropolises were portrayed in works that chronicle life in countries where *masificación* had started earlier. *Papeles de recienvenido* (1929, Papers of Newcomer) by Macedonio Fernández is a saga of intellectual urbanization; in his humorous yet sarcastic chronicles, the Argentine writer coined the term '*recienvenidez*' (quality of being a newcomer) to caricature the parochialism of intellectuals arriving in Buenos Aires who try desperately to leave behind their provincial background (Fernández, 1968, p. 14). Also in Buenos Aires, social climbers, foreigners and outsiders intertwine in situations described by Roberto Arlt in *Aguafuertes porteñas* (1933, Buenos Aires Etchings).[20]

The sophistications of the capital city are familiar to once privileged, but now

Figure 4.4. Cartoon of Juan Bimba, who needs the student's instruction and is told that their newspaper has been cancelled by the government. Drawing by Mariano Medina Febres (MEDO), originally published on 9 June 1937. (*Source*: Medina, 1991)

impoverished characters like Teresa Iturrigorriaga, protagonist of Joaquín Edwards Bello's *La chica del Crillón* (1935, The *Crillón* Girl). Though she is seduced by the glamour around one of Santiago's main hotels, the lacklustre flapper is forced to let a room to a student who demands 'social justice' for 'the masses' in a capital stricken by the Great Depression (Edwards, 1935, 2010, pp. 85–88). From an opposite side of Santiago, Edwards Bello had earlier recreated in *El roto* (1920, The Pleb), the sordid *conventillos* that turned into shantytowns.[21]

With touches characteristic of José María Arguedas's social denouncement, the mass of newcomers also appears in *Yawar fiesta* (1941) through *cholos* (of Indian origin) and outsiders drawn to the outskirts of sprawling Lima. And so it happened with black and popular characters swelling the segregated Havana recreated by Alejo Carpentier in *Écue-Yamba-Ó* (1933), another *avant-garde* example of city dwellers and immigrants adjusting to Latin America's new metropolitan life.

Americanismo, Modernismo, Muralismo

In the inter-war years, there was an international appetite for Latin America and other regions untouched by the miseries of World War I. In this respect, Jean Franco pointed out that early-twentieth-century *nativismo* was fuelled by the alleged decline of Western civilization denounced by Spengler in his eponymous classic (Spengler, 1918–1922, 1998). At the same time, anti-modernist pleas by authors like D.H. Lawrence, Hermann Keyserling and Waldo Frank exalted indigenous forms of *americanismo* (Franco, 1967, pp. 70, 118–119).

In accordance with this ethos, much of the transition of the lettered city into the revolutionized one involved an *avant-garde* reinterpretation of Latin America's vernacular and indigenous motifs. This is the case of Oswald de Andrade's manifestos 'Pau-Brasil' (1924, Brazil Wood) and 'Antropófago' (1928, Cannibal), as well as Mario de Andrade's novel *Macunaima* (1928). But regardless of its search for primitive roots, Brazil's *modernismo* was led by sophisticated urban elites who could only flourish in the cosmopolitan atmosphere of Rio and São Paulo. Proclaiming its cultural primacy, the latter hosted the 1922 Week of Modern Art, which also featured artists like Tarsila do Amaral (Franco, 1967, pp. 108–111; de Almeida, 2002).

Championed by Diego Rivera, José Clemente Orozco and David Alfaro Siqueiros, all sponsored by Vasconcelos from the Ministry of Education, Mexico's *muralismo* (muralist movement) was another example of blending primitive and *avant-garde* forms.[22] By the late 1920s, once official support was obtained, the objectives achieved by *muralismo*, like Brazilian modernism, prove that these movements, nativist and innovative alike, contributed with their iconography to the economic, political and intellectual nationalism through the mid-twentieth century (Williamson, 1992, p. 512).

Vanguards, Roots and Races

The mass metropolises also fostered the reinterpretation of nineteenth-century movements that had underpinned Latin America's national literature, such as *costumbrismo* and regionalism (see pp. 20–21, 37–38). This was the case with the Boedo group in Buenos Aires, and the *Babel* and *Sur* (South) magazines. The latter were founded by Victoria Ocampo, with the collaboration of well known writers, including Macedonio Fernández, who revisited provincial and traditional topics (Franco, 1967, pp. 104–107).[23] Others like Adolfo Bioy Casares and Jorge Luis Borges preferred more urban and cosmopolitan images.

There was also the influence of Latin American writers based in Paris and other foreign capitals. They combined, in precursors of what would be called 'magical realism' (Anderson Imbert, 1976), approaches and techniques from surrealism and dada with symbols inherited from native traditions. Besides the Peruvian poet César Vallejo and the Chilean Vicente Huidobro, Paris was home to storytellers such as the Cuban Alejo Carpentier and Miguel Ángel Asturias, author of *Leyendas de Guatemala* (1929, Guatemala Legends), who influenced the Venezuelan Arturo Uslar Pietri.

These authors' return to a vernacular catalogue was also perceivable in diverse genres whose indigenous themes were different from nineteenth-century treatment. This was the case in Peru with the aforementioned Arguedas and Ciro Alegría's *La serpiente de oro* (1935, The Golden Snake) and *El mundo es ancho y ajeno* (1941, Wide and Alien is the

World). In his 1948 foreword to the tenth edition of *El mundo*, the author characterized secular *indigenismo* as different from nineteenth-century *indianismo* (Alegría, 1948, 1955, pp. 13–14), which had been imbued with romanticism and torn between the antinomies of Europeanism and *costumbrismo*, civilization and barbarism (see pp. 17–21). And to complete this artistic renewal based on Latin America's racial roots, the *passion noire* that was also present in cubism and *modernismo* penetrated the music of Brazil's Heitor Villa-Lobos and the Afro-Cuban motifs in Carpentier's works.[24]

Emerging Social Sciences

Beyond music, painting and literature, the intellectuals' revival of indigenous motifs invigorated Latin America's nascent social sciences, some of whose leaders participated in both cultural movements and academic milieus. Still rooted on nineteenth-century trends such as positivism, by the 1930s a generation of works emerged in Latin America which was representative of the new approaches which came together in the emerging social sciences (Morse, 1978).[25] Examples included Gilberto Freyre's *Sobrados e mucambos* (1936), Sergio Buarque's aforementioned *Raízes do Brasil*, as well as Ezequiel Martínez Estrada's *Radiografía de la pampa* (1933, The Pampa's Radiography) and *La cabeza de Goliat* (1940, Goliath's Head), and Benjamín Subercaseaux's *Chile o una loca geografía* (1940, Chile or a Crazy Geography).

Although they were not focused on cities or urbanization, some of these works reviewed territorial and social processes with new vocabularies, mainly borrowed from sociology, anthropology and social psychology. This was the case with Freyre's *Sobrados* and *Casa-grande e senzala* (1933, Masters and Slaves), where Herbert Spencer's evolutionist influences were applied in a new interpretation of Brazil's racial and social *mestiçagem* (miscegenation); the Portuguese, indigenous and black components would have resulted in an 'agrarian, slave-dominated and hybrid' society (Freyre, 1933, 2000, pp. 235–236). Meanwhile, Buarque's *Raízes* replaced nineteenth-century and positivistic inconsistencies with concepts drawn from the cultural sociology of Wilhelm Dilthey, Georg Simmel and the Frankfurt School, all of them familiar to Buarque, who lived in Germany between 1929 and 1930 (Damazio, nd, pp. 31–32). Buarque's notion of *raíz* also detected atavistic impediments to the urban modernization advocated by functionalist sociology and demanded by Vargas's *Estado Novo* (Buarque, 1936, 2005; Candido, 1967, 2005, pp. 13, 20).

Focused more on the metropolitan way of life and its tensions with the provinces, the analyses of Martínez Estrada and Subercaseaux seemed to point to the capitals' new social and territorial structures, echoing the approaches of German sociology. Originally a chapter of the 1933 *Radiografía*, Martínez's essay about 'Goliath's Head' pioneered the description of Buenos Aires as a 'psychological phenomenon' and hub of Argentine 'intelligentsia', but also the epicentre of the hustle and bustle, the 'haste' and 'mechanic life'. The capital was likewise the main stage of mercantilism and instrumentality in human relations, reminiscent of features characterized by Simmel and Spengler for the *Weltstädte* or world cities (Martínez Estrada, 1940, 1983, pp. 21,

36, 48; Simmel, 1903, 1969; Spengler, 1918–1922, 1998, II, p. 158). Along this same line, Subercaseaux appealed to biological and Spengler-like images: Santiago had passed from being an 'old hamlet' to representing a 'populous adult'; but despite having a 'great city soul', it lacked 'life overall' (Subercaseaux, 1940, 2005, pp. 111, 126). The territorial imbalances caused by the 'mutilated octopus' are tinged with drama in Subercaseaux's metaphors; but instead of using the image of the hypertrophied head, the Sorbonne-trained psychologist referred to 'a heart too weak for a giant body: blood does not arrive everywhere and the extremities get cold' (Subercaseaux, 1940, 2005, pp. 126–128).

Ranging from the artistic vanguards that sought the recovery of vernacular motifs from the New World, to the historical, sociological and geographical works that analysed urban and national realities with fresh categories drawn from social sciences, the inter-war climate thus enriched the imaginary and discourses about Latin America's mass metropolises and *masificación*. And it can also be said that the feedback between vanguards and social sciences paved the way for the emergence of urbanism as a discipline.

Urban Reforms and the Emergence of *Urbanismo*[26]

Academic and Professional Breakthroughs

Population growth evinced the urgency of adopting urban reforms and plans, which were carried out by local governments, foreign maestros and native professionals. Although many of the last were still sent to study or train in Europe or the United States, some had graduated from the architectural faculties recently founded in local universities that, by that time, had started to offer their first courses on urban planning and design.[27] One of the earliest courses was introduced in 1928 at the School of Architecture of the University of Chile by Alberto Schade Pohlenz, author of a 1923 plan for Santiago. Strongly influenced by Camillo Sitte's artistic approach, his syllabus inspired a similar programme at the Catholic University in 1929 (Hofer, 2003, pp. 74–75). Promoted by the Austrian urbanist Karl Brunner – invited to the country by Ibáñez's administration – at this time the Institute of Urbanism was founded and the *Ley General de Construcciones y Urbanizaciones* (General Law of Buildings and Urban Development) was passed, followed by the celebration of the country's first Congress of Architecture and Urbanism in 1934 (Pavez, 1992; 2009–2010).

Mexico was also early to mature in academic terms, with changes in the architectural practice and teaching furthered by the Revolution; these included the course 'City Planning and Civic Art', inaugurated in 1926 at the National School of Fine Arts. José Luis Cuevas Pietrasanta was in charge until 1929, when he was replaced by Carlos Contreras – founder of the journal *Planificación*. Led by the Asociación Nacional para la Planificación de la República Mexicana (ANPRM, National Association for the Planning of the Mexican Republic), the celebration of the first national planning conference in 1930 and the passing of a general law on planning in the same year, confirm Mexico's pioneering development of a professional and legal groundwork (Contreras, 2003; Valenzuela-Aguilera, 2013).

Though advances were hindered by political instability and the *Estado Novo*, whose authoritarian centralism favoured national over local reforms, Brazil also showed signs of administrative, professional and academic institutionalization of *urbanismo*. Following the creation of the short-lived National Association of Town Planning in 1927, another step towards its acceptance as a public issue was marked by the 1932 setting up of the Department of Municipal Administration, which aimed at providing assistance to local governments (Rezende, 2012). Confirming that the prefects of Brazilian cities have often been technical experts in addition to civil servants, Luíz de Anhaia Mello, author of *Problemas de urbanismo* (1929, Problems of Town Planning), not only organized in São Paulo a Congress of Housing but also a Week of Urbanism in Salvador de Bahia in 1935. By then, the Prefect Francisco Prestes Maia had presented his famous *Plano de Avenidas da Cidade de São Paulo* (1930, Avenue Plan of São Paulo, figure 4.5). In addition to the creation of polytechnic schools in Rio, São Paulo, Recife, Salvador, Belo Horizonte and Porto Alegre (Gomes, 2005, p. 13), in 1931 Lúcio Costa reformed Rio's Escola Nacional de Belas Artes (ENBA, National School of Fine Arts) and included urbanism and landscape courses within a curriculum intended to make the teaching of architecture independent from plastic arts (Pereira, 2003, pp. 79–80).

In the case of Argentina, after the creation of the Commission of Building Aesthetic in 1925,[28] the interest in urbanism was demonstrated by the invitations to Le Corbusier and Werner Hegemann to visit the capital in 1929 and 1931, respectively (see p. 84). The latter's proposals were promoted from the Office of the Plan created in 1932 and chaired by Carlos della Paolera, the father of the new discipline in Argentina. Developed between 1922 and 1928 as his doctoral thesis at the Parisian Institut d'Urbanisme, della Paolera's Master Plan for the Buenos Aires Agglomeration (figure 4.6) not only included the historic core but also the regional conurbation, in line with the ideas of

Figure 4.5. Cover of Francisco Prestes Maia's *Estudo de um plano de avenidas para a Cidade de São Paulo*. São Paulo: Melhoramentos, 1930.

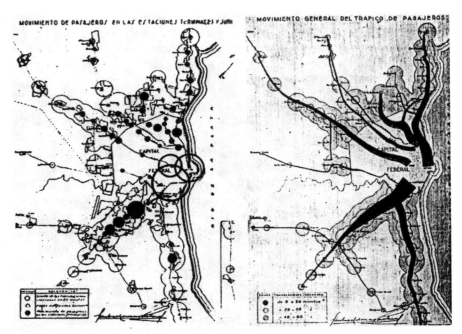

Figure 4.6. Regional analyses of commuters' flows in Carlos della Paolera's plan. (*Source*: Randle, 1977)

Patrick Geddes (Caride, 2002–2004). Courses on urbanism were pioneered by della Paolera himself at Rosario's Universidad del Litoral in 1929, and at the University of Buenos Aires (UBA) in 1933, thus paving the way for the celebration of Argentina's first Congress of Urbanism in 1935 (Randle, 1977).

Creole and Foreign-Advised Urban Plans

In common with academic and professional *urbanismo*, Latin America's planning administration did not take shape until the second half of the 1920s, when urban problems came to the fore in the emerging welfare states. Most of the national or municipal town planning offices in Santiago, Montevideo, Buenos Aires, Mexico City, Rio, Lima, Bogotá and Caracas were a joint effort between local and national governments, new professional associations, and urban research centres (Violich, 1944, pp. 157–170). Indigenous urban planners, some of them also acting as administrative heads, urban designers and promoters, emerged from these offices to take charge of elaborating the first plans for the sprawling metropolises, including the aforementioned Carlos Contreras in Mexico City, Mauricio Cravotto in Montevideo, Carlos della Paolera in Buenos Aires, Luiz de Anhaia Mello and Francisco Prestes Maia in São Paulo, Pedro Martínez Inclán in Havana, and Leopoldo Martínez Olavarría in Caracas.

From the late 1920s these early plans from local administrations seemed to crown the institutionalization of urbanism. Indeed, one could say that, unlike Britain and

Germany – where the discipline's consolidation was based on legislative reform, either municipal or national (Sutcliffe, 1981) – Latin America's *urbanismo* appeared associated with plans that were often hailed as birth certificates or manifestos of the new practice, regardless of their legal status or implementation. Combined in some cases with urban planning techniques arriving from North America, different traditions of European urbanism were incorporated into the planning agendas of the new institutions, and this often involved visits by famous *urbanistas* as advisers for those first plans. Although influenced, as Contreras himself recognized, by his experience in New York,[29] it can be said that the plan for Mexico's Federal District was the most autochthonous of this first generation in Latin America, considering that Contreras was in charge of the coordination, without foreign assistance (Valenzuela-Aguilera, 2013). Also lecturer at the National University's High School of Fine Arts, Contreras had participated in preliminary studies for the plan since 1925, which were published in the first issue of *Planificación* in 1927 and displayed at the First Exhibition on City Planning held in the capital the same year. But the legal status as *Plano Regulador* and Contreras's appointment as Head of the Commission attached to the Secretary of Communications and Public Works had to wait for the approval of the *Ley sobre planeación de la República* (1930, Act of the Republic's Planning), one of Latin America's earliest nationwide legislations on this matter (Contreras, 1939, 2003, p. 131; 2003, pp. 85, 91). Another example of local *urbanismo* without the direct participation of foreigners took place in São Paulo, where the *Plano de Avenidas* was launched, as mentioned, by Prestes Maia in 1930 (figure 4.5). In the 1920s Prestes had prepared blueprints influenced by the functionalism of Eugène Hénard and Joseph Stübben, but the 1930 plan also incorporated references to Philadelphia's comprehensive planning and Harland Bartholomew's pioneering works on automobile flows (Pereira, 2010, pp. 99–101).

Unlike Mexico City and São Paulo, other Latin American cities opted to invite foreign advisers to help produce their first plans. Let us try to summarize these experiences while grouping them according to the architectural and planning trends that the emissaries were representing of (Almandoz, 2010*b*).

The École Française d'Urbanisme Tradition

Still capitalizing on the eclectic side of French urbanism in the aftermath of Latin America's *Bella Época*, conspicuous representatives of what Choay labelled the École Française d'Urbanisme (EFU) were invited to participate in proposals and plans for some capitals (Choay, 1983, pp. 252–258). Jean-Claude Nicholas Forestier visited Buenos Aires in 1924, when some of his ideas, inspired by the City Beautiful, were incorporated into the first 'Organic Project' elaborated by the Commission of Building Aesthetic (Gorelik, 1999, pp. 318–330; Berjman, 1998, pp. 215–267). Also with Forestier's collaboration, the Plan for the Beautification and Enlargement of Havana was published and included in the *Ley de Obras Públicas* (Act of Public Works) issued in 1925 by Gerardo Machado's government (Duverger, 1995).

The EFU tradition seemed to renew and enlarge its repertoire during Léon

Jaussely's visit to Montevideo in 1926, when the founder of the Sociéte Française des Urbanistes (SFU) demonstrated his opposition to the colonial grid and preference for the introduction of garden city principles in urban expansion. Showing a more modernist image while in Buenos Aires, Jaussely not only advocated the need to consider the future of the southern metropolis within its regional hinterland, but also introduced zoning as a means of escaping from the centre and searching for open spaces where new buildings could be combined with parks (Gutiérrez, 2010, pp. 64–66).

Invited by the Prefect Antônio Prado Junior and the Rotary Club to coordinate a technical team between 1926 and 1930, Alfred Agache masterminded a plan for Rio, whose methodology included geographical surveys and a well-documented contextualization reminiscent of Geddes's recommendations for civic studies (Agache, 1932, I).[30] At the same time, Agache saw the Brazilian metropolis as a laboratory, where he could experiment with circulation axes drawn from Eugène Hénard's proposals, as Le Corbusier would also do on his visits (Pereira, 1995). Notwithstanding the adoption of some of its proposals in the late 1930s, Agache's plan has been reckoned, from a broader perspective, as a belated attempt by the *República Velha*'s oligarchy to control Rio's structure, which was already being transformed by industrial modernization and *masificación* (Abreu, 1988, p. 86).

The last example of the EFU's eclectic tradition can be found in the first plan for Caracas (1939), drawn up by the Directorate of Urbanism of the capital's Federal District. Since the creation of the office in 1937, the team of local experts had been boosted by the advice of the Paris-based office of Henri Prost, whose junior associates, Jacques Lambert and Maurice Rotival, were sent to Caracas to coordinate the mission.

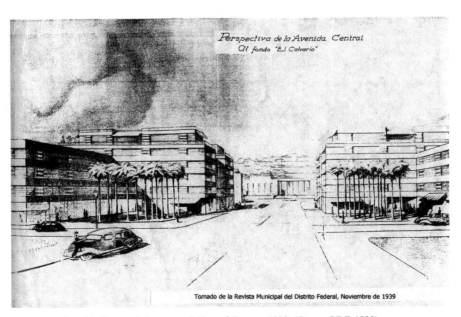

Figure 4.7. Avenida Central, Monumental Plan of Caracas, 1939. (*Source*: GDF, 1939)

The foreign advisers combined most of the EFU's ingredients, which made possible the import of Haussmann's ideas into the Venezuelan capital (Almandoz 2006a, pp. 323–339). Indeed, the Prefect of the Seine was invoked many times in the so-called Monumental Plan of Caracas (1939), while the Parisian example was often used to draw different conclusions about the plan's major dilemma between urban renewal and urban extension of the centre. Partially implemented in the 1940s, the final project opted for a sort of renewal aimed at solving the growing traffic problems with the creation of eastward corridors, presided over by a monumental Champs-Elysées-like Avenida Central (GDF, 1939; figure 4.7).

Corbusian Modernism

In contrast to the EFU's academicism, fresh ideas of the Congrès Internationaux d'Architecture Moderne (CIAM) were what South Americans tried to get by inviting Le Corbusier to visit Buenos Aires, Montevideo, São Paulo and Rio. Sponsored by the *avant-garde* Society of Friends of Art and the School of Architecture, Le Corbusier's 1929 visit was ignored by the Central Society of Architects and its *Revista de Arquitectura* (Journal of Architecture) (Pérez, 1991). He presented a preconceived version of the 1925 'Plan Voisin de Paris', which had attempted the introduction of 'a business city at the heart of town'. This was a progressive initiative which, Le Corbusier claimed, had been rejected by the Parisian academic establishment. But his vision was that the *Plan Voisin* could succeed in the New World; that, with its massive city of towers dominating the Atlantic, the Buenos Aires of more than 3 million people could become 'one of the most deserving cities of the world', replacing the metropolitan role of New York, which had merely been 'the first gesture of contemporary civilization' (Le Corbusier, 1930, pp. 167, 172–174, 202).

By focusing on his own visions for the Argentine capital, Le Corbusier probably tried to avoid any polemic with the proposals of Forestier and Jaussely, and he was to do the same with Agache's plan for Rio (Pérez, 1991, pp. 25–27). Paying tribute to Pereira Passos's determination for transforming the *Cidade Maravilhosa* in the 1900s (see pp. 35, 36), the highlight of Le Corbusier's proposal was the famous viaducts that were residential buildings at the same time. Sketches of these buildings epitomized thereafter the carioca architectural modernity, whose first symbols had been the skyscrapers of Copacabana and Cinelândia (Tsiomis, 1998). Whereas Agache had seen the Brazilian capital as a sort of laboratory, during his visits in 1929 and 1936 Le Corbusier conceived it as a 'manifesto', where he unfolded modernist principles drawn from Hénard's proposals, while introducing elements from the *villes radieuses* that in some way anticipated the evolution of metropolitan Rio (Pereira, 1995, pp. 102–104).

In his *Précisions sur un état présent de l'architecture et de l'urbanisme* (1930), Le Corbusier reported his 1929 tour with an enthusiasm that mirrored his belief in the mission of French urbanism abroad, no matter what the differences among its representatives. In view of all these stimulating experiences, the champion of modernism confirmed that he had perceived in South America a renewed energy capable of doing away with all academic methods in architecture, '…the methods from the stone age that have survived until Haussmann…' (Le Corbusier, 1930, pp. 12–14). Le Corbusier's enthusiasm seemed to prefigure, likewise, Latin America's fascination with modernism in the decades to come, when it would be converted to a fetish or delusion of modernization and development (see pp. 99–106).

Städtebau Representatives

Veterans of the German-speaking world also fostered the nascent *urbanismo* of Latin America. In Argentina, Werner Hegemann was hosted by The Friends of the City, a pragmatic society which was not satisfied with either the EFU's proposals or Le Corbusier's prefabricated plans. The man responsible for the invitation was the aforementioned Carlos della Paolera, who knew of both Hegemann's scientific and humanist approach to planning. During his four months in Buenos Aires, Rosario and Mar del Plata, Hegemann tried to be tactful in relation to proposals by former visitors, while focusing on the unique aspects of the Argentine context; his proposal for a *Plano Regulador* was definitely a more comprehensive and down-to-earth instrument than Le Corbusier's architectural sketches (Collins, 2005, pp. 252–265; Tartarini, 1995, pp. 58–59, 61–63).

Karl Brunner arrived as the last descendant of an Austrian-German lineage that dated back to Sitte and Otto Wagner. However, as in the case of Hegemann, his conception of the nascent discipline as a 'science' overcame the artistic antecedents and anticipated the forthcoming engineering-oriented practice, as it was summed up in articles resulting from his lectures (Brunner, 1930, for instance). Going beyond this conception, and considering the Chilean capital's lack of urban spaces and landmarks, Brunner's 1933 plan for Santiago proposed 'to architecturalize' the layout and to configure new axes and centres. He also put great emphasis on shaping the city with open spaces and districts, the main of which was the Barrio Cívico around the presidential palace of La Moneda (Figueroa, 1995*b*) (figure 4.2). In addition to his achievement in securing the approval of his plan in 1939, throughout the 1930s Brunner contributed, as was noted above, to the consolidation of urban planning in Chile (Pavez, 2009–2010). During the same decade, he masterminded both the municipal office and plan for Bogotá, where he had translated his *Manual de Urbanismo* – a very popular textbook among Latin American planners (Brunner, 1939–1940). Although in 1941 Brunner also drew up a plan for Panama City and was still active in the region, his scientific conception of urbanism, like the EFU academicism, began to be replaced by a more functional modernism.

Despite its shortcomings and colonial echoes, it can be said that the inter-war wave of foreign advisers, most of them Europeans as we have seen, helped to shape Latin America's first generation of urban plans – regardless of the fact that most of them remained unrealized proposals. From theoretical and methodological references to practical instruments, the interaction between local teams and foreign experts strengthened *urbanismo* in professional and academic circles. However, the forthcoming transit into *planificación* and *planejamento*, with epistemological, technical and territorial changes involved, was to occur amidst post-war Americanization and modernism, as we shall see in the next chapter.

Notes

1. The first sections of this chapter rely on passages from Almandoz (2013a, pp. 179–189, 212–219; 2013b).
2. Panama was a Colombian province in the Central American isthmus.
3. In Venezuela Standard Oil and the Rockefeller Foundation instigated improvements to infrastructure and campaigns against yellow fever, malaria and other diseases.
4. In contrast to the pseudo-history recounted by Darío, Rodó and Ugarte – according to which all Hispanic Americans had been 'aggrieved by Uncle Sam's big stick' – the Americans' participation in the war had proved their international idealism.
5. Estrada's regime inspired Miguel Ángel Asturias's famous novel *El señor presidente* (1946, Mister President).
6. With the reform, about a third of the population received land (Suchlicki, 1996, 2008, p. 120).
7. The constitution made explicit the state's obligation to 'the protection of work, industry and welfare, especially regarding healthy accommodation and economic livelihood, so that each inhabitant is provided with a minimal wellbeing, adequate to his personal needs and those of his family' (quoted in Villalobos, 1979, 2010, p. 186).
8. This unrest was fuelled by intellectuals such as Leopoldo Lugones, Ricardo Rojas and Manuel Gálvez, who saw the uncontrolled immigration as a threat to traditional values.
9. It ranged from the Communist Party founded in 1922 to the Brazilian Integral Action inspired on Italian fascism.
10. APRA was strengthened by the incorporation of prominent intellectuals such as Antenor Orrego and José Carlos Mariátegui.
11. Andean military had ruled Venezuela since 1899.
12. 'Proceso del pensamiento venezolano' (1937).
13. 'Rumbo y problemática de nuestra historia' (1947). Picón's plea was analogous to those of Vasconcelos and Reyes in Mexico.
14. The *masificación* (overcrowding) was manifest from the late 1920s, when political, social and economic changes were fuelled by the Great Depression and interwar turbulence. By then, according to Romero, 'urban problems were multiplied by demographic growth, social differentiation and, sometimes, ideological differentiation among groups'; that resulted in the cities no longer being 'strictly cities but a juxtaposition of anomic ghettos, cut off from each other' (Romero, 1984, pp. 19, 322).
15. Here urbanization went from 7.2 per cent to 11.6 per cent over the same period.
16. Honduras's Tegucigalpa was even smaller at 50,000 inhabitants.
17. As shown by Gorelik (1999, pp. 357–386) in the case of Buenos Aires, from the *barrio* stemmed a *masificada* yet vernacular culture, with genuine and locally-based expressions from sport and music to literature. For the role of foreigners in the definition of São Paulo's *bairros* and their popular culture, see Lanna *et al.* (2011).
18. This section and the next rely on passages from Almandoz (2013a, pp. 219–263).
19. Juan Bimba was also a motif in Andrés Eloy Blanco's poetry (Blanco, 1997, pp. 201–203).
20. Arlt's chronicles were originally published in the *El Mundo* newspaper.
21. Edwards's novel introduced the theme of urban poverty and proletarian life, not only in Chilean literature – where it was to be continued by Nicomedes Guzmán's *Los hombres oscuros* (1939, The Dark Men) and *La sangre y la esperanza* (1943, Blood and Hope) – but also in the Latin American novel more generally (Brushwood, 1975, 1993, pp. 31–37).

22. Ranging from traditional Mexican engraving to European post-impressionism and fauvism, the movement crystallized by the 1920s, when the Painters' Union decided to place murals in major public buildings that were offered by Vasconcelos from the central government (Tedesco, 2004, pp. 409, 419–425).
23. Others included Ricardo Güiraldes, Benito Lynch, Horacio Quiroga and Silvina Ocampo, Victoria's sister.
24. After Carpentier, Fernando Ortiz, Lydia Cabrera and Nicolás Guillén consolidated the cult of Caribbean Negritude which still exists today.
25. In the previous decade, José Ingenieros *La evolución de las ideas argentinas* (1918–1920, The Evolution of Argentine Ideas), Jorge Basadre's *La multitud, la ciudad y el campo en la historia del Perú* (1929, The Crowd, the City and the Countryside in Peru's History).
26. I rely on passages from Almandoz (2010*b*, pp. 31–39; 2013*a*, pp. 232–263). Depending on the context, the word *urbanismo* will sometimes be translated as town planning or urbanism.
27. Technical journals with an increasing urban agenda also started publication throughout Latin America during the first decades of the twentieth century: among them were *La Ciudad* (1929) in Buenos Aires; *Planificación* (1927) and *Casas* (1935) in Mexico; *Ciudad y Campo* in Lima; *Zig-zag*, *ARQuitectura* (1935) and *Urbanismo y Arquitectura* (1939) in Chile; *Architetura no Brasil*, *Revista Brasileira de Engenharia* and *Urbanismo e Viação* in Brasil; and *Revista Técnica del Ministerio de Obras Públicas* and *Revista Municipal del Distrito Federal* (1939) in Caracas.
28. The CBA was headed by the governor, Carlos Martín Noel.
29. New York's regional plan was coordinated by the Englishman, Thomas Adams, former secretary of the Garden City Association and administrator of Letchworth (1903–1906).
30. From a theoretical perspective, the French edition of the plan – *La remodelation d'une capitale* (1932) – claimed to combine biological concepts derived from Poëte's evolutionism with scientific methods taught at the École Supérieure d'Urbanisme – which probably prevented it from conveying a more modern message (Agache, 1932, I, pp. xviii–xx, 93).

Chapter 5

Developmentalism, Modernism and Planning

Industrialization, Urbanization and Development[1]

50 anos em 5
    Juscelino Kubitschek's presidential slogan

From the end of World War II until the mid-1960s, Latin America's largest countries showed relative prosperity, marked by significant economic expansion and sustained urbanization. Fuelled by the massive markets targeted by the import substitution industrialization (ISI), Brazil and Mexico reached a yearly growth of 6 per cent, which made them look like model economies on the eve of 'taking off' towards development, in terms of Walt Whitman Rostow's famous phases discussed below (Rostow, 1990). Even though the Southern Cone countries had been more dynamic in the inter-war period, they still maintained an economic expansion of 4 per cent (Clichevsky, 1990, pp. 22–23). Meanwhile, epitomized by the windfall of oil-producer Venezuela, the surplus yielded by the export of raw materials financed a second generation of ISI also in Colombia and Peru, in all of which the rate of industrial growth almost doubled that of the primary sector (Williamson, 1992, pp. 334–335). For the rest of the countries, the increase of manufacturing and the decrease of agriculture in the Gross Domestic Product (GDP) was a trend from the 1940s (Roberts, 1978, pp. 62–63).

Economic growth was accompanied by demographic transition: while the continent's average percentage of urbanization was 47 by 1960, over half of the population of Uruguay (80.4), Argentina (66.2), Chile (59.2) and Venezuela (56.4) already lived in urban centres by 1955 (Harris, 1971, p. 31) (Appendices table 1). Brazil and Mexico were not demographically urban because of their huge populations spread across vast territories, although they boasted long since some of the world's biggest metropolises: Mexico City and Rio de Janeiro were just below and above 3 million, respectively, while São Paulo had already spiralled to 2.5 million. This first rank of Latin America's metropolitan areas was still led by the Gran Buenos Aires, which amounted to 4.7 million. The proportion of 'metropolitan population' – living in cities over 100,000 inhabitants – increased from 21.2 per cent in 1950 to 27.4 per cent in 1960; meanwhile urban primacy grew in all Latin American countries, except Haiti's Port-au-Prince and Bolivia's La Paz (Harris, 1971, pp. 35, 167, 172–173, 186).

Economic Nationalism, Populism and ECLAC

Demographic transition and modernization were imbued with an 'economic nationalism' shared by Latin America's socialism and liberalism alike. The political spectrum ranged from the already-mentioned populist regimes of Mexico's Lázaro Cárdenas (1895–1970), Argentina's Juan D. Perón (1946–1955) and Brazil's Getúlio Vargas (1882–1954), to the progressive yet brutal dictatorships of the Dominican Republic's Rafael L. Trujillo (1930–1961), Cuba's Fulgencio Batista (1940–1944, 1952–1959) and Venezuela's Marcos Pérez Jiménez (1952–1958). Framed within F.D. Roosevelt's Good Neighbour policy (see pp. 65–66), their common agenda of *desarrollismo* (developmentalism) was backed since 1948 by the creation of international agencies such as the Organization of American States (OAS) and the Economic Commission for Latin America and the Caribbean (ECLAC), both sponsored by the United Nations (UN) and the USA's growing interest in the region's agricultural, mineral and industrial exploitation.

Headquartered in Santiago de Chile and led by Raúl Prebisch – former director general of Argentina's Central Bank – the ECLAC was a cornerstone of Latin America's post-war developmentalism, aimed at implementing ISI and other economic policies that consolidated the corporate state in industrializing countries until the mid-1960s, when the 'easy phase' of ISI was over (Williamson, 1992, pp. 338–339; Edwards, 2009, p. 71).[2] ECLAC's Keynesian programmes were associated with different models of state intervention advocated by economists such as Gunnar Myrdal and Albert Hirschman (de Mattos, 2010, p. 34), but it was Prebisch's ideas that prevailed. His *desarrollismo* relied on two premises: firstly, economic development was based on technical progress, which was concentrated in advanced countries and was slowly transferred to the periphery. However, 'such problems would be resolved if developing countries were able to reach significant industrial progress, given that industrialization was the leverage of development and the best mechanism to channel the diffusion of technologic progress' (Montoya, 2006, p. 28). Secondly, the impossibility of analyzing the dynamics of developing countries without considering their position in the world economy, and this reinforced ECLAC's *centre/periphery* conception; i.e. a centre with an economically diverse yet technologically homogeneous structure, with high levels of productivity in all sectors, in contrast to a periphery specialized in export staples with low productivity (Montoya, 2006, p. 24).

In addition to these economic tenets, the ECLAC's rationale ran parallel to and in concert with the emergence of populism in Latin America's major economies, a populism whose success 'rested to a great extent on the capacity of industrialization to create employment in the cities' (Roberts, 1978, p. 71). The 'populist political philosophy' of this period was intimately related to the belief that difficulties of development would be overcome 'with concerted effort from government and an aware citizenry'; this duet ultimately related to 'the nationalist solution to underdevelopment', which was also stressed in Africa and Asia in the post-war period, and was represented in Latin America by ECLAC as its main think tank (Roberts, 1978, pp. 74–75).[3]

Modernization and Development

Besides the relationship between industrialization, urbanization and populism, the post-war pursuit of progress in the world's less advanced regions also involved modernization and development. Linkages and tensions between the latter terms entail a string of theories and authors already referred to (see Chapter 1); by the mid twentieth century, the discussion was revived by the structural functionalism of Talcott Parsons and the developmentalism of Rostow (Weiner, 1966). Used by the Kennedy administration and highly influential in Latin America, Rostow's economic-oriented theory offers the advantage of making explicit relations with the urban transition, while its historical approach sheds light on the challenges for Latin America's development in relation to other regions of the world.

Mexico and Argentina having 'taken off' in the 1950s, Rostow pointed to Venezuela and Brazil as the flyers of the following decade, escorted by Colombia, Chile and the Philippines; in all of them, the indicator of take-off was the fact that more than 25 per cent of the GDP went to investment (Rostow, 1990, pp. 44, 127). Yet development was not secured by an irreversible moment of *despegue*, as 'take-off' is known in Spanish, but required a long and intense process of economic, social and political change, articulated in the phases explained by Rostow in *The Stages of Economic Growth* (1960). Combining elements of economic and political history with sociological descriptions, he studied and grouped the cases of 'traditional societies' which, from late-eighteenth century England onwards, had modernized their agrarian and industrial sectors; those societies later increased their investment, as required by the take-off, in order to achieve a 'drive to maturity', not only economic but also social and political, all of which should be maintained throughout two generations or fifty years of sustained well-being, before finding their path towards permanent development (Rostow, 1990, pp. 10–12). Until then maturity was incomplete and nations that had taken off were still regarded as 'developing countries' or 'transitional societies', among other categories then applied in different contexts, from Taiwan and South Korea to India and Turkey (Reissman, 1964; Davis, 1965, 1982).

Among developing countries, Brazil, Venezuela, Chile and Colombia were outstanding in Latin America; even though by the 1960s, according to Rostow's stages, Argentina and Mexico had already taken off, their maturity had not been reached – and would not be for the rest of the century. The explanation of why maturity was not attained in Latin American nations after several decades of alleged *despegues* is very complex. As Rostow observes, once the take-off has occurred there are many decisions to adopt and balances to keep regarding the priorities of development. For instance, the diffusion of modern technology and the increase in growth rate, on one hand, and rising per capita consumption, on the other; or the increase in social welfare expenses without excessive expansion in state bureaucracy, are typical obstacles on the path to development. On top of that, scenarios are made more complex by the particular political and social situations that each country must face (Rostow, 1990, pp. 14–16). So, considering all these challenges and factors, let us try to explore how imbalance in urbanization in relation to the productive sector is at the root of the immature take-offs in Latin America in the mid twentieth century.

Fifty Years in Five

Juscelino Kubitschek's famous slogan when campaigning for the Brazilian presidency –epigraph '*50 anos em 5*'– arguably was a leitmotif to *desarrollismo* in this period. One could put forward, as an initial hypothesis, that in Latin America's major economies there were attempts to compress Rostow's fifty-year drive to maturity, as if it were possible to jump directly into development and modernization without going through structural adjustments and progressive growth. But far from that, diverse factors, from economic and political to social and urban, hindered the drive to maturity.

Mexico's Corporate State

Since the 1930s, when the Party of the Mexican Revolution (PRM) provided stability, the so-called 'reformist' phase had founded landmarks of the public apparatus, including the National Financial Company, the petroleum company (PEMEX), the Bank of Mexico, the National Bank of Agricultural Credit, the Bank of Credit for Ejidos (communal land), the Regional Schools of Agriculture, and the Bank of Works and Services (Cosío, 2005*b*, p. 139; Quiroz, 2008, p. 126). Mexico thus became a typical corporate state, controlling enterprises in 'strategic sectors', namely those with special impact in the industrial lines of production. Following ECLAC guidelines, such a policy relied on the belief that the private companies would be unable to undertake major projects, either financially or administratively. And this belief was reinforced by the fear that – according to the economic nationalism of the period – strategic sectors might end up in the hands of foreign investors (Edwards, 2009, p. 77).

After Lázaro Cárdenas's social reforms (see pp. 66–67), during the administration of Manuel Ávila Camacho (1940–1946), 'new emphasis was placed on economic growth based on more productivity and less distribution of wealth' (Suchlicki, 1996, 2008, p. 126). Although this economic growth was sustained from the mid-1930s to the 1960s, reaching 6 per cent during the 1940s, it was at the cost of social and territorial inequities (Cosío, 2005*b*, pp. 141–143). Reaching its peak during the administration of Miguel Alemán (1946–1952) with its ambitious programme of public works – including the University City and the Pan American motorway – that policy of alleged 'consolidation' of development and modernization was to be tempered and even questioned in years to come (Suchlicki, 1996, 2008, pp. 97–98, pp. 127–128).

Perón's New Argentina

Fuelled by the instability and decline initiated in the so-called 'infamous decade' of the 1930s (see pp. 68–69), populism had gained ground in Argentina, as evidenced by Juan

Domingo Perón's rise and reforms. The scarcity of imported goods during World War II had prompted the emergence of small and medium industries which were favoured during his tenure as Secretary of Work, from the beginning of the 1943 revolution. This industry-based 'New Order' represented an alternative to the traditional agrarian sector, associated with the oligarchy. Undermining established communist or socialist unions by the creation of new ones, Perón also encouraged the migration of peasants and *descamisados* (shirtless) desperate to become part of the productive sector and absorbed into the urban mass (Luna, 1993, 2005, pp. 210–211; Romero, 2008, pp. 259, 268–269). Accompanied by his second wife, Eva (Evita) Duarte, Perón's first presidential platform was provided by the Labour Party jointly with contingents from traditional radicalism and the grassroots organizations supportive of the charismatic *caudillo*. The 'New Argentina' began with Perón's first administration on 4 June 1946, a regime that was to seek greater control with the help of the centralist constitution introduced in 1949 (Luna, 1993, 2005, pp. 213–215, 231; del Pozo, 2002, pp. 150–151).

The economy of Perón's first tenure (1946–1952) was typically nationalist and state-dominated. Several activities previously under private and foreign domain, such as the British railways and gas, were handed over to the public sector; the state's presence was also reinforced through the nationalization of the Central Bank, the setting up of the Industrial Bank and the flagship airline Aerolíneas Argentinas. Also the Argentine Institute of Promotion and Exchange (IAPI) was created in order to showcase and sell national produce abroad (Luna, 1993, 2005, pp. 220–222).

The economic bonanza after World War II was mirrored in the ambitious goals of the first Plan Quinquenal (1947–1951, Five-Year Plan) based on the expected rise of meat and wheat exports. However, the value of these staples declined after 1949, when the United States was able to provide them to Europe on more advantageous terms. Amid this post-war international climate, and accordingly with its reticence regarding world superpowers, the *peronismo* then advocated a so-called Third Position, allegedly independent from the growing polarization between the United States and the Soviet Union (Luna, 1993, 2005, p. 233). Although this Third Position was rather rhetorical and did not lead to Argentina's confrontation with North American interests, it was a breakthrough for the Non-Aligned Movement.

The New Argentina's triumphalism and industrialism during Perón's first presidency had to be toned down in the second (1952–1958), which was also shadowed from the beginning by Evita's death. A devalued peso and soaring inflation forced moderation of the goals of the Second Five-Year Plan (1952–1957), while the *peronismo*'s nationalist rhetoric ended up aligned with the United States and allowed Standard Oil to exploit the country's hydrocarbons (Halperin, 1967, 2005, pp. 479–482). A tense conflict with the Catholic Church was the last catalyst for the *coup d'état* which toppled the regime on 21 September 1955. By then the promising course of Argentina's take-off a decade earlier seemed lost.

Brazil: From Vargas to Kubitschek

Perhaps less evident than in Mexico and Argentina, the corporatism of Getúlio Vargas's *Estado Novo* (1937–1945) included technical training of the bureaucracy through the

Administrative Department of Public Service (DASP, 1938), as well as reinforcing industry with the creation of the National Steel Company in 1941. Meanwhile, trade difficulties during World War II accelerated the ISI, contributing to apparent industrial prosperity that raised manufactures to the second place in exports, after coffee. However, the short-term and artificial facilities provided to local producers, including exchange control and lack of competitiveness, was not enough to prevent recurrent inflation and reduced purchasing power of the Brazilian market (Prado, 1968, 1999, pp. 112–118).

Imbued with Vargas's populism during the *Estado Novo*, which sought to gain the support of the urbanizing mass, Brazilian *desenvolvimento* after World War II was at the crossroads between agricultural and industrial orientations; the latter faced in turn the alternatives of nationalism and the penetration of foreign capital as the engine of development. While Gaspar Dutra's government (1946–1951) declared itself overtly in favour of industrial predominance (del Priore and Venancio, 2010, pp. 263–264), Vargas's last mandate (1951–1954) – democratically constituted and less authoritarian than the *Estado Novo* – pursued a more balanced and nationalist development. This was manifest in the creation of the *Banco Nacional de Desenvolvimento Econômico* (BNDE, National Bank of Economic Development) and state intervention in key sectors such as iron and steel industry, petrochemicals, transport and energy. Such corporatism was boosted with the new state company Petrobras (1953), inspired by Vargas's famous slogan '*O petróleo e nosso*' (Petroleum is ours). But fears that Brazil might become a union-dominated republic, similar to Perón's Argentina, undermined Vargas's support by diverse groups, including the Army's High Command, whose request for the President's resignation prompted his suicide in the early morning of 24 August 1954 (Schneeberger, 2003, pp. 319–320).

Though open to foreign capital, Juscelino Kubitschek's government (1956–1961) promoted continental funding through what later became the Inter-American Bank of Development (IBD). JK – as he was popularly known – epitomized the industrialism of the period with his aforementioned slogan, '*50 anos em 5*'. But this daydream was not going to be so doable. Supported by the so-called *tripé* or tripod, JK's economic model favoured associations of Brazilian private companies with multinational and state corporations, the latter being responsible for producing energy and industrial inputs. Such joint ventures seemed to work in the short term, while national rates of economic growth reached between 7 and 10 per cent; but in the long run they brought about an indebtedness resulting from the foreign companies' higher productive capacity amid favourable conditions, while national firms continued to import industrial inputs in many sectors (Prado, 1968, 1999, p. 125; del Priore and Venancio, 2010, p. 268).

Relying on the 'Goals Plan' that combined improvement in education with the growth of basic industry, JK's administration undertook a vast programme of construction of roads, hydroelectric plants, aeronautic projects and car manufacturing. Bolstering Brazil's sluggish north through the *Superintêndencia para el Desenvolvimento do Nordeste* (SUDENE, Administrative Division for the Northeastern Development), the invigoration of the central Goias territory was crowned with the creation of Brasilia (see pp. 104–106), which epitomized the endeavour to transform physical environment as a manifestation of development (Schneeberger, 2003, pp. 321–323; Moraes, 2004, p. 99).

Chile: The Popular Front and Beyond

Unlike Argentina and Brazil, where the unrepresented mass was the 'engine of populism' during the 1940s and 1950s, in Chile 'the importance of several political parties of diverse origin and style, where middle groups were able to develop', kept the country away from populist predominance (de Ramón, 2006, p. 147). After the weakening of radical support during Alessandri's second presidency (1932–1938), the so-called 'State of compromise' was reached with the Popular Front's rise to power in 1938. This coalition inaugurated a period of relative stability, politically and economically, under the government of Pedro Aguirre Cerda (1938–1941) and the moderate guidance of the radicalism that he represented,[4] while the 'urban unionized mass' was incorporated into public life through the Socialist and Democrat parties (Aylwin et al., 1990, 2008, pp. 146–147; de Ramón, 2006, p. 144). The president aptly summed up the plural yet nationalist nature of his coalition in a message delivered in May 1939: 'Our Popular Front is nothing else than a conglomerate of progressive forces, essentially patriotic and comprehensive of the time that the Republic goes through, without direct or indirect concomitance with any foreign influence...' (Aguirre quoted in Aylwin et al., 1990, 2008, p. 290).

But the Popular Front's nationalism was not that radical in economic terms. Accelerated by the 1939 earthquake and founded with a US credit, the Corporation of Promotion of Production (CORFO, 1939) was fundamental for the statist model that was being shaped from the 1920s onwards. CORFO implemented sound measures in the industrial, energy and mining sectors, including the creation of ENELCA (National Enterprise of Electricity, 1944), the National Enterprise of Petroleum, the Pacific Steel Company, and CODELCO (Company of Copper Marketing) (Villalobos, 1979, 2010, pp. 195–198). However CORFO was unable to overcome the backwardness of agriculture, partly because of the political interests associated with land tenure (de Ramón, 2006, pp. 154–158, 174–175; Aylwin et al., 1990, 2008, pp. 173–179).

Several other factors prevented the country from achieving economic development. On the one hand, the inability of the emerging middle class to transform itself into an entrepreneurial bourgeoisie – a hindrance shared with other Latin American countries that industrialized earlier (Pinto, 1962, pp. 182–190). On the other hand, propensity for inflation persisted throughout the 1940s, 1950s and 1960s, reaching an average of 17.6, 38.2 and 24.9 per cent, respectively. In addition to mounting political instability, economic and social weakness made Chileans believe that changes had to come through more radical means than transforming national structures, as the Popular Front had tried to do (de Ramón, 2006, pp. 176–179).

Colombia: Before and After the Bogotazo

In conditions similar to Chile, Colombia's presidential tenures succeeded according to the constitution from the 1930s through the mid-1940s, with predominance of the

Liberal Party over the Conservative. Reminiscent of Chile's Frente Popular, the Liberal governments of Alfonso López Pumarejo (1934–1938; 1942–1945) were supported by the Communist Party, while launching an agrarian reform comprised in the so-called 'ongoing revolution' that tried to eradicate the colonial structures and to guide the country towards modernization (Ocampo, 1994, 2007, p. 291; del Pozo, 2002, p. 146). For that purpose, López advocated a more productive conception of property that he defined as based 'on the *social function* that it performs', while its possession consisted 'of the economic exploitation of the land through positive facts, different from those entitled by its dominion' (López quoted in Ocampo, 1994, 2007, p. 292).

While envisaging an agrarian reform oriented towards a so-called New Colombia, the National Front which backed López Pumarejo fostered an urbanizing mass combining rural immigrants and the workforce unionized since 1936 in the CTC or Confederation of Colombia's Workers. With urbanization above 30 per cent by 1938, the 'new order' of López Pumarejo's first government not only had to recognize the political force crystallized by the CTC, but also the threat presented by the shantytowns surrounding Bogotá, Medellín, Cali and Barranquilla, which sheltered more than 100,000 inhabitants in each city (Ocampo, 1994, 2007, pp. 300–301).

A partial response to this challenge was the constitutional reform of 1936, whereby universal and direct suffrage for municipal elections was introduced (Ocampo, 1994, 2007, pp. 296–297). Delayed during the presidency of the also-liberal Eduardo Santos (1938–1942) – known as the 'Great Pause', because of the slowdown of political and economic changes – the reformism of López Pumarejo's second government was thwarted by hardships resulting from World War II. There were also conflicts between the liberals' more and less conservative wings, which split the party between the factions led by Gabriel Turbay and Jorge Eliécer Gaitán, respectively. With López's resignation and the completion of Alberto Lleras Camargo's tenure (1945–1946), the liberal cycle initiated in the 1930s finished with the arrival of the conservative Mariano Ospina Pérez to the presidency (1946–1950).

The slow process of social change in Colombia's oligarchic structure was truncated on 8 April 1948 with the murder of Gaitán, a liberal hopeful and most likely winner of the 1950 elections. Showing the charisma of a Colombian Perón, Gaitán's assassination triggered the so-called *Bogotazo*, when more than 500 people died and nearly 150 buildings were set on fire (Arturo, 2002, pp. 390–391) (figure 5.1). Beyond the capital, the episode not only reignited the fight between conservatives and liberals, but also unleashed urban violence and rurally-based guerrilla war in several regions. However, in contrast to this political and social unrest, in the decade after 1945, the coffee boom and ECLAC-like developmentalism propelled an annual per capita GDP growth of 3.9 per cent and increase in investments of 20 per cent, mainly in the industrial sector (Ocampo, 1994, 2007, p. 298–391).

The short-lived regime of Laureano Gómez (1950–1953) exacerbated the instability following Gaitán's assassination, said to have been carried out by the conservatives. Afterwards, the Peron-like 'reformist militarism' of Gustavo Rojas Pinilla (1953–1957) was an attempt to quash political violence, which claimed 200,000 victims nationwide

Figure 5.1. Bogotazo, 9 April 1948. (*Source*: http://elespectador.com)

since the *Bogotazo* (del Pozo, 2002, p. 147; Ocampo, 1994, 2007, p. 301). However the guerrillas, whose grievances resulted from unequal land tenure and the protracted agrarian reform, persisted for decades to come, with more dramatic expressions than in other parts of Latin America (Halperin, 1967, 2005, pp. 508-509) (see also pp. 114, 148–149).

Pérez Jiménez's Venezuela

Despite the impediments to Venezuela's belated yet sudden urbanization, Pérez Jiménez's dictatorship (1952–1958) epitomized the linkages between economic developmentalism, nationalism and infrastructure amelioration that were manifest in Latin America's larger countries. Through the 'doctrine' of Nuevo Ideal Nacional (NIN, New National Ideal), Pérez Jiménez tried to leave behind Venezuela's sluggishness, in his own words, 'with the celerity required to overcome the gap that distanced ourselves from moderately developed countries' (Pérez, 1955, p. 68). While huge oil concessions, mainly in the western state of Zulia and the eastern of Anzoátegui, were granted in the 1950s to Shell, Creole and other foreign corporations, the ISI was bolstered in the country's northern strip with projects of the Corporación Venezolana de Fomento (CVF, Venezuela's Corporation of Promotion).

Relying on an ambitious programme of European immigration and public works, the 'rational transformation of the physical environment and the improvement of moral, intellectual and material conditions of the country's inhabitants', seeking 'full possession of our territory', were for him the NIN's social and physical aims (Pérez, 1955, pp. 30, 85) (see also pp. 102–103). By the end of his regime, he claimed not only to have converted Venezuela into a 'prestigious nation', but also to have positioned it as 'Latin America's first economic power', with one of the highest economic growth and per capita incomes in the world (Tenreiro, 1995, pp. 12–13, 22).

The *coup d'état* that ousted Pérez Jiménez on 23 January 1958 began a new political cycle in Venezuela, more influenced by the corporatism and populism that had permeated other Latin American states after World War II. Once the repressive machinery of the progressive dictatorship was dismantled, it was no longer possible for one of Latin America's richest countries to keep pursuing economic growth and infrastructure improvement, while the political and social demands of the urbanizing mass were neglected (Carrera, 1988, pp. 177–178). It was then necessary to accelerate the transition of the welfare state, which that post-Gómez Venezuela had started, into a social-oriented and democratic one (Brewer-Carías, 1975, p. 167).

This shift was undertaken by successive Venezuelan governments from the 1960s, in contrast to other Latin American countries, like Argentina and Brazil, where dictatorships were about to cancel some of the guarantees and benefits achieved by corporatism and populism. At the same time the dependence of Venezuela's economic growth on public works and the building sector was comparable to the case of Mexico, where construction cushioned the deficiencies of industrialization by absorbing excessive immigration from the countryside. In this respect, by the late 1950s Latin American countries in the process of taking off, including Chile and Colombia, shared imbalances in their developmentalism, which impeded the completion of 'fifty years in five', according to JK's daydream in Brazil. But to understand the impossibility of this shortened drive to maturity it is necessary to look also at elements from Latin America's demographic transition and social modernization, as we do in the next section.

Asynchronies in Urbanization and Modernization

In demographic, social and cultural terms, some differences between Latin America's developing countries and societies that had modernized earlier must also be taken into account to explain the failure in the former's take-off and drive to maturity. Indeed, from the early 1960s the connection between industrialization, urbanization and modernization was analysed by Leonard Reissman, Kingsley Davis and others, from the standpoints of social change and demographic transition, relying on the examples of the North Atlantic countries that had industrialized in the nineteenth century (Davis, 1965, 1982; Reissman, 1964; Weiner, 1966). From that literature it could be inferred that Latin America's developing nations were on the path to urbanization and industrialization, but they actually suffered from distortions by comparison with experiences of modernization in Europe, North America and other parts of the world.

Some of those distortions and imbalances were the reasons for the conference on 'Problems of Urbanization in Latin America' held in Santiago de Chile in June 1959 and sponsored by the UN, the OAS and ECLAC. Though recognizing that 'urbanization was an unavoidable consequence of economic development', Philip Hauser – chair of the conference and head of the University of Chicago's Department of Sociology –

pointed out that, 'especially in countries scarcely developed', it was necessary 'to channel that process so that negative effects could be minimized' (Hauser, 1967, pp. 22–23).

Following the functionalist rationale that had also inspired Rostow's model, Hauser concluded that it was 'evident that two of the most serious problems that Latin America will have to face in the immediate future will be how to create means to obtain capital goods required for augmenting production, as well as how to improve the yield of capital resources available' (Hauser, 1967, p. 33). Hauser's approach also coincided with ECLAC's conception of development as based on the continuation and deepening of the ISI – a view that would be questioned by governments and experts in the early-1970s (see pp. 123–128, 138–139).

Push–Pull Effect

There were other problems besides political instability and insufficient industrialization, most of which related to the fact that Latin America's urban population overall had grown faster than the general one: the increases during the 1950s were 56 per cent in the former compared to 30 per cent in the latter (Harris, 1971, p. 44) (Appendices table 2). On the one hand, the fledgling industrialization had not preceded but *followed* an excessive urbanization, so the ISI was not the equivalent of an 'industrial revolution' with its dynamic effects on the economic system and demographic transition and flows (Williamson, 1992, p. 333). As happened elsewhere in what came to be known as the Third World, instead of *pulling* waves of population to cities, which could be absorbed by manufacturing and other productive sectors, most of Latin America's rural–urban migration was *pushed* by a countryside that had been abandoned after the urban-focused policies of corporate states (Potter and Lloyd-Evans, 1998, pp. 12–13).

The adoption of ISI had aggravated the rural crisis in many countries which had not undergone land reforms: not only did the agricultural labour force decline between 1945 and 1962, but its productivity in terms of per capita GNP was, at best, less than a quarter of the USA's for the same period (Harris, 1971, p. 74; Williamson, 1992, pp. 337–338). As a result, Latin America's rural 'depopulation' from the 1950s through the 1970s was relatively higher than that experienced by Britain and Germany during the industrial revolution (Roberts, 1978, pp. 91–92).

On the other hand, levels of urbanization almost doubled industrial participation in the economies of Argentina, Chile, Venezuela, Colombia and Brazil, according to 1950s censuses (Harris, 1971, p. 85). Such levels could not be absorbed by the productive system, so in the long term generated 'urban inflation' or 'hyper-urbanization', as would happen in other parts of the Third World (Potter and Lloyd-Evans, 1998, pp. 14–15). Or, as Germani pointed out in relation to the also called *sobreurbanización*, the real problem stemmed from the combination of 'under-industrialization' and under-development of manufacturing and agriculture, respectively (Germani, 1969, p. 199). In the decades to come, this surplus of unproductive population living in cities could only be accommodated in slums, shantytowns and the informal economy (see pp. 129–133).

According to Germani there were other 'asynchronies' in the economic structure of

Latin America and in other parts of the Third World. The main one was the coexistence of patterns of modern consumption with 'archaic' production and other economic hindrances, along with the *sobreterciarización* or excessive growth of the administrative and services sector (Germani, 1969, pp. 10–11). As a result of the less dynamic way industrialization had taken place in underdeveloped areas in general and Latin America in particular, this oversized sector usually hid a 'pseudo-tertiary' group, composed of those who, like domestic servants and street vendors, did not work in modern services and usually occupied marginal positions in the social system and urban structure (Germani, 1969, p. 173).

Dual Societies

Extending into social and cultural domains, some of Latin America's demographic asynchronies stemmed from the different ways in which industrialization and urbanization occurred and influenced one another in the nineteenth and twentieth centuries. In addition to the larger populations of the twentieth century was the fact that the delay in industrial maturity had not prevented demographic transition in developing countries (Appendices table 2). This transition was accelerated by rural–urban migration and the widespread penetration of media totally unknown in the nineteenth century. However, demographic transition and *masificación*, which began in most of Latin America after the 1930s (see pp. 70–74), did not imply a decrease in birth rates. The sole exceptions to this trend were Argentina and Uruguay, whose fertility from the late nineteenth century went down (Germani, 1969, pp. 170–172, 178, 180–181; Blanco, 2006, pp. 207–208).

In terms of social change, the post-war period witnessed, even in Latin America's most advanced countries, a 'second generation' of urban proletariat and other 'modern' groups who often coexisted with 'archaic' and destitute populations in the countryside, who were not organized or even aware of their political and economic rights (Germani, 1969, p. 55). Likewise, the emergence of a 'mass society' permeated by technologically-advanced media and consumerist patterns contrasted with 'marginal' settlements lacking minimum standards of living, both in cities and the countryside (see pp. 128–133). In addition to 'internal inequalities' between urban and rural, advanced and backward regions, these were all factors that shaped 'dual societies' in most of Latin American countries (Germani, 1969, pp. 55–57).

In spite of this duality, Latin America's modernization in the twentieth century was the first to go beyond the elites and 'central areas' of the countries, so the social 'mobilization' that it brought about prompted a series of conflicts due to clashing interests and 'inconsistencies' between the groups, especially after World War II (Germani, 1969, pp. 76–77). In the political arena, some of the cancellations or reversals of rights and breakthroughs took place as the *coups d'états* and revolts referred to above. In social and cultural domains, clashes were fuelled by the *masificación* and mostly corresponded to what Romero labelled 'the revolution of expectations', by which lower-income and marginal groups tried to reproduce the consumption patterns of the middle and upper classes (Romero, 1984, p. 366).

So returning to Rostow's requirements for development, one could say that this revolution of expectations in the economies that took off in the 1940s and 1950s occurred without the bases of industrial maturity and robust welfare states. And we could also conclude with Germani that the asynchronies 'between economic development, modernization and demographic growth put developing countries in general, and Latin American in particular, before an unprecedented situation in history' (Germani, 1969, p. 185).

From Academicism to Functional Modernism

In those decades of Latin America's developmentalism, some of the asynchronies and mismatches between urbanization and industrialization were manifest in the duality between, on the one hand, the *avant-garde* modernism boasted by some cliques and projects in the cities, and on the other, the flimsy modernization achieved in education and culture of the mass (García Canclini, 1990, p. 19). The asynchronies were also noticeable in architecture and town planning, where the *modernismo* of some public works was mistaken by political elites for the completion of social modernization and economic development (Almandoz, 2006b, pp. 96–100; 2007). Departing from this hypothesis, the purpose of this section is to look at some urban projects that were representative of Latin American *modernismo* yet misleading as expressions of development. We also intend to see how they illustrated another phase of functional *urbanismo*, some of whose ingredients came from the USA, unlike the European-oriented academicism prevailing during the 1930s (see pp. 80–85).

Architectural modernism showcased the rapid modernization pursued by economic developmentalism, whose nationalist ingredients coloured vernacular and genuine *modernismos* in some of Latin America's developing countries. The peculiarity of this 'alternative modernism' reached its peak where the 'alliance between modernizing governments and modernist architects' was in tandem, as happened in Mexico, Brazil and Venezuela, whose university cities, housing projects and administrative buildings were ranked among the world's best examples of the modern movement (Fraser, 2000, pp. 15–18).

International interest in reporting and explaining Latin America's modernism, especially from the US, was remarkable. Architects such as Mexico's Juan O'Gorman, Brazil's Lúcio Costa and Oscar Niemeyer, followed by Venezuela's Carlos Raúl Villanueva, were catalogued in the exhibitions 'Brazil Builds' (Goodwin, 1943) and 'Modern Architecture in Latin America since 1945', organized by New York's Metropolitan Museum of Modern Art (MOMA), the latter with the famous critic Henry-Russell Hitchcock as curator (Hitchcock, 1955). The enthusiasm for Latin America extended to other cultural and technical manifestations: from literature, music and cinema, to the eagerness of US-based firms to work for local and regional bodies of planning in Latin American countries (Gomes and Huapaya, 2009, pp. 153–154).

Founded in New York in 1941 by Catalan architect Josep Lluís Sert and Leipzig born American architect Paul Lester Wiener, Town Planning Associates (TPA)

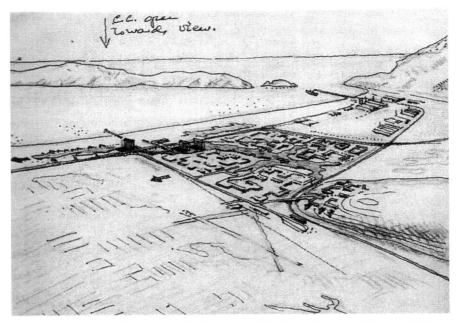

Figure 5.2. A view of TPA's project for Chimbote, Peru, 1948. (*Source*: Gomes and Huapaya, 2009)

provides several examples of the USA's technical promotion of CIAM principles; their long-standing and diverse portfolio included the new city of Tumaco (1948) on the Colombian coast, as well as business districts and residential units in Colombia's Medellín (1948), Venezuela's Maracaibo (1950) and Peru's Lima (1951). Besides Brazil's *Cidade dos Motores* – see below – another outstanding project of TPA in Latin America was Chimbote, commissioned in 1948 by Peru's National Bureau of Urban Planning and Santa's Peruvian Corporation (Huapaya, 2009; Gomes and Huapaya, 2009, pp. 161–163, figure 5.2).

Mexico City

Even before the eclipse of academic urbanism, the left-wing rationalism of Hannes Meyer, former Bauhaus Director, stood out when he lived in Mexico for a decade following a prolonged stay in Stalin's USSR. The social housing and public institution projects in which he collaborated not only helped a shift towards the more vernacular architecture produced during and after the Cárdenas years, but also radicalization of the professional milieu, with the foundation of the Association of Socialist Architects and the High School of Urbanism (Gorelik, 2005, pp. 121–122; Tomas, 1993, pp. 80–81). After Cárdenas's presidency, Meyer's influence faded and 'socialist architects' lost power and scattered. They gave way to a Corbusian modernism whose early skyscrapers and housing schemes were designed by a new generation led by Mario Pani, Enrique del Moral and Juan Sordo Madaleno. Following CIAM principles, they

Figure 5.3. Rectorado or Presidentship of the Ciudad Universitaria, Mexico City, with mural by David A. Siqueiros. (*Photo*: Andrés Téllez, 2010)

often used the zoning to break up the traditional *damero*, as was epitomized, during Alemán's progressivism, in the Ciudad Universitaria (University City) project, a masterpiece of *modernismo* that reinterpreted the native iconography (Ochoa, 1993, pp. 91–92; Valenzuela-Aguilera, 2013) (figure 5.3).

Buenos Aires and Bogotá

Functional modernism in other Latin American capitals was enriched during the 1940s, especially by the visits of CIAM luminaries as advisors to new planning institutions, some of which passed from the local to the national administration. Prepared in his Parisian *atelier* in the rue de Sèvres – with the collaboration of Argentine architects Juan Kurchan and Jorge Ferrari Hardoy, leaders of the *avant-garde* Austral Group – Le Corbusier's second proposal for Buenos Aires incorporated some lessons learnt during his 1929 visit. In addition to greater contextualization, it included the skyscrapers of the business city planted on an artificial island in the river La Plata, the opening of a big north–south avenue, the construction of housing blocks to minimize urban land use, and stringent zoning regulations never before applied in Argentina (Liernur and Pschepiurca, 2008, pp. 177–217). Following functionalist precepts of the Athens Charter and the Radiant City (Le Corbusier, 1941, 1971, pp. 37, 99) – which replaced the pre-eminence of *Plan Voisin* in the 1929 proposal – the functionalist comparison with the human body was stressed, while the circulation network was an analogy of the 'cardiac system' (Caride, 2002–2004, p. 218).

With the creation of the Oficina del Plano Regulador de Bogotá (OPRB, Bureau of Bogotá's Master Plan) in 1948, Le Corbusier was chosen as the 'technician of high international reputation' to be hired. Intended to refresh an environment tired of Karl Brunner's *Städtebau*, the result of such appointment was the Director Plan, completed in Paris in 1949 and made official by decree the year after (Suárez, 2006, pp. 70–71). Le Corbusier travelled to the Colombian capital five times between 1947 and 1951, when he tried to realize his old project of the *grand immeuble* (big building), an edifice 'characterized by its intention and not by its size', supposed to harbour – again according to the Athens Charter precepts – ministries in the capital's historic and administrative centre (Arias, 2008, pp. 23–28). Although the *grand immeuble* was never built, the *Plano Regulador* was completed from New York between 1950 and 1952, coordinated by Sert and the TPA. However, in addition to being produced in the turbulent years after the *Bogotazo*, the plan was opposed by landowners and professionals, and was put aside during Rojas Pinilla's regime (Arias, 2008, p. 19).

Havana and Caracas

While Le Corbusier travelled to Bogotá, CIAM's theoretical presence was consolidated with the Spanish edition of the *Charte d'Athènes*, published in Argentina in 1954, completed with its Cuban adaptation in Pedro Martínez Inclán's *Código de Urbanismo*. After visits to Havana by modernists such as Richard Neutra (1945), Walter Gropius (1945) and Josef Albers (1952), CIAM's leadership among younger generations of Cuban architects went to Sert, advisor to the new Junta Nacional de Planificación (JNP, National Board of Planning) created in 1955 by Batista's dictatorship (Hyde, 2012). In Sert's 1957 proposed master plan the former image of Havana as a Nice of the Caribbean was replaced by the myth of Las Vegas or Miami. It featured a regional centre of tourism that included a complex of hotels, a Corbusian business city, and CIAM-inspired grids for the working-class residential suburbs (Scarpaci et al., 2002, pp. 78–88).

Arriving in Venezuela in the late 1940s, particularly during Pérez Jiménez's NIN, functionalist planning was advocated by Sert, and also by Robert Moses, Francis Violich and Maurice Rotival. All advised on the housing projects of the Banco Obrero (BO, Workers' Bank), epitomized by the high-rise blocks originally named 2 December – in commemoration of Pérez Jiménez's arrival to power, later renamed 23 January (figure 5.4). Villanueva's masterpieces during this period included the Ciudad Universitaria - initiated by Medina Angarita but completed during the dictatorship – where sculpture and painting were integrated with the modernist architecture.

The foreign experts also advised the Comisión Nacional de Urbanismo (CNU, National Commission of Planning), created in 1946 and responsible for the Planos Reguladores for Caracas (1951) and several other Venezuelan cities (Almandoz, 2002–2009, II, pp. 119–126; Almandoz, 2006a, pp. 346–350). In addition to Violich's emphasis on zoning as a centrepiece of functional segregation and planning control, a new and denser version of the neighbourhood unit – originally proposed by the American planner Clarence Perry – was adapted for the Venezuela context by CNU advisors, especially by Sert (Villoria-Siegert and Almandoz, 2002). Violich later summarized –

Figure 5.4. Aerial view of the 23 de Enero superblocks, Caracas, c. 1970. (*Source*: Arturo Almandoz Archive)

in relation to his Venezuelan experience at the CNU – the disciplinary shift that took place in those decades of developmentalism. What he said can be predicated of other Latin American capitals: 'A latter-day Beaux Arts movement inspired the late 1930s, and a social orientation, the mid-1940s, only to give way in the early 1950s to a functional approach drawing on North American techniques' (Violich, 1975, p. 285).

Brazil

Following the introduction of international modernism to São Paulo in 1923 by the Russian Gregori Warchavchik, CIAM representatives and Le Corbusier's proposals for Rio fuelled the functionalist momentum that reached climax in Lucio Costa's and Oscar Niemeyer's Brasilia. After the sketches of viaducts serving as high-rise residences, produced during his 1929 visit, Le Corbusier went back in 1936 to Brazil, where some of his proposals were more in tune with local reality (see pp. 83–84). In the capital, the

Figure 5.5. Ministry of Education and Health, Rio de Janeiro. (*Source*: Hitchcock, 1955).

Ministry of Education and Health building realized the tenets of *Vers une architecture* (1923), namely: *pilotis*, free façade, free plan, glazed walls and roof top gardens (Fraser, 2000, p. 156) (figure 5.5).

Imbued with the industrialism and developmentalism of those decades, an experience that confirms Brazil's fascination with CIAM's functionalism was the *Cidade dos Motores* (City of Engines, figure 5.6), a settlement for 25,000 people to provide homes for workers at an aeronautic factory north of Rio de Janeiro. The president of the Brazilian association of airplane manufacturers commissioned TPA to undertake the project. This was thanks to Wiener's contacts with the US State Department which was interested in strengthening the aviation industry in a country needed as an ally during World War II. Although Washington's 'involvement' is understandable on geopolitical grounds, it is more difficult to explain on technical ones, unless the seduction of CIAM-related luminaries is taken into account because, as Fraser points out, 'by 1942 Brazilian architects were well-informed on town-planning issues, so they were hardly in need of foreign leadership' (Fraser, 2000, p. 207).

The new capital city of Brasilia was a return to a nineteenth-century idea for a new capital then known as Planaltina. Although Le Corbusier was consulted about the project during his 1929 visit, it really gained momentum with industrialization and developmentalism after World War II, when functional modernism provided an

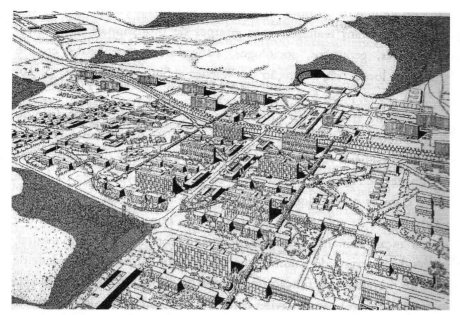

Figure 5.6. TPA's project for the City of Engines, Rio de Janeiro, 1945, including civic centre, factories and residential districts. (*Source*: Gomes and Huapaya, 2009)

impressive wrapping. Under the guidance of Costa and Niemeyer, Brasilia's national team finally showed that Brazilian architects and planners could achieve international acclaim without the help of foreign maestros. Having worked with Kubitschek when he was mayor of Belo Horizonte, Niemeyer was responsible for many of Brasilia's buildings, laid out within Costa's plan. The plan's aircraft-like shape has been interpreted not only as a reference to Le Corbusier's cult for that machine (Le Corbusier, 1931, 1986, pp. 107–127) and the rationality of the Roman *castrum*, but also as an allusion to Brazil's alleged take-off and drive for development. The functionalist principles of segregation and the predominance of express ways were displayed along the civic-commercial axis and in the *superquadras* of the residential wings. The *superquadras* are similar to the blocks adopted by Sert and Wiener in the *Cidade dos Motores*, following the principles of neighbourhood units and provided with communal services (Fraser, 2000, pp. 227, 235; Urban, 2012, pp. 79–99) (figure 5.7).

Fraser's assessment of Kubitschek's capital could apply to other Latin American rulers and projects of that period: '[he] saw Brasilia as a way of breaking with the roots of the past, of promoting industrialization, stimulating economic growth and encouraging regional development' (Fraser, 2000, p. 216). But curiously, in addition to not being the result of a proper regional proposal – as we shall further discuss in the next section – Brasilia was, like Latin America's *modernismo*, an illusion in the sense that it was mistaken as the completion of economic development and social modernization. Both, however, proved to be far more complex than building a capital city in five years.

Figure 5.7. Plaza of the Three Powers and National Congress, Brasilia. (*Source*: Roberto Segre Archive)

Between *Urbanismo* and Planning, City and Region[5]

It is not a coincidence that the term *urbanismo*, adopted during the 1920s and 1930s in Latin America, tended to be replaced, after World War II by *planificación* or *planeamiento* in Spanish, and by *planejamento* in Portuguese. In addition to theoretical and disciplinary distinctions that apply to other contexts (Taylor, 1998; Hebbert, 2006, for instance), that terminological transition was reinforced in Latin America by the displacement of the poles from which modernity was imported: as had happened in medicine and engineering, academic urbanism which until the late 1930s had come mostly from Europe, gave way to a package of master plans, zoning ordinances and planning-related instruments and institutions that were mainly channelled through the USA (Harth-terré, 1961, pp. 64, 124–126; Randle, 1968, pp. 20–25).

Towards Regional Planning

In those decades of US-backed developmentalism, Latin America's transition from *urbanismo* to *planificación* and *planejamento* was also reinforced by techniques and ideas drawn from regional planning, as happened in other contexts after World War II (Taylor, 1998, pp. 59–91). Such a shift does not mean, however, that the idea of the *region* had not been present before as an *extension*, so to speak, of city and metropolitan planning. In this respect Karl Brunner's famous *Manual de Urbanismo* (see pp. 84–85) – did not emphasize the region as a territorial entity, though it did recognize 'regional planning' as a new technique whose antecedents dated back to Robert Schmidt's planning of the Ruhr basin and Geddes's civic studies of Edinburgh. However contemporary breakthroughs in that field were being led, for Brunner, by experiences of the Regional Planning Association of America (RPAA) in New York and California (Brunner, 1939–1940, II, pp. 189–190). It was not the *urbanista* but the *planificador* the professional expected to coordinate the economic goals of regional planning, though part of its instruments, such as satellite towns and green belts, could work together with traditional urban planning (Brunner, 1939–1940, II, pp. 138–177).

At the same time, regional considerations had been incorporated into the field studies and theoretical frameworks of some of the first plans for Latin American capitals, from Carlos Contreras's and Carlos della Paolera's plans for Mexico City and Buenos Aires, to Donat-Alfred Agache's and Maurice Rotival's plans for Rio and Caracas, respectively (see pp. 82–83). The case of Rotival is especially significant in terms of the transition in the scale and approach. During his first visit to Caracas in the late 1930s, he coordinated a plan in the tradition of monumental urbanism, where regional considerations were not of much importance. But the second time, when he was hired by the Venezuelan government to advise the CNU, Rotival no longer wanted to be branded as *urbaniste*; by then he considered himself a *planificateur*, namely the more all-round professional who, in the US, 'was placed to the right of the President, the state governor or the city mayor' (Rotival, 1964, p. 42; Violich, 1975, p. 285; Almandoz, 2006a, pp. 348–350).

Brazil

Brazil and Mexico can be regarded as early examples of the transition of the discipline and the widening of its territorial scope. However these changes were not free from misconceptions and controversies among groups involved in regional planning, as the case of Brasilia showed. In spite of the founding in 1956 of the *Companhia Urbanizadora da Nova Capital do Brazil* (Novacap, Development Company for Brazil's New Capital), which appeared to be a regional corporation, the new body acted more like a firm running a design competition and the construction of a project. Regional considerations of the plan were neglected. Gilberto Freyre, a leading figure in Brazil's social sciences, criticized the company for not having incorporated more economists, ecologists, and social scientists. Arguing that the integration of diverse professional teams would have greatly prolonged the project – against Juscelino Kubitschek's feverish haste – Costa's reply was not only clever but representative of the changing condition of *planejamento* by then: the new capital city was not supposed to be 'the outcome but the cause of the regional plan' (Fraser, 2000, pp. 220–230).

Although regional factors were not fully incorporated into the planning of the capital, widening of the urban scale and changes in approach were taking place in some other Brazilian cities (Rezende, 2012). After Prestes Maia's tenure as mayor (1938–1945), São Paulo's *planejamento* was no longer conceived only in terms of public works and roads, but included new instruments and methods championed by Anhaia Mello from the General Division of Planning created in 1947. Among these were US inspired zoning and the framing of the metropolitan area within its hinterland, following the lessons from The Regional Plan of New York (Feldman, 2005, pp. 20–23, 28, 46–55).

The transition from urbanism into *planejamento* was accelerated by the visits of French Dominican, Father Joseph Lebret to São Paulo and other Brazilian cities, where he advocated, through the *Sociedade para a Análise Gráfica e Mecanográfica Aplicada aos Complexos Sociais* (SAGMACS, Society for the Graphical Analysis and Applied Research of Social Complexes), the assimilation of principles from economic and regional planning in the control of sprawling metropolitan areas (Lamparelli, 1998; Leme, 1999a, p. 26).

Among such areas was the capital of the Bahia state, where from 1946 to 1952 the regional tenets of Patrick Geddes, Ernest Burgess and Lebret were applied by the *Escritório do Plano de Urbanismo da Cidade de Salvador* (EPUCS, Bureau of the Urban Plan of Salvador) (Gomes, 2005, p. 25). With influences ranging from Marxism and Frédéric Le Play's reformism, to François Perroux's contemporary theories of regional poles (Perroux, 1955), Lebret's Economy and Humanism Movement and the SAGMACS pioneered the post-war improvement in the quality of life and 'spatialization' of development, through an early *aménagement du territoire* (town and country planning) closely linked to social sciences (Lamparelli, 1998).

Mexico

Another early example of regional planning was in Mexico, where Carlos Contreras championed the passing of the 1933 *Ley de planificación y zonificación del Distrito Federal y Territorios de la Baja California* – a law that provided the first legal framework for regional planning (Contreras, 1939, 2003, p. 131). By the 1940s, Mexico's regional development plans were inspired by the experience of the Tennessee Valley Authority (TVA); later tenets from Perroux's theory of development poles were incorporated, particularly in the case of the Lázaro Cardenas industrial port and the tourist resort of Cancun, by the 1970s (Quiroz, 2008, pp. 57, 60).

Mexico also saw the early adoption of the term *planeación* in place of *urbanismo*, in contrast to other Latin American countries where the EFU and CIAM had been stronger (see pp. 80–84). This change was perhaps brought about by the influence of the International Housing and Town Planning Congresses (IHTPC), whose sixteenth conference in 1938 was convened by Contreras in Mexico City. While EFU and CIAM were perceived as expressions of the local-based *urbanisme*, IHTPC advocated the techniques of urban and regional planning; the latter were expounded in Contreras's *Planificación* journal, whose approach was highly influential and prevailed in the long term (Sánchez, 2008, pp. 267–268).

Although the replacement of *urbanismo* by *planificación* may have been different in other countries, over time this change took place throughout Latin America roughly following the rationale of the Mexican case. Beyond the modification in the name, understandable in a post-war climate of North American influence, this substitution also corresponded, as this chapter has tried to show, to structural shifts in the discipline;

they included the transition from academicism into modernism, increased city size and the emergence of the region as the main focus of planning. However, the integration of regional planning with goals of economic development, both becoming part of national *planificación* or *planejamento* were to occur later, as we shall see in the next chapter (see pp. 133–136).

Notes

1. I rely here on passages from Almandoz (2008*a*; 2011; 2013*a*, pp. 267–276).
2. The end of the 'easy' phase of ISI has been summed up by Williamson in the following terms: 'By the end of the 1950s the more advanced countries had reached the limit of their internal market in what is generally known as the "easy" phase of import substitution: the production of non-durable consumer goods such as textiles and leatherware. Since much manufactures are labour-intensive and low-technology, factories were able to absorb the migrants from the countryside fairly easily while the internal market was still expanding' (Williamson, 1992, p. 339).
3. Indeed, Prebisch and ECLAC's *desarrollismo* inspired in the region, and especially in the Southern Cone countries, a series of institutions and, most importantly, 'an intellectual society' comprising economists, sociologists and historians, among new generations of scholars and professionals that represented a flowering of Latin America's social sciences from the 1950s (Blanco, 2006, p. 206).
4. Aguirre's presidential period was supposed to last until 1944, but he died of tuberculosis in 1941.
5. This section relies on passages from Almandoz (2006*b*; 2010*c*).

Chapter 6

Between Cold War and Third World

The Cuban Revolution breaks through the barriers of the news media and spreads its truths like a shower of dust among the American masses anxious for a better life. Cuba is the symbol of new nationhood and Fidel Castro is the symbol of liberation.

E. Che Guevara, *Guerrilla Warfare* (1961)

Revolution and Alliance in the Backyard[1]

Washington's Errors

As the benefits of the Good Neighbourhood faded away and the Cold War had begun, Washington made several errors in relation to Latin America, which had come to be known as the US's *patio trasero* (backyard). An early example of anti-communist penetration had taken place in Chile where, in 1948, tensions unleashed by the Iron Curtain led the government of Gabriel González Videla (1946–1952) to pass the *Ley de Defensa de la Democracia* (Defence of Democracy Act). This established 'limited pluralism' of political parties, 'coercive vigilance over the union movement' and the proscription of the Partido Comunista (PC, Communist Party), despite the fact that it was part of the coalition that made possible González's triumph (Aylwin *et al.*, 1990, 2008, pp. 134, 166).

The government's progressive reforms included the creation of the State Bank, agrarian improvements, a plan for low-cost housing, and workers' compulsory unionization. According to communist senator, poet and later Nobel laureate Pablo Neruda, the last, in particular, had threatened the privileges of the 'old feudal oligarchy' and 'the agents of North American imperialism represented in mighty companies' (Neruda, 1982, pp. 290, 292).[2] These US interests allegedly determined González's 'betrayal' and the radical turn of his regime, according to Neruda's accusations in 1947, and precipitated the loss of his parliamentary immunity together with the PC's proscription the following year (Neruda, 1982, pp. 312–340).[3]

Prompted by the leftist inclinations of Jacobo Arbenz's government in Guatemala (1951–1954), fighting the communist threat maintained its place on the US agenda in its *patio trasero*. At the Tenth Inter-American Conference held in Caracas in 1954, Washington tried to suppress the non-intervention in the nations' internal affairs – a principle that had been agreed at the 1948 conference in Bogotá and incorporated into the OAS Charter. This pressure partly explains the revolts during Richard Nixon's visit to Lima and Caracas in 1958; in Caracas he was spat at and violent mobs rocked his car, preventing the official motorcade from completing itineraries. Returning from exile to Caracas that same year, after Pérez Jiménez's overthrow in January, Rómulo Betancourt disagreed with the 'hatred' that 'communist minorities' exhibited against 'everything that is North American'. However, he lashed out at the Pentagon's turning a blind eye to the dictatorships of Fulgencio Batista in Cuba (1952–1959), Rafael Leónidas Trujillo in the Dominican Republic (1930–1961) and Pérez Jiménez in Venezuela (Betancourt, 1958, p. 21).[4]

Some positive lessons, nonetheless, were drawn from Nixon's infamous tour when the Eisenhower administration (1953–1961) regarded it in hindsight. Having made loans and grants of $12.6 billion worldwide between 1954 and 1958, the US government had only given 7 per cent of that aid to Latin America. Thus a significant step taken by Washington after Nixon's trip was to create – following a similar initiative undertaken for the Near East – the Inter-American Development Bank (IADB), aimed at making loans across the region to boost infrastructure projects in transport, health and education (Taffet, 2007, pp. 14–18). The Americans thought that such programmes would be enough to calm the anti-Yankee malaise, amend past errors and secure the backyard against communism – but they were mistaken.

The Cuban Revolution

Having witnessed the overthrow of Arbenz's government in Guatemala by a CIA-organized operation, Ernesto Guevara was radicalized when he, like many other foreigners, had to flee the Central American country. In Mexico, the Argentine-born doctor met Fidel Castro and in 1956 joined the 26 July Movement and *Granma*'s expedition[5] of eighty-two rebels to fight against Batista's dictatorship in Cuba (del Pozo, 2002, pp. 156, 219). While the corrupt regime was playing in the Havana of rumbas, casinos and prostitution, the insurgence was being incubated in the island's countryside. From the mountains of Sierra Maestra, 'Che' Guevara[6] not only acted as the rebels' doctor, but also became one of the Cuban Revolution's heroes, alongside Castro and Camilo Cienfuegos. After Batista's escape on 1 January 1959 and the new government was installed, Guevara occupied significant positions, such as head of the Industrial Department of the Instituto Nacional para la Reforma Agraria (INRA, National Institute for Agrarian Reform), President of the National Bank and Minister of Industry. Revered already as a revolutionary champion in Latin America and the Third World, Che Guevara had published a series of diaries and manuals about the armed subversion, including *Guerra de guerrillas* (1960, Guerrilla Warfare), which summarizes the Cuban Revolution's first measures and their immediate impact.

Despite the initial enthusiasm following the demise of Batista's regime, this process soon worried the Cuban establishment and Western powers. As Guevara recalled: 'The first alarm bell for the parasitic classes of the country sounds with the rent law, the reduction of electricity rates, and the intervention in the telephone company and the subsequent reduction in call charges – all decreed in rapid succession' (Guevara, 1960, 2009, p. 141). From then on, the fear of 'communism' was accelerated by Castro's approach to the Soviet Union, Poland and China in search of oil, loans and technology first, and the unmasking of his Marxist-Leninist ideology later (Williamson, 1992, pp. 448–450; del Pozo, 2002, p. 220). At this time, the agrarian reform in the 114,000 km² island was further proof of the revolution's communist nature and scope, whose main difference from earlier revolutions in Latin America was, according to Che, its radical fight against foreign corporations and 'the big Creole *latifundistas*' (Guevara, 1960, 2009, p. 143).

Passed in May 1959, the INRA's first law 'established a maximum property size of just 402 hectares, a limit that would be further reduced in 1963 to 67.1 hectares by the Second Agrarian Reform Law'; state control thereby increased to 70 per cent of all arable land (Scarpaci et al., 2002, p. 134). Cuba's early agrarian reform not only affected the land possessions and sugar production of the United Fruit Company – as had occurred in Arbenz's Guatemala – but also the estates of the Rockefellers and the Deutsch group, among other foreign investors. In addition to banning Soviet oil from being refined by US companies based in Cuba, the reaction of the Eisenhower administration was to stop buying sugar from the island in 1961, although 60 per cent of the business was in American hands. This decision and the total embargo on US imports to the island were deemed by Cubans a declaration of war; tensions escalated with the US-backed attempt to invade Bahía de Cochinos in April 1961, the missile crisis in October 1962, and Cuba's expulsion from the OAS the same year. The Cuban Revolution's destiny as a communist battleground of the Cold War was thus sealed in its early years (del Pozo, 2002, pp. 219–220; Williamson, 1992, p. 449).

The Alliance for Progress

After the Cuban Revolution, one of Washington's first responses was to create the military School of the Americas, based in Panama and whose purpose was to professionalize the armies from Latin American countries that now fought guerrillas (Edwards, 2009, p. 68). In order to forestall further leftist revolutions, the new administration of John F. Kennedy (1961–1963) also decided to promote the so-called Alliance for Progress (AFP), heir to Monroe's Pan-Americanism and Roosevelt's Good Neighbourhood. Inspired by the *Non-communist Manifesto* of W.W. Rostow (see pp. 89–90),[7] the US$ 20 billion package sought to boost the ISI and regional development, encourage land reform and reduce social inequalities through US help to new democratic governments. At a White House ceremony on 13 March 1961, President Kennedy described the programme's essence in terms of 'homes, work and land, health and school' for the continent (quoted in Taffet, 2007, p. 201).

The AFP was not unilaterally devised from Washington, but resulted from the interaction between Kennedy's advisors and Latin American planners such as ECLAC's Raúl Prebisch and IADB's Felipe Herrera (Consalvi, 2011; Taffet, 2007, pp. 30–31).[8] Shaped in the *Punta del Este Charter* – signed at the presidential meeting in the Uruguayan resort in August 1961 – the AFP was presented as a non-interventionist initiative, especially after the Bay of Pigs fiasco in April the same year. This is why the Bogota Act of OAS and the Pan American Operation promoted by Brazil's Kubitschek were referred to as background in the Charter, while the US only appeared as a *primus inter pares* (Halperin, 2005, pp. 539–540; Taffet, 2007, pp. 30–33, 206–209).

Although it was maintained during the administration of Lyndon Johnson (1963–1968), the AFP lost momentum after JFK's assassination and it competed for priority in foreign aid once the US entered the Vietnam War in 1965. Presidents of countries that benefited from the programme, such as João Goulart and Juan Bosch, were perceived as sympathizers with the communist left and advocates of anti-imperialist rhetoric, which eventually led to Washington's support for the *coup d'état* in Brazil and the invasion of the Dominican Republic (Taffet, 2007, pp. 6–8). Meanwhile, other regional leaders and beneficiaries of the AFP, such as Chile's Eduardo Frei, criticized the programme for not incorporating organizations representative of civil society, like trade unions and student associations (Edwards, 2009, p. 70). Over time, the AFP was undermined from different sides: south of Rio Grande, it came to be perceived as a plan for helping US exports to Latin American countries, while stoking the latter's endemic mismanagement of funds (Aylwin *et al.*, 1990, 2008, p. 198). From within the US, Washington's conservative policy-makers started to look at the AFP as wasted money, especially in the heat of a Vietnam War that had become hugely expensive by the late 1960s (Edwards, 2009, p. 70).

AFP, Coups and Communism

Considering, on the one hand, the turbulence and insurgence prompted by the Cuban Revolution and the Cold War, and on the other, the economic and political agenda set up by the AFP, let us look at the different situations of some Latin American countries.

Mexico: Miracle versus Massacre

Boosted by a visit from President Kennedy in 1961, Mexico's developmentalism reinforced socially-oriented goals during the administration of Adolfo López Mateos (1958–1964); according to AFP guidelines, the government resumed programmes of literacy and agrarian reform, while recognizing the Cuban regime as legitimate. Despite these left-leaning gestures, the PRI's political establishment was shaken by the students' protests in 1968, during the government of Gustavo Díaz Ordaz (1964–1970), when on 2 October the Tlatelolco massacre tainted Mexico's Olympic Games. The massacre and the students' movement resulted in the Movimiento de Acción Revolucionaria (MAR, Revolutionary Action Movement) with its Maoist tendencies, based in the southern state of Guerrero (Suchlicki, 1996, 2008, pp. 130–135; Meyer, 1973, 2005, pp. 149–150). The unresolved controversies from that period brought about another crisis during the administration of Luis Echeverría (1970–1976), when the *desarrollismo* distanced itself from the social legacy that previous administrations had respected after Cárdenas's corporate state (see pp. 66–67, 90).

Notwithstanding the 7 per cent growth reached by the early 1970s, the weakening of the economy was accelerated by the inflation unleashed after the 1973 oil crisis (see pp. 138–139, 143–144); at the same time, the ISI was not able to invest more in intermediate and capital goods, despite the protectionist policies that caused considerable indebtedness (Quiroz, 2008, p. 68). The devaluation of the peso, on 31 August 1976, put an end to the apparent Mexican miracle that had been trumpeted during the 1968 Olympic Games and the 1970 World Cup (Meyer, 1973, 2005, pp. 149–153). In spite of some adjustments then introduced, from 1976 onwards, 'while many clamored for greater state intervention in the economy and more populist policies', Mexico's model was to show a relative decline in the state involvement with some privatization and foreign investment (Suchlicki, 1996, 2008, pp. 130–132).

Colombia's National Front and Violence

Beset by violence after Gaitán's death in 1948, Colombia needed reforms that to some degree continued transformations introduced by Rojas Pinilla's left-wing dictatorship (see pp. 94–95). The National Front Pact signed by conservatives and liberals in 1957 was inaugurated with the presidency of the liberal Alberto Lleras Camargo (1958–1962), which adopted rigorous economic planning in accordance with the AFP and ECLAC. During the so-called 'developmentalist decade', economic goals were continued by the conservative administration of Guillermo León Valencia (1962–1966), followed by the liberal Carlos Lleras Restrepo (1966–1970). The constitutional reform promoted by the latter, approved in 1968, strengthened the presidential authority and reinforced the State's role as planner (Ocampo, 1994, 2007, pp. 302–304).

As the country became predominantly urban during the National Front governments, Colombia remained one of Latin America's most institutional and technocratic states, whose main weakness stemmed from the unsolved problems of land reform, rural guerrilla and urban violence. In this respect, the bipartisanship of the National Front incubated the 'discontent of the urban masses' and the ensuing emergence of the Alianza Nacional Popular (ANAPO, Popular National Alliance) under the leadership of Rojas Pinilla (Halperin, 1967, 2005, p. 621). Having apparently triumphed in the 1970 elections, this party was nonetheless impeded from coming to power, which ignited the subversive Movement 19 April (M–19). Other guerrilla groups had appeared since the mid-1960s: the Fuerzas Armadas Revolucionarias de Colombia (FARC, Colombia's Revolutionary Armed Forces), of Marxist orientation and backed by the USSR; and the Ejército de Liberación Nacional (ELN, National Liberation Army), which emulated Cuban guerrillas (del Pozo, 2002, p. 204).[9] Despite economic and constitutional stability, the violence fuelled by those movements was to shake Colombia's political and social life until the 1990s (see pp. 148–149).

Brazil: The Installation of the Military

In the midst of the Cold War, Jânio Quadros increased fears of communism in Brazil during his seven-month presidency in 1961. He resumed diplomatic ties with the USSR and commercial exchange with Mao's China, while approaching the Non-Aligned Movement, which became the political nucleus of the Third World. A Brazilian decoration bestowed on Che Guevara as Cuban Minister was a catalyst for his resignation. This was also fuelled by recession and inflation left by Kubitschek's expansionism, while his popular and parliamentary support plummeted. In order to control inflation, stimulate growth and curb public expenses, João Goulart's government (1961–1964) implemented a Triennial Plan coordinated by Celso Furtado, a left-wing member of ECLAC and champion of the Theory of Dependence that was about to emerge (see below, pp. 126–128). The nationalization of oil refineries and expropriation of land alongside railways and roads were decisions that, together with suspicions over an agrarian reform led by Goulart's communist sympathizers, undermined the backing of the bourgeoisie, the congress and armed forces. All those factors prompted the exile of 'Jango', as Goulart was nicknamed, and the establishment of a military junta – the first to disrupt the democracy promoted by the AFP (Schneeberger, 2003, pp. 326–327; del Priore and Venancio, 2010, pp. 274–275).

Presided over by General Humberto Castelo Branco between 1964 and 1967, the first dictatorship of this cycle combined elements of developmentalism and the welfare state, such as the 'Programa de Ação Econômica do Goberno' (PAEG, Programme of the Government's Economic Action) and the new *Banco Nacional de Habitação* (BNH, National Bank of Habitation), which aimed at dealing, for the first time, with the mounting deficit in housing, partly aggravated by rural–urban migration. But the regime also adopted authoritarian measures: combating guerrillas with US support, strengthening of centralism to the detriment of local and federal competences, and delaying agrarian reform (Schneeberger, 2003, pp. 328–331; del Priore and Venancio, 2010, pp. 282–283).

Emulating Kubitschek's period, mammoth projects such as the Trans-Amazonian road were undertaken during the military government of Garrastazu Médici (1969–1974). Industrial growth in this period, reaching 10 per cent in 1973, was hailed as an 'economic miracle', crowned by Brazil's triumph in Mexico's World Cup in 1970. Nevertheless, the re-adoption of the model of *tripé* or tripod – associations of Brazilian private companies with multinational and state enterprises – brought about indebtedness similar to the late Kubitschek years (del Priore and Venancio, 2010, p. 284). Meanwhile, for strategic and economic reasons that were summarized in the slogan 'Security and Development', political repression, torture and kidnapping, censorship of the media, and socio-demographic disparities were maintained or aggravated. When referring to these disparities, Garrastazu had to accept: '*O país vai muito bem, mas o povo vai mal*' (The country is doing very well, but the people go wrong), which seemed to acknowledge the social malaise caused by military-led developmentalism (Schneeberger, 2003, pp. 334–335).

Argentina: From Frondizi to Onganía

In the wake of the so-called Liberator Revolution that toppled Perón in Argentina – characterized by the return to a version of the 1853 Constitution and the proscription of *peronismo* from the political scene – the government of the radical Arturo Frondizi (1958–1962) promised to go back to social stability and economic growth. In accord with the AFP, the new president advocated developmentalist policies in agriculture, mining and industry in order to overcome stagnation. Economic goals were strengthened by a law to boost foreign investment, which jumped from $20 million in 1957 to $348 million by 1961 (Romero, 1994, 2013, pp. 140–142). However, critics regarded this legislation as contradicting Frondizi's anti-monopolist position when he campaigned for the presidency. Fuelled by this controversy and the anti-imperialist climate brought about by the Cuban Revolution, the first outbreaks of guerrilla activity in Tucumán in 1959 prompted the activation of the repressive Plan de Conmoción Interna del Estado (Plan of the State's Internal Commotion (Romero, 1946, 2008, pp. 272–273).

Frondizi's government bore the burden of having attracted many Peronists and having a pact with the deposed leader – then exiled in Madrid – to unite for elections (Luna, 1993, 2005, p. 269). This situation tainted the regime until its fall in 1962 and also undermined the presidency of Arturo Illía (1963–1966). Closer to ECLAC guidelines and less favourable to foreign investment, Illía softened the proscription of *peronismo*,[10] and this catalysed his overthrow by a military junta presided over by Juan Carlos Onganía (Romero, 1994, 2013, pp. 138–139, 148–150).

Unlike Castelo Branco's economic policies in Brazil, Onganía's regime (1966–1970) did not pursue developmentalism, while the social unrest mounted. Guerrilla activities in Tucumán were followed by further outbreaks in Salta, echoed by students' and workers' rebellions in Rosario in May 1969, and eventually by the *Cordobazo* at the end of the same month. Representing renewed and dramatic expressions that the radicalism and Peronism had shaped in previous decades, those popular movements contributed to reconciling Argentina's two main political trends, while undermining the military order. The new scenario of coalition led to the declaration of the so-called 'people's time', on 11 November 1970, a manifesto that made possible the brief return to democracy (Romero, 1946, 2008, p. 288–292).

Venezuela's Puntofijo Pact

After Pérez Jiménez's overthrow in January 1958, Rómulo Betancourt's government (1959–1964) advocated Venezuela's greater participation in the oil industry.[11] The leader of Acción Democrática (AD, Democratic Action) did not deem it timely, however, to nationalize the oil resources, which would have been 'a leap in the dark', given that 98 per cent of Venezuela's income came from oil (Betancourt, 1958, pp. 88, 91–92).[12] The deepening of the ISI was present in Betancourt's corporate state through the development of metallurgy and petrochemical industries, mainly south of the Orinoco (see below, pp. 135–136).[13] Using funds provided by the UN and AFP, another cornerstone of the social-democratic government was the land reform, especially considering that there was, according to Betancourt, 'a dangerous ebullition in the Venezuelan countryside' that seemed to confirm the Americans' fears of revolutions (Betancourt, 1958, pp. 55–56). Although the president approved an Agrarian Reform in 1960, which was much praised during the Kennedys' visit in December 1961, it did not deter rural backwardness and migration to the cities (Ledezma, 1993, p. 202).

In the political arena, Betancourt distanced his government from the radical left, by stating that AD was not communist, and after signing the Puntofijo Pact in 1958 with Venezuela's major political parties – the Christian Democratic COPEI and the radical URD – in order to prevent further dictatorships (Betancourt, 1958, pp. 129, 133). Betancourt's position prompted the secession of AD's leftist factions, which allied with the Partido Comunista de Venezuela (PCV, Venezuela's Communist Party), while others opted for fighting with guerrilla groups. Although the AD government of Raúl Leoni (1964–1969) permitted the participation of subversive factions in the 1968 election, it had also allowed brutal repression of the guerrillas by the military and intelligence services. These conflicts continued despite the 'pacification' policy carried out during the presidency of Rafael Caldera (1969–1974), the first to take COPEI to power (Ledezma, 1993, pp. 188–192). In spite of internal upheavals, the oil-rich nation was to remain as one of Latin America's most stable societies in decades to come, especially after left-wing dissidents were assimilated in the *status quo* of 1970s Gran Venezuela. However, the resentment caused by the exclusion of radical parties from the Puntofijo Pact remained dormant until the bonanza was over in the 1980s (see pp. 152–154).

Chile: from Alessandri to Allende

Jorge Alessandri Rodríguez's government (1958–1964), though leaning to the right, lived up to its socially-oriented promises and to the AFP agenda. In 1962 Alessandri passed the first legislation on agrarian reform that introduced two pivotal institutions: the Corporación de Reforma Agraria (CORA, Corporation of Agrarian Reform) and the Instituto de Desarrollo Agropecuario (INDAP, Institute of Agricultural Development). But it was during the administration of Eduardo Frei Montalva (1964–1970) when a Law of Agrarian Reform was finally approved in 1965; 540,000 hectares of rural land were expropriated that same year and 525,000 the following one, all boosted by legislation on the peasantry's right to unionize (de Ramón, 2006, pp. 160–162).

Even though 3.4 million hectares had been expropriated and 413 unions constituted up to 1970 (Aylwin *et al.*, 1990, 2008, p. 222–226), the agrarian reform slowed down, as happened in other Latin American countries. However this situation changed with the Unidad Popular's (UP, Popular Unity) rise to power in 1970, when illegal occupation of land was led by the Movimiento de Izquierda Revolucionaria (MIR, Movement of the Revolutionary Left). A similar process of expropriation occurred with the so-called 'chilenización del cobre' (making copper Chilean) initiated by Frei in 1966 and accelerated by the 'total nationalization of the big mining' during Salvador Allende's government (1970–1973) (de Ramón, 2006, pp. 162–165; Aylwin *et al.*, 1990, 2008, p. 228).

The UP's arrival to power in 1970 closed the political cycle initiated by the Popular Front in 1938, which had to a great extent gravitated around the middle class and the Radical Party (see pp. 68, 93). However, the early 1970s scene was far from similar, with a stronger presence of communists and socialists and a revolutionary project set in perspective by Allende in the following terms: 'We do not want a repetition of the Popular Front, which sought to improve the regime and maintain the system. We want to change the regime and the system in order to constitute a new society upon economic bases utterly different' (Allende quoted in de Ramón, 2006, pp. 188–189). Curiously, the UP leader proposed at the same time to work 'with the tools and mechanisms provided by democratic and bourgeois institutions, subject to Chilean traditions, a revolution of *"empanadas* (pastries) with red wine", as he liked to say, thereby highlighting the joyful and festive character with which he wished to brand his revolution' (de Ramón, 2006, p. 191).

By November 1971, Allende claimed to have nationalized 90 per cent of banks and expropriated seventy strategic enterprises, while the agrarian reform had been 'deepened' with more than 2,400,000 hectares expropriated (Allende, 2008, p. 14).[14] Also in that year 167 enterprises passed to public hands, augmented by 151 the following year, while intervention in the banks was stepped up. The state's presence grew with the nationalization of copper, coal, iron and saltpetre, alongside the extension of the agrarian reform together with expropriations and invasions, which reached 10 million hectares by 1973.[15] Meanwhile 600 per cent inflation was triggered by, on the one hand, the decline in production and the ensuing scarcity of goods, and on the other, by the exchange control over the peso and the black market generated (Edwards, 2009, p. 127). This situation was aggravated by political turbulence in the streets, which prompted the middle classes to withdraw their backing for the UP, as was evinced in the results of the 1973 municipal elections. Allende's allegedly festive revolution ended up without social support and was cut short by a coup on 11 September when he committed suicide in La Moneda palace (see pp. 139–140); so 'the empanadas and wine kept waiting their opportunity', as de Ramón paraphrased the president's slogan (de Ramón, 2006, pp. 191–194).

Guerrillas, Anti-Imperialism and Revolution

Allende's revolution represented not only the closure of the socialist cycle initiated by the Frente Popular, but also the best known communist response to changes proposed by the AFP (figure 6.1). The UP's Marxist option had also manifested throughout subversive movements and anti-imperialist stances that had been deeply rooted in the region since the 1950s (see above, pp. 110–112) and would remain so in the following decades. Let us consider in this section some of the claims and grievances of Latin America's revolutionary left, together with the critique that, prompted by Cold War tensions and the contradictions of the Cuban Revolution, emerged among different intellectual groups.

Figure 6.1. 'Nobody will stop the revolution'. Poster by Vicente Larrea and Hugo Larrea, photo by Hugo Lagos. (*Source*: Archivo de Originales SLGM. FADEU. Pontificia Universidad Católica de Chile)

Silent Vietnams

In the wake of the Cuban Revolution, armed insurgence was invoked as the way out from inequality and imperialism for the diverse flanks of Latin America's left wing. When the AFP Charter was to be signed in Punta del Este in 1961, a bearded Che in battle dress officially representing the Cuban government warned that 'if there were not urgent measures to meet the demands of the people', Cuba's example could 'take root in the countries of Latin America' (Guevara in Taffet, 2007, p. 35). This crusade against monopoly and imperialism had gathered support in Asia and Africa, some of

Figure 6.2. 'Viet Nam ... a war that sends blacks to combat yellows, allowing whites to keep what they have stolen from reds'. Poster by Vicente Larrea and Hugo Larrea, photo by Hugo Lagos. (*Source*: Archivo de Originales SLGM. FADEU. Pontificia Universidad Católica de Chile)

whose decolonized nations had met in 1955 in Bandung, Indonesia, to launch the Non-Aligned Movement. After organizing a Tricontinental Conference in Havana in 1965, Che Guevara became a pioneer of this Third World crusade, with his experiences in Congo (1965) and Bolivia (1966); fighting in the latter against René Barrientos's regime (1964–1969), he wanted to transform it into a South American Vietnam (Guevara, 1960, 2009, p. 146) (figure 6.2).

Triggered by the Cuban Revolution and communist expansion, the Catholic

Church had meanwhile undertaken the so-called *Aggiornamento* aimed at bringing it up to date with the social development in Latin America, thereby propitiating curious forms of 'Christian revolutionary nationalism' in the 1960s (Ocampo, 1994, 2007, p. 304). Colombian Camilo Torres Restrepo[16] and Brazilian Hélder Câmara were early exponents of the so-called 'Third World priests' who spread throughout Latin America, their preaching 'torn between the Gospels and the Communist Manifesto' (Romero, 1946, 2008, 298). In this respect it is worth remembering that Che himself had brought near those two seemingly opposed archetypes of social liberation by stating that 'the guerrilla fighter, as the conscious element of the vanguard', had to display 'the moral conduct of a true priest of the desired reform' (Guevara, 1960, 2009, p. 49). Guerrillas and clergy were thus among the ingredients of Liberation Theology that came out of Latin America's 1968 Episcopal Conference in Medellín, Colombia, and thereafter inspired subversive movements amongst some Catholics across the Third World.

Subversion and revolution were also justified on political and economic grounds by Allende before the UN General Assembly in 1972: still suffering from the post-war financial order created in Bretton Woods, the Latin American subcontinent had become 'the main field of action for economic imperialism' (Allende, 2008, p. 62).[17] As Che had claimed in relation to Bolivia, the Chilean President appealed to the image of a 'silent Vietnam' in describing his own country's war against foreign states and corporations that opposed the nationalization of copper and other communist policies (Allende, 2008, p. 47).[18] Although Chile never became a battleground for guerrillas as such, other Latin American countries did, as we have seen, and could therefore be regarded as silent Vietnams that battled imperialism and foreign intervention.

Following the death of Che Guevara in the Bolivian jungle in 1967 in a CIA-backed ambush, the Nixon administration came to represent the most perverse face of imperialism in the region. Latin Americans' antipathy towards Washington was augmented by US attempts to impede Allende's arrival to power through the Operation Track II, supported by the CIA and endorsed by Secretary of State, Henry Kissinger (de Ramón, 2006, p. 187). Meanwhile US National Security advice continued to be given to governments that fought guerrillas, such as Stroessner's in Paraguay and Onganía's in Argentina. And last but not least, there was the blatant complicity with the military juntas that ejected leftist governments, such as José Torres's (1970–1971) in Bolivia, Allende's in Chile and Juan Velasco Alvarado's (1968–1975) in Peru.

The Critique by the Left-Wing Intelligentsia

In the midst of the procommunist and anti-American climate fuelled by guerrillas and imperialism, some intellectuals dared to voice their criticisms of the Cuban Revolution and its influence in Latin America. The revolutionary establishment started to age and show its shortcomings and abuses, and this dampened the initial enthusiasm of left-wing intelligentsia, including members of Latin America's literary boom.[19] This was what happened to Jorge Edwards when, in 1971, he arrived as Chile's ambassador to

Havana, a mission that only lasted three months and was reported in *Persona non grata* (1973) – the book that first adopted a critical stance and was initially proscribed by the international left. While rejecting the Cuban government's intentions that Chile should become 'South America's first Vietnam', Edwards paralleled the bureaucratic Castro and the Revolution that had lost 'freshness and rapture' with the 'relentless deterioration' of the city that he had first visited during a writers' congress in 1968 (Edwards, 1973, 2006, pp. 22, 297).

It was the same Revolution that, having repelled the Bay of Pigs invasion, maintained its popularity, but later radical intellectuals who disliked Cuba's support for the Soviet's Prague actions became disenchanted. As the island's economic situation deteriorated, the 'demoralization' grew when, by 1970, Cuba's *zafra* or sugar cane harvest did not reach 10 million tons, 'despite the crucial significance that Castro had attached to the figure' (Williamson, 1992, p. 453).[20] When Heberto Padilla and other Cuban writers were forced to disown their own works, in May 1971 international intellectual celebrities, who had initially hailed the Cuban Revolution, published a letter of protest where the episode was equalled to 'the most sordid moments of Stalinism, its prefabricated trials and witchhunts' (Vargas Llosa, 2009, p. 118). Signatories included Italo Calvino and Carlos Fuentes, Simone de Beauvoir and Jean-Paul Sartre, Marguerite Duras and Pier Paolo Pasolini, Alain Resnais and Juan Rulfo. They were led by Vargas Llosa – up to then a revolutionary stalwart – who in vain exhorted Castro 'to avoid in Cuba the dogmatic obscurantism, cultural xenophobia and repressive system that Stalinism imposed in socialist countries, where events similar to those happening now in Cuba were flagrant manifestations' (Vargas Llosa, 2009, p. 118).[21]

From Noble Savages to Guerrilleros

There was also the critique by liberal intellectuals such as the Venezuelan Carlos Rangel, whose *Del buen salvaje al buen revolucionario* (1976, From the Noble Savage to the Good Revolutionary) set Latin America's armed subversion in historical and mythical perspective.[22] The book expounded controversial theses, such as claiming that 'because of the noble savage myth, the West suffers an absurd guilt complex, intimately convinced of having corrupted with its civilization other people of the Earth gathered under the denomination of "Third World"' (Rangel, 1976, 2005, p. 41). The quintessential incarnation of Rousseau's myth of the *bon sauvage* was the bearded Fidel emerging from Sierra Maestra, combating not only Batista's Cuba, but also Yankee imperialism (Rangel, 1976, 2005, p. 152) (figure 6.3). Another expression of the myth rooted in the Enlightenment was the *guerrillero* (guerrilla fighter), who was idealized by Che Guevara with sacred missions such as being 'the guardian angel' of the peasant, to whom the former should provide the 'orientation' proper of a 'social reformer' (Guevara, 1960, 2009, pp. 50–51).

After the mythical experiences in Sierra Maestra, Cuban guerrillas thus acquired a 'Utopian strain' across Latin America: they recalled the 'millenarian zeal which had motivated the ascetic missionaries of Spain, who wanted to evangelize the Indians in

Figure 6.3. 'Homeland or Death. We shall overcome', Fidel Castro's slogan. Poster by Vicente Larrea and Hugo Larrea, photo by Hugo Lagos. (*Source*: Archivo de Originales SLGM. FADEU. Pontificia Universidad Católica de Chile)

order to build a New World free from the sins of the old' (Williamson, 1992, pp. 447–448). And such a Utopia was to be built, in the twentieth century, by the *guerrillero* and his Marxist Revolution against imperialism and destitution (Almandoz, 2002–2009, III, pp. 109–113).

The Failure of Industrialization and the Distortions of Urbanization

ISI Constraints

Political turbulence and armed subversion were woes that Latin America added to more structural problems, such as truncated industrialization and excessive urbanization, which it shared with other parts of the Third World. As anticipated (see pp. 139–140), from the late 1950s, the ISI had already shown fatigue that was to some extent the natural result of the distortions that the model had suffered. ECLAC strategists had initially recommended that 'protectionist measures had to be strictly temporary', while being applied in key sectors with dynamic effects on the production line (World Bank, 1993, pp. 24–25). At the same time, duties charged on imports – aimed at protecting national produce – had to be very selective in the case of staples and high enough to provide protection, but low enough to foster efficient local productivity. Since neither of those conditions was met in the long term, the ISI brought about instead the disincentive of exportations, high currency exchange rates and slow creation of employment, while non-productive sectors of the economy expanded (World Bank, 1993, p. 55; Edwards, 2009, pp. 73–74).

Thus, despite the AFP aid and ISI's long presence in the largest economies, by the late 1960s industrialization had neither diversified nor consolidated in Latin America, especially in terms of intermediate goods and machinery. The weakness of economic integration within the region, the small size of some of the national markets and the disadvantage of most of the countries in competing with international manufacturers[23] are other factors which explain the ISI's structural and contextual constraints (Williamson, 1992, pp. 339–340). Aimed at enlarging the market for ISI produce, the creation of the Andean Pact in 1969 – grouping Bolivia, Chile, Colombia, Ecuador, Peru and eventually Venezuela – also proved to be insufficient, as had been the protectionist strategy (World Bank, 1993, pp. 25–26).[24]

Having defended the model over decades, the 'external constriction' of the ISI had to be recognized by ECLAC at a mid-1970s meeting in Trinidad, where the main constraint was attributed to the fact that industries producing capital and intermediate goods were 'lagging behind those of durable and non-durable consumer goods' (ECLAC, 1979, pp. 76–77). While much of the region had become politically closer to the Group of 77 or Non-Aligned Countries, Latin America's Third World condition was ratified in economic terms by another ECLAC conference in La Paz, Bolivia, in 1979; here inequities of income between cities and countryside was highlighted as one of the most dramatic indicators of underdevelopment (ECLAC, 1979, p. 170).

Concentration and Primacy, Migration and Poverty

The weakening of ISI thus fractured the fragile support that industrialization had provided in post-war decades to the urbanization process, which for Latin America as a whole rose from 57.4 per cent in 1970 to 65.4 per cent in 1980 (Clichevsky, 1990, p. 42). Far above Africa and Asia, Latin America was the most urbanized region of the Third World (Drakakis-Smith, 1990; Potter and Lloyd-Evans, 1998, pp. 24–25).

Throughout most of the 1970s, Latin America's rates of urban growth were six times higher than the rural ones (Clichevsky, 1990, p. 48) (Appendices tables 1 and 2), which indicated massive rural–urban migration. On top of that, most of this population was highly concentrated in certain areas: by 1970 not only did Latin America boast three of the Third World's five megalopolises with populations of over 8 million (Clark, 2000, p. 46), but by 1980 more than a half the populations of Argentina, Brazil, Mexico, Venezuela, Chile and Colombia lived in metropolitan areas with more than 100,000 inhabitants (Clichevsky, 1990, p. 54).

Mid twentieth-century urban growth and migration increased the national primacy of traditional metropolises: between 1950 and 1980, the population of Greater Buenos Aires rose from 4,603,000 inhabitants to almost 10 million, Mexico City from 2,223,000 to 14,750,000, Lima from 835,000 to more than 5 million, Bogotá from 525,000 to 4,169,000 (figure 6.4), Guadalajara from 378,000 to 2,467,000 and Medellín from 256,000 to 2,071,000 inhabitants (Hardoy, 1997, p. 271). As an example of national primacy, in a country that had surpassed 70 per cent urbanization by 1970, Santiago was home to 32 per cent of the national population, and spread over an area that increased from 21,389 hectares in 1960 to 44,165 in 1982 (Aylwin *et al.*, 2008, pp. 254, 257; Hardoy, 1997, p. 271) (figure 6.5).

Further, attempts to move the ISI from light to intermediate manufacture aggravated Latin America's urban distortions. One of the main effects was that 'the rising tide of fugitives from the crisis in the countryside could not be absorbed by industry in the cities, so that during the 1960s urban unemployment began to soar' (Williamson, 1992,

Figure 6.4. Bogotá's centre, photograph by Germán Téllez, 1975. (*Source*: Téllez, 1988)

Figure 6.5. Santiago's centre, circa 1980. (*Source*: Archivo de Originales SLGM. FADEU. Pontificia Universidad Católica de Chile)

pp. 339–340). By the early 1970s it was also evident that, beyond the Americanized bourgeoisie and middle classes, the 'modernizing style of development' of the previous decades had not spread its benefits to other strata of population, especially to the growing mass of 'urban poverty' which was fuelled by rural–urban migration (Clichevsky, 1990, p. 25).

Three decades after the beginning of the ISI and one after the AFP, 40 per cent of Latin American families continued to live below the poverty line, a proportion that reached 62 per cent in rural areas (ECLAC, 1979, p. 160). The rigidity and inertia in the distribution of income during the 1960s was confirmed at another ECLAC meeting in Guatemala in 1977: the poorest half of the Latin American population had only received 14 per cent of the income; 20 per cent of the inhabitants absorbed another 14 per cent, while the remaining 30 per cent captured 72 per cent (ECLAC, 1979, p. 93). This impoverishment was the most dramatic in the Third World: Latin America was the only undeveloped region where the share of income received by the poorest 20 per cent of the population declined over the 1960s and 1970s, going from 3.7 per cent in 1960 to 2.9 in 1978 (World Bank, 1993, p. 118).[25]

The School of Dependence

The constraints of the ISI and the failure of modernization, along with Latin America's rapid and colossal urbanization undermined the ECLAC approach of post-war decades (see pp. 87–89, 96–99). From the 1960s, it became necessary to look for sociological rather than economic explanations for the imbalances and contradictions that prevented Latin America from achieving development. In the midst of this malaise, the Theory of Dependence reinterpreted ECLAC's centre/periphery antinomy as a structural hindrance that could only be overcome through State intervention (Williamson, 1998, pp. 334–335). The *dependentista* approach was not originally opposed to ECLAC initiatives, including the ISI, but as the latter proved to be exhausted, Dependency Theory became a predominantly Marxist response to capitalist developmentalism (Almandoz, 2006b, pp. 104–105; 2008b, pp. 163–164).

With pioneering contributions from André Gunder Frank, Theotonio Dos Santos, and later by Celso Furtado, Fernando H. Cardoso and Enzo Faletto, the theory turned into a Marxist school of social sciences. It provided a framework for understanding Latin America's backwardness during the colonial and republican eras, including the economic, political and social dimensions of underdevelopment (Cardoso and Faletto, 1969). As to the *urbanización dependiente* or dependent urbanization, the deficiencies and imbalances of cities were interpreted by Kaplan (1972) and Quijano (1977), while historical analysis of Latin America's weak city systems – configured according to the export necessities of the Iberian metropolises in colonial times (see pp. 15–17) – was carried out by Rofman (1977).[26]

Marking Latin America's intellectual climate until the early 1980s, belief in Dependency Theory was not limited to Marxists or socialists, but influenced a diverse political spectrum, from social and Christian democrats to populists and conservatives (Vargas Llosa, 2009, pp. 301–302).[27] Also it reinforced the nationalist orientation of some governments opposed to foreign investment in the exploitation of raw materials and industrial development (del Pozo, 2002, pp.177–179).

From *Vecindades* to Shantytowns

Culture of Poverty and Marginality

While some districts of Latin America's metropolises exhibited the Americanized modernization with high street shops and department stores, bourgeois suburbs and supermarkets (figure 6.6), others displayed backwardness and destitution. Regarded as one of the most flagrant failures of modernization and developmentalism, this duality spurred a long-lasting political and academic debate over the causes of, and possible solutions to, what came to be known first as the 'culture of poverty', and later as 'marginality'.

Oscar Lewis's *The Children of Sánchez* (1961) became the manifesto of Latin America's culture of poverty. Relying on oral history and other anthropological methods, he paints a vivid picture of the poverty in Mexico City's *vecindades*, descendants of the *conventillos* in existence since the late nineteenth century (see pp. 33–37, 59–61). Lewis's description of life in the *vecindad* or tenant house of Casa Grande, very close to the Zocalo plaza, reveals a world of rural-like shabbiness with hints of modern metropolitan facilities and services, as were to be found in Latin American central districts and shanties since the 1950s (Lewis, 1961, p. xiv). Partly because it originated in the ghettos, the culture of poverty developed as a 'subculture of the national one' in which the survival and

Figure 6.6. Sabana Grande High Street in Caracas, postcard by K. Weidmann, c. 1960. (*Source*: Arturo Almandoz Archive)

adaptation to the precariousness of everyday life and environment were perpetuated in a fatalistic way (Roberts, 1978, p. 140).

As the more comprehensive and prevailing approach in the 1970s, especially among the School of Dependence, marginality was summarized by Roberts as 'consisting in the lack of participation of low-income groups in education, in their "traditional" attitudes and in their lack of access to education, health care and adequate standards of consumption'. From this perspective, marginality was 'an unfortunate and avoidable consequence of rapid urban growth in the situation of underdevelopment', but was 'remediable through social welfare and educational programmes and through the creation of job opportunities' (Roberts, 1979, p. 139). Echoing David Harvey's conception of the international capitalist system as one where the wealth of urban centres is based on creating scarcity at the periphery (Harvey, 1973), urban poverty was, in the marginality approach, not only a matter of family income, but also conditioned by spatial location in the city and its ensuing inaccessibility to proper housing and public services (Roberts, 1979, p. 137).

While Lewis depicted Mexico City's central *vecindades* in the 1950s,[28] Latin America's disenfranchised were later displaced to shantytowns. These included Peru's

Figure 6.7. *Barrio de ranchos* (shantytown) in Caracas, adjacent to the Parque Central towers, photograph by Roberto Loscher, *c*. 1975. (*Source*: Mendoza, 1980)

barriadas, Brazil's *favelas*, Mexico's *colonias proletarias*, Venezuela's *barrios de ranchos*, Chile's *poblaciones callampa* and Argentina's *villas miseria*, among other manifestations (Harris, 1971, pp. 208–223). Depending on the city's topography, some of these were located not in the misery belt on the periphery, but intermingled with upper-class districts, as typically happens in Rio and Caracas (figure 6.7).

Causes and Manifestations

In his comparative study of the structure of Latin America's primate cities, the initial reasons for the poor population's peripheral location were summarized by Walter Harris in the following terms:

> (a) the existence of land of little economic value, for either commercial or agricultural purposes on the outskirts of the city…; (b) the availability of large spaces of public land in the periphery; (c) the existence of a large housing shortage which has led to much overcrowding of the central areas, which allows little space for residential building in locations taken up by commercial and government use; (d) the fact that most of the low-income groups have come from rural areas and prefer the peripheral areas, where they at least have their own shelter and sometimes a small lot to cultivate. (Harris, 1971, pp. 208–211)

Latin America's marginality seemed to increase more dramatically in cities that had a high rate of urban growth without significant industrialization. This was the case in Mexico City, Rio, Lima and Caracas, where 24.9, 38, 21.5 and 38.5 per cent of inhabitants lived in squatter settlements, according to UN data of the 1950s and early 1960s. But marginality was not limited just to capitals with scarce industrialization: by the early 1960s ECLAC recognized the magnitude of marginal settlements in Latin American capitals generally, including those of the Southern Cone, which previously seemed to be unaffected (ECLAC, 1963). In Greater Santiago – where central *conventillos* had originally absorbed urban poverty – the population in *callampas* had risen from 34,678 in 1952 to 53,401 families in 1961; this persuaded the government to commission the Corporación de la Vivienda (CORVI, Housing Corporation) with an aggressive programme of low-cost housing (ECLAC, 1963, pp. 5–7).

Fuelled by the country's mounting political tensions over land reform, Chile can also be regarded as an example of how the causes and manifestations of the marginal population escalated into the national agenda (see pp. 117–118). Since the late 1950s, squatters who took part in *tomas de terreno* (land seizures), epitomized by the famous invasion of La Victoria in 1957, were not evicted by the authorities.[29] The invasions worsened during the following decade, reaching thirty-five in 1969 alone; meanwhile, Eduardo Frei's Christian democrat government responded with the so-called 'operations', whereby semi-urbanized land was handed over for self-build by occupants, on the basis of long-term mortgages (Gross, 1991, nd, pp. 145, 155–157).

Reinforcing the socialist role of the welfare state, the Allende administration undertook housing and other programmes for *poblaciones callampa* with the support of corporations associated with the Ministry of Housing and Urbanism (MINVU), alongside the Oficina de Planificación (Odeplan, Bureau of Planning) (figure 6.8). All

Figure 6.8. *Población callampa* next to Pablo Neruda sector, Santiago, 1979. (*Source*: Archivo de Originales SLGM. FADEU. Pontificia Universidad Católica de Chile)

this contributed to a major trend in Chilean urban policy: as was demonstrated in the case of Santiago, grassroots organizations and social movements (Castells, 1976, pp. 413–469), usually sponsored by communist and left-wing political parties alongside labour unions, managed to link the urban conflict with the political one (Roberts, 1978, p. 156). During this period, this linkage was found to varying degrees throughout Latin America, where the revolutionary ethos found a cause in the urban and economic distortions dramatized by marginality (Castells, 1980).

Migration and Exclusion

Rural–urban movements in Latin America mostly proceeded from depressed and remote regions and corresponded to low-income populations that sought better conditions in major cities (Cerrutti and Bertoncello, 2003, p. 8; Roberts, 1978, p. 99). Lured in part by the consumer and cultural opportunities they saw or heard about on the radio, TV and other media (Germani, 1969, p. 141), the numbers of people immigrating from the countryside accounted for 44 per cent of Latin America's urban growth between 1952 and 1960, and 32 per cent between 1960 and 1982 (Hardoy, 1997, p. 271).

In addition to the large numbers of migrants, there were other general trends in the shantytowns of Latin America's major metropolises that confirmed the effects of poverty and marginalization. Integration of the resident population into the formal economy was weakened over time: as happened in the *villas* of Buenos Aires, the *favelas* of São Paulo and the *barriadas* of Lima, the low-income yet unionized contingents of the 1960s and 1970s tended to be replaced by informal and unemployed population by the 1980s (Clichevsky, 2003, p. 348; Taschner, 2003, p. 330; Calderón, 2003, pp. 385–386). As to insertion within the urban structure, although many of Rio's *favelas* and Caracas's *barrios* remained embedded on inner hills (figure 6.7), overall illegal settlements moved towards the periphery. But these marginal or peripheral locations differ from the ghetto-like insertion of poverty pockets within the sprawling and fragmented structure, as would happen in some Latin American metropolises after neoliberal reforms of the late 1980s (Sabatini and Salcedo, 2011, pp. 333, 343) (see also pp. 158–160, 177–179).

Housing Deficit and Governmental Responses

Despite the massive influx of the poor into Latin American cities, official responses were not effective, which increased the housing deficit, especially in those cities where there was little industrialization. Lima's case is representative of the initial delay to tackle the housing problem: between 1949 and 1956, 45,712 dwellings were built, while the population increased by 76,000 households; by 1960, while the Peruvian capital's population grew at 5 per cent, less than four dwellings per 1,000 inhabitants were constructed and the marginal population reached 20 per cent by 1964 (Harris, 1971, pp. 209, 216). The 1961 *Ley de Barrios Marginales* (LBM, Law of Marginal Barrios) was an early measure aimed at tackling the explosive growth of the previous decade, but it allowed the sprawl of eighty-three new *barriadas* during the rest of the 1960s. Although

Velasco Alvarado's leftist dictatorship claimed to be the 'institutional promoter' of the 'Pueblos Jóvenes' (Young Towns), there was no effective response to the mounting housing deficit. Relying on the LBM, later military regimes tried to ameliorate the *barriadas* or *bolsones* while evicting the population of the *barriadas* located on urban land with high commercial value (Calderón, 2003, pp. 378–379).

Although present from the 1890s, Rio's *favelas* were not recognized as a problem by local or national governments until the 1930s, when censuses revealed that they were home to over 14 per cent of the urban population. By then, their 'political visibility' at the beginning of Vargas's *Estado Novo* made them part of the housing question with the passing of the *Código de Obras* (Code of Works) in 1937 (Pereira da Silva, 2012, pp. 311–318). Compulsory relocation programmes were implemented by the military from 1964, when nearly 175,000 inhabitants of eighty *favelas* were moved to peripheral sites. However, given the precarious conditions of the new residences, a significant number either returned to central *favelas* that had not been demolished or eventually constructed new ones elsewhere (Vaz and Jacques, 2003, pp. 266–269; Ribeiro, 2003, p. 306).

The experience of relocation in Pérez Jiménez's Caracas appeared more successful, given that most of the population did stay in the high-rise blocks of 23 de Enero, which became a continental reference (see figure 5.4 and pp. 102–103). Reaching a density of about 620 inhabitants per hectare, Villanueva's buildings were provided with infrastructure facilities and communal services, but they lacked adequate transport links with employment areas (Harris, 1971, p. 214; López Villa, 1986; 1994). However in later democratic years, Venezuela's shortage of low-cost housing became notorious: in Gran Caracas alone there were 580,000 *ranchos* or shacks by the mid-1960s and they were home to 22 per cent of its population. As the tip of an iceberg, this massive amount of informal housing confirmed a deficit that amounted to 800,000 units by the end of Betancourt's presidency (Martínez, 1996, p. 57; OMPU, 1972, pp. 57–58).

Venezuela's housing shortage was perhaps representative of that of Latin America as a whole in the decades to come: during the 1960s and 1970s only three housing units per 1,000 inhabitants were built, whereas ten were required; this led to an accumulated deficit of 20 million units by 1970, in a region whose population already amounted to 283 million (Hardoy, 1997, p. 272). Meanwhile, the problem of marginality, which was to change its denomination, remained a symbol of Latin America's Third World type urbanization (see pp. 123–126).

Central Planning and Regional Development

Despite the failure of the ISI and the distortions of urbanization, the state's central planning and regional projects stood out as a significant component of Latin America's corporate model of development from the 1930s. Regional plans for national capital cities became a part of national development goals by the early 1960s, when a system of centralized *planificación* or *planejamento* was institutionalized or at least envisaged in the largest countries. This integration can be regarded as another phase in the lengthy process of epistemological change and spatial enlargement from the city-focused *urbanismo* to regional planning, and eventually to nationwide *ordenamiento* (town and country planning, see pp. 106–109). The possible illustrations for this process are countless, but are only touched upon here: first we show that some systems of regional or national planning, generated under different influences and strategies, were mainly around the capital cities; secondly, a more detailed examination of Venezuela's Ciudad Guayana reveals a flagship project of this period with its ideals of regional poles of development, which was, however, masterminded from a centralized apparatus of planning.

Around the Capitals

Mexico and Brazil had pioneered the enlargement of the metropolitan scale and the 'spatialization' of development as channels for regional planning in Latin America (see pp. 107–109). Trying to catch up with the needs of the sprawling metropolis, Mexico City's early platform for regional planning was boosted with the 1953 *Ley de Planificación del Distrito Federal* (Planning Act of the Federal District) and the 1970 *Ley Orgánica del Gobierno del Distrito Federal* (Organic Act of the Federal District's Government); meanwhile, economic development goals were incorporated into territorial *planeación* following the Soviet model (Bataillon and Rivière, 1973, pp. 100–101; Sánchez, 2008, pp. 267–268). In *Brazil*, the strengthening of planning from the local level included the Rio-based *Instituto Brasileiro de Assistência aos Municipios* (IBAM, Brazilian Institute for Municipal Assistance, 1946), which counted on the support of the US Agency of International Development (USAID). Setting aside the experience of Brasilia's Novacap, the institutionalization of planning at a federal level only occurred in 1972 with the *Coordenadoria Geral de Planejamento* (COGEP, General Coordination of Planning) (Feldman, 2005, pp. 46–47). Planning was then regarded as 'an authoritarian and repressive practice' associated with Brazil's military regimes (Leme, 2003, pp. 121–122).

Headed by the economist Lauchlin Currie, a World Bank mission arrived in *Colombia* in 1949 with a 'Programa de Fomento' or Four Point Programme comprising a series of recommendations in different fields, some of them linking economic growth with comprehensive planning. For that purpose the Departamento Nacional de Planificación (DNP, National Department of Planning) was created in 1958, followed by the Centre of Development Research of Colombia's National University by the beginning of the 1960s (Ramírez, 2010). With similar experiences in Peru and Cuba (see pp. 99–100, 102), these national departments and regional development corporations became cornerstones for connecting economic and social development, on the one hand, with the urban and planning system, on the other. While the Soviet model was a reference, they also followed the examples from the United States post Roosevelt's TVA, and in Europe after World War II (Hall, 1974, 1992, pp. 74–76).

The administration of capital regions was also a way of linking economic development and central planning. In Chile, in order to tackle a metropolis that, according to the 1960 census, neared 2 million inhabitants and whose *comunas* or counties had increased from seventeen to thirty-five, Santiago's *Plan Regulador Intercomunal* (PRIS, 1960, figure 6.9)

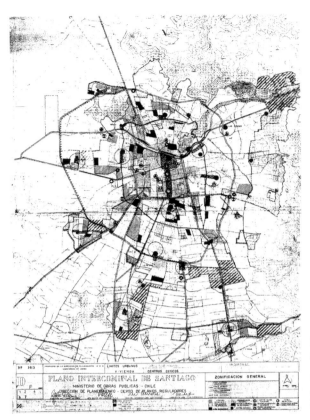

Figure 6.9. Santiago's *Plan Regulador Intercomunal* (PRIS), 1960. (*Source*: Observatorio Urbano, Ministerio de Vivienda y Urbanismo (MINVU), http://www.observatoriourbano.cl)

proposed several corridors, forest reserves, ring roads and the reorganization of industrial activity along new 'cordons'. While urban planning ideas were drawn from Patrick Abercrombie's Greater London Plan, among other influences, the PRIS economic tenets and policies were established according to CORFO goals (see p. 93). Though it was not part of an integrated system, the PRIS resulted from the strengthening of the planning function in the *Ley General de Construcciones y Urbanización* (1953, General Law of Buildings and Urbanization), and was also boosted by the CORVI or Housing Corporation and the Planning Direction of the Ministerio de Obras Públicas (MOP, Ministry of Public Works). The PRIS prefigured the regional planning to be instituted from 1965 by ODEPLAN or National Bureau of Planning) (de Ramón, 2000, pp. 215, 225–231; Gross, 1991, nd, pp. 145–148, 153).[30]

In the case of Buenos Aires, after Carlos della Paolera's first attempts, it was not until 1943 that the industrial and economic goals of quinquennial plans provided a framework of regional planning for the eventual creation of the Gran Buenos Aires (1948), with a population of 4,723,918. However, given Argentina's political upheavals during the Perón years and later, the integration of economic and regional planning was not resumed until 1963, when the Consejo Nacional de Desarrollo (CONADE, National Council of Development) was created (Lombardo, 1999, pp. 22–23, 49–53).

Ciudad Guayana

Regional poles as part of a central planning system became a priority in Betancourt's Venezuela, where the CNU or National Planning Commission was replaced by CORDIPLAN or Central Office of Coordination and Planning; the latter recognized 'the importance of the spatial question for national planning' and that the city system provided 'the master notion of *ordenamiento territorial*' (Fossi, 1989, p. 480). After the restoration of democracy, Betancourt's agenda included the ISI initiated by Pérez Jiménez's NIN, which had favoured the country's north–central axis along the coast (see pp. 116–117). By developing the steel and iron industry south of the Orinoco river,[31] the social-democratic government aimed at strengthening the industrial muscle with metal, petrochemical and machinery production (figure 6.10).

The region's development relied on the creation of the Corporación Venezolana de Guayana (CVG, Guayana's Venezuelan Corporation) in 1960; the CVG's flagship project was the design of Ciudad Guayana following University of Harvard and Massachusetts Institute of Technology modernist orientations. The local team was headed by General Rafael Alfonzo Ravard – an MIT graduate who had made the original contact with the foreign advisers. Among the latter Lloyd Rodwin stood out: like Ravard also a military man, with a Masters in land economics, he founded and directed the two academic institutions' Joint Center for Urban Studies (JCUH). Rodwin was key to dealing with the CVG's aim 'to convert general plans into specific projects, each of them with its own budget, and a schedule with the precise time for completing works' (Rodwin, 1982, pp. 126–127). The JCUH also recruited John Friedmann, who elaborated the *ad hoc* notion of *core region*, drawn from Perroux's developmental poles, applied to a

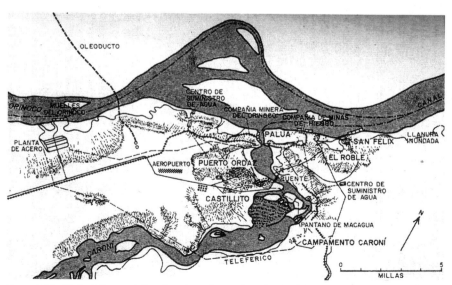

Figure 6.10. Ciudad Guayana's location along the southern bank of the Orinoco River, 1960. (*Source*: Rodwin, 1982)

territory with plenty of mining resources and water facilities, but lacking crops and food (Friedmann, 1965; Perroux, 1955).

Following the constitution of the CVG in 1960 and the arrival of the experts, Ciudad Guayana began to grow beyond the original plan and had to absorb, like Brasilia, the workers involved in the city's construction and the informal population attracted by the project. The original estimates suggested that Ciudad Guayana would have 166,000 inhabitants in 1966 and 400,000 by 1975; the metropolitan area actually lagged behind these figures, with 152,575 in 1971 and 332,516 by 1981 (Negrón, 2001, pp. 184–186). Despite its decrease in industrial productivity, the fact that Ciudad Guayana had become Venezuela's sole metropolitan area south of the Orinoco made its founders think that it had achieved its role as regional pole in demographic terms – though it could not claim the same concerning the development of heavy industry (Rodwin, 1982, p. 119).

Beyond this debate on the city's achievements, to render in urban design the guidelines of national development was deemed by Rodwin as the greatest 'lesson' learnt by him and his JUCH colleagues in the Ciudad Guayana mission (Rodwin, 1982, p. 133). It was a connection between economic goals and territorial occupation that could not always be established in other examples of regional development in the era of Latin America's central planning and developmentalism. This was partly because of the failings of the ISI, the distortions of urbanization, and the oversized bureaucracy that planning relied upon. Accelerated by the oil crisis, dictatorships and the neoliberal ethos of the late 1970s, both industrialization and central planning were about to be removed as cornerstones of the State-led model of development that had prevailed in Latin America since the 1930s, as we shall see in the next chapter.

Notes

1. A preliminary version of the first sections of this chapter appeared as Almandoz (2010d; 2011; 2013c).
2. 'La crisis democrática en Chile es una advertencia dramática para nuestro continente' (1947).
3. 'Yo acuso' (6 January 1948).
4. Much of the military strength of these regimes stemmed from their adherence to the 1951 Mutual Security Act that Washington had approved during the Korean War (de Ramón, 2006, p. 213).
5. The *Granma* – as in the abbreviation of 'grandmother' – was a yacht stealthily bought in Mexico by the Cuban rebels from an American enterprise. The movement was named after the attack to the Moncada barracks in Santiago de Cuba, on 26 July 1953, by 160 insurgents led by 26-year-old Fidel Castro. Although it failed, the 'quixotic Moncada attack and the official terror that it provoked served to turn Fidel Castro into a nationalist hero' (Williamson, 1992, p. 444).
6. As he was nicknamed by comrades, according to Argentina's popular form of addressing.
7. Rostow was a presidential advisor of the Kennedy administration.
8. Arthur Schlesinger and George McGovern were among the Kennedy advisors.
9. There also was the Ejército Popular de Liberación (EPL, Popular Army of Liberation), influenced by Maoism.
10. The *peronismo* was channelled through the Justicialista party and the Unión Popular.
11. This was traditionally decided by the international cartel or major companies of the black gold.
12. 'El petróleo en la economía venezolana' (15 September 1958).

13. The ISI had mainly favoured Venezuela's northern area during Pérez Jiménez's NIN.
14. Speech of 4 November 1971.
15. This was equivalent to 60 per cent of Chile's agricultural land.
16. Torres joined Colombia's ELN.
17. Discourse of 4 December 1972.
18. Speech of 2 December 1972.
19. Between the 1960s and 1970s, Latin America's so-called 'literary boom' gathered a group of novelists whose work achieved editorial success worldwide. It included Colombia's Gabriel García Márquez, Peru's Mario Vargas Llosa, Argentina's Julio Cortázar, Guatemala's Miguel Ángel Asturias, Cuba's Alejo Carpentier and Mexico's Carlos Fuentes. Their work was highly experimental and controversial in political terms (Brushwood, 1975, 1993, for instance).
20. Not only had the structure of the economy been badly damaged by the obsessive concentration on sugar, but the shortfall was a sign that the country was incapable of overcoming the productive stagnation which had afflicted its economy since the 1920s' (Williamson, 1992, pp. 453–454).
21. 'Carta a Fidel Castro' (May 20, 1971), pp. 117–119.
22. Also Arturo Uslar Pietri (1979a; 1979b) explored the problematic nature of the myths of the noble savage, utopia and revolution in the very land where they originated.
23. Then flooded with produce made in Hong Kong, Taiwan and the rest of East Asia.
24. As were the Central American Common Market (MCC), the Latin American Association of Free Trade (ALALC, later ALADI) and, later on, the Latin American Economic System (SELA).
25. According to the so-called Gini coefficient for measuring disparity of income – a statistical index ranging from 0 through 1, where values closer to the latter mean a wider disparity – by the early 1970s distribution of income had not improved but worsened in Latin America: 0.63 in Brazil – even higher than in the previous decade; 0.47 in Colombia, 0.44 in Costa Rica and 0.49 in Venezuela. Only Argentina and Urugay remained steady with 0.42 and 0.33 respectively (Edwards, 2009, p. 55).
26. This was one of the few attempts to render more geographical the school's lack of spatiality in its approach (Almandoz, 2006b, pp. 105–106; 2008b, pp. 164–165).
27. 'Entre la libertad y el miedo' (October 1988), pp. 295–309.
28. Analogous to Lima's *corralones*, *casas de vecindad* in Caracas and *conventillos* in other contexts.
29. A settlement was even later founded in the La Victoria site in commemoration.
30. ODEPLAN mirrored ECLAC policies.
31. This was the least populated area of Venezuela since colonial times.

Chapter 7

Dismantling a Model

But what mattered to me was that the Independence of the IMF and the World Bank were maintained... The intractable problems of Third World poverty, hunger and debt would not be solved by misdirected international intervention, but rather by liberating Enterprise, promoting trade – and defeating socialism in all its forms.

Margaret Thatcher, *The Downing Street Years* (1993)

From the Oil Crisis to the Lost Decade

The collapse of Latin America's ISI and the state-led model of development inherited from the inter-war period were catalysed by international factors. Significant among the latter was the fuel crisis brought about by the 1973 war in the Middle East, which quadrupled the prices established by the Organization of the Petroleum Exporting Countries (OPEC). While the 20-day conflict almost caused another confrontation between the USA and the USSR, OPEC's measure had lasting and catastrophic effects worldwide, including on Latin America's inflation-stricken economies.

Expectations about the region's significance within international economy had diminished after the post-war developmentalism and modernization. The decrease in Latin America's exports within the world total – down from 13.5 per cent in 1946 to 5.1 per cent in 1970 (del Pozo, 2002, p. 176) – aggravated the burden of foreign debt, which had threatened the republics ever since political independence. The 'immature takeoffs' of Latin American countries after their alleged 'drive to maturity' – paraphrasing Rostow's stages of growth (see pp. 89–90) – was in contrast to the success of East Asian nations (Almandoz, 2011; 2013c). Even though some of these had suffered wars or gained independence only after World War II, just when major Latin American economies undertook the ISI, the Asian bloc recovered rapidly. Not only in inflation control and income distribution, the contrast was regarded in hindsight by the World Bank in terms of economic and export growth:

> Although the two groups of countries had similar rates of growth in 1965–80 – Latin America with a 6 percent annual average and East Asia with 7 percent – their export performance was astonishingly different. As exports grew at an annual average rate of 10 percent in East Asia, they declined at a pace of 1 percent a year in Latin America. (World Bank, 1993, p. 27)

In spite of the reluctance of nationalist governments to accept foreign capital, loans from international private banks soared. These reached more than 50 per cent of Latin America's Gross National Product (GNP) overall by 1980, as was the case in the largest economies such as Mexico and Argentina, with the exception of Brazil. Slower rates of GNP growth caused the regional average to fall from 4.5 per cent in the 1970s to 1.3 per cent the following decade, when annual hyperinflation spiralled to more than 2,000 per cent in Argentina, Brazil and Peru (del Pozo, 2002, pp. 179–180). While local currencies remained overvalued, there was a severe flight of capital out of Latin America from the late 1970s through the mid-1980s, which prompted several governments to adopt exchange controls (Edwards, 1996, pp. 22–23). This is why the 1980s was dubbed as Latin America's 'lost decade', especially when compared with the astounding development achieved by the Asian 'tigers' of South Korea, Singapore Malaysia, Indonesia and Thailand.

In the political arena, economic woes and Cold War tensions had undermined governments hit by imperialism and guerrillas (see Chapter 6). This malaise turned some of Latin America's most stable democracies into dictatorships, as was prefigured in Brazil in 1964 and later confirmed in Chile, Argentina and Uruguay. These cases sparked a critique of the functionalist rationale of developmentalism and modernization: the 'optimistic' assumption that 'a greater socioeconomic development would be followed by increased probability of the emergence and consolidation of political democracy' had not taken into account that such development instead engendered 'a process of greater political populism' (Romero, 1999, pp. 182–183). In Latin America's Third World reality of growing economic difficulties and territorial imbalances, such populism unleashed social demands that could not be satisfied in a democracy. Unlike Mexico and Venezuela – where oil alleviated social tensions until the 1980s – Southern Cone dictatorships emerged as 'bureaucratic-authoritarian regimes' that wiped out former political establishments while redefining the 'corporate state' in Latin America (Roberts, 1978, pp. 170–172; O'Donnell, 1982). Led by the Chilean dictatorship, some of these regimes claimed to have initiated the dismantling of Latin America's model of development dating back to the 1930s, whereas other countries coped with terminal manifestations of that model, as we intend to show next.

Pinochet's Chile and the Chicago Boys

The *coup d'état* that ousted Salvador Allende from power on 11 September 1973 was justified by General Augusto Pinochet as vital in rescuing the country from becoming a 'Communist Paradise', before it was 'irreparably late' (Pinochet, 1980, pp. 13–15). Reviving the political conservatism and economic liberalism masterminded by Diego Portales at the dawn of the Chilean republic (see pp. 26–27), the *de facto* regime became market-oriented in terms of economics. After Milton Friedman's visit to Santiago in March 1975, when he had an interview with General Pinochet, the University of Chicago Professor recommended a 'shock treatment ... to end the inflation and establish the basis for economic recovery and growth'; fundamental to both goals 'was a drastic cut in government spending, since the inflation was clearly being driven by the need to print money to finance a major government deficit' (Friedman and Friedman, 1998, pp. 399–400).

In his memoirs, however, Friedman emphasized that Chile's 'Chicago Boys' who had studied in his school and worked for the military government, had 'already reached their conclusions' before his visit. Indeed, with the arrival of Sergio de Castro as Minister of Economy (1974–1976) and leader of the group, the market-oriented programme had started with the liberalization of prices and restitution of private property, the opening to foreign investment, and the rescue of entrepreneurial confidence through the reduction of expenditure on education, health and retirement pensions. The last two were handed over to private companies and funds, while large public enterprises such as railways were deprived of finance until their eventual liquidation (Villalobos, 1979, 2010, pp. 208, 212). The reduction in the state's participation in the economy – which had reached 40 per cent of GNP by the early 1970s – reduced the fiscal deficit and prevented hyperinflation (Rosende, 2007, p. 19).

As a key figure in a USAID-sponsored deal between the University of Chicago and Chile's Catholic University Departments of Economics, Arnold Harberger's teachings on government finance and the social effects of public policy were influential for more than fifty Chilean professionals who had studied in Chicago (de Castro, 2007; Edwards, 2009, pp. 124–125). His lessons included disincentive of the sluggish ISI and the strengthening and renewal of neglected sectors, such as agriculture, forestry and fisheries (World Bank, 1993, p. 62). These shifts were trumpeted in the political arena and, despite the fact that recovery was still insecure, from the mid-1970s Pinochet's Chile was regarded as another example that draconian economic reforms can be undertaken by authoritarian regimes.

Once the early imbalances caused by the liberal programme were controlled – especially in terms of unemployment and poverty – by 1977 economic growth reached 8.3 per cent; meanwhile the inflation fell to 30 per cent, after spiralling to 343 per cent in 1975. These early achievements led the military to proclaim the Chilean 'miracle' – at least until 1982, when the debt crisis surfaced as in other Latin American countries (de Ramón, 2006, pp. 264–266) (see also pp. 143–144, 146–148). By then the regime's abuses were appalling: in addition to more than 30,000 exiles and the 2,296 cases of human rights violations perpetrated mainly by the Dirección de Inteligencia Nacional (DINA, Direction of National Intelligence),[1] the state's social welfare expenditure per capita had been slashed by 20 per cent between 1974 and 1982. As unemployment reached almost 34 per cent – and up to 50 per cent in *callampas* and working-class *barrios* – the alleged Chilean miracle only flourished among the upper classes' consumerism (de Ramón, 2006, pp. 240, 266–267).

Brazil: Cruzeiro, Cruzado and New Cruzeiro

After the economic expansion during Garrastazu Médici's tenure, Ernesto Geisel's government (1974–1979) suffered the effects of soaring oil prices. Amidst restrictions over energy consumption and a negative balance of trade, the external debt reached US$45,000 million and the inflation was unleashed again. This turmoil fuelled protests to make the military regime less rigid, which were focused around São Paulo's metallurgical union led by Luiz Inácio Lula da Silva. As a response to these pressures, João Baptista Figueiredo's government (1979–1985), appointed by the Electoral College but not democratically elected, allowed some relaxation of controls on society. This included new political parties, in addition to those in existence since 1964, alongside an amnesty that encouraged the return of thousands of exiles. As recession reached –4.2 and –2.9 per cent in 1981 and 1982, respectively, the country's commercial deficit and the high cost of oil continued inflating the external debt; Brazil had therefore to knock at the IMF door (Schneeberger, 2003, pp. 336–338; del Priore and Venancio, 2010, p. 287).

Democracy finally returned with the government of José Sarney (1985–1990), whose 'plan Cruzado' – named after the new currency that replaced the devalued *cruzeiro* – brought about positive results by 1986, which led the new president to claim erroneously that inflation was 'a thing of the past'. But it was just another case of counting chickens before they are hatched: not only did inflation reappear, but also the new currency was devalued yet again, prompting the application of another 'plano Verão' in the summer of 1989. This included a monetary reconversion into the *cruzado novo* or new cruzado that deleted three zeroes from the old one. While this plan failed too and the inflation escalated to 1,000 per cent by the end of 1989, the major legacy of Sarney's tenure was the 1988 Charter or 'Courage Constitution', as it was called by its champion Ulysses Guimarães (Schneeberger, 2003, pp. 341–342; del Priore and Venancio, 2010, p. 289).

Argentina: the Last Perón, Military Process and Democratic Renewal

Allowed by the Great National Agreement promoted by the conciliatory government of General Alejandro Lanusse (1971–1973), Perón's long-awaited return was accelerated by Héctor Cámpora's victory in the elections of March 1973. The *peronistas'* political manoeuvres included the resignation of the puppet president less than two months later. New elections in September were easily won by Perón, with his third wife Isabel as vice president. As part of the Programme of Reconstruction and National Liberation, Perón's government promoted socially-oriented works alongside an increase in public sector jobs and enterprises, which certainly reactivated the economy yet augmented the deficit. The inflation which followed was exacerbated by the oil crisis and the European Common Market restrictions on imports of Argentine beef (Romero, 1994, 2013, pp. 180–198). Social unrest was fuelled by the political polarization between the *montonera* left and the far right led by the Triple A (Argentine Anti-communist Action).

The demise of the last Perón regime was brought about by his death in June 1974 and the rise to the presidency of his third wife and now widow, Isabel. Her two years in power initiated the cycle of persecution and torture, with more than 800 *desaparecidos* or missing persons and 500 murders (Martínez, 2007). Repression worsened after the *coup d'état* on 24 March 1976, which introduced a military junta headed, until 1981, by General Jorge Videla, whose Process of National Reorganization raised the so-called *desaparecidos* to 30,000 (Romero, 1994, 2010, pp. 207, 210). The regime's euphoria over Argentina's triumph at the World Cup in 1978 was preceded by an IMF loan and the first results of the 'Chicago-school' plan masterminded by the Minister of Economy, José Alfredo Martínez de Hoz. The plan sought to counteract Peronist policies and to dismantle the statist and populist model promoted from the 1940s (Rosende, 2007, p. 19).

However, unlike the Chilean experience, market principles were not cemented in the long run, given Argentina's high concentration of wealth in few hands, the persistence of state-owned companies – usually controlled by senior members of the military – and the increase in public expenditure. A bank collapse in 1980 was followed by 100 per cent devaluation of the peso the next year, accompanied by 400 per cent inflation; and the debt crisis evident in the early 1980s: US$8,500 million in 1979, it jumped to US$25,000 million in 1981 and US$45,000 million in 1984 (Romero, 1994, 2013, pp. 210–216).

Undermined by the debt crisis, the military junta was confronted by the opposition coalesced around the Multipartidista or multi-party coalition and the Madres of the Plaza de Mayo who routinely protested about the disappearance of their children (Kaiser, 2008). Once General Leopoldo Galtieri assumed power, the regime's decisive gamble came with the Falklands War, declared when Britain responded to the Argentine invasion of the islands on 2 April 1982. Notwithstanding the junta's repeated attempts, it was impossible to get Washington's support at special meetings of the Organization of American States; meanwhile, the British military invasion of Port Stanley led to Argentina's unconditional surrender on 14 June 1982, with 700 dead and 1,300 wounded (Romero, 1994, 2013, pp. 231–235; Thatcher, 1993, pp. 173–235).

After the political and economic debacle prompted by the Falklands War, democracy was restored with the UCR government of Raúl Alfonsín (1983–1989), when the civilian enthusiasm was increased by the return of scientists, academics and intellectuals exiled since the 1960s. However, this 'cultural modernization' did not prevent the economic weakening caused by 600 per cent hyperinflation and the increase in the external debt. In order to combat both woes, the Plan Austral, launched in May 1985, created a new currency with the same name, whose value nevertheless plummeted by the end of the same year. In the midst of political and military unrest, another devaluation of the reinstated peso, in February 1989, fuelled a 200 per cent inflation followed by widespread looting. This paved the way for the rise of a 'renewed *peronismo*' led by Carlos Menem, so confirming the cyclical nature of Argentina's political history (Romero, 1994, 20103, pp. 244–246, 256–258, 266–267).

From the Gran Venezuela to the Black Friday

Not even the so-called Gran Venezuela – beneficiary of the soaring oil prices that strangled the neighbouring countries' economies – was able to escape from the failure of the state-led developmentalism and the lost decade. Capitalizing on Rafael Caldera's unfulfilled promises and Acción Democrática's (AD's) strengthening as a political party, Betancourt's protégé, Carlos Andrés Pérez (CAP) gained a landslide victory in the 1973 elections. It was a peak of the AD-COPEI bipartisanship resulting from the Puntofijo Pact, which dominated the political establishment until the late 1980s (Ledezma, 1993, pp. 194–195) (see also pp. 116–117). With US$45,000 million of supplementary income, CAP's first government (1974–1979) created the Fondo de Inversiones de Venezuela (FIV, Venezuela's Investments Fund), aimed at managing the surplus earnings resulting from high oil prices. This windfall was increased by the nationalization of iron and petroleum in January 1975 and 1976, respectively. These were historic landmarks in a period of mammoth projects and economic and social euphoria known as the Gran Venezuela, whose manifesto was the Fifth Plan of the Nation, masterminded by the CORDIPLAN minister Gumersindo Rodríguez (Arráiz, 2007, pp. 179–180). Yet CAP's buoyant government triggered a disproportionate growth of both central and decentralized public administration: while ninety bodies had been created in the 1960s, that number jumped to 154 state-owned enterprises, twenty-eight mixed ones and thirty autonomous institutes in the 1970s (Stambouli, 2002, p. 154).

Inheriting from CAP a 'mortgaged Venezuela' with a public debt reckoned as more than US$25,000 million, Luis Herrera's COPEI government (1979–1984) promised to adapt the economy to reality by eliminating subsidies and liberating prices, though inflation already amounted to 20 per cent (Stambouli, 2002, pp. 145–146). However, the Herrera administration was not only unable to cope with the mounting external debt, but also had to devalue the bolivar on 18 February 1983, known thereafter as the Viernes Negro (Black Friday). Since the 1960s, the national currency had remained at 4.3 bolivars per US dollar, thus becoming a cornerstone of the seeming democratic stability of the so-called Saudi Venezuela, whose oil-fuelled bonanza had enabled the country to avoid the hyperinflation and dictatorships of its South American neighbours.

In addition to the currency's dramatic depreciation that marked the rest of the decade, corruption scandals continued during the Herrera administration and worsened during that of AD's Jaime Lusinchi (1984–1989), despite the fact that both presidents' electoral pledges included their eradication (Ledezma, 1993, pp. 184–190). Venezuela's Puntofijo-based democracy thus went from collective disenchantment to frustration, aggravated by the unaffordable expansion of the bureaucracy. Public expenditure drained international reserves from US$10,000 million at the beginning of the decade to only US$300 million in 1988 (Stambouli, 2002, pp. 155–158). By then, the bolivar had been further devalued and the inflation rose to 42 per cent – an unheard-of level for the former Gran Venezuela, whose per capita income was seriously diminished after being at the top in Latin America (Edwards, 2009, p. 239).

Mexico: The Outbreak of the Debt Crisis

A similar case of devaluation occurred in Mexico at the end of Echeverría's presidency, on 31 August 1976, when the peso fell from 12.5 per US$ to 20 and later to 22; it unleashed a collapse that exacerbated the balance of payments deficit, mainly caused by an excess in imports over tourism-related income. While inflation rose after the oil crisis and the ISI showed its exhaustion, there was an outflow of foreign exchange and the external debt escalated from US$4,200 million in 1971 to US$11,600 million in 1975 (Meyer, 1973, 2005, p. 152; Suchlicki, 1996, 2008, pp. 135–136). But the 1970s discovery of petroleum and gas reserves heralded an opportunity for financial recuperation: Petróleos Mexicanos (PEMEX) was boosted with proven reserves totalling 5.4 billion barrels in 1973, 11 billion in 1977 and 60 billion in 1980 (Meyer, 1973, 2005, p. 153).

Mexico became the world's first exporter of petroleum outside OPEC; its GDP rose by 8 per cent and unemployment was reduced by a half during the early years of José Lopez Portillo's administration (1976–1982). But, as had happened in Venezuela, Mexico's black gold bred corruption and increases in bureaucracy, while traditional inequities in income distribution were far from reduced. On the contrary, 'long-standing income-concentration was intensified in 1971–1980 due to soaring inflation, inadequate tax reforms, and failure to tackle the basic structural problems of the economy, especially the low productivity of large sectors of agriculture'; by 1977, 50 per cent of low-income population received only 13.5 per cent of the national income, while for the upper 10 per cent it was 46 per cent (Meyer, 1973, 2005, pp. 153–154). By the end of López Portillo's extravagant period, the peso had depreciated by 176 per cent, salaries plummeted and the public deficit amounted to 18 per cent of the GDP. These conditions led the government to adopt desperate measures, such as nationalizing private banks and controlling the exchange of foreign currency in order to curtail the flight of capital (Suchlicki, 1996, 2008, pp. 140–141).

Unable to support its 1,155 state-owned enterprises, the debt crisis of August 1982 announced not only Mexico's entrance into the lost decade, but also Latin America's showdown with its creditors in the international arena (Edwards, 1996, p. 17; Edwards 2009, p. 84). Negotiations were not only to confirm the collapse of the state-led model of development of previous decades, but also to confront the region with the West's 1980s neoliberal ethos (del Pozo, 2002, p. 182).

Between New Right and Neoliberalism

A Hot Spot of the Cold War

Waging further battles of the Cold War against Soviet communism, Western politics was highly influenced in the 1980s by the New Right alliance between Margaret Thatcher as Britain's Conservative Prime Minister (1979–1990) and US Republican President Ronald Reagan (1981–1989). According to the former's assessment when taking office, despite economic aid and military intervention led by the US, the democratic and capitalist West was 'slowly but surely losing' the Cold War against the axis articulated between the Third World and USSR-based communism, which in Latin America counted on the Cuban stronghold and other outposts (Thatcher, 1993, pp. 156–157,

171). After interventions of the Nixon years (see pp. 119–121), Washington's strategy in Latin America began to change with the policy of Human Rights Respect adopted during Jimmy Carter's administration (1977–1981). The signing of the treaty for the devolution of the Panama Canal with Omar Torrijos's regime (1969–1981) was especially regarded as a goodwill gesture towards a region that no longer wanted to be the US's backyard. But the communist block did not seem to send equally conciliatory signals. There was Soviet aid to Velasco Alvarado's dictatorship in Peru (1968–1975), along with the subversion in Central America; competing with the USSR, China meanwhile strengthened ties with Latin American embassies which also resumed relationships with Havana and called off the blockade decreed by the US (del Pozo, 2002, pp. 171–173).

After Allende's suicide, strongholds of communism moved northwards, and Latin America's left-wing agenda diversified. From Argentina's Perón and Mexico's Echeverría to Venezuela's CAP, during the 1970s presidents in the region advocated causes of the Third World and Non-Aligned Movement as a way of placating demands of local leftist factions (Suchlicki, 1996, 2008, p. 136). Meanwhile communist subversion rekindled with the war led in El Salvador by the FMLN or Farabundo Marti Front for National Liberation, and with the coming to power of Nicaragua's FSLN (Sandinist Front of National Liberation) in 1979, once the Somoza dynasty was deposed. By then it was clear that Soviet arms were being sent via Cuba to Salvadoran guerrillas, as Thatcher read in US intelligence reports. This is why, at the first meeting between Thatcher and Reagan, both regarded Central America as one of the hottest spots of the Cold War in the Third World (Thatcher, 1993, p. 158).

The influence of the Cold War continued to reverberate in Central America and the Caribbean during the 1980s. On the one hand, both the FSLN and the FMLN were strengthened and officially recognized by administrations such as Mexico's López Portillo and France's François Mitterrand (Suchlicki, 1996, 2008, pp. 139). There was, on the other hand, Reagan's counteroffensive through the Contras paramilitary, the invasion of Grenada in 1983, Washington's lack of support for Argentina in the Falklands War, and the capture of Panama's General Manuel Noriega in 1989. However, diplomacy was more powerful than bravados, mostly thanks to the Contadora Group, constituted in 1983 by the governments of Colombia, Mexico, Panama and Venezuela. The resolution of Central America's conflicts was reached thanks to the negotiations led by the Contadora Group, later cemented by the FSLN's electoral defeat in Nicaragua in 1990 and El Salvador's peace treaty in 1992. By then the Cold War was ending in the world and in Latin America – though violence and subversion were to take on new forms in the latter (see pp. 176–177).

IMF, World Bank and the Cancun Summit

While Washington intervened in Latin America's politics during the 1980s, the New Right conditioned, in the economic arena, the response to the debt crisis and the ensuing liberalization in the region. According to Margaret Thatcher's memoirs, she was aware of the strategic link between Third World finance and international geopolitics during the Cold War. Especially after the Soviet-led conflict in Afghanistan which began in 1979, she foresaw how the former alliance between the USSR and the Third World was being debilitated. A decade before the fall of the Berlin Wall and the disintegration of the Soviet Union, she anticipated the 'earthquake' that would allow the consolidation of neoliberalism and free-market reforms among countries which had formerly lent towards communism, including some of Latin America (Thatcher, 1993, p. 171).

In view of her misgivings about Latin America and the strategic importance of the debt crisis, it is understandable that in the 1981 summit held in Cancun, Mexico – one of the first focused on the North-South dialogue – Thatcher defended the independence of the International Monetary Fund (IMF) and the World Bank, which developing countries wanted to subordinate to the UN. The autonomy of the IMF and the WB as had been conceived at Bretton Woods, finally confirmed in the summit's communiqué, was an achievement that Lady Thatcher was proud of – as we can see in the epigraph to this chapter (Thatcher, 1993, pp. 169–170) – and proved to be influential for the forthcoming liberalism throughout Latin America and other regions of the Third World.

While remaining autonomous, something more significant occurred in relation to the IMF and the World Bank during the time of Thatcher and Reagan. Despite having been promoted by John Maynard Keynes at Bretton Woods as a body aimed at stimulating the governments' aggregate demand in order to prevent crises such as that of 1929, in the 1980s the IMF, along with the World Bank, were to become 'missionary institutions' of neoliberal practices. And the traditional distinctions between their functions – the IMF was supposed to control countries' macroeconomics while the World Bank dealt with their 'structural issues' – were blurred and became progressively intertwined (Stiglitz, 2003, pp. 11–14).

The Brady Plans and the Washington Consensus

As Thatcher anticipated, throughout the lost decade regional and international factors made the arrival of liberalism in Latin America inevitable. Although representing the first steps towards dismantling the statist model of development, some of the economic measures involved (see pp. 138–144) proved to be unorthodox adjustment policies which failed to curb the inflation, but became a feature of Latin American economies. Furthermore, cuts in public expenditure by more than 20 per cent in several countries led only to a substantial decline in real wages and the deterioration of infrastructure, without reducing the magnitude of the public sector (Edwards, 1996, pp. 18–19, 26–27, 33, 39–40; 2009, pp. 78, 85). As these piecemeal economic policies failed from Mexico to Argentina, the international scene had changed significantly as revealed in a World Bank report on Latin America's debt crisis and lost decade:

> Once the programs' failure was clear, politicians turned to the stellar performance of East Asian countries as examples worth considering, even emulating. Latin American leaders

were especially impressed by East Asia's rapid recovery after the brief slowdown early in the debt crisis. The advice and assistance of multilateral institutions were also important. The World Bank, by focusing on long-term programs, emphasized the need for deep structural transformations. It also continued its insistence on the need to develop poverty-alleviating programs, thus changing the way several countries design social policy. The largely successful Chilean experience became a model for many countries, and the collapse of the Soviet Union pulled the rug out from under the Marxist camp that had long advocated replacing markets with central planning. The Spanish experience with economic reform under socialist leader Felipe González also became an important factor that influenced economic thinking in many countries. (World Bank, 1993, pp. 23–24)

Influenced by the changes on the international scene, the so-called Brady Plan – named after the US Secretary of the Treasury, Nicholas Brady, who masterminded it – emerged as the main exit to the debt crisis. It was based on the rationale of reducing the credits and enabling the defaulting countries to issue dollar-denominated bonds to be traded on emerging-market stock exchanges. Signed with the governments of Mexico (1989), Venezuela (1990), Uruguay (1991), Argentina and Brazil (1992), among others, national agreements were elaborated by the World Bank and the IMF with the advice of a new generation of Latin American professionals trained in the USA and Europe. They imposed fiscal discipline, open international trade, financial liberalization and privatization, while recognizing that macroeconomic stability was a requirement for growth (World Bank, 1993, pp. 23–24; Edwards, 2009, pp. 86–87).

The Brady Plans signed with different republics also sealed the so-called Washington Consensus. Such denomination reflected the degree of strategic importance with which, from 1989, US-based institutions – such as the World Bank, the IMF, the IDB and the Treasury itself – regarded Latin American and other Third World economies ravaged by debt (Stiglitz, 2003, pp. 16–17; Edwards, 2009, p. 90). The consensus comprised macroeconomic stability, poverty alleviation, reduced economic role of the state, and openness of trade. In order to achieve these goals – especially the last – new trade agreements were promoted, such as the Common Market of the South (MERCOSUR, its initials in Spanish), formed in 1991 by South America's largest and smallest economies (Argentina and Brazil, Uruguay and Paraguay). Also the Andean Pact and the Central American Common Market (CACM) were revitalized in 1990 and 1991, respectively (World Bank, 1993, pp. 24, 67–71). Through these measures and policies, the Brady Plans and the Washington Consensus tried to put an end to the lost decade, which were also 'the culmination of Latin America's affair with protectionism and the economic strategies based on the government's preponderant role' (Edwards, 2009, p. 89).

National Packages and Prescriptions

In view of Latin America's deep-rooted history of corporativism and populism, the results of these so-called *paquetes* (packages), *recetas* (prescriptions) and reforms dictated by the Washington Consensus were diverse, intriguing and even adverse, depending on the time when they were implemented, their duration and the political stability of each nation, as can be seen below.

The Chilean Miracle

After the setbacks of earlier years (see pp. 139–140), Chile's miracle was back on track by the mid-1980s, making it unnecessary to sign any plan with the IMF and World Bank. Completion of payments to these institutions, return to economic growth, privatization of further public enterprises and the strengthening of non-traditional agro-industrial exports were among the policies of Hernán Büchi as Minister of Finance. Notwithstanding the economic achievements that the Pinochet regime relied on for the 1989 plebiscite, inflation was above 20 per cent and unemployment over 10 per cent, while the huge 'social debt' was denounced by the Concertación de Partidos por la Democracia (Parties' Association for Democracy) after more than a decade of dictatorship (de Ramón, 2006, p. 293).

The Concertación's victory on 5 October 1989 demonstrated that political reforms were perceived as necessary to spread the benefits of the economic miracle. However, there also was awareness that social welfare could only be reached if the military's neoliberal policies were retained – a lesson that the restored democracy proved to have learnt. Indeed, when the Concertación's first government – presided over by Patricio Aylwin – came to power in 1990, it decided to maintain the economic modernization without falling into populist orientations that were still latent in Latin America. Although Aylwin's administration (1990–1994) was 'willing to modify the economic model in order to tackle serious issues such as the structure of the public health and the education systems, it opted for a "gradualist approach", expanding social expenditure in a "fiscally responsible way" in order to avoid inflation' (de Ramón, 2006, pp. 293). Despite the yawning inequity of income, and poverty which reached 23.2 per cent by 1996, as economic growth kept at 7 per cent during the first half of the decade, later Concertación governments maintained the modernization of the agro-export model through training and technical advances, productivity and international competitiveness (Edwards, 2009, p. 138).

When General Pinochet died in 2006, Vargas Llosa wrote for Spanish-language newspapers a vitriolic obituary in which he criticized the atrocities perpetrated by 'the tyrant' and the corruption of his entourage. However, Vargas acknowledged that the Concertación's decision to combine new 'political democracy' with inherited 'market economy' was the only way for Chile to leave behind 'that underdevelopment that still most of Latin American countries squelch in' (Vargas, 2009, p. 97).[2]

Colombia: Not Quite Pandemonium

Less intense than in neighbouring countries, Colombia's debt crisis was nonetheless evident during Belisario Betancur's government (1982–1986): it amounted to US$8,396 million in 1983 and forced the government to accept IMF recommendations from the year after, though the republic never stopped complying with its financial duties, as happened in Chile (Edwards, 2009, p. 152). Meanwhile, the spread of violence engulfed Bogotá: perpetrated by the M-19 on 6 November 1985, the seizure of the Palace of Justice, the very centre of the capital, put an end to the government's peace negotiations with the guerrilla movements. Besides the subversion fuelled by the latter since the 1970s, drug cartels and paramilitary groups were new scourges of the 1980s, which increased the violence's death toll throughout three decades to 100,000 (del Pozo, 2002, p. 204). Nonetheless, economic growth by the late 1980s reached 3.4 per cent per year – above Latin America's average of 1.5 per cent – while annual inflation remained at 20 per cent, well below the continent's 200 per cent average during the lost decade (Ocampo, 2007, pp. 323–325, 338–339).

All in all, late-1980s Colombia was not quite the pandemonium portrayed by Hollywood movies and tabloid journalism, showing instead signs of institutional and territorial renewal that paid off by the end of the century. Indeed, despite the unspeakable violence and social instability, regional and local autonomy was boosted during Virgilio Barco's government (1986–1990) with the promulgation of the Statute of Decentralization in 1987 (Ocampo, 2007, pp. 326–329). While the M-19 was dismantled in 1990 and institutionalized as the Democratic Alliance under the guidance of Antonio Navarro Wolff, the New Liberalism broke Colombia's traditional bipartisanship of conservatives and liberals and won elections. César Gaviria's administration (1990–1994) led the so-called *gran revolcón* (great romp) of institutions, epitomized by a Constituent Assembly. Initially hailed as a refreshing initiative on the continental scene, Colombia's 1991 constitution became one of the Americas' longest; it comprised many economic and social rights that served as models for populist charters to be passed the following decade (Edwards, 2009, pp. 157–158) (see also pp. 165–166).

Brazil: From the Impeachment to the Plan Real

Latin America's early 1990s neoliberal climate seemed in tune with the short-lived government of Fernando Collor de Mello (1990–1992) – the first president democratically elected in Brazil since 1964 (see p. 115). With the conservative support of the Rede Globo media corporation, Collor triumphed following a campaign featuring industrial modernization and market-oriented policies. Although labelled a 'right-wing populist' because he came to power with a discourse against traditional monopolies and political parties, his economic programme was neoliberal and relied on three axes: the 'shock policy' against inflation, the privatization of major public enterprises and the state's modernization. The former brought moderate results initially, lowering inflation from 2,900 per cent in 1990 to 430 per cent the following year; but it spiralled again in 1992 to 950 per cent and 2,000 in 1992. However, challenging Getúlio Vargas's dogma that 'state-owned enterprises were fundamental for development', Collor's privatization programme was more successful; it included several aeronautic and mining companies that opened the doors for the penetration of private and foreign capital during the following decade (Edwards, 2009, p. 276).

But Collor's attempt to modernize the Brazilian state was cut short by an impeachment brought by the Congress on 29 December 1992 on charges of corruption. Endemic from the early republican times, the scourge of corruption fuelled a constitutional plebiscite in April 1993 over Brazil's type of state and form of government. With abstention reaching almost 30 per cent, two-thirds of voters confirmed nonetheless their adherence to the republican system, yet a significant 10 per cent still longed for the monarchy as a way of overcoming Third World woes (Schneeberger, 2003, pp. 341–343). But some economic stability was reached during the administration of Itamar Franco (1992–1994), with the so-called Plan Real launched on 1 July 1994 by the Treasurer Fernando Henrique Cardoso. Stepping aside from his former stance within the School of Dependence (see pp. 126–128), Cardoso created a new currency with the same name that eliminated indexation as a compensatory mechanism of inflation. The Plan Real also reduced fiscal deficit and fixed the exchange rate in relation to the US dollar. On those grounds, the inflation was reduced to 64 per cent by 1994 – a relatively low value by contemporary standards (Edwards, 2009, p. 277). However, new economic problems were to arise by the end of the decade, when neoliberal policies were to be overhauled (see pp. 171–172).

Mexico: GATT, OECD, NAFTA – and Tequila

Despite a gloomy beginning marked by the debt crisis inherited from previous administrations, Miguel de la Madrid's government (1982–1988) initiated Mexico's economic shift 'to put ... the house in order': several programmes 'restructured the public sector, reduced costs, increased honesty and efficiency, and generated revenues through fiscal reforms' (Suchlicki, 1996, 2008, p. 142). The relative success was recognized by the international community when accepting Mexico into the General Agreement on Tariffs and Trade (GATT) in 1985.

Thanks to changes in the political establishment, the PRI's progressive and modernizing wing was taken over by Carlos Salinas de Gortari, while 'the ideological ills and defects – populism, statism, socialism, economic nationalism' were passed on to the Partido Revolucionario Democrático (PRD, Democratic Revolutionary Party) led by Cuauhtémoc Cárdenas (Vargas, 2009, p. 64).[3] With a moderate growth of 2.8 per cent, Salinas's administration (1988–1994) achieved significant breakthroughs in the neoliberal reforms: 1,115 enterprises were sold – which represented 85 per cent of the state's assets – while inflation was reduced from 150 to 12 per cent (Suchlicki, 1996, 2008, p. 145). Such advances were crowned, on the international stage, with the signing of the Brady Plan, Mexico's admission to the Organization for Economic Cooperation and Development (OECD), and joining North American Free Trade Agreement (NAFTA).

Salinas's economic reforms were hailed, whereas Mexico's lack of real political renovation was criticized. Besides President Clinton's support for NAFTA's enlargement, financial agencies such as the World Bank and the IMF trumpeted the

'Mexican miracle' – supposed to be Latin America's first successful case of free-market and democracy-based modernization, unlike Pinochet's Chile (World Bank, 1993, pp. 63–71; Edwards, 2009, p. 175). However, in those years of euphoria, Vargas Llosa spoiled the party: acknowledging the PRI's social and cultural accomplishments in post-revolutionary Mexico (see pp. 66–67, 90), he denounced the fact that the ruling party had established 'the perfect dictatorship' over six decades: 'the corruption resulting from this political monopoly has been internalized by institutions and everyday life in an unparalleled way, what has created one of the most irreducible hurdles for the country's genuine democratization' (Vargas, 2009, p. 64).

But such institutional obstacles did not seem to worry Margaret Thatcher, who contrasted the Third-World Mexico which she had criticized during the 1981 North-South Summit in Cancun (see pp. 145–146), with the neoliberal country that she visited in 1994. Without even mentioning the insurgence of the Ejército Zapatista de Liberación Nacional (EZLN, Zapatista Army of National Liberation) from January 1994, Thatcher belittled the importance of the peso crisis and the Tequila effect that broke at the end of the same year, when the Mexican currency lost two-thirds of its value pegged to the US dollar (Thatcher, 1995, pp. 582–583). And yet, those were early symptoms of economic, political and social woes that, despite its belonging to the GATT, the OECD and NAFTA, prevented Mexico from achieving the status of a developed country.

Argentina: Menem's Decade

Carlos Menem's first presidency (1989–1995) in Argentina looked like another successful dismantling of Latin America's corporatist model of development. The laws of Economic Emergency and State Reform made possible the privatization of large public enterprises, such as the telephone company ENTEL and the flagship carrier Aerolíneas Argentinas, followed by others in roads, television, railways and petroleum. However, corruption scandals dampened the initial momentum of privatization. As a part of the economic plan masterminded by the Harvard-educated minister Domingo Cavallo, the 1991 Law of Convertibility established the conversion of the austral into the peso and the latter's parity with the US dollar. The main purpose of the law was to control Argentina's recurrent problems of excessive printing of money and fiscal deficit, thus allowing the country to benefit from the Brady Plan (Romero, 1994, 2013, pp. 272–274). Cavallo's package included the privatization of further public enterprises, from the postal service to nuclear power stations, while international trade was strengthened, especially with MERCOSUR. Thanks to all those reforms, Argentina's inflation shrank from more than 2,000 per cent at the beginning of the decade to barely 3 per cent in 1994; meanwhile, the GDP growth reached 11 per cent in 1990 and remained at 6 per cent in 1993, 8 per cent in 1994 and 5 per cent in 1996 (Edwards, 2009, pp. 198–200).

Showcased by the easy wealth of Menem's entourage, those dazzling years concealed the profound distortions in the reform process. Besides the shares that the state and unions kept for themselves in the privatization of major enterprises, a Fiscal Pact was negotiated with the provinces that complied with the capital's political clientelism. At the same time, with unemployment stuck over 10 per cent since 1993, other economic indicators signalled Argentina's weakness in the mid-1990s. The peso's overvaluation made national goods and services more expensive and diminished exports, while the new dependency on foreign mutual funds increased the external vulnerability of the Argentine economy. This Achilles heel became apparent during the recession caused by the Tequila crisis, aggravated by 18 per cent unemployment. Curiously, this juncture reinforced the electorate's perception that Menem's leadership was necessary to get through the turbulence, which prompted his election for a second term (Romero, 1994, 2013, pp. 275–280, 287).

Unlike his first tenure, when he appeared charismatic and in confident control of his party and the media, Menem's second term (1995–1999) was marked by a defensive attitude towards growing economic upheavals and political attacks. Although the 8 per cent GDP indicated that the Tequila crisis was over by 1997, the 15 per cent unemployment and the US$ 100,000 million debt signalled the debacle. On the political front, the Peronist clientele ferociously opposed the IMF prescriptions implemented by Cavallo, who left the cabinet in 1996. From then on, currency devaluations in emerging markets like Russia, Thailand and Brazil prompted the transgression of the Law of Convertibility and a 4 per cent fall in GDP by 1998. Social opposition to mounting redundancy caused by privatizations spiralled meanwhile, epitomized by the *piqueteros* (picket organizers) – the new face of millions of Argentinians opposed to a decade of Menem's neoliberal package (Romero, 1994, 2013, pp. 287–291).

Venezuela: IESA Boys, Caracazo and 1992 Coups

IMF and World Bank packages were volatile when implemented too late and drastically after a relative bonanza, as happened during CAP's second government in Venezuela (1989–1993), marked by lootings, social unrest and military coups. CAP thought that his charisma sufficed to reverse AD's oil-funded populism, which had reached its peak during the 1970s Gran Venezuela. Instead of relying on high-ranking members from his party's machinery, CAP recruited a group of young technocrats from the Caracas-based Instituto de Estudios Superiores de Administración (IESA, Institute of High Studies on Management) to mastermind the neoliberal reforms (Stambouli, 2002, pp. 173–175). But this replacement was opposed by AD cliques, inasmuch as technocratic changes were regarded suspiciously by a society reluctant to come to terms with the end of the Saudi Venezuela after Black Friday (see pp. 142–143).

The IESA Boys' package comprised freezing public employment, adjusting telephone and electricity tariffs, privatizing several enterprises and raising the price of food and fuel. The increase in petrol prices triggered a 30 per cent increment in the public transport fares, sparking riots in Guarenas – a dormitory town of the Gran Caracas and epicentre of the revolts of 27 and 28 February 1989, which left between 800 and 1,000 dead. The so-called *Caracazo* (figure 7.1) evinced not only the economic disappointment and desperation among popular sectors, but also signalled deeper conflicts between the party-based agenda and the 'programmatic rationality' of CAP

Figure 7.1. El Caracazo, 27–28 February 1989. (*Photo*: Francisco Solórzano. *Source*: *El Nacional* Archive)

and the IESA Boys (Stambouli, 2002, p. 183). These conflicts could no longer be swept away in a country fed up with the bipartisanship inherited from the Puntofijo Pact, which had already disenchanted the working class and poor (Arráiz, 2007, p. 191) (see also pp. 116–117).

In the wake of the *Caracazo*, CAP and the IESA ministers tried to offset the social effects of the package, accelerating at the same time the decentralization process (see p. 161), until further political setbacks aborted the reforms. While the President returned from the World Economic Forum (WEF) in Davos on the early morning of 4 February 1992, a group of Army officers of the Movimiento Bolivariano Revolucionario 200 (MBR200, Revolutionary Bolivarian Movement) initiated a *coup d'état* from the barracks in Maracay, Valencia and Maracaibo. However, Commander Hugo Chávez was unable to seize the capital's Miraflores Palace. When he appeared that morning before the TV cameras acknowledging his inability to accomplish the military goals, 'for the time being', Chávez put a face to the political changes claimed: the *comandante*'s popularity came instantly and only increased with his imprisonment during the mid-1990s. He was then perceived as Venezuela's saviour, in contrast to corrupt traditional parties and leaders (Arráiz, 2007, p. 195; Torres, 2010, pp. 167–170).

As the Venezuelan economy grew at almost 10 per cent in that fateful 1992, Caracas's population had to endure, on the early morning of 27 November, a second coup attempt, this time carried out by air force officers. The episode aggravated the political instability which led to the President's impeachment in May 1993, charged with embezzlement. CAP's political assassination was another blow to the Puntofijo establishment, which Rafael Caldera was to close with his second presidency (1994–1999), despite having been one of the signatories of the 1958 pact (Arráiz, 2007, pp. 197–200).

Peru's Fujishock and Beyond

By the late 1980s, Peru was suffering political instability and economic disarray, fuelled by terrorist groups. Allegedly inspired by the Maoism of China's Cultural Revolution and Cambodia's Khmer Rouge, the ruthless tactics of Sendero Luminoso (Shining Path) were backed, from 1983, by the MRTA or Tupac Amaru Revolutionary Movement, descendant of the Cuban guerrillas and similar to Colombia's M-19 (Vargas, 2009, p. 144;[4] Rosas, 2010, pp. 290–291). After the debacle of Alan García's first administration (1985–1990) – which had to nationalize the banking system and suspend debt payments to international creditors – the electoral contest was between the famous writer Mario Vargas Llosa and the unknown engineer Alberto Fujimori (Rosas, 2010, pp. 297–303). The latter's victory in the second round was made possible by the votes of those who rejected the neoliberal package announced by Vargas's right-wing coalition (del Pozo, 2002, p. 236).

Ironically, the new president, who was of Japanese descent, implemented a so-called Fujishock from August 1990, by which state subsidies on basic products and services were cancelled, so their prices increased abruptly. The drastically liberal programme resulted in GDP reaching an accumulated growth of 32.1 per cent between 1993 and 1996 (Ludeña, 2011, pp. 80–86). On the political front, Fujimori's rhetoric against APRA and traditional parties was radicalized with the so-called *autogolpe* or self-inflicted coup of 1992, when the president, backed by the military, dismantled the legislative and judiciary powers, which were allegedly perceived as corrupt by the population. Also a new constitution was passed in 1993. Partly as an acknowledgement to Peru's successful war on coca cultivation and terrorism, the presidential coup was eventually recognized by George Bush's administration (1989–1993), though relations were to sour during Fujimori's second term (1995–2000) (Rosas, 2010, pp. 303–315).

Despite upheavals in Peru and other countries, when looking with hindsight at the application of neoliberal packages, Thatcher reckoned that Latin America had done the right thing by dismantling the centralist model inherited from Iberian colonialism. However, aware of the turmoil caused by the Fujishock and probably also of CAP's aborted reforms in Venezuela, she echoed the Washington Consensus policy-makers when stating that 'political stability' was 'necessary if the full benefits of free-enterprise are to overcome the legacy of "mercantilism"' (Thatcher, 1995, p. 583; World Bank, 1993). But events of the rest of the decade and the start of the new century were to prove that, apart from Chile and Brazil, political stability was far from being achieved in other Latin American countries which, on the contrary, became strongholds of the neoliberal refusal.

The Completion of Urbanization: From Demography to Globalization

From Rural–Urban to Inter–Urban Migration

Amid the economic woes and political turbulence of Latin America's lost decade urbanization reached 71.4 per cent by 1990 (Clichevsky, 1990, pp. 67–69). Slower population growth caused by lower fertility and less rural–urban immigration, resulted in 'smaller increases in the levels of urbanization and the much smaller rates of growth for many of the region's larger cities' (United Nations, 1996, pp. 42–43). Meanwhile, Latin America's 'million cities' concentrated 29 per cent of the population by 1990 and 45 per cent by the end of the decade, more than the total rural population (United Nations, 1996, pp. 47–48; Clark, 2000, p. 24) (see also Appendices tables 1 and 2).

While rural–urban migration in Latin America accounted for 46.4 per cent of the urban growth in the 1950s and 38.4 in the 1990s, most territorial and demographic changes were caused by inter–urban migration, which especially favoured medium-sized cities of between 50,000 and 500,000 inhabitants (Cerrutti and Bertoncello, 2003, pp. 8, 11, 17). Besides the dismantling of the ISI and the metropolises' industrial base, the stronger attraction of medium-sized and 'million-cities' over larger metropolises has been explained by the latter's deterioration in terms of worn-out infrastructure

Figure 7.2. La Hoyada station, Caracas metro, 1989. (*Source*: Archivo de Originales SLGM. FADEU. Pontificia Universidad Católica de Chile)

and declining living standards, which led to the shift from rural–urban to inter-urban migration (Clichevsky, 1990, p. 47; Portes and Roberts, 2008, pp. 31–34).

Despite the oil crisis and the lost decade, lower urban investment in Latin America did not entirely halt infrastructure development in major cities, especially metro systems (Hardoy, 1997). They ranged from São Paulo's in 1974 and Santiago's in 1975 – which somewhat proclaimed the militaries' miracles – to Caracas's in 1983, the same year as the Black Friday devaluation (figure 7.2). The limited improvement of public infrastructure was in many cases surpassed by private investment in shopping centres, corporate towers (figure 7.3) and landmarks that heralded the neoliberal cycle (figure 7.4). However, while major flows of population kept moving to intermediate cities, the lacklustre renewal of Latin America's metropolitan image in the 1980s was undermined by the growth of unemployment and poverty. Not until the following decade would there be significant strategic planning projects in major capitals (see pp. 158–160).

Figure 7.3. ENTEL Tower, Santiago, view from Alameda Bernardo O'Higgins, circa 1975. (*Source*: Archivo de Originales SLGM. FADEU. Pontificia Universidad Católica de Chile)

Figure 7.4. Santiago Centro building, Santiago, 1980s. (*Source*: Archivo de Originales SLGM. FADEU. Pontificia Universidad Católica de Chile)

The Urbanization of Poverty

An early 1980s ECLAC report acknowledged that there had been no reduction in Latin America's poverty compared with the previous decade, when nearly 40 per cent of the population lived in such conditions; on top of that, 20 per cent were considered 'indigent', that is their income levels were so low that they could not afford to feed themselves adequately (ECLAC, 1981, pp. 8–9). Throughout the decade, privatization and the demolition of the public bureaucracies, which had swollen the tertiary sector, raised levels of unemployment above 20 per cent, producing alarming growth in absolute poverty and the informal economy and conditions worse than in the Great Depression after 1929 (del Pozo, 2002, p. 181; Bourguignon, 1998, p. 4).[5]

Also as a consequence of the debt crisis, Latin America's socio-economic standards deteriorated throughout the 1980s, when per capita GDP declined in the majority of countries (United Nations, 1996, p. 45) (see also Appendices table 3). By the mid-1990s, Latin America, together with sub-Saharan Africa, were the two developing regions where the poverty was higher than in the previous decade. According to World Bank figures, the region had gone from 91 million people living in absolute poverty in 1987, to 110 million in 1993 – an increase from 22 per cent to 23.5 per cent of the total population. So it was no surprise that Latin America and the Caribbean held 'the most pronounced income disparity of all developing regions of the world' (Javed Burki, 1998, p. 8). Social inequities sharpened in the largest countries throughout the rest of the decade: by the late 1990s incomes for the richest quintile of the population – which absorbed more than 40 per cent of the national income – was fifteen times higher than that of the poorest quintile (del Pozo, 2002, pp. 237–238, 242; Portes and Roberts, 2008, p. 53).

As for urban poverty as such, its incidence in Latin America rose from 25 per cent of households in 1980 to 34 per cent in 1990, while rural poverty remained stable over the same period. Further, when considering that, according to World Bank data, 59 per cent of the poor population lived in cities by 1990, it could be said that the lost decade brought about the 'urbanization of poverty' resulting, to a great extent, from rural migration of previous decades (Valdés and Wiens, 1998, p. 108; Javed Burki, 1998, p. 8). Far from producing a 'spill over of growth', as had been expected, in many capitals neoliberal reforms accentuated the proportions of informal work, poverty and social inequity. Effects on the urban environment were dramatic, particularly in terms of the invasion of the public space by street vendors and informal activities, alongside the establishment of gated communities in both residential districts and squatter settlements (Grimson, 2008, pp. 10–11).

Spatial Resurgence: Urban Centres and Strategic Planning

Latin America's 1970s malaise following the failure of modernization and developmentalism was aggravated during the lost decade by the dismantling of the statist model. While central planning systems were downsized and reoriented following neoliberal strategies, the replacement of both the Dependence's Marxist approach and economically-oriented *planificación* ran parallel to the resurgence of Latin America's spatial planning practices (Almandoz, 2008*b*, pp. 168–169).

In tune with the growing awareness of the importance of historical and cultural heritage for the city's variety (Rowe and Koetter, 1981; Kostof, 1992, for instance), Latin America's emerging concern about the rescue of historic centres again bridged town planning with urban design. A first generation of traditional Latin American centres which underwent regeneration included Brazil's Salvador de Bahia, Colombia's Cartagena (figure 7.5), Panama City, Antigua, Ecuador's Quito (figure 7.6), Puerto Rico's San Juan and Mexico's Guanajuato, Zacatecas, Taxco and San Miguel Allende. By the late 1970s, thirty-two of the 164 centres declared by UNESCO as Cultural Heritage of the Humanity were to be found in the region (González, 2002, pp. 158, 175, 199). Such awareness helped to reinforce heritage considerations in urban proposals and plans (Hardoy *et al.*, 1981; Hardoy and Satterthwaite, 1986).

Meanwhile, the rejection of normative and centralized *plans* tended, in accordance with the neoliberal ethos, to favour instead the *projects* of 'strategic' planning and/or *gestión* (management). With its origins in the Harvard Business School, this new trend was understood as a 'continual process of decision-making' aimed at realizing economic development at the local level, while adopting a sustainable stance in respect of the environment (Hoshino, 1997, p. 38; Edralin, 1997, p. 49). In contrast to the subordination of the urban space within regional planning and territorial *ordenamiento* from the 1960s through the early 1980s (see pp. 133–136), strategic planning often highlighted spatial landmarks and urban design. These were epitomized in great private initiative projects, though still framed within 'the regulatory and driving role of public administration', according to Jordi Borja (Borja, 1997, pp. 89–90). Imitating the renowned examples of Barcelona, Valencia and Lisbon – where urban competitiveness and marketing were capitalized – Rio, Bogotá, Medellin, Buenos Aires and Santiago,

Figure 7.5. Central Street, Cartagena de Indias, Colombia. (*Photo*: Juan Camilo Pardo, 2010)

Figure 7.6. Rocafuerte Street, central Quito, Ecuador, *c*. 1980. (*Source*: Arturo Almandoz Archive)

among others, became exponents of the new trend from the late 1980s. At the same time these cities benefited from favourable junctures resulting from democratic and/ or constitutional renewal, amidst neoliberal prosperity (Borja, 1997, pp. 87, 95–96; Duque, 2013).

Elsewhere, capital regeneration was undertaken through the modernization of surface transport, as in the case of buses and trams in Quito in the mid-1990s (Carrión, 1997) and the so-called Transmilenio or Bus Rapid Transit (BRT) system launched in Bogotá in 2000 (figure 7.7). Further, strategic projects such as Puerto Madero in Buenos Aires, promoted by both private and public agents, signalled the return of Latin American *urbanismo* to the city and the spatial fabric which had been ignored by normative planning and territorial *ordenamiento* (Almandoz, 2006b, pp. 110–114). This happened too with the so-called 'parochial plans' in Caracas in the mid-1990s, though many of these did not materialize (Almandoz, 2000, pp. 160–164).

Figure 7.7. Transmilenio stop, Street 26, Bogotá. (*Photo*: Andrés Téllez, 2011)

Despite its restitution of spatial and monumental values, strategic planning – as the sole 'efficient means' of urban intervention recognized by neoliberalism and globalization – was questioned because of its indiscriminate assumption of market and management principles to attract visitors, following the 'spectacularization' of Barcelona and other European cities based on tourism (Vainer, 2000, pp. 78, 80–82; Vaz and Jacques, 2006).

Decentralization, Territorial Restructuring and Peripheral Globalization

Following recommendations of the IMF and World Bank, some Latin American countries' neoliberal packages of the late 1980s and 1990s were accompanied by the decentralizing reforms aimed at strengthening regional and local administrations (Roberts and Portes, 2008, pp. 512–513; Claverie, 2011). However, these were seldom allocated sufficient material and financial resources to provide services and accomplish duties adequately (Hoshino, 1997, p. 37). This was the case in Brazil, for instance, where the New Republic established by the 1988 Constitution returned many of the municipal competences taken over by the dictatorships' centralism, but the decentralization process was undermined by the economic crisis until the following decade (Moraes, 2004, pp. 101, 142).

A different scenario unfolded in Venezuela, where the long-lasting centralism started to be offset by the COPRE or Commission for the State's Reform from the 1980s. In the wake of the *Caracazo*, constitutional changes in the early 1990s comprised municipal and provincial elections to strengthen democracy and implement liberal reforms, but they proved belated and insufficient to placate political unrest (Arráiz, 2007, pp. 188–189, 193–195). Partly serving as example for the Venezuelan process, a timelier and deeper reform had taken place in Colombia with the aforementioned 1991 Constitution which boosted regional and local governments (Ocampo, 1994, 2007, pp. 363–365).

Even though territorial policies were minimized in the post-Fordism that accompanied Latin America's neoliberalism, new public investment was concentrated on road and technological infrastructure, services to private companies and promotion of small and medium enterprises (SME). In a more selective and competitive way than in the era of ISI and developmentalism, investments often favoured cities and regions oriented towards the countries' export businesses (de Mattos, 2010, pp. 53–58). While affecting the migration flows and cities' hierarchy, territorial results and the effects of those export-oriented practices reinforced regional disintegration and disparities, as happened in Brazil's dynamic south in relation to the sluggish north (Moraes, 2004, pp. 102–103; Portes and Roberts, 2008, pp. 38–40). In countries exporting natural resources with little added value, such as Chile, new investments were located in production and export outposts nationwide. Instead in Mexico, more oriented towards manufacturing, corporations tended to concentrate in the northern states along the US border, with advantages such as 'entrepreneurial capacity, favourable working environment, availability of cheap workforce, access to communication means and expeditious link to importing markets' (de Mattos, 2010, pp. 60–61).

Alongside decentralization and territorial restructuring, the replacement of industrial by tertiary bases oriented towards globalization can be said to be another geographical manifestation of the dismantling of Latin America's economic model of growth from the 1980s (Montoya, 2006, p. 12). As strongholds of this shift, by the early 1990s, major metropolises such as São Paulo, in a first category, followed by Buenos

Aires, Mexico City, Rio, Santiago and Caracas, in a secondary one were ranked among the 'world cities' of 'semi-periphery' countries (King, 1991, pp. 124–125). However, the precariousness of this peripheral globalization was evident by the fact that the number of transnational corporations with premises in those metropolises was dramatically lower than in their counterparts in the developed world (Clark, 2000, pp. 140, 149). At the same time, fledgling economic indicators of Latin America's seemingly global cities were dampened by criminality, social unrest and lack of governance. Fuelled by reactions to neoliberal packages, these woes appeared by the mid-1990s as national problems whose most dramatic stages were precisely metropolitan areas, as we shall see in the next chapter.

Notes

1. According to the so-called *Rettig Report*, elaborated by the Comisión Nacional de Verdad y Reconciliación (1991, National Commission of Truth and Reconciliation), appointed by the Chilean government in 1990. Available at: http://www.ddhh.gov.cl/ddhh_rettig.html.
2. 'Las exequias de un tirano' (December 2006).
3. 'La dictadura perfecta' (May 1992).
4. 'Los buenos terroristas' (December 1999).
5. Absolute poverty was measured 'by the proportion of population below US$75 a month at 1991 prices' (Bourguignon, 1998, p. 4).

Chapter 8

New Century and Old Demons

> ... the way globalization has been managed, including the international trade agreements that have played such a large role in removing those barriers and the policies that have been imposed on developing countries in the process of globalization, need to be radically rethought.
>
> Joseph E. Stiglitz, *Globalization and Its Discontents* (2003)

Post-Liberalism and Neo-Populism

Frustrated Transitions

Much of Latin America's shift to the left in the early twentieth century can be attributed to the disenchantment with neoliberal and globalizing practices introduced from the late 1980s by the Washington Consensus. Masterminded by the IMF and the World Bank, these sought to reduce fiscal deficit, eliminate barriers to international trade, privatize public enterprises and liberate the cost of goods and services (see pp. 146–147). Latin America's traditional protest which used to target the privileged upper classes and political establishment, in reaction to these packages shifted to the states' technical-bureaucratic elites, from the 1989 *Caracazo* (figure 7.1) to the popular revolts in Buenos Aires in 2001 (Roberts and Portes, 2008, pp. 510–511).

Regardless of the explosive effects of some of these market-oriented packages, their eventual failure has been explained, from a liberal standpoint, by their being limited, incomplete and uncompetitive when compared with those in South East Asia and other parts of the world. In order to understand this, it is necessary first to recognize that the transition pursued by Latin America's programmes can be framed within three phases triggered by so-called 'creative destruction',[1] followed by institutional modernization and consolidation of development (Edwards, 2009, pp. 20–28). And this is a situation which did not arise in most Latin American countries, since reforms were introduced *from outside* to economic structures that retained many of their inherent weaknesses.

Without the experience of creative destruction – with the exception of Chile, where the radical programme of liberalization played the role of it – Latin America's largest economies became secondly 'frustrated' in their transition towards modernization and development. Social and political opposition became manifest once the economic growth that had deceived rulers and experts in the early 1990s slowed (World Bank, 1993, pp.

56–77). This is why the social and political measures that the 1996 Annual World Bank Conference on Development in Latin America and the Caribbean recommended most countries to adopt were not implemented. Key among the measures prescribed was the implementation of 'second-generation reforms' – which would probably affect the interests of the unions and political parties – in order 'to dismantle the populist state'. The reformed state should support 'a fundamental change in the role of government – from being an owner and operator to being a policy-maker and a regulator', and in its new role the government should work 'closely with the private sector to develop a competitive, outward-looking, and employment-generating economy' (Javed Burki, 1998, p. 8).

However most of these ideas remained wishful thinking in terms of political and social reforms, partly because conservative sectors perpetuated a 'false dichotomy between social policy and growth' (Hommes, 1998, pp. 11–12). Alongside institutional shortcomings in the judiciary and property rights, economic problems also persisted and strangled reforms in countries whose currencies were pegged to the US dollar, while questionable privatization of public services was often reduced to a mere conversion from public into private monopolies (Edwards, 2009, pp. 93–94, 102–107, 189).

Promised Land of Anti-Globalization and Neo-Populism

In spite of the structural deficiencies of its reforms, by the mid-1990s World Bank economists thought that Latin America exhibited a number of 'positive developments' and had learnt many lessons – including that 'protectionism' had become 'an ugly word' (Cardoso, 1998, pp. 34–35) – while liberalization and direct investment had taken root throughout the region. Furthermore, there was the false belief that policy-makers had abandoned 'populism and follow up on their words in the real world and not just in Washington meeting rooms' (World Bank, 1993, p. 23).

But the World Bank experts were mistaken in the sense that populism was to resurface alongside state corporatism, launching an era of post-liberalism. Issues neglected by neoliberalism, such as the importance of public services, national sovereignty and strategic resources that must remain under the state's control, came to the fore once more (Grimson, 2008, pp. 16–17). This U-turn responded, on the one hand, to an unfulfilled challenge that the World Bank itself had anticipated in relation to Latin America's social structure: 'unless the social dimensions of development are dealt with rapidly, the reforms will be politically unsuitable in the long run' (World Bank, 1993, p. 34). On the other, Latin America's shift to the left was fuelled by disenchantment with globalization, given its failure to reduce poverty while increasing inequity. These criticisms of the 'broken promises' of 'global institutions', especially of the IMF and its alleged goal of international stability, gathered force when voiced by Joseph Stiglitz, former policy-maker of the Washington Consensus and Senior Vice President of the World Bank (Stiglitz, 2003, pp. 3–25).

These factors all help to explain why, at the beginning of the twenty-first century, Latin America began a cycle of neo-populism that, prompted by economic and political upheavals in several countries, fuelled the reaction against neoliberalism. From a macroeconomic standpoint, populism has been characterized as a practice that emphasizes the growth and distribution of income while playing down inflationary risks, restrictions on international trade and the concern for reaction of financial markets and bodies to governmental policies. Although welcomed by the masses, 'populist episodes' inexorably lead to accelerated inflation, unemployment and devaluation of salaries, given that they are usually funded by public indebtedness and printing money (Edwards, 2009, p. 23). Although Latin America's 2000s populism exhibited more 'fiscal prudence' and awareness of inflation than in the past, 'neo-populist' governments have tried to curb the hazards artificially by introducing price controls, nationalization of private companies and other regulations (Edwards, 2009, p. 230).

Still in the economic domain but looking at social and political demands, Latin America's neo-populism is also related to Alain Touraine's notion of 'grand refusal', understood as 'the reaction of the masses in social movements to the oppressive conditions caused by global neoliberalism' (Irazábal, 2008, p. 11; Touraine, 1999, pp. 154–158). Epitomized in 'extraordinary events' taking place in public spaces, such reactions have materialized 'a vision for alternative socio-political projects' that arguably convert Latin America into a sort of Promised Land of anti-globalization, post-liberalism and neo-populism (Irazábal, 2008, p. 26). Examples of those protests include the EZLN's seizure of Mexico City's Zocalo in March 2001 (Tamayo and Cruz Guzmán, 2008), the revolts that toppled Fernando de la Rúa in Argentina in December 2001 (Pírez, 2009), and the Caracas marches in support of Hugo Chávez in 2002–2004 (Irazábal and Foley, 2008) (see pp. 169–171).

Aspirational Constitutions and Nationalisms

In Latin America's historic populism, charismatic leaders endeavoured to gain the support of the urbanizing masses by promising them economic benefits, as happened with Vargas in Brazil and Perón in Argentina (Williamson, 1992, pp. 346–351; Romero, 1999, pp. 159–160) (see also pp. 50, 90–92). Such an appeal to the underdogs and lower-income groups has usually been exerted through a de-legitimization of established political parties along with an attack on representative democracy. This is why populist regimes have traditionally become autocratic and authoritarian, from Fujimori in Peru to Chávez in Venezuela. As the incarnation of Latin America's neo-populism, the latter has been labelled as a mixture of Peron and Che Guevara (Adler, 2004). It is necessary to distinguish, though, the *de facto* rise to power of populist leaders in the past from the electoral and institutional mechanisms used by more recent generations, backed by the new constitutions that they have promoted, reformed or tailored (Edwards, 2009, pp. 226, 230–231).

As in the recent cases of Venezuela, Ecuador and Bolivia, those *presidentialistas* or presidential-driven charters have been conceived as easily amendable and relatively unfinished constitutions that incorporate the aims of the socialist projects within which they have been framed. The most emblematic example was Venezuela's 1999 constitution, reformed 10 years later in order to permit the indefinite re-election of the President and other high-rank posts (Edwards, 2009, pp. 19, 232; Quenan, Velut and Allou, 2011, p.16). Besides the three traditional branches – executive, legislative and judicial – those constitutions have opted for incorporating the citizens' and electoral powers, thereby reinforcing populist mechanisms for the leaders' consultations to their grassroots. Partly following the Colombian example, those 'aspirational constitutions' have also included economic and social benefits that, in the US and other countries representative of the so-called 'protective constitutions',[2] are implemented through organic laws and specific regulations. The economic and social-oriented agendas of aspirational constitutions have resulted in excessively long and ambitious documents (Edwards, 2009, pp. 232–234).

However, supporters argue that Latin America's most recent constitutions, including those of Brazil and Peru, make possible a 'performative citizenship' that consecrates 'the right to be different from the dominant national community' in terms of ethnicity or sexual orientation, among other social rights (Irazábal, 2008, pp. 17–18). This trend is also in tune with the changing agenda of 'collective action' in Latin America's metropolises, which has moved from the class-driven movements prevailing up to the 1980s, to civil society's demands for citizenship and participative democracy (Roberts and Portes, 2008, pp. 525–526). At the same time, these constitutions have boosted the decentralization process initiated in many countries in the 1980s – with the exception of Pinochet's Chile – and have relied on European – mainly French – examples (Claverie, 2011, pp. 162, 167).

As is sometimes reflected in the constitutional reforms, neo-populism has revived old demons from Latin America's republican history, such as *indigenismo*, militarism and nationalism, whose invocation as a 'panacea for our problems' had been denounced by Vargas Llosa in relation to the rhetoric of Venezuela's Chávez and Bolivia's Evo Morales (Vargas, 2009, p. 245).[3] Such nationalism now lashes out at capitalism, globalization, US imperialism and its 'pawns' – to use Chávez's expression – whose failures have allegedly been evident from the 1990s crises through the 2008 crash and its ensuing depression (Edwards, 2009, pp. 282; Adler, 2004; Romero, 1999, pp. 184–185). Although it has been tempered in other countries – as in Lula's Brazil, where global corporations have sometimes become targets of anti-imperialist critique – the attack on the alleged hegemony of the United States and the legacy of the Washington Consensus remains a feature of old-fashioned left-wing nationalism (Surel, 2011, p. 152; Torres, 2010). It all configures an updated political mythology that – as was seen in the anti-Yankee ethos after the Cuban Revolution – echoes the 1900s *arielistas*' images of Caliban and the Golden Calf (see pp. 42–44).

Incomplete Reforms

Latin America's post-liberalism, and in some cases reversal to populism after the controversial packages of the 1990s has developed in different ways, depending on the political and financial upheavals each country went through. Bearing in mind that these national processes have occurred over different time spans and at varying speeds, let us outline here (see also pp. 146–154) how Latin America's incomplete economic reforms of the 1990s, fuelled by the international reaction against neoliberalism and globalization (see pp. 163–166), framed the countries' trends at the start of the twenty-first century.

Tequila Hangover in the Two Mexicos

An early and decisive setback was experienced in Salinas's México, which championed Latin America's adoption of the Brady Plan and free-market reforms after the lost decade (see pp. 150–151). While the country's entrance to the OECD and NAFTA was being celebrated, the first blow came with the Chiapas Indians' uprising under the guidance of the so-called Sub-commander Marcos in 1994; this episode not only revived the strategies of 1960s guerrillas but also made plain that they were not exterminated with Central America's peace accords of the early 1990s (Suchlicki, 1996, 2008, p. 150). Two Mexicos coexisted thereafter: on the one hand, the modern country on the brink of joining the First World, on the other, the 'quasi-feudal' nation reminiscent of the *porfiriato* (see pp. 29–30, 47–49). Whereas many analysts disregarded the Chiapas events as something folkloric, others perceived in them 'the fragility of the Mexican road towards a free-market economy' (Edwards, 2009, pp. 171–172).

Alongside the Chiapas insurgents – whose makeshift camp in Mexico City's Zocalo became an emblem of anti-global movements worldwide (Tamayo and Cruz-Guzmán, 2008) – there were the long-lasting economic effects of the Tequila crisis triggered at the end of 1994, when the peso lost two-thirds of its value against the US dollar. Both events unleashed the first wave of criticisms against market-oriented reforms in Latin America, especially given that Mexico was supposed to be its first democratic success, after Pinochet's Chile. On top of that, in March of the same *annus terribilis* the PRI candidate, Luis Donaldo Colosio, was assassinated, in what was a precursor to the political and drug-related violence of today's Mexico (Suchlicki, 1996, 2008, pp. 4–5, 150–151; Edwards, 2009, pp. 172–173).

Even though Ernesto Zedillo's administration (1994–2000) established a pact between government, unions and entrepreneurs to maintain salary increases and inflation at 4 per cent, the Tequila hangover led to an initial 15 per cent devaluation of the peso, which then lost half of its value in the following six months (Edwards, 2009, pp. 182, 185; Suchlicki, 1996, 2008, p. 156). Economic growth was re-established in the second half of the decade, but as this was very dependent on US dynamism, and deceleration in the US economy by 2000 also affected that of Mexico (Quenan and Torija-Zane, 2011, p. 47). Despite the launch of the Programme of National Solidarity, PRONASOL was monopolized by the PRI clientele during the governments of Salinas and Zedillo, according to critics (Sosa, 2000, pp. 72–73). Since the mid-1990s the proportion of population below the poverty line was more than 25 per cent, while layoffs in privatized or downsized companies resulted in the loss of 400,000 jobs (Suchlicki, 1996, 2008, pp. 145–146). Such gloomy indicators were very different from expectations created by neoliberal reforms and membership of NAFTA, and only fuelled the critics' rhetoric about inequities between the two Mexicos.

From the Gran Revolcón to the Plan Colombia

Colombia was another case where reforms slowed. Under the aegis of a 'social democracy' defined in the 1991 constitution, César Gaviria's 'Pacific Revolution' promised to overcome the problems of a nation of thirty-two million, 40 per cent of whom were considered poor (Ocampo, 1994, 2007, pp. 350–351, 370). In economic terms, Gaviria's government followed the neoliberal agenda of the Club Suizo (Swiss Club), so called after the Bogotá restaurant which was often the meeting place of a group headed by Minister of Finance and Public Credit, Rudolf Hommes. Such an agenda comprised the liberalization of trade through lowering import duties, alongside weakening the Colombian peso in order to favour exports, and abolition of the currency exchange controls which had been in place for decades (Edwards, 2009, pp. 154–155, 160).

Despite its alignment with the Washington Consensus, Colombia's free trade did not achieve the expected commercial results, but instead had a negative impact on traditional producers. There was also union opposition to the privatization of big enterprises, such as the telephone company Telecom, where a strike in April 1992 paralyzed a country already stricken by the guerrilla war and drug trafficking. These problems combined to undermine the hesitant support for neoliberalism by leftist groups – attracted by Ernesto Samper, former Minister of Development who turned into a maverick – as Gaviria's *gran revolcón* lost momentum and ended as another truncated programme of reforms in Latin America (Edwards, 2009, pp. 160–168).

Notwithstanding the assassination, on 12 December 1993, of the notorious Pablo Escobar, head of the Medellín Cartel, the government of Ernesto Samper (1994–1998) was deemed the peak of the so-called *narcodemocracia* (drug democracy). Scandal surrounding the financing of his electoral campaign through money laundering tarnished the reputation of the president himself. However, Samper's Colombia showed signs of economic recovery, while the free market was combined with 'social capitalism' (Ocampo, 1994, 2007, pp. 377, 381). Nonetheless, protectionism prevailed overall and growth shrank to less than 2 per cent between 1997 and 1998, which signalled Colombia's first recessive trend since the 1930s (Edwards, 2009, p. 168; Quenan and Torija-Zane, 2011, p. 63).

Towards the end of the decade, Bill Clinton's second administration (1997–2001) helped with the problem of drug trafficking through the Plan Colombia (1999–2000), providing US$1 billion of the US$7.5 billion cost of the programme together with military advice (Ocampo, 1994, 2007, p. 408). Thus Andrés Pastrana's administration (1998–2002) seemed to return to past associations with the Americans, as had been the case during the so-called Dance of the Millions of the 1920s (see pp. 63–64). Even though President Clinton made clear that the plan was not another Vietnam, it positioned Colombia as the third international recipient of US military aid, after Israel and Egypt (Edwards, 2009, p. 169). Meanwhile, the message sent by the FARC commander Manuel Marulanda to a negotiation meeting with the government in January 1999, sounded prophetic and defiant for Colombia's twenty-first-century democracy after decades of guerrilla war:

> We want peace without hunger, without repressive laws, without press censorship; with land, health, housing, well-being, employment; economic growth with social development, right to life and sovereignty. Big investments from the State are required for that purpose, with the contribution of the international community, which does not mean interference in our country's internal businesses. (Marulanda quoted in Ocampo, 1994, 2007, p. 399).

From Caldera's Agenda Venezuela to Chávez's Restoration

Gained with only 30 per cent of the votes and 40 per cent abstention – indicators of the disenchantment with the Puntofijo establishment – Rafael Caldera's victory in Venezuela's 1993 elections could be said to be pyrrhic. The so-called Agenda Venezuela promoted foreign investment, especially joint ventures with the state-owned PDVSA in the oil industry. But the 1994 crisis in the financial sector – when more than thirteen banks required government intervention – was a major blow for an economy also shaken by the Tequila effect. Echoing the pacification policy that *guerrilleros* benefited from during his first presidency in the early 1970s (see pp. 116–117), Caldera pardoned those involved in the 1992 military coups, though he knew that Hugo Chávez was the leader of the 'anti-politics' aimed at throwing out the democracy that Caldera's generation had established (Stambouli, 2002, p. 218; Arráiz, 2007, pp. 201–204) (see also pp. 152–154).

After CAP's neoliberal package of the early 1990s, Caldera's administration, rather than following, stepped aside from the Washington Consensus guidelines. Thus, despite having signed another agreement with the IMF in 1996, by the end of the decade Venezuela was regarded as 'the country where fewer liberal reforms had been adopted than anywhere in Latin America' (Edwards, 2009, p. 257). In the political arena, it should be remembered that constitutional changes of the late 1980s and early 1990s boosted municipal autonomy in order to revitalize democracy, but this proved to be insufficient to calm the unrest. Meanwhile, neighbourhood associations constituted in the 1970s and 1980s – which had acted as grassroots for local participation – were co-opted by political parties, thus obstructing one of the few remaining channels of democratic renewal (García-Guadilla, 2003, pp. 438–439). And last but not least, economic, social and political malaise was aggravated by a dramatic increase in violence: with the highest figures in Latin America, Venezuela experienced a 200 per cent growth in homicides by 1999 (Sanjuán, 2000, p. 81).

Together these factors paved the way for Hugo Chávez's leadership, whose political career took off after his release from prison in 1994, with the support of civil and military groups clamouring for a military alternative to bipartisanship and corruption (González, 2005, pp. 107–116; Almandoz, 2012, pp. 17–19). To eradicate the Fourth Republic's woes,[4] Chávez promised a new constitution as his political banner, while the abandonment of globalization was offered in economic terms. Having called the national assembly so as to elaborate a constitution as soon as he took office – in which his supporters obtained 95 per cent of the seats – in 1999 Chávez's so-called Bolivarian Revolution fulfilled the promise of passing a charter based on a 'participative democracy' that took over from the representative one, thereby launching the Fifth Republic (Torres, 2010; García-Guadilla, 2012, pp. 178–171). But economic policies were far more radical than electoral promises: they returned to old-fashioned strategies of nationalization of businesses and public services alongside price controls, while social programmes were initiated through the so-called *misiones* or missions in health, education, poverty and other critical areas (see pp. 173–174). Chávez's missions were initially praised for being more assertive than previous governments' approaches to social exclusion, but later criticized for their administration from the central government with populist criteria reminiscent of the clientele-based aid and participation of traditional parties (Naím, 2013; Krauze, 2008, pp. 84–88).

While the regime radicalized its socialist and autocratic stance, tensions with the opposition escalated, especially regarding PDVSA's politicization and its loss of technocratic management since nationalization in the 1970s; massive protests and confrontations culminated in the events of April 2002, when the military high command withdrew its support for the president, who allegedly resigned (figure 8.1). The unconstitutional measures of the short-lived government that followed prompted the

Figure 8.1. Demonstration against Chávez, Francisco Fajardo Motorway, Caracas, 2002. (*Photo*: CC Carlos Granier-Phelps)

caudillo's restoration two days later after what came to be labelled by official supporters as a *coup d'état*, whereas the opposition claimed it had been a power vacuum (Stambouli, 2002, pp. 216–219; Irazábal and Foley, 2008, pp. 152–155).

Argentina's Corralito and Beyond

By the end of the 1990s, when the radicalist Fernando de la Rúa was inaugurated as President (1999–2001), Argentina's export income had diminished, the fiscal deficit reached 71 per cent and the government's debt was 51 per cent of the GDP. Even with a special IMF loan, by 2001 the world's financial crises aggravated those internal weaknesses and raised unemployment to 15 per cent. That year US$18 million fled the country; in December Domingo Cavallo – also minister during Menem's administrations (see pp. 151–152) – froze bank deposits – the so-called *corralito* – while the IMF suspended its cash flow in view of the imminent collapse. Popular protest prompted de la Rúa's resignation on 20 December 2001, triggering a governmental crisis that defeated four presidents in a few days. Argentina declared its default in meeting international commitments, while the peso was devalued by 40 per cent and the people suffered a 'poverty shock' (Edwards, 2009, pp. 202–205, 209; Quenan and Torija-Zane, 2011, p. 55).

As the dollar-driven economy struggled with the devalued peso, the provisional government of Eduardo Duhalde (2002–2003) blamed foreign banks and international corporations for the catastrophe, though much of this had been caused by the previous governments' lack of fiscal discipline. With unemployment reaching 20 per cent and social unrest mounting, it was easier to point the finger at the financial agencies, especially for Duhalde's *justicialista* government, which followed Perón's traditional reluctance to the IMF's intervention in Argentina (Edwards, 2009, pp. 210–213) (see also pp. 90–91, 141–142). The Peronist-style anti-globalization discourse continued during the administration of Néstor Kirchner (2003–2007), who gained power with a record low of only 22 per cent of votes, after Menem's withdrawal in the second electoral round. Alongside the relative economic recuperation during his term, Kirchner's leftist stance, close to Chávez's, was probably what contributed most to increase his popularity by the end of his term (Edwards, 2009, p. 216; Quenan and Torija-Zane, 2011, p. 55).

Brazil: From Cardoso to Lula

A former theorist of the School of Dependence (see pp. 126–128), Fernando H. Cardoso continued, during his double term as president (1994–2002), with Brazil's economic stabilization and moderate liberalism, which included the privatization of telecommunications, electricity and railways. Even though GDP remained positive throughout the 1990s, the effects of Mexico and Argentina's financial turmoil, along with the emergence of the Movimento dos Sem-Terra (MST, the Landless Movement) – secular expression of Latin America's protracted land reform – were reminders that neoliberalism was far from a panacea (Schneeberger, 2003, pp. 347–350; del Priore and

Venancio, 2010, pp. 291–292). The fragility of the reforms was revealed during the exchange crisis of 1999, when the Brazilian real lost 20 per cent of its value, and the Central Bank allowed it to float in the market. Such measures helped to reduce inflation to 10 per cent between 2001 and 2002, while economic growth maintained a modest yet significant 2 per cent per annum (Edwards, 2009, p. 278).

Economic stability made possible a landmark presidency in Brazil: Luiz Inácio Lula da Silva's inauguration in January 2003 not only meant the Partido dos Trabalhadores' (PT, Workers' Party) long-awaited victory, but also 'the rise to power of the revolutionary generation of the 1960s' (del Priore and Venancio, 2010, p. 293). Given the electoral campaigns in which he participated, there was the fear that Lula might become the political reincarnation of Getúlio Vargas or João Goulart, or an emulator of Chávez. However, unlike Chávez's anti-American rhetoric and communist leanings, Lula opted for a productive *modus vivendi* with the United States, openness to foreign investment and orientation of the Brazilian model towards the socialist democracies of Western Europe (Edwards, 2009, pp. 282–285). Always concerned about controlling inflation that he knew affected lower-income groups most, Lula's administration launched the PAC (2007–2010, Plan for Accelerating Growth), associated by some critics with Latin America's failed developmentalism of the 1950s and 1960s (del Priore and Venancio, 2010, pp. 294–296). However, far from repeating historical mistakes, the Lula model resulted in a more balanced and socially-oriented alternative to implementing reforms in the post-liberal era (see pp. 180, 183–184).

Poverty Alleviation and Fragmented Metropolises

Before addressing the latest political and economic changes, this section outlines how the neoliberalism of the 1990s and early 2000s affected Latin America's urban societies and metropolitan structures. Following an exploration of the extent to which urban populations became the main beneficiaries of social programmes managed by national administrations, there is a brief comparison between the fragmented metropolitan structures brought about by neoliberal policies and the dual cities characteristic of the state-led *desarrollismo* (see pp. 124–133, 155–158).

Home to 584 million people unevenly distributed across the territory and 8.1 per cent of the world's population, Latin America began the 2000s as a continent completing a demographic transition characterized by lower fertility and mortality rates (Appendices tables 1 and 2). Such conditions bring about the positive fact that, helped by lower growth rates and reduced rural–urban migration, living standards have generally increased: by 2005 most of the population lived in upper middle income (UMC) economies according to the World Bank (World Bank, 2006, p. 287) (Appendices table 3).[5] But on the flip side, demands for social security and housing, among other needs, are also greater, particularly as life expectancy is now over seventy in most countries. Further, despite relative development, Latin America is still a continent of significant socio-economic contrasts, from the most unequal nations – Brazil, Chile, Colombia

– to the least – Costa Rica, El Salvador, Uruguay and Venezuela (Quenan, Velut and Allou, 2011, pp. 12–15).

Social Programmes: Between CCTP and Missions

According to ECLAC and SELA (Sistema Económico Latinoamericano y del Caribe or Latin American Economic System), poverty in the continent and the Caribbean reduced by 11 per cent between 2002 and 2010, when it amounted to 32 per cent of the population; there has, however, been a relative increase in extreme poverty, mainly due to soaring food prices. The reduction in the magnitude and intensity of poverty has been explained by the region's economic growth between 2003 and 2008, the decrease in fertility rate and related 'demographic dividend', alongside socially-oriented programmes transferring public resources to the poor sectors who are increasingly aware of their rights (Cosío-Zavala, 2011, pp. 98, 106; Guaregua, 2011; Lautier, 2011, pp. 279, 290).[6]

Partly following World Bank and IMF recommendations, since the 1990s social programmes to tackle poverty and its related manifestations and causes – mainly illiteracy and malnutrition – have been implemented in the region with varying success at the national level and repercussions on urban dynamics (Roberts and Portes, 2008, pp. 538–539). One such arrangement, the so-called Conditional Cash Transfer Programmes (CCTP) target poor families – usually represented by women, who are more reliable householders – which receive economic aid from the government; in return CCTP stipulate that families must comply with requirements such as sending children to school and providing them with medical care according to governmental guidelines. Mexico's 1997 *Progresa* (Progress) pioneered the CCTP for rural areas, extending it during Vicente Fox's administration (2000–2006) as *Oportunidades* (Opportunities, 2002) for marginal urban sectors (Lautier, 2011, pp. 254–255, 261–262). 'Social Commitment for Quality Education', health insurance for poorest families, and home ownership for low-income households are other social programmes (Suchlicki, 1996, 2008, pp. 164–165).

Brazil's social programmes have also been effective since the 1990s, when the Cardoso administration adopted the so-called *Bolsa Escola* (School Allowance) and *Bolsa Alimentação* (Food Allowance). On the basis of these and following the CCTP rationale, in 2002 the Lula administration created the *Fome Zero* (Zero Hunger) and the *Bolsa Família* (Family Allowance), which allegedly benefited eleven million people and contributed hugely to presidential popularity (del Priore and Venancio, 2010, pp. 294–296). Thanks to these programmes, Brazil's inequity in income distribution was reduced by 4.6 per cent between 1995 and 2004 (Edwards, 2009, pp. 280–282). The economic and political success of Mexican and Brazilian CCTP inspired other programmes in the region, such as Argentina's *Familias* (Families), Colombia's *Familia en Acción* (Family in Action) and Chile's *Puente* (Bridge), *Chile Solidario* (Solidarity Chile) and *Ingreso Ético* (Ethical Income) (Lautier, 2011, pp. 267–268).

Different from the CCTP, Chávez's Venezuela implemented successful literacy policies, such as the so-called Robinson Mission, while other programmes in high school and university education, namely the Ribas and Sucre missions, have been controversial. In addition to favouring government partisans or *chavistas*, the populist nature of these programmes is confirmed by the fact that – besides there being no conditions for beneficiaries, as in the CCTP – they have often been funded from the executive. This means that they have not been budgeted by the central administration, in spite of using up to 25 per cent of national income, while financial support for schools and hospitals built by previous administrations has been drastically reduced (Krauze, 2008, pp. 84–85). Remarkable in urban terms was the first part of the so-called *Misión Barrio Adentro* (Mission inside the Shantytown), aimed at providing preventive and ambulatory medicine to the eight million people living in uncontrolled shanties across Venezuela (Edwards, 2009, pp. 262–263, 283). However, critics object that the 1,500 outpatient centres – mostly staffed by 11,000 Cubans – were built at the expense of the maintenance of 583 hospitals and 4,000 *ambulatorios* (centres for ambulatory medicine) built before Chávez's came to power in 1999 (Krauze, 2008, p. 85).

Urban Contrasts and Public Investments

Despite the implementation of CCTP and other social programmes, inequality is still significant in Latin America. About 31 per cent of its population – some 138 million – live in 'marginal' settlements or *barrios* without drinking water, electricity, sanitation or proper building materials; they also suffer from overcrowding, location on unstable land and/or land tenure problems (Paquette, 2011, p. 305). The housing deficit problem is similarly overwhelming, both in terms of new dwellings required and the renovation of the existing ones. It is true that there have been considerable improvements in uncontrolled settlements, especially regarding the provision of water and electricity, but sanitation and accessibility remain highly deficient. It is also true that, mainly as a consequence of the lower migration from the countryside, the growth rate of marginal population has decreased, but is still substantial in countries that underwent neoliberal programmes in the 1990s, such as Argentina, Colombia and Peru (Paquette, 2011, pp. 304–305; Clichevsky, 2003, pp. 352, 356).

As a response to marginality and housing deficits, during the last two decades some Latin American countries, backed by the World Bank, have changed the approach to these problems: social housing production has passed to the private sector, while the public sector has focused on financing the beneficiary lower-income population. Pioneered in Chile in the 1980s, such a scheme has been adopted since the 2000s in Mexico and Brazil, where the housing production has reached almost a million units per annum. The state's new role as financing agent has not prevented its involvement in other traditional programmes for marginal areas, such as the improvement of *barrios* and legalization of land tenure (Paquette, 2011, pp. 306–308). National and local governments have also tried to address the accommodation demands of middle classes by promoting and subsidizing residential regeneration of so-called *pericentros* or inner districts around historic centres. These programmes could be said to have been initiated in the 1980s with the rescue of central districts and the relocation of street vendors, as in the pioneering cases of Ecuador's Quito (figure 7.6) and Brazil's Salvador de Bahia (see pp. 158–160). Backed by neoliberal reforms, the 'return to the centre' was promoted as an investment policy in Santiago in the 1990s (figure 8.2) and in Mexico City in the 2000s through the construction and renewal of housing units. Beyond the success of those programmes in the real-estate market, urban effects have been questioned in terms of the artificial increase of land value and gentrification, without significantly gaining residential population or improving quality of life in central areas (Paquette, 2011, pp. 310–312).

Figure 8.2 Parque Los Reyes, central Santiago. (*Photo*: Ximena Arizaga; by courtesy of Ximena Arizaga and Andrea Rojas, 2013)

Figure 8.3 Metrocable or cableway, Santo Domingo station, Medellín, Colombia. (*Photo*: CC SajoR)

Also transport infrastructure has attracted resources from national and local governments. After the example of Bogotá's Transmilenio in 2000 (figure 7.7), nearly fifteen cities, including Santiago, Mexico City and Lima, have adopted bus rapid transit (BRT), which allegedly is more sustainable and less invasive than metros. However, new underground lines have been built in São Paulo, Buenos Aires, Santiago, Lima, Mexico City and Caracas, and also in Caracas a *metrocable* or cableway to serve *barrios* on the hillsides was inaugurated in 2010, following the example of a similar system introduced in Colombia's Medellín in 2004 (figure 8.3). Meanwhile, the privatization of motorways has continued to be a transport policy in countries with market-oriented systems, such as Chile, Peru and Colombia (Paquette, 2011, pp. 298–303).

Globalization Undermined by Informality and Violence

Although weakly integrated into globalization, Latin American cities have shown some competitiveness in attracting foreign enterprises and capital; their best assets have been their 'non-transferable features', such as the natural environment in Rio de Janeiro and Santiago, urban life in Buenos Aires and historical heritage in Mexico City (de Mattos, 2010, pp. 246–247). Much of the weakness stems from the fact that, despite the diversification in the region's exports, most still depend on natural resources whose prices fluctuate sharply, whereas commercial services and industrial staples are not competitive in international markets (Quenan and Torija-Zane, 2011, p. 65). Another problem for the globalization of Latin American cities has been the persistence of the informal economy and its new 'proletariat' (Portes and Roberts, 2008, pp. 66–67). In addition to the usually low productivity of SMEs and informal enterprises, the 'unfair competition' of the informal sector of the economy is often permitted by national and local authorities, or at least indirectly facilitated by the complicated red tape required to legalize activities (Quenan and Torija-Zane, 2011, p. 51). In many cases, the hypertrophy and ramification of the informal sector facilitate the exposure to or connection with international organized crime through commercial piracy, prostitution, arms trafficking and, especially, drug trafficking (de Mattos, 2010, pp. 250–251).

Nurtured by other factors such as military repression, guerrilla wars and poverty increase, the escalation of violence in Latin America has also been linked to the social inequality brought about by neoliberal policies (Concha-Eastman, 2000, p. 40; Portes and Roberts, 2008, p. 65). In some cases this violence is rooted in previous conflicts, as happened in Colombia, where rural-based guerrillas of the FARC, ELN and M-19, despite displaying a left-oriented political discourse, were infiltrated by drug trafficking and right-wing paramilitary organizations from the 1980s (Pizarro, 2000, pp. 61–62). With 100,000 victims since the 1960s and seventy-three homicides per 100,000 inhabitants, 1980s Colombia exhibited one of the continent's highest rates of criminality, which spurred migration from the countryside into cities that were relatively controlled by the state (see pp. 148–149). Analogous situations occurred in Nicaragua, El Salvador and Guatemala, as well as in Peru's areas penetrated by Sendero

Luminoso, where subversive movements 'found an important ally in the coca industry' (Rosas, 2010, p. 300; del Pozo, 2002, p. 204).

Following the introduction of the Plan Colombia, much of the *narcoviolencia* has moved to Mexico's northern states of Sinaloa and Chihuahua; in 2008 alone Ciudad Juárez, the capital of Chihuahua, suffered 6,000 drug-related deaths (Edwards, 2009, p. 300). From the south, meanwhile, in the states of Chiapas, Guerrero and Oaxaca, the guerrilla violence led by the EZLN from 1994 onwards has been confronted by the Mixed Operations Brigades, among other military and paramilitary organizations promoted since 1996 by the central government to the detriment of local and regional police forces. It all frames a confused political and military scene in which, under the pretext of 'public safety' and the necessity of safeguarding conditions for foreign investment and tourism, civil rights are severely undermined (Sosa, 2000, pp. 76–77; Gourdon, 2011, pp. 138–139).

Related to political violence, 74 per cent of the world's firearms homicides were in Latin America, according to 2010 figures from the UN Office on Drugs and Crime (UNODOC). With 82.1 homicides per 100,000 inhabitants, Honduras heads the list for regional violence, followed by El Salvador with 66 and Venezuela with 49, which represents a change in relation to the previous decade, when Colombia and Brazil were ranked in the highest (UNODOC, 2011, pp. 9–10, 25). Growing in frequency since 1995, a quarter of the homicides in Latin America and the Caribbean are related to organized crime, while in Central America the main cause is drug trafficking and local conflicts remaining from previous decades (UNODOC, 2011, pp. 10–11, 24–25). Increasing violence and unresolved corruption make governments appear ineffective, and, while at the same time the press and the media denounce the situation, images of violence, desperation and hopelessness are reinforced. Thus corruption, violence and crime unleash a menace that undermines Latin America's weakest democracies, while turning them into a test bed for other forms of governance. These often result from the interaction between national and local administration, on the one side, and civil society, on the other (Rotker, 2000, pp. 11, 16; Surel, 2011, pp. 149–150).

Urban Mosaics and Gated Communities

Combining signs of globalization with informality, often aggravated by political violence and crime, most Latin American cities stage the development and underdevelopment that their countries fluctuate between, but beyond that transitional condition, other general trends are difficult to pinpoint. Pushed by the 'centrifugal dynamics' of residential groups or 'dispersal' that persisted throughout the twentieth century in the biggest cities (Amato 1970; Bataillon and Rivière, 1973; Hardoy, 1997; Cerrutti and Bertoncello, 2003; Diez, 2007, for instance), a predominant feature arguably is the so-called 'fragmented' metropolis that now shows a more scattered and contrastive segregation than in the 'polarized' city of previous decades (Bähr and Borsdorf, 2005, pp. 212–213) (see also pp. 124–126, 128–133).[7] That fragmentation is nowadays marked by stronger barriers, contrasts and inequalities between the 'gated communities' and sectors that compound the urban mosaic (Roberts and Portes, 2008, pp. 528–529; Sabatini and Salcedo, 2011, p. 332).

The trend towards gated communities on the periphery of cities has intensified mainly in response to insecurity and congestion in their centres (Ludeña, 2011, pp. 80–81). Examples of 'private satellite towns' can be found in Alphaville in São Paulo, Nordelta in Buenos Aires and Piedra Roja in Santiago (de Mattos, 2010, pp. 261–262). However, gated communities have existed longer and with more dramatic manifestations in highly-contrastive and delinquency-stricken capitals such as Caracas, where the private enclosure of affluent suburbs dates back to the late 1980s (García-Guadilla, 2012). Partly due to its topography, the structure of Caracas is analogous to Rio's 'model of segregation', where those from very different social groups coexist in close spatial proximity; this closeness allows workers from *favelas* and *barrios* to access the labour market in the consolidated city (Ribeiro, 2003, pp. 305, 308).

The construction of shopping centres and high-rise office complexes that reproduce the architectural vocabulary of globalization is often reinforced, in the context of Latin America's contrastive metropolises, by security reasons that undermine high street public life. Such structures reach their zenith in Santiago's Costanera Center (figure 8.4), at 300 m South America's tallest skyscraper. However, in those parts of Latin America where neoliberalism has been opposed, there have been movements to recapture public

Figure 8.4 Costanera Center, Santiago. (*Photo*: CC Cristofer Daniel Ortega Urrutia)

Figure 8.5 Plaza Mayor and the cathedral, Lima. (*Photo*: CC Victoria Alexandra González Olaechea Yrigoyen)

spaces despite the 'spatial barriers' imposed by crime, segregation and gentrification. This 'street politics' has manifested in 'extraordinary events', such as the occupation of Mexico City's Zocalo by the Zapatistas or the marches for and against Chávez in Venezuela (see figure 8.1), all aimed at recovering democracy and citizenship in public spaces (Irazábal, 2008, pp. 14–16). Lima's Plaza Mayor provides another example but of a rather different nature: after the invasion of street vendors and merchants in the 1970s – most of them migrants from the Peruvian countryside – the 'synergy' among municipal government and social and economic groups made possible the regeneration of the centre in the mid-1990s (figure 8.5). But far from gentrifying the central district, this urban renewal invigorated the social and political significance of the Plaza Mayor and its surroundings, as demonstrated during the protests that prompted the demise of Fujimori's regime in 2000 (Chion and Ludeña, 2008, pp. 110–112; Ludeña, 2011, pp. 81, 95–98) (see also p. 154).

Trends of the 2000s

New Liberal Culture and New Left

By the mid-2000s, Latin America's political map seemed dominated by leftist governments, from Lula's Brazil and Kirchner's Argentina, via Chávez's Venezuela, to

Tabaré Vázquez's Uruguay. This 'political chessboard' was seconded by Ricardo Lagos's moderate socialism in Chile and offset by more conservative governments in Mexico, Colombia and Peru. In most countries, prior to the financial crisis in the United States and Europe, the biggest challenges were unemployment and insecurity, at least according to the Grupo de Diarios de América (GDA, Americas' Group of Newspapers, 2010). As pointed out above (see pp. 163–166), much of the leftwards shift was due to the resentment against neoliberal recipes of the 1990s, which were questioned by critics who advocated the adoption of economic globalization in a more equitable way (Touraine, 1999; Stiglitz, 2003).

Notwithstanding this political picture dominated by the left, observers such as Vargas Llosa noticed, in 2000s Latin America, a 'liberal culture' permeating socialist leaders and parties which had earlier advocated populism and nationalism. After Chile's Ricardo Lagos, who was always moderate, the best exponent of that new liberal culture was Brazil's Lula. As a candidate Lula 'preached a populist doctrine of economic nationalism and the left's traditional hostility towards the market', yet as president he turned into 'a militant of fiscal discipline, a promoter of foreign investment, of private enterprise and globalization' (Vargas, 2009, p. 333).[8] Such liberal culture among socialist regimes is concomitant with a 'new Latin American left', whose faces included the aforementioned rulers, completed by the later examples of Peru's Alan García in his second term, Uruguay's José Mujica and Brazil's Dilma Rousseff. Most significantly, despite having been members of guerrilla movements in their countries, Mujica and Rousseff share an adoption or continuation of the so-called 'Lula model' (GDA, 2010).

Leaders of Latin America's new left understand 'the importance of the market economy' without demonizing globalization, though they do criticize the financial excesses that generated the 2008 financial crisis. They also recognize innovation, efficiency and productivity as fundamental to economic success. While criticizing Anglo-Saxon capitalism and believing that more governmental regulation and intervention are required in order to reduce inequity, they are not staunch socialists and emulate 'policies of Western European social democracies' (Edwards, 2009, p. 20). In the geopolitical domain, Latin America's liberal culture has been accompanied by a shift in the attitude towards the United States, which in turn has understood that promotion of dictatorships is not the solution, as it used to be in the Cold War (Vargas, 2009, pp. 334–335). The United States has rather become a major ally, sponsor and adviser in terms of national security and the fight against crime in the cases of Colombia, El Salvador and other Central American governments (Surel, 2011, p. 152).

Despite this new climate, Washington retains for staunch radicals like the late Chávez and his followers, headed now by Bolivia's Evo Morales, resonances of the early-twentieth-century Caliban. Let us not forget in this respect that, in September 2006, in his intervention before the UN General Assembly in New York, Chávez referred to George W. Bush as 'the devil' (Momentos, 2013). This somehow echoed the anti-Yankee resentment of Venezuela's 1900s president Cipriano Castro, and other Latin American leaders of the Belle Époque and the rest of the century, as well as the *arielistas*' misgivings regarding the Colossus of the North (see pp. 39–44).

Economic Recovery and Perspectives

Latin America's new liberal political and economic trends were facilitated by an average growth rate of 5 per cent between 2003 and 2008. This growth was partly propelled by Asian demand, mainly Chinese, but was due more to the favourable terms of trade – especially in South America – than to the inflow of investment. However this commercial and financial openness has not eradicated protectionism, either in less interventionist countries – Chile, Mexico, Colombia and Peru – or in Brazil, which maintains ingredients of its mid-twentieth-century developmentalism when safeguarding national industry. But the most radical cases are Argentina and Venezuela, where much of the mid-2000s economic growth was due to the recovery of the internal demand after the crises suffered at the beginning of the decade (Quenan and Torrija-Zane, 2011, pp. 25–26, 30–32; Lyons and Magalhães, 2012).

During the boom, the investment rate in Latin America overall increased from 18 per cent of the GDP in 2001–2002 to 21 per cent in 2008, on the eve of the financial crash. At the same time, while the region's external debt was reduced, the internal one rose in cases such as Brazil. Even during the recession that followed the 2008 crisis, Latin America was arguably one of the world's least affected regions, only experiencing a brief recession of about 2 per cent in 2009; this was partly due to the fall in Mexico's GDP, which suffered the effects of its proximity to the United States. South America is instead more oriented towards China, which by 2015 may rank as the region's second commercial partner. The risk of this association lies in its being based on the exportation of raw materials, whose effects in the productive chain are sparse, especially when other staples of more aggregated and technical value are not diversified (Quenan and Torija-Zane, 2011, pp. 37, 68, 56–57, 72).

Besides its dependence on the exportation of commodities, other restrictions remain regarding Latin America's economic development. One of which is the high degree of macroeconomic volatility in contrast to low rates of growth, when compared with other emerging areas, notably Asia. There is also the low productivity in non-agricultural industries, mainly because of the lack of technological development and innovation. The latter can be inferred through the meagre budget allocated to research and development, which for Latin America altogether barely reached 0.7 per cent of GDP, whereas in South Korea, an outstanding example, it was more than 3 per cent. In addition, there is the region's low productive investment. Although this grew from about 17 per cent of the GDP in 2003 to 20 per cent in 2008, it is still below the 21 per cent reached during the ISI-driven period between 1950 and 1980, and is less than that of other emerging regions (Quenan and Torija-Zane, 2011, pp. 73–76).

Chile: Crossing the Third Wall

As the champion of Latin America's liberal culture and fight against underdevelopment, Chile has maintained neoliberal reforms and political stability since the 1990s. This combination has framed what president Michelle Bachelet called in her first term

(2006–2010) the 'central line' of a post-dictatorial Concertación that was predominantly socialist until Sebastián Piñera took over from her (Bachelet quoted in Correa, 2009). Besides democratic renewal and free-market economy, the increase in productivity is also at the basis of Chile's progress in terms of Schumpeter's phases of transition into growth and prosperity (see pp. 163–164). The country's public investment in machinery, equipment and infrastructure rose from 18 per cent in 1989 to 26 per cent by the mid-1990s. Together with economic growth that reached 7 per cent for the rest of the decade, these factors headed the nation – the only one in Latin America – into the 'second phase' of the transitional reforms; then 'the most important sources of growth are a combination of an improvement in productivity with an increase in the productive capacity through the accumulation of capital' (Edwards, 2009, p. 138). However, such economic growth was less dynamic between 2000 and 2007, when it reached an average 3.7 per cent, which made analysts rank it as 'solid' economy that was slowing down (Quenan and Torija-Zane, 2011, p. 29).

It is true that yawning gaps in income distribution persisted, which held Chile's Gini coefficient at 0.55 in 2003 (Edwards, 2009, p. 138). However, according to government figures, the population below the poverty line was reduced from 19 per cent in the mid-1990s to 15 per cent in 2011 (World Bank, 2006, p. 290). Having reached a per capita income above US$11,500 by 2005 and US$15,000 by the end of Bachelet's first term, comparable to some developed countries, together with an index of International Human Development (IHD) of 0.802 (PNUD, 2011) (see Appendices table 3), Chile was able to join the OECD in 2010. However, aware of the earlier failures of developing countries in the region, President Piñera confirmed that beyond being an active democracy and an open economy, Chile needs to cross the 'third wall' in its path towards development; by which he meant 'an efficient State capable in the fight against poverty and in the promotion of greater equal opportunities' (Piñera, 2011). It remains to be seen how long Chile will take to cross that third wall of inequality and become Latin America's first developed country, now that it has returned to socialist leaning, with the election of Michelle Barchelet for a second term (2014–2018).

Mexico against Kidnapping, Siesta and Dinosaurs

Not all liberal reforms in the 1990s proved as successful as Chile's. Perhaps Mexico is the country that, after its celebrated admission to the OECD and NAFTA, came to epitomize Latin America's frustrated development (see pp. 150–151, 167–168). Even though Vicente Fox – former Coca Cola executive – was elected president in 2000 with the support of the Partido de Acción Nacional (PAN, National Action Party), the PRI's populist influence persisted, along with more leftist factions represented by Andrés Manuel López Obrador. Economic growth meanwhile fell to an average 1.9 per cent between 2000 and 2008 (Edwards, 2009, p. 186). Part of this slowdown was because much of Mexican industrial produce competes with Chinese manufactures, which prompted the migration of many factories to Asia (Suchlicki, 2008, p. x). With the economic growth further reduced to 1 per cent by 2008, the country was also the epicentre of the H1N1 epidemic that affected tourism from 2009. Meanwhile, drug-related violence and decline in oil production accelerated Mexico's loss of leadership in world forums, especially during the presidency of Harvard-graduate Felipe Calderón (2006–2012), another PAN leader and former member of Fox's cabinets. The 'lost opportunities' have been said to result from Mexico's 'abduction' or control by *carteles* – not only drug cartels, but also 'private enterprises, unions, political groups, universities, communication means and professional associations that limit competition within their respective domains' (Naím, 2010).

Although Mexico reached an IHD of 0.770 by 2011 – fifty-seventh in the world (PNUD, 2011) (see Appendices table 3) – per capita income is still only one-sixth of that in the United States. At the same time, the fact that more than 20 per cent of the population remains below the poverty line since 1999, accounts for the uncontrolled emigration towards the north (World Bank, 2006, p. 291; Suchlicki, 2008, p. xi). The decline in economic growth and increase in poverty by 30 per cent during the last decade made PAN's Mexico appear to be taking a prolonged 'economic siesta' on the eve of the 2012 presidential contest (Palou, 2012). When the PRI candidate, Enrique Peña Nieto was elected, the Mexican intellectual Enrique Krauze paraphrased Vargas Llosa's 1992 assertion that Mexico was 'the perfect dictatorship' (Vargas Llosa, 2009, p. 64) (see also p. 151); he called it 'the imperfect democracy', inferring that the result signalled a democratic yet daunting scenario. Without ignoring the progress throughout the PAN era in terms of the autonomy of State powers, the PRI's challenge in its comeback is to reduce poverty, to eradicate the clientele-driven politics promoted by traditional 'dinosaurs' from provincial governments and unions, and to fight the vast monopolies that dominate the private sector (Krauze, 2012). From that perspective, the victory of Peña Nieto, 'grandson of the PRI' – playing with his second surname, which means 'grandson' in Spanish – is regarded as the crossroads between academic technocrats and PRI dinosaurs (Bastenier, 2012).[9]

Brazil: The Country of the Present

Having been derided over decades as 'the country of the future' – due to its recurrent yet frustrated take-off as an industrial and modernist giant – Brazil emerged as Latin America's power in the 2000s, in contrast to ailing Mexico and Argentina. With almost 25 per cent of the Brazilian population below the poverty line in 1995, there have been considerable improvements since the Cardoso administration, mainly because the existing forty million poor inhabitants now represent a lower proportion of the population, while the per capita income reached US$8,320 by 2005 (World Bank, 2006, pp. 288–290). Lula's sound social policies, alongside control of inflation and cancellation of the debt with the IMF, coincided with achieving self-sufficiency regarding fuel consumption (del Priore and Venancio, 2010, p. 300; Rodríguez, 2010, p. 2). Trying to escape from the curse of embezzlement and corruption that has haunted some petroleum-rich countries, after his re-election in 2006 Lula outlined the different scenario envisaged for Brazil's exploitation of its resources: 'Unlike traditional oil-producer states with large reserves, little technology and industry, a small internal market and much instability, we count on big reserves but have high technology, a diversified industrial basis, a vast internal market and, above all, stability' (Lula quoted in Rodríguez, 2010, p. 1).

The magnitude and importance of Brazil's economy has also been recognized on the international scene by its inclusion in the BRICS group, alongside Russia, India, China and South Africa. Between 2003 and 2008 the country grew at an annual average of 3.9 per cent, which was slightly slower than other BRICS members but still significant (Edwards, 2009, pp. 255–285). Helped by China's purchase of its commodities, Lula's Brazil expanded by 5 per cent in 2008, with twenty million people moving out of poverty, despite the effects of the forthcoming world crisis on its financial sector and economy (Naím, 2010). The growing volume of foreign investment suggests that moderate socialism can be attractive to global capital, and this is partly because the PT's social and political agenda, initially feared as the reincarnation of populism and nationalism, has respected the economic openness bequeathed by Cardoso (del Priore and Venancio, 2010, p. 295).

So Brazil is no longer 'the country of the future' but of the present, while its future continues to be promising and spectacular, especially with its hosting of the 2014 World Cup and 2016 Olympic Games. However, Brazil's economic growth, largely dependent on raw materials exports, the protection of some national industries, and the promotion of consumption through credit, had slowed to 2.7 per cent by 2011. At the opening of Dilma Rousseff's PT government (2011–2015), caution about economic expansion has been accentuated by misgivings concerning the country's capacity for internal saving and investment that could result in economic growth less dependent on foreign capital (Quenan and Torija-Zane, 2011, p. 46; Lyons and Magalhães, 2012). It is to be hoped that Rio's Olympic extravaganza does not become another mirage for Brazilian developmentalism, just as Brasilia's mid-twentieth modernism was mistaken for proof of maturity after the take-off (see p. pp. 103–106).

Argentina's Sisyphean Toil

Despite the traumas left by the 2001 crisis, by 2005 Argentina had a per capita income of US$13,920 and an IHD of 0.765, both among Latin America's highest (World Bank, 2006, p. 288; PNUD, 2011) (Appendices table 3). However, these figures masked the relative deterioration in the quality of life in the country and of its continental and international image, which were evident from, for instance, the decrease in foreign investments, which prior to the 2001 crisis had kept Argentina among the world's fifteen top recipients. And even though the economy grew 8.3 per cent between 2004 and 2008, this was the consequence of the dramatic contraction during the early years of the decade (Edwards, 2009, pp. 217, 297) (see also p. 171).

Reminiscent of Peron and his wife Isabel in the early 1970s (see pp. 141–142), the Argentina of Cristina Fernández de Kirchner – elected in 2007 as her husband's successor to the presidency – has deepened the conflicts caused by Peronist practices and populism. The country has also lost continental leadership and has aligned itself with anti-global positions promoted from Chávez's Venezuela. This is the case, for instance, with taxes on primary exports, which are allegedly diverted to the urban clientele of *kirchnerismo*, fuelling strikes and protests in the agrarian sector, which also brought the country to a standstill in March 2008. In view of such a dismal panorama, the migration of producers to neighbouring countries has resulted in Argentina losing its traditional leadership in the agrarian sector, to be overtaken by Brazil as Latin America's main beef exporter (Edwards, 2009, p. 219). Since her re-election in 2011, Mrs Kirchner has continued with the populist policy of nationalization of private enterprises – including the polemical case of the oil producer YPF, affiliate of the Spanish Repsol – as well as the return to draconian measures such as currency exchange controls, which so far has proved to be, as in previous episodes, ineffective in preventing the capital flight.

Despite substantial inflation and loss of economic and political leadership, Argentina still benefits from the social progress achieved in previous decades, which enabled it to boast an IHD of 0.797 in 2011 – forty-fifth in the world and second after Chile in Latin America (PNUD, 2011) (Appendices table 3). Thus, with hindsight, the continuing efforts of the country, which on several occasions almost achieved modernization and development and has shown resilience and recuperation after crises, have been compared by Argentine historian Luis Alberto Romero to 'a Sisyphean toil' (Romero, 1994, 2013, p. 295). It is an image that, *mutatis mutandis*, can be predicated for other Latin American countries.

Venezuela's Bolivarian Revolution

Although a secondary country for most of the twentieth century, Venezuela has become one of Latin America's best-known political test beds, mainly because of its eventful recent history and the anti-global stances of Chávez's Bolivarian Revolution (Irazábal and Foley, 2008, pp. 160–163). Particularly after the long yet unsuccessful general strike called by the opposition between 2003 and 2004, Chávez's 'Socialism of the Twenty-First Century' came closer to communism, including his failed attempt in 2007 to reform the constitution via referendum (Torres, 2010, pp. 186–187; Momentos, 2013). Regardless of this setback, the caudillo's discourse and actions turned more radically against capitalism, imperialism and globalization, while becoming politically closer to a 'presidential absolutism' (García-Guadilla, 2012, pp. 178–182; Gourdon, 2011, pp. 132–133). Due to their strong social orientation and the country's high income – oil prices went from US$15 in 1999 to US$135 in 2008 – the Revolution's *misiones* reduced poverty from more than 50 per cent of the population in 2003 to 27.6 in 2008. However, such a decrease has not been accompanied by the provision of employment and proportional alleviation of hunger, as was recommended by the UN Millennium Goals (Edwards, 2009, pp. 265–269; Cosío-Zavala, 2011, p. 100). However, in reaching an IHD of 0.735 and the seventy-third position in 2011, Venezuela had advanced in human development but reduced in social equity (Cardona, 2011).

In macroeconomic terms, Chávez's populist policies generated 30 per cent inflation by 2005, the highest ever seen in Latin America. Price regulations and currency exchange controls – implemented in 2003 as a reaction to the opposition's general strike – have often produced shortages of food and other basic items (Edwards, 2009, pp. 256, 264; Momentos, 2013). Despite the country's high oil revenue, the population's per capita income by 2005 was US$6,440, still below South American counterparts (World Bank, 2006, p. 289). After an average economic growth of 3.5 per cent between 1999 and 2007, Venezuela's GDP expanded 10.4 per cent from 2004 through 2008, largely as a consequence of the contraction during the 2002–2003 oil stoppage and general strike (Edwards, 2009, pp. 265, 297; Momentos, 2013). In retaliation to these events, the government sacked more than 17,000 highly qualified oil industry employees; they were also harassed and prevented from getting another job in their own country, forcing them to emigrate to Mexico, the Middle East and elsewhere.

Venezuela's brain drain continued after Chávez's re-election in October 2012 with nearly 55 per cent of the votes, which confirms the popular support that his Bolivarian Revolution held. Despite his death on 5 March the following year, his handpicked successor, Nicolás Maduro, seems to continue the *chavismo*'s costly combination of populism and clientelism, amidst increasing protests over shortages of goods, mounting inflation and uncontrolled violence.[10] The country has meanwhile been accepted in MERCOSUR, taking advantage of the temporary suspension in June 2012 of Paraguay – whose congress fiercely opposed Venezuela's access to the bloc because of Chávez's undemocratic credentials. Beyond the debatable economic benefits that this association will represent to the country, its left-wing radicalism is unlikely to be moderated by its partners from MERCOSUR and UNASUR (Union of South American Nations). The latter has mediated after the regime's brutal repression of civil protests since February 2014, which staunch critics like Vargas Llosa deem a 'totalitarian' threat not only to Venezuelan opposition but also to the region's 'fragile and weak' democracies (quoted in Collyns, 2014). Despite political criticisms, the Bolivarian Revolution has become referential for other countries in Latin America, from small states like Bolivia, Ecuador and Nicaragua, to more distant giants like Argentina, in all of which social inequities have been reduced by the most in the region (Cosío-Zavala, 2011, p. 101).

Between Statism and Free Market

As a reaction to Bolivarian Venezuela and its followers, other countries seem to have accelerated their neoliberal reforms. Colombia continued its fight against guerrilla and *narcotráfico* during the administrations of Álvaro Uribe (2002–2010), when the per capita income reached US$7,400 by 2005 and the poverty was reduced from 64 per cent in 1999 to 42.8 per cent in 2008 (World Bank, 2009, pp. 288, 290; Cosío-Zavala, 2011, p. 100). After the economic expansion between 2002 and 2008, especially in the energy and construction sectors, the country recovered from recession and, during the government of Juan Manuel Santos (2010–2014) seems to maintain the same model of development, which will require further investment and internal saving (Quenan and Torija-Zane, 2011, p. 63). Also aligned in this direction is Peru, where the administration of Ollanta Humala (2011–2016) – despite coming to power with the support of the PNP or Peruvian Nationalist Power, initially feared as an extension of the *chavismo*'s anti-global position – has distanced itself from the Bolivarian Revolution. Furthermore, the country has reinforced its move towards the free market, though in addition to 36.2 per cent of poverty by 2008, it will have to continue coping with the informal economy and the remains of terrorism (Ludeña, 2011; Cosío-Zavala, 2011, p. 100).

Some Central American countries also embraced democracy and the free market after the era of guerrillas and civil wars that ended in the early 1990s, though their progress along this way has been hindered by structural deficiencies or political hesitations. Liberal culture early penetrated El Salvador, for instance, where President Alfredo Cristiani (1989–1994) launched a programme of economic openness and modernization inspired by the Chilean model, and actually advised by former Chicago Boys. Having reached an average annual growth of 6.8 per cent between 1992 and 1995, in contrast to 2.5 per cent during the previous five years, the tiny republic was not able, however, to renovate its infrastructure through investment. Aggravated by China's competition to Salvadoran *maquilas*, the infrastructure deficiency, together with institutional weakness and persistent corruption, has hindered economic modernization. In the social domain, 47 per cent of the population remained under the poverty line in 2008 – even more than the 43 per cent during the war in the late 1980s – while the Gini coefficient was 0.52 (Cosío-Zavala, 2011, p. 100; Edwards, 2009, pp. 143–145). Persistence of poverty and corruption, alongside deficiencies in education, has also challenged the development of Panama, which adopted the US dollar as a national currency and resumed control of the canal in 1999. Achieving 8 per cent economic growth from 2005 through 2010, the country of 3.5 million inhabitants has experienced a profound process of liberalization of its tertiary-oriented economy, aspiring to emulate the model of Singapore (GDA, 2011).

Not only demonstrated by the economic alignment of Nicaragua and Bolivia with Venezuela's Bolivarian Revolution, the dilemmas between statism and free market have also affected the political stability of other Latin American countries. After the dictatorships, civil wars and guerrilla threats of the Cold War, followed by the presidential impeachments of the early 1990s, the fragile constitutional continuity of some Latin American countries has been tested recently by other upheavals. Following Chávez's alleged 'resignation' in 2002, the impeachments of Manuel Zelaya in Honduras in June 2009 and of Fernando Lugo in Paraguay in June 2011 – sanctioned by the judiciary and the legislative powers, respectively – were denounced by presidential supporters as right-wing manoeuvres against the state-led and socialist projects represented by those leaders (Gourdon, 2011). Beyond the polemics about their constitutionality, those events certainly reflect the fears of communism among conservative sectors, whereas, on the opposite side of the political spectrum, imperialism and now globalization continue to be demonized by the radical left. At the same time, those episodes highlight the historical disagreements and obstacles still haunting democratic development. Having recently celebrated two centuries of republican life, most Latin American republics, now demographically urbanized, still face the dilemma of whether modernization and development are to be attained through free-market or state-oriented models.

Notes

1. A phrase coined by the Austrian economist Joseph Schumpeter, 'Creative Destruction' describes the traumatic condition by which economic growth is often catalysed. As 'the essential fact about capitalism', in Schumpeter's words, this revolution of the economic structure must be brought about *from within*, incessantly destroying the old one' (Schumpeter, 1943, 2010, p. 73).
2. The 'aspirational constitutions' are deemed as descendant from J.J. Rousseau's social contracts, unlike the 'protective constitutions' that try to preserve the nation's historic achievements and conquests, the main of which is Montesquieu's three-power state (Edwards, 2009, pp. 233–234; Brewer-Carías, 1975).
3. 'Raza, botas y nacionalismo' (January 2006).
4. There had been four republics in Venezuelan history since the first was declared in 1811; the Fourth Republic, established by the 1961 constitution and shaped politically by the 1958 Puntofijo Pact that followed Pérez Jiménez's dictatorship (see pp. 116–117), became the political establishment abhorred by Chávez and his followers.
5. World Bank groups of economies include low income (LIC), US$875 per annum or less; lower middle income (LMC), $876–3,465 per annum; upper middle income (UMC), $3,466–10,725 per annum; high income (HC), $10,726 per annum or more.
6. As a consequence of the decrease in fertility rate and the completion of demographic transition, the 'demographic dividend' is a limited period during which dependent population lowers in relation to those in productive age (Cosío-Zavala, 2011, p. 95).
7. These authors distinguish four periods and 'models' for the physical and social structures of Latin American cities: the 'compact' colonial city; the 'sectorial' city (1820–1950); the 'polarized' city (1950–1990), and the 'fragmented' city (Bähr and Borsdof, 2005).
8. 'Confesiones de un liberal' (March 2005).
9. Peña Nieto has also confessed to being an admirer of past president Ávila Camacho as exponent of the prosperous Mexico of the 1940s (see p. 90).
10. According to UNODOC's 2013 report, Venezuela has become the world's second most violent country after Honduras, holding a rate of 57 homicides per 100,000 inhabitants (Molina, 2014).

Appendices

Initials and Acronyms

AD	Democratic Action (Venezuela)
AFP	Alliance for Progress
ALALC, ALADI	Latin American Association of Free Trade
APRA	America's Revolutionary and Popular Alliance (Peru)
BO	Workers' Bank (Venezuela)
BRICS	Brazil, Russia, India, China, South Africa
BRT	Bus Rapid Transit
CCTP	Conditional Cash Transfer Programmes
CIA	Central Intelligence Agency (USA)
CIAM	Congresses of International Modern Architecture
COPEI	Social Christian Party (Venezuela)
CORFO	Corporation for the Promotion of Production (Chile)
DASP	Administrative Department of Public Service (Brazil)
ECLAC, CEPAL	Economic Commission for Latin America and the Caribbean
EFU	École Française d'Urbanisme or French School of Urbanism
ELN	National Liberation Army (Colombia)
EZLN	Zapatista Army of National Liberation (Mexico)
FARC	Colombia's Revolutionary Armed Forces
FMLN	Farabundo Marti Front for National Liberation (El Salvador)
FSLN	Sandinist Front of National Liberation (Nicaragua)
GATT	General Agreement on Tariffs and Trade
GDP	Gross Domestic Product
Habitat	United Nations Centre for Human Settlements
ICA	International Congress of Americanists
IDB, IADB	Inter-American Development Bank
IESA	Institute of High Studies on Management (Venezuela)
IHD	International Human Development
IHTPC	International Housing and Town Planning Congresses
IMF	International Monetary Fund
ISI	Import Substitution Industrialization
M–19	Movement 19 April (Colombia)
MBR200	Revolutionary Bolivarian Movement (Venezuela)
MCC, CACM	Central American Common Market
MERCOSUR	Common Market of the South

MRTA	Tupac Amaru Revolutionary Movement (Peru)
NAFTA	North American Free Trade Agreement
NIN	New National Ideal (Venezuela)
OEA, OAS	Organization of American States
OECD	Organization for Economic Cooperation and Development
OPEC	Organization of the Petroleum Exporting Countries
PAN	National Autonomist Party (Argentina)
PAN	National Action Party (Mexico)
PC	Communist Party (Chile)
PDVSA	Venezuela's Petroleum Company
PEMEX	Mexican Petroleum
PETROBRAS	Brazilian Petroleum
PRD	Democratic Revolutionary Party (Mexico)
PRI	Revolutionary Institutional Party (Mexico)
PT	Workers' Party (Brazil)
SELA	Latin American Economic System
SME	Small to Medium-Sized Enterprises
TPA	Town Planning Associates
TVA	Tennessee Valley Authority (USA)
UCR	Radical Civic Unity (Argentina)
UN	United Nations
UNASUR	Union of South American Nations
UNESCO	United Nations Educational, Scientific and Cultural Organization
UP	Popular Unity (Chile)
USAID	US Agency for International Development
USSR	Union of Soviet Socialist Republics
WB	World Bank
WEF	World Economic Forum

Dramatis Personae

Abercrombie, Sir Patrick (1879–1957) English town planner and literary critic
Agache, Donat-Alfred (1875–1959) French urbanist
Aguirre Cerda, Pedro (1879–1941) Chilean lawyer, minister and President
Alberdi, Juan Bautista (1810–1884) Argentine political thinker
Albers, Josef (1888–1976) German-born American artist and educator
Alegría, Ciro (1909–1967) Peruvian writer and politician
Alemán, Miguel (1900–1983) Mexican lawyer and President
Alessandri Palma, Arturo (1868–1950) Twice President of Chile
Alessandri Rodríguez, Jorge (1896–1986) Chilean engineer, entrepreneur and President
Alfaro, Eloy (1842–1912) President of Ecuador
Alfonsín, Raúl (1927–2009) Argentine lawyer, UCR leader and first democratic President after the military Proceso
Allende, Salvador (1908–1973) Chilean physician, leader of the UP and President
Altamirano Talavera, Luis (1876–1938) Chilean military
Alvear, Torcuato de (1822–1890) Argentine politician and mayor of Buenos Aires
Amaral, Tarsila do (1886–1973) Brazilian painter, founder of Modernism
Andrade, Mario de (1893–1945) Brazilian writer, founder of Modernism
Andrade, Oswald de (1890–1954) Brazilian poet, founder of Modernism
Anhaia Mello, Luís de (1891–1974) Brazilian urbanist, politician and academic
Arbenz, Jacobo (1913–1971) Guatemalan military and President
Arcaya, Pedro Manuel (1874–1958) Venezuelan sociologist, minister and diplomat of the Gomez regime
Arguedas, José María (1911–1969) Peruvian writer and anthropologist
Aristiguieta Montero, R., Venezuelan politician
Arlt, Roberto (1900–1942) Argentine writer
Asturias, Miguel Ángel (1899–1974) Guatemalan writer and Nobel laureate
Ávila Camacho, Manuel (1896–1955) Mexican military and President
Aylwin, Patricio (1918–) Chilean lawyer and first President after Pinochet's dictatorship
Azuela, Mariano (1873–1952) Mexican physician and writer

Bachelet, Michelle (1951–) Chilean physician, diplomat and twice President
Balmaceda, José Manuel (1840–1891) 11th President of Chile
Barbosa, Rui (1849–1923) Brazilian lawyer, politician and minister
Barco, Virgilio (1921–1997) Colombian engineer and President
Bardet, Gaston (1907–1989) French urbanist and writer
Barrientos, René (1919–1969) Bolivian military and de facto President
Bartholomew, Harland (1889–1989) American urban planner
Basadre, Jorge (1903–1980) Peruvian historian and minister
Bassols, Narciso (1897–1959) Mexican lawyer and politician
Batista, Fulgencio (1901–1973) Cuban military, President and dictator
Batlle y Ordóñez, José (1856–1929) Leader of the Colorado Party and twice President of Uruguay
Beauvoir, Simone de (1908–1986) French philosopher and feminist
Belaúnde Terry, Fernando (1912–2002) Peruvian architect and twice President
Bell, Purl Lord (1886–1930) American diplomat
Benjamin, Walter (1892–1940) German-Jewish literary critic and philosopher
Bernard, Émile (1868–1941) French painter and architect working in Mexico

Betancourt, Rómulo (1908–1981) Venezuelan politician, writer and twice President
Betancur, Belisario (1923–) Colombian lawyer, writer and President
Bilbao, Francisco (1823–1865) Chilean politician and writer
Bioy Casares, Adolfo (1914–1999) Argentine writer
Blanco, Andrés Eloy (1897–1955) Venezuelan poet, humorist and politician
Blanco Fombona, Rufino (1874–1944) Venezuelan poet and novelist
Blest Gana, Alberto (1830–1920) Chilean novelist and diplomat
Boari, Adamo (1863–1928) Italian architect and engineer established in Mexico
Bolívar, Simón (1783–1830) Venezuelan military and liberator of Bolivia, Colombia, Ecuador, Peru and Venezuela
Borges, Jorge Luis (1899–1986) Argentine writer
Borja, Jordi (1941–) Spanish sociologist, politician and former mayor of Barcelona
Bosch, Juan (1909–2001) Dominican lawyer, historian, writer and President
Bouvard, Joseph Antoine (1840–1920) French architect and landscape designer
Bowen, Herbert Wolcott (1856–1927) US Envoy Extraordinary and Minister Plenipotentiary to Venezuela
Brady, Nicholas (1930–) American economist and Secretary of the Treasury for the Ronald Reagan and George Bush administrations
Brito, Saturnino de (1864–1929) Brazilian sanitary engineer
Brunner, Karl (1887–1960) Austrian town planner working in Chile, Colombia and Panama
Buarque de Holanda, Sergio (1902–1982) Brazilian social scientist and writer
Büchi, Hernán (1949–) Chilean engineer and minister of the Pinochet regime
Bulnes, Francisco (1847–1924) Mexican writer and politician
Burchard, Martin, French developer established in São Paulo
Burgess, Ernest (1886–1966) American sociologist and member of the Chicago School
Bush, George (1924–) 41st President of the United States
Bush, George W. (1946–) 46th President of the United States

Cabrera, Lydia (1899–1981) Cuban anthropologist and writer
Caldera, Rafael (1916–2009) Venezuelan lawyer, sociologist and twice President
Calderón, Felipe (1962–) Mexican lawyer, PAN co-founder and President
Calles, Plutarco Elías (1877–1945) Mexican educator, military and President
Calvino, Ítalo (1923–1985) Italian journalist and writer
Câmara, Helder (1909–1999) Brazilian bishop and theologian of the Liberation
Cámpora, Héctor (1909–1980) Argentine dentist and President in 1973
Canal Feijoo, Bernardo (1897–1982) Argentine lawyer and writer
Cané, Miguel (1851–1905) Argentine writer, diplomat and politician
Cárdenas, Cuauhtémoc (1934–) Mexican engineer, politician and founder of the Democratic Revolutionary Party (PRD)
Cárdenas, Lázaro (1895–1970) Mexican military and President
Cardoso, Fernando H. (1931–) Brazilian sociologist, member of the School of Dependence and twice President
Carmagnani, Marcello (1940–) Italian economic historian specialized in Latin America
Carpentier, Alejo (1904–1980) Cuban journalist and writer
Carranza, Venustiano (1859–1921) Mexican revolutionary and President
Carril, Bonifacio del (1911–1994) Argentine lawyer, minister and diplomat
Carvajal, Carlos (1872–1950) Chilean engineer

Castelo Branco, Humberto (1897–1967) Brazilian military and de facto President
Castro, Cipriano (1858–1924) Venezuelan military and President
Castro, Fidel (1926–) Cuban military and leader of the Revolution, later prime minister and President of the country
Cavallo, Domingo (1946–) Argentine economist, minister and politician
Cerdá, Ildefonso (1815–1876) Spanish urban planner designer of Barcelona's *ensanche*
Chávez, Hugo (1954–2013) Venezuelan military and three-time President
Choay, Françoise (1925–) French architectural and urban historian
Cienfuegos, Camilo (1932–1959) Cuban revolutionary
Cleveland, Grover (1837–1908) 22nd and 24th President of the United States
Clinton, William 'Bill' (1946–) 42nd President of the United States
Collor de Mello, Fernando (1949–) Brazilian politician and President
Colosio, Luis Donaldo (1950–1994) Mexican economist, politician and PRI candidate
Comte, Auguste (1798–1857) French philosopher and founder of positivism
Coni, Emilio (1855–1928) Argentine physician
Contreras Elizondo, Carlos (1892–1970) Mexican architect and town planner
Correa, Rafael (1963–) Ecuadorian economist and President
Cortázar, Julio (1914–1984) Belgian-born Argentine writer and author of the novel *Rayuela*
Costa, Lúcio (1902–1998) French-born Brazilian architect, designer of Brasilia
Cravotto, Mauricio (1863–1962) Uruguayan architect and urbanist
Cremonesi, Ignazio (1866–1949) Italian architect established in Chile
Cristiani, Alfredo (1947–) Salvadoran businessman and President
Cruz, Oswaldo (1872–1917) Brazilian physician and epidemiologist
Cunha, Euclides da (1886–1909) Brazilian sociologist, engineer and writer
Currie, Lauchlin (1902–1993) Canadian-born American economist working in Colombia as WB representative

D'Annunzio, Gabriele (1863–1938) Italian nationalist and writer
Darío, Rubén (1867–1916) nom de plume of Félix Rubén García Sarmiento, Nicaraguan poet and journalist
Darwin, Charles (1809–1882) English naturalist founder of the Evolutionist theory
Daudet, Alphonse (1840–1897) French novelist
Dávila Boza, Ricardo (1850–1937) Chilean physician and public health expert
Davis, Kingsley (1908–1997) American sociologist
de Castro, Sergio (1930–) Chilean engineer, economist, academic and minister of the Pinochet regime
de Mattos, Carlos Uruguayan-born architect, planner and academic working in Chile
de Ramón, Armando (1927–2004) Chilean historian and academic
Delgado Chalbaud, Carlos (1909–1950) Venezuelan military and president of junta
Díaz, Porfirio (1830–1915) Mexican military and President
Díaz Ordaz, Gustavo (1911–1979) Mexican lawyer and President
Díaz Rodríguez, Manuel (1871–1927) Venezuelan writer
Dilthey, Wilhelm (1833–1911) German historian and philosopher
Domínguez, Cipriano (1904–1995) Venezuelan architect
Dos Santos, Theotonio (1936–) Brazilian sociologist and founder of the Theory of Dependence
Doyère, Emilio, French architect resident in Chile

Duhalde, Eduardo (1941–) Argentine lawyer and President
Duras, Marguerite (1914–1996) Nom de plume de Marguerite Donnadieu, French writer and film director
Dutra, Gaspar (1883–1974) Brazilian military and President

Echeverría, Esteban (1805–1851) Argentine writer
Echeverría, Luis (1922–) Mexican lawyer and President
Edwards, Jorge (1931–) Chilean journalist, writer and diplomat
Edwards, Sebastián (1953–) Chilean economist, academic and novelist
Edwards Bello, Joaquín (1887–1968) Chilean writer
Egaña, Mariano (1793–1846) Chilean lawyer and author of constitution
Eisenhower, Dwight D. (1890–1969) American General and 24th President of the United States
Ernesto, Pedro, Brazilian politician
Escobar, Pablo (1949–1993) Colombian politician, entrepreneur and drug trafficker, founder of the Medellin Cartel
Estrada Cabrera, Manuel (1857–1924) Guatemalan President
Eyzaguirre, Jaime (1908–1968) Chilean historian

Faletto, Enzo (1935–2003) Chilean historian and sociologist, member of the School of Dependence and ECLAC
Fasileau-Duplantier, Amon, French-born developer established in Costa Rica
Fernández, Macedonio (1874–1952) Argentine writer
Ferrari Hardoy, Jorge (1914–1977) Argentine modernist architect, member of the Austral group
Figueiredo, João Batista (1918–1999) Brazilian military and President
Forestier, Jean-Claude Nicholas (1861–1930) French landscape architect
Fox, Vicente (1942–) Mexican businessman and President that ended the PRI hegemony
France, Anatole (1844–1924, Anatole François Thibault) French writer
Franco, Itamar (1930–2011) Brazilian politician and President
Franco, Jean (1924–) British-born academic and critic on Latin American literature
Frank, André Gunder (1929–2005) German sociologist, founder of the School of Dependence
Frank, Waldo (1889–1967) American writer
Fraser, Valerie, English art historian and academic specialized in Latin America
Frei Montalva, Eduardo (1911–1982) Chilean lawyer and President
Freud, Sigmund (1856–1939) Austrian neurologist, founder of psychoanalysis
Freyre, Gilberto (1900–1987) Brazilian anthropologist and academic
Friedman, Milton (1912–2006) American economist, academic and Nobel laureate
Friedmann, John (1926–) Austrian-born American planner and academic
Frondizi, Arturo (1908–1995) Argentine lawyer and President
Frontin, André Paulo de (1860–1933) Brazilian engineer
Fuentes, Carlos (1928–2012) Mexican writer
Fujimori, Alberto (1938–) Peruvian engineer and President of Japanese descent
Furtado, Celso (1920–2004) Brazilian economist and minister, member of the School of Dependence

Gache, Samuel (1859–1907) Argentine physician

Gaitán, Jorge Eliécer (1903–1948) Colombian politician whose murder unleashed the Bogotazo
Gallegos, Rómulo (1884–1969) Venezuelan novelist and President
Galtieri, Leopoldo (1996–2003) Argentine military and president of junta
Gálvez, Manuel (1882–1962) Argentine writer
García, Alan (1949–) Peruvian lawyer, sociologist and twice President
García Calderón, Francisco (1883–1953) Peruvian historian and diplomat
García Márquez, Gabriel (1927–2014) Colombian writer and Nobel laureate
García Moreno, Gabriel (1821–1875) Twice President of Ecuador
Garnier, Charles (1825–1898) French architect
Garrastazu Médici, Emílio (1905–1985) Brazilian military and de facto President
Gaviria, César (1947–) Colombian economist, President and Secretary General of the OAS
Gayol, Roberto (1857–1936) Mexican engineer
Geddes, Patrick (1854–1932) Scottish biologist, sociologist and urbanist
Geisel, Ernesto (1907–1996) Brazilian military and President
Germani, Gino (1911–1979) Italian sociologist established in Argentina
Gil Fortoul, José (1861–1943) Venezuelan lawyer and sociologist and collaborator of the Gómez regime
Gómez, Juan Vicente (1908–1935) Venezuelan military and President
Gómez, Laureano (1889–1965) Colombian engineer and President
Gómez Carrillo, Enrique (1873–1927) Guatemalan writer
González Videla, Gabriel (1898–1980) Chilean lawyer and President
Gorelik, Adrián (1957–) Argentine architect and urban historian
Gropius, Walter (1863–1969) German modernist architect, founder of the Bauhaus School
Goulart, João (1919–1976) Brazilian left-wing politician and President
Guerrero, Vicente (1782–1831) Mexican politician
Guevara, Ernesto 'Che' (1928–1967) Argentine-born leader of the Cuban Revolution
Guillén, Nicolás (1902–1989) Cuban poet and political activist
Guimarães, Ulysses (1916–1992) Brazilian lawyer and politician, champion of the 1988 Constitution
Güiraldes, Ricardo (1886–1927) Argentine writer
Gutiérrez, Lucio (1957–) Ecuadorian engineer, military and President
Guzmán Blanco, Antonio (1829–1899) Three times Venezuelan President

Habsburg, Maximilian of (1832–1867) Austrian-born Emperor of Mexico
Harberger, Arnold C. (1924–) American economist and academic
Hardoy, Jorge Enrique (1926–1993) Argentine architect and urban historian
Harth-Terré, Emilio (1899–1983) Peruvian architect and writer
Harvey, David (1935–) British geographer and social scientist
Hauser, Philip (1910–1994) American demographer and academic
Haussmann, George E., Baron (1809–1891) French politician, Prefect of the Seine during the Second Empire
Haya de la Torre, Víctor (1895–1979) Peruvian politician and founder of APRA
Hegemann, Werner (1881–1936) German town planner and writer
Hénard, Eugène (1849–1923) French urbanist
Henríquez Ureña, Pedro (1889–1959) Dominican philologist, critic and writer

Herrera, Felipe (1922–1996) Chilean lawyer, economist and politician
Herrera Campins, Luis (1925–2007) Venezuelan lawyer and President
Hirschman, Albert (1915–) German economist specialized in development
Hitchcock, Henry-Russell (1903–1987) American art historian and curator
Ho Chi Minh (1890–1969) Vietnamese revolutionary and President
Hommes, Rudolf (1944–) Colombian economist, academic and Treasurer of the Gaviria administration
Howard, Ebenezer (1850–1928) English social reformer and advocate of the Garden City
Huerta, Victoriano (1854–1916) Mexican revolutionary and President
Huidobro, Vicente (1893–1948) Chilean poet
Humala, Ollanta (1962–) Peruvian retired military and President

Ibáñez del Campo, Carlos (1877–1960) Chilean military and twice President
Illía, Arturo (1900–1983) Argentine physician and President
Iturbide, Agustín de (1783–1824) Mexican military, politician and regent

Jaussely, Léon (1875–1933) French architect and urbanist
Jecquier, Émile (1866–1949) French-born Chilean architect
Juárez, Benito (1806–1872) Mexican lawyer, reformer and President
Justo, Agustín Pedro (1876–1943) Argentine military, diplomat and President

Keiserling, Hermann (1880–1946) German philosopher
Kennedy, John F. (1917–1963) 35th President of the United States
Keynes, John Maynard (1883–1946) English economist
Kidd, Benjamin (1858–1916) British sociologist and philosopher
Kirchner, Cristina Fernández de (1953–) Argentine lawyer and first woman elected President
Kirchner, Néstor (1950–2010) Argentine lawyer and President
Kissinger, Henry (1923–) German-born American diplomat and Nobel laureate, US Secretary of State
Krauze, Enrique (1947–) Mexican engineer, historian and editor
Kubitschek, Juscelino (1902–1976) Brazilian President and sponsor of Brasilia
Kurchan, Juan (1913–1972) Argentine modernist architect, member of the Austral Group

Lagos, Ricardo (1938–) Chilean lawyer, economist, diplomat and President
Lambert, Jacques (1891–?) French urbanist working in Chile and Venezuela
Lanusse, Alejandro (1918–1996) Argentine military and President
Larraín Bravo, Ricardo (1879–1945) Chilean architect specialized in hygiene
Lastarria, José Victorino (1817–1888) Chilean politician and writer
Lawrence, David Herbert (1885–1930) English writer
Lebret, Joseph (1897–1966) French Dominican father and economist, advocate of the Economy and Humanism movement
Le Corbusier (1887–1965), (Charles Édouard Jeanneret) Swiss-born French architect and urbanist, pioneer of modern architecture
Legarreta, Juan (1908–1934) Mexican architect
Leguía, Augusto (1863–1932) Peruvian businessman, minister and President

Leoni, Raúl (1905–1972) Venezuelan lawyer and President
Le Play, Frédéric (1806–1882) French engineer, sociologist and economist
Lerdo de Tejada, Miguel (1812–1861) Mexican minister and liberal politician
Lesseps, Ferdinand de (1805–1894) French entrepreneur and diplomat
Lewis, Oscar (1914–1970) American historian and anthropologist, advocate of the culture of poverty
Liceaga, Eduardo (1839–1920) Mexican physician
Lima Barreto, Alfonso de (1881–1922) Brazilian writer
Limantour, José (1854–1935) Mexican politician and Secretary of Finance during the Porfiriato
Lleras Camargo, Alberto (1906–1990) Colombian lawyer and twice President, first Secretary of the OAS
Lleras Restrepo, Carlos (1908–1994) Colombian lawyer and President
López, Lucio (1826–1894) Uruguayan-born politician and writer established in Argentina
López Contreras, Eleazar (1883–1973) Venezuelan military and first President after the Gómez regime
López Mateos, Adolfo (1910–1969) Mexican lawyer and President
López Obrador, Andrés Manuel (1953–) Mexican politician and former mayor of Mexico City
López Portillo, José (1920–2004) Mexican lawyer and President
López Pumarejo, Alfonso (1886–1959) Colombian entrepreneur and twice President
Lugo, Fernando (1951) Paraguayan sociologist, former bishop and President
Lugones, Leopoldo (1874–1938) Argentine writer and politician
Lula da Silva, Luiz Inácio (1945–) Brazilian syndicalist, founder of the PT and twice President
Luna, Félix (1925–2009) Argentine historian and writer
Lusinchi, Jaime (1924–) Venezuelan pediatrician and President
Lynch, Benito (1880–1951) Argentine writer

Machado, Gerardo (1871–1939) Cuban military and President
Machado de Assis, Joaquim (1839–1908) Brazilian writer
Madero, Francisco (1873–1913) Mexican lawyer, revolutionary and first President of the Revolution
Maduro, Nicolás (1962–) Venezuelan syndicalist, politician and President
Mao Zedong (1893–1976) Chinese revolutionary, chairman of the Communist Party and Founder of the Popular Republic of China
Marcos, Sub-commander Combat name of Rafael Sebastián Guillén, Mexican revolutionary, leader and spokesman of the EZLN
Mariátegui, José Carlos (1895–1930) Peruvian writer and communist thinker
Mármol, José (1818–1871) Argentine writer and politician
Martí, Agustín Farabundo (1893–1932) Salvadoran communist politician
Martí, José (1853–1895) Cuban political hero of Independence and modernist writer
Martínez de Hoz, José Alfredo (1925–) Argentine economist and minister of the military Proceso
Martínez Estrada, Ezequiel (1895–1964) Argentine writer
Martínez Inclán, Pedro (1883–1957) Cuban architect and urbanist
Martínez Olavarría, Leopoldo (1919–1992) Venezuelan architect and urbanist

Marulanda, Manuel or Tirofijo (1930–2008) Combat names of Pedro Antonio Marín, Colombian revolutionary, co-founder and commander of the FARC
Marx, Karl (1818–1883) German philosopher and father of scientific socialism and communism
Maupassant, Guy de (1850–1893) French writer
Mazzini, Giuseppe (1805–1872) Italian politician and hero of the Risorgimento
McGovern, George (1922–2012) American historian and politician
McKinley, William (1843–1901) 25th President of the United States
Medina Angarita, Isaías (1897–1953) Venezuelan military and President
Medina Febres, Mariano (1912–1976) Venezuelan physician and cartoonist also known as Medo
Menem, Carlos Saúl (1930–) Argentine congressman and twice President
Meneses, Guillermo (1911–1978) Venezuelan writer
Meyer, Hans Emil 'Hannes' (1889–1954) Swiss architect and director of Bauhaus
Mirbeau, Octave (1848–1917) French writer
Mistral, Gabriela (1889–1957) Nom de plume de Lucila Godoy, Chilean pedagogue, poet, diplomat and Nobel laureate
Mitre, Bartolomé (1821–1906) Argentine military, historian and President
Mitterrand, François (1916–1996) French socialist politician and twice President
Monroe, James (1758–1831) Fifth President of the United States and sponsor of the Monroe Doctrine
Montesquieu, Charles de Secondat, Baron de (1689–1755) French political philosopher
Montigny, Grandjean de (1776–1850) French architect established in Rio
Montt, Manuel (1809–1880) Twice President of Chile
Moral, Enrique del (1906–1987) Mexican architect
Morales, Juan Evo (1959–) Bolivian syndicalist and President
Morris, Ira Nelson (1857–1942) American traveller
Morse, Richard (1922–2001) American scholar and humanist
Moses, Robert (1888–1981) American urban planner and 'master builder' of New York City
Mujica, José (1935–) Uruguayan revolutionary, politician and President
Mulhall, Michael G. (1836–1900) British traveller and envoy
Mumford, Lewis (1895–1990) American journalist, humanist and scholar
Myrdal, Gunnar (1898–1987) Swedish economist and Nobel laureate

Navarro Wolff, Antonio (1948–) Colombian engineer, politician and former leader of the M-19
Neruda, Pablo (1904–1973) Nom de plume de Ricardo Neftalí Reyes, Chilean writer, politician, diplomat and Nobel laureate
Neutra, Richard (1892–1970) Austrian modernist architect
Niemeyer, Oscar (1907–2012) Brazilian modernist architect and designer of Brasilia
Nixon, Richard (1913–1994) American lawyer and 37th President of the United States
Noriega, Manuel (1934–) Panamanian military and dictator ousted from power by a US invasion
Nothmann, Victor, German entrepreneur established in Brazil between 1859 and 1905

Obregón, Álvaro (1880–1928) Mexican military, revolutionary and President
Ocampo, Silvina (1903–1993) Argentine writer

Ocampo, Victoria (1890–1979) Argentine intellectual and founder of Sur magazine
O'Gorman, Juan (1905–1982) Mexican architect and painter
O'Higgins, Bernardo (1778–1842) Chilean military, liberator and director of the country
Oliveira Viana, Francisco de (1883–1951) Brazilian sociologist and historian
Olmsted, Frederick Law (1822–1903) American landscape designer
Onganía, Juan Carlos (1914–1995) Argentine military and de facto President
Orozco, José Clemente (1883–1949) Mexican painter and muralist
Orrego, Antenor (1892–1960) Peruvian politician and writer
Ortega, Daniel (1945–) Nicaraguan revolutionary and twice President
Ortiz, Fernando (1881–1969) Cuban anthropologist and writer
Ortiz Monasterio, Manuel, Mexican architect
Otero Silva, Miguel (1908–1985) Venezuelan journalist and writer
Oyarzun Philippi, Rodulfo (1895–1985) Chilean architect, urbanist and academic

Padilla, Heberto (1932–2000) Cuban writer and dissident
Palafox, Silvano, Mexican architect
Pani, Mario (1911–1993) Mexican architect
Paolera, Carlos della (1890–1960) Argentine architect and urbanist
Pardo Bazán, Emilia (1851–1921) Spanish writer and scholar
Park, Robert E. (1864–1944) American sociologist, member of the Chicago School
Parker, Richard Barry (1867–1941) English architect and town planner
Parsons, Talcott (1902–1979) American sociologist and academic
Pasolini, Pier Paolo (1922–1975) Italian film director and writer
Pastrana, Andrés (1954–) Colombian lawyer, journalist and President
Paz, Octavio (1914–1998) Mexican writer, diplomat and Nobel laureate
Pedro I (1798–1834) Portuguese-born Emperor of Brazil and King of Portugal
Pedro II (1825–1891) Emperor of Brazil
Peña Nieto, Enrique (1966–) Mexican lawyer and President
Pereira de Sousa, Washington Luís (1869–1957) Brazilian lawyer, historian and President
Pereira Passos, Francisco (1836–1913) Brazilian engineer and prefect of Rio
Pérez, Carlos Andrés (1922–2010, CAP) Venezuelan politician and twice President
Pérez Galdós, Benito (1843–1920) Spanish writer
Pérez Jiménez, Marcos (1914–2001) Venezuelan military and twice President
Perón, Eva Duarte de (1919–1952) Argentine actress and First Lady as Perón's wife
Perón, Isabel Martínez de (1934–, nee María Estela Martínez) Argentine politician, vice-president and President
Perón, Juan Domingo (1895–1974) Argentine military and three times President
Perroux, François (1903–1987) French economist and advocate of the Poles of Development
Perry, Clarence (1872–1944) American urban planner and advocate of the Neighbourhood Unit
Picón Salas, Mariano (1901–1965) Venezuelan writer and diplomat
Piñera, Sebastián (1949–) Chilean economist, businessman and President
Pinochet Ugarte, Augusto (1915–2006) Chilean military and dictator
Pinto Santa Cruz, Aníbal (1919–1996) Chilean economist and member of ECLAC
Pocaterra, José Rafael (1889–1955) Venezuelan writer
Poëte, Marcel (1866–1950) French urbanist and historian

Pombal, Marquis of (1699–1782, Sebastião José de Carvalho e Melo) Portuguese statesman
Portales, Diego (1793–1837) Chilean businessman, politician and minister who masterminded the 1833 Constitution
Prado, Paulo (1869–1943) Brazilian businessman, patron and writer
Prado Júnior, Antônio (1880–1955) Brazilian engineer, entrepreneur and politician
Prado Júnior, Caio (1907–1990) Brazilian Marxist historian
Prebisch, Raúl (1901–1986) Argentine economist, minister and Secretary General of ECLAC
Prestes, Luis Carlos (1898–1990) Brazilian military and communist leader
Prestes Maia, Francisco (1896–1965) Brazilian engineer, urbanist and prefect of São Paulo
Prost, Henri (1874–1959) French urbanist
Puga Borne, Federico (1855–1935) Chilean physician and congressman

Quadros, Jânio (1917–1992) Brazilian politician and President
Quevedo, Miguel Ángel (1859–1946) Mexican engineer and campaigner for the flora
Quiroga, Horacio (1878–1937) Uruguayan writer working in Argentina

Rama, Ángel (1926–1983) Uruguayan critic and scholar
Ramírez, Sergio (1942–) Nicaraguan lawyer, politician and writer
Ramos, Julio (1957–) Puerto Rican literary critic and academic
Randle, Patricio, Argentine historian and academic
Rangel, Carlos (1929–1988) Venezuelan journalist and writer
Ravard, Alfonzo (1919–2006) Venezuelan military and manager
Rawson, Guillermo (1821–1890) Argentine physician, politician and minister
Razetti, Luis (1862–1932) Venezuelan physician and sanitation campaigner
Reagan, Ronald (1911–2004) American actor, politician and twice President
Redfield, Robert (1897–1958) American anthropologist and ethnolinguist
Reissman, Leonard (1921–1975) American sociologist and academic
Renan, Ernest (1823–1892) French historian and philosopher
Resnais, Alain (1922–2014) French film director
Reyes, Alfonso (1889–1959) Mexican writer and diplomat
Rivas Mercado, Antonio (1889–1959) Mexican engineer and architect
Rivera, Diego (1886–1957) Mexican painter and muralist
Roca, Julio (1843–1914) Argentine military, leader of PAN and twice President
Rodó, José Enrique (1871–1917) Uruguayan writer and politician
Rodrigues Alves, Francisco (1848–1919) Brazilian lawyer and President
Rodríguez, Gumersindo, Venezuelan economist, politician and minister
Rodríguez de Francia, José Gaspar (1766–1840) Paraguayan ruler also known as 'Doctor Francia' or 'the Supreme'
Rodwin, Lloyd (1919–1999) American planner and academic
Rojas, Ricardo (1882–1957) Argentine journalist and writer
Rojas Pinilla, Gustavo (1900–1975) Colombian military, engineer and de facto President
Romero, José Luis (1905–1977) Argentine historian and academic
Romero, Luis Alberto (1944–) Argentine historian and academic
Romero, Silvio (1851–1914) Brazilian writer
Roosevelt, Franklin D. (1882–1945) 32nd President of the United States
Roosevelt, Theodore (1858–1919) 26th President of the United States

Rosas, Juan Manuel de (1763–1867) Argentine military, dictator and leader of the confederation
Ross Santa María, Gustavo (1879–1961) Chilean politician and Finance minister
Rostow, Walt Whitman (1916–2003) American economist, scholar and political adviser
Rotival, Maurice (1892–1980) French engineer, urbanist and academic
Rourke, Thomas, Nom de plume of Daniel Joseph Clinton, American writer
Rousseau, Jean-Jacques (1712–1776) Swiss-born French philosopher of the Enlightenment
Rousseff, Dilma (1947–) Brazilian economist, revolutionary and first female President
Rúa, Fernando de la (1937–) Argentine lawyer and President that resigned after protests in 2001
Rulfo, Juan (1917–1986) Mexican writer and photographer

Sáenz Peña, Roque (1851–1914) Argentine lawyer, leader of the UCR and President
Saint Simon, Claude Henri (1760–1825) French philosopher of utopian socialism
Salinas de Gortari, Carlos (1948–) Mexican economist and President
Sampaio, Carlos (1866–1930) Brazilian engineer and prefect of Rio
Sampaio, Theodoro (1855–1937) Brazilian engineer specialized in sanitation
Samper, Ernesto (1951–) Colombian economist, diplomat and President
Sandino, Augusto César (1895–1934) Nicaraguan revolutionary opposed to the occupation by the USA
Santos, Juan Manuel (1950–) Colombian journalist, economist and President
Saravia, Aparicio (1856–1904) Uruguayan caudillo founder of the National Party
Sarmiento, Domingo Faustino (1811–1888) Argentine writer and President
Sarney, José (1930–) Brazilian lawyer and President
Sartre, Jean-Paul (1905–1980) French existentialist philosopher
Schade Pohlenz, Alberto (1882–1961) Chilean architect, urbanist and academic
Schaedel, Richard (1920–2005) American anthropologist and scholar
Schlesinger, Jr, Arthur (1917–2007) American historian and political advisor
Schmidt, Robert (1869–1934) German city and regional planner
Schumpeter, Joseph (1883–1950) Austrian-born American economist and political scientist
Scipio the African (236–183 BC) Roman general who defeated Hannibal in the Second Punic War
Scruggs, William Lindsay (1836–1912) American lawyer and diplomat to Colombia and Venezuela
Semprún, Jesús (1882–1931) Venezuelan writer and diplomat
Sert, Josep Lluís (1902–1983) Spanish-born modernist architect working in the US and Latin America
Sierra, Justo (1848–1912) Mexican writer, politician and minister of the Porfiriato
Silva, José Asunción (1865–1896) Colombian writer
Simmel, Georg (1858–1918) German philosopher and sociologist
Siqueiros, David Alfaro (1896–1974) Mexican painter and muralist
Sitte, Camillo (1843–1903) Austrian art historian, architect and city planning theoretician
Sjoberg, Gideon, Swedish sociologist and academic
Solano López, Francisco (1827–1870) Paraguayan military and second President
Sordo Madaleno, Juan (1916–1985) Mexican architect
Soria, Arturo (1844–1920) Spanish engineer and town planner

Spencer, Herbert (1820–1903) British biologist and social scientist
Spengler, Oswald (1880–1936) German historian and philosopher
Stalin, Joseph (1878–1953) Russian revolutionary and premier of the USSR
Stiglitz, Joseph (1943–) American economist, academic, former WB vice president and Nobel laureate
Stroessner, Alfredo (1912–2006) Paraguayan military and dictator
Stübben, Joseph (1845–1936) German town planner
Subercaseaux, Benjamín (1902–1973) Chilean sociologist and writer
Sutcliffe, Anthony (1942–2011) English urban historian

Taine, Hippolyte (1828–1893) French critic and historian proponent of naturalism and positivism
Thatcher, Margaret, Baroness (1925–2013, née Roberts) British conservative Prime Minister
Tisserand, L.M., French academic and promoter of the denomination 'Latin America'
Tönnies, Ferdinand (1855–1936) German sociologist, introducer of the distinction between Gemeinschaft (community) and Gesselschaft (society)
Torres Restrepo, Camilo (1929–1966) Colombian priest and guerrilla fighter
Torrijos, Omar (1929–1981) Panamanian military and de facto president who promoted the 1979 treaty for the devolution of the canal
Touraine, Alain (1925–) French sociologist and academic
Trujillo, Rafael Leónidas (1891–1961) Dominican military and dictator
Turbay, Gabriel (1901–1947) Colombian physician and politician
Turner, Frederick Jackson (1861–1932) American historian and scholar

Ugarte, Manuel B. (1875–1951) Argentine writer, diplomat and politician
Uribe, Álvaro (1952–) Colombian lawyer and President
Uriburu, José Félix (1868–1932) Argentine military and de facto President
Uslar Pietri, Arturo (1906–2001) Venezuelan writer, politician and diplomat

Vallejo, César (1892–1938) Peruvian poet
Vallenilla Lanz, Laureano (1870–1936) Venezuelan sociologist and politician of the Gomez regime
Vargas, Getúlio (1882–1954) Brazilian lawyer and twice President
Vargas Llosa, Mario (1936–) Peruvian-Spanish writer, presidential candidate and Nobel laureate
Vargas Vila, José María (1860–1933) Colombian writer
Vasconcelos, José (1882–1959) Mexican politician and philosopher of indigenismo, cultural leader of the Revolution
Vázquez, Tabaré (1940–) Uruguayan physician and President
Vicuña Mackenna, Benjamín (1831–1886) Chilean politician, historian and governor of Santiago
Videla, Jorge (1925–) Argentine military and president of junta
Villa, Pancho (1878–1923) Nickname of José Doroteo Arango, Mexican revolutionary
Villa-Lobos, Heitor (1887–1957) Brazilian composer
Villanueva, Carlos Raúl (1900–1975) Venezuelan architect
Viola, Rafael (1924–1994) Argentine military and president of junta
Violich, Francis (1911–2005) American urban planner and academic

Wagner, Otto (1841–1918) Austrian architect and town planner
Warchavchik, Gregori (1896–1972) Russian modernist architect working in Brazil
Wiener, Paul Lester (1895–1967) German modernist architect
Wilde, Oscar (1854–1900) Irish-born English writer and poet
Wilson, Woodrow (1856–1924) 28th President of the United States
Wirth, Louis (1897–1952) American sociologist and member of the Chicago School

Yáñez, Enrique (1908–1990) Mexican architect
Yrigoyen, Hipólito (1852–1933) Argentine politician, leader of the UCR and twice President

Zapata, Emiliano (1879–1919) Mexican revolutionary
Zedillo, Ernesto (1951–) Mexican economist and President
Zelaya, Manuel (1952–) Honduran politician and deposed President
Zumeta, César (1860–1955) Venezuelan writer and diplomat

Table 1. Urban and rural population of Latin American countries, 1950–2010 in thousands

Countries and Areas Latin America	1950	1955	1960	1965	1970	1975	1980	1985	1990	1995	2000	2005	2010
Total population	156120	178802	205916	237200	273520	315889	365098	390512	429775	468889	507932	546385	583699
Urban population	61371	77063	96572	119362	146344	178435	216172	266416	305252	343909	380274	418119	454838
Rural population	94751	101739	109344	117838	127176	137454	148896	124096	124524	124980	127658	128266	128862
Urban percentage	39	43	47	50	54	56	59	68	71	73	75	77	78
Argentina													
Total population	17189	19122	20956	22909	24937	27068	29334	30305	32527	34768	37032	39302	41474
Urban population	11038	12657	14161	15767	17431	19179	21043	25731	28256	30715	33166	35590	37891
Rural population	6151	6465	6795	7142	7506	7889	8291	4574	4271	4053	3865	3712	3583
Urban percentage	64.2	66.2	67.9	68.8	69.9	70.9	71.7	85	87	88	90	91	91
Bolivia													
Total population	3013	3322	3696	4136	4658	5277	6000	5895	6573	7414	8329	9275	10229
Urban population	778	915	1104	1345	1652	2040	2514	2978	3657	4480	5383	6321	7259
Rural population	2235	2407	2592	2791	3006	3237	3486	2917	2915	2934	2945	2954	2970
Urban percentage	25.8	27.5	29.9	32.5	35.5	38.7	41.9	51	56	60	65	68	71
Brazil													
Total population	52178	60453	70309	81300	93752	107863	123566	135262	148030	159608	170693	181604	192240
Urban population	16083	21526	28329	36026	44926	55207	66779	96068	110579	123776	136337	148366	159748
Rural population	36095	38927	41980	45274	48826	52656	56787	39195	37451	35832	34356	33238	32492
Urban percentage	30.8	35.6	40.3	44.3	47.9	51.2	54.0	71	75	78	80	82	83
Chile													
Total population	6073	6761	7627	8567	9636	10872	12300	12047	13100	14210	15211	16136	17010
Urban population	3327	4005	4861	5791	6850	8024	9274	9775	10848	11987	13034	14018	14956
Rural population	2746	2756	2766	2776	2786	2848	3026	2272	2251	2223	2177	2118	2054
Urban percentage	54.8	59.2	63.7	67.6	71.1	73.8	75.4	81	83	84	86	87	88
Colombia													
Total population	11679	13441	15468	17787	20514	23774	27691	31659	34970	38542	42321	46039	49665
Urban population	4253	5574	7134	8958	11161	13865	17163	21184	24251	27773	31516	35262	38959
Rural population	7426	7867	8334	8829	9353	9909	10498	10475	10719	10769	10805	10778	10707
Urban percentage	36.4	41.5	46.1	50.4	54.4	58.3	62.1	67	69	72	74	77	78
Costa Rica													
Total population	801	984	1206	1467	1769	2110	2491	2642	3049	3554	4023	4453	4857
Urban population	232	297	377	494	647	836	1071	1184	1423	1725	2029	2331	2634
Rural population	569	687	829	973	1122	1274	1420	1458	1626	1829	1994	2122	2223
Urban percentage	29.9	30.1	31.3	33.7	36.6	39.6	43.0	45	47	49	50	52	54

continued on page 205

continued from page 204

Cuba													
Total population	5508	6127	6797	7523	8307	9146	10034	10115	10628	10964	11201	11372	11516
Urban population	2753	3261	3816	4423	5083	5792	6546	7246	7948	8505	8951	9308	9607
Rural population	2755	2866	2981	3100	3224	3354	3488	2870	2680	2459	2250	2063	1909
Urban percentage	50.0	53.2	56.1	58.8	61.2	63.3	65.2	72	75	78	80	82	83
Dominican Republic													
Total population	2243	2587	3030	3588	4277	5124	6174	6376	7110	7823	8495	9123	9708
Urban population	482	634	834	1096	1435	1874	2444	3332	3821	4466	5111	5739	6341
Rural population	1761	1953	2196	2492	2842	3250	3730	3043	3289	3357	3385	3383	3368
Urban percentage	21.5	24.5	27.5	30.5	33.6	36.6	39.6	52	54	57	60	63	65
Ecuador													
Total population	3197	3691	4317	5036	5909	6933	8080	9099	10264	11460	12646	13798	14899
Urban population	878	1100	1423	1803	2297	2898	3573	4672	5684	6785	7930	9079	10201
Rural population	2319	2591	2894	3233	3612	4035	4507	4427	4581	4675	4716	4720	4698
Urban percentage	27.5	29.8	33.0	35.8	38.9	41.8	44.2	51	55	59	63	66	68
El Salvador													
Total population	1868	2142	2490	2914	3417	4022	4730	4769	5110	5669	6276	6875	7441
Urban population	515	595	721	892	1105	1378	1708	2239	2543	2978	3467	3977	4487
Rural population	1353	1547	1769	2022	2312	2644	3022	2530	2567	2691	2809	2898	2954
Urban percentage	27.6	27.8	29.0	30.6	32.3	34.3	36.1	47	50	53	55	58	60
Guatemala													
Total population	2805	3258	3765	4343	5053	5906	6942	7738	8749	9976	11385	12952	14631
Urban population	674	886	1124	1403	1780	2262	2885	2904	3327	3854	4483	5174	5932
Rural population	2131	2372	2641	2940	3273	3644	4057	4834	5422	6122	6902	7778	8699
Urban percentage	24.0	27.2	29.9	32.3	35.2	38.3	41.6	38	38	39	39	40	41
Haiti													
Total population	3380	3722	4140	4645	5255	6001	6912	6134	6942	7622	8357	9151	9994
Urban population	340	401	513	683	927	1274	1749	1671	2118	2612	3185	3826	4522
Rural population	3040	3321	3627	3962	4328	4727	5163	4464	4823	5010	5172	5325	5471
Urban percentage	10.1	10.8	12.4	14.7	17.6	21.2	25.3	27	31	34	38	42	45
Honduras													
Total population	1428	1660	1950	2315	2750	3266	3879	4186	4879	5654	6485	7347	8203
Urban population	249	321	432	593	797	1051	1367	1579	1989	2510	3126	3825	4582
Rural population	1181	1339	1518	1722	1953	2215	2512	2608	2889	3144	3359	3521	3621
Urban percentage	17.3	19.3	22.2	25.6	29.0	32.2	35.2	38	41	44	48	52	56
Mexico													
Total population	26366	30612	36018	42681	50733	60554	72659	75465	83226	91145	98881	106147	112891
Urban population	12144	15397	19741	25268	32105	40626	51340	51764	59464	66902	74601	81995	88979
Rural population	14222	15215	16277	17413	18628	19928	21319	23701	23762	24244	24280	24152	23912
Urban percentage	46.1	50.3	54.8	59.2	63.3	67.1	70.7	69	71	73	75	77	79

continued on page 206

206 • Modernization, Urbanization and Development in Latin America, 1900s–2000s

continued from page 205

Nicaragua													
Total population	1060	1245	1477	1754	2083	2474	2938	3404	3827	4426	5074	5800	6529
Urban population	297	383	502	638	819	1047	1343	17499	2011	2387	2807	3290	3791
Rural population	763	862	975	1116	1264	1427	1595	1655	1817	2039	2267	2511	2739
Urban percentage	28.0	30.8	34.0	36.4	39.3	42.3	45.7	51	53	54	55	57	58
Panama													
Total population	797	923	1055	1209	1387	1591	1823	2167	2398	2631	2856	3067	3266
Urban population	282	363	447	548	669	811	975	1121	1289	1466	1646	1824	2000
Rural population	515	560	608	661	718	780	848	1046	1109	1165	1210	1243	1266
Urban percentage	35.4	39.3	42.4	45.3	48.2	51.0	53.5	52	54	56	58	59	61
Paraguay													
Total population	1397	1565	1768	2007	2296	2645	3065	3609	4219	4828	5496	6216	6980
Urban population	392	444	508	583	674	785	920	1621	2052	2531	3085	3708	4388
Rural population	1005	1121	1260	1424	1622	1860	2145	1988	2167	2297	2411	2508	2592
Urban percentage	28.1	28.4	28.7	29.0	29.4	29.7	30.0	45	49	52	56	60	63
Peru													
Total population	7969	8790	10025	11650	13586	15869	18527	19492	21569	23532	25662	27804	29885
Urban population	2498	3003	3904	5021	6345	7935	9782	12929	14814	16759	18555	20425	22289
Rural population	5471	5787	6121	6629	7241	7934	8745	6564	6755	6773	7106	7379	7597
Urban percentage	31.3	34.2	38.9	43.1	46.7	50.0	52.8	66	69	71	72	73	75
Uruguay													
Total population	2195	2348	2491	2647	2802	2960	3126	3009	3106	3218	3337	3455	3566
Urban population	1734	1887	2030	2186	2341	2499	2665	2684	2812	2950	3089	3218	3340
Rural population	461	461	461	461	461	461	461	324	294	268	248	237	226
Urban percentage	79.0	80.4	81.5	82.6	83.5	84.2	85.3	89	91	92	93	93	94
Venezuela													
Total population	4974	6049	7331	8722	10399	12434	14827	17138	19502	21844	24170	26468	28716
Urban population	2422	3414	4611	5844	7300	9052	11031	13986	16365	18748	21129	23491	25804
Rural population	2552	2635	2720	2878	3099	3382	3796	3152	3137	3096	3041	2977	2912
Urban percentage	48.7	56.4	62.9	67.0	70.2	72.8	74.4	82	84	86	87	89	90

Source: Own elaboration based on data from Harris (1975), ECLAC (1999) and Latin American and the Caribbean Demographic Observatory (2009).

Table 2. Urbanization, growth and level of transition, 1950–2010

Countries and Stage of Urban Transition	Urban population (percent)							Annual growth rate (per 100 inhabitants)						
	1950	1960	1970	1980	1990	2000	2010	1950–1960	1960–1970	1970–1980	1980–1990	1990–2000	2000–2010	1950–2010
Advanced urban transition														
Argentina	64.2	67.9	69.9	71.7	87	90	91	3.0	2.2	2.3	1.9	1.4	1.54	2.0
Chile	54.8	63.7	71.1	75.4	83	86	88	3.9	3.0	2.8	1.8	1.6	1.83	2.5
Uruguay	79.0	81.5	83.5	85.3	91	93	94	–	0.9	1.0	1.0	0.4	0.80	0.8
Venezuela	48.7	62.9	70.2	74.4	84	87	90	6.5	4.8	3.9	3.1	3.0	3.11	4.1
Right Urban Transition														
Brazil	30.8	40.3	47.9	54.0	75	80	83	5.0	5.1	4.3	2.9	2.4	2.29	3.7
Colombia	36.4	46.1	54.4	62.1	69	74	78	4.4	4.3	2.7	1.9	2.4	2.43	3.0
Cuba	50.0	56.1	61.2	65.2	75	80	83	2.9	2.7	2.3	–	1.1	1.30	2.1
Mexico	46.1	54.8	63.3	70.7	71	75	79	4.8	4.7	4.5	2.7	2.3	2.54	3.6
Peru	31.3	38.9	46.7	52.8	69	72	75	3.6	4.9	3.5	2.8	2.1	2.42	3.2
Moderate Urban Transition														
Bolivia	25.8	29.9	35.5	41.9	56	65	71	–	2.4	–	4.3	3.6	2.24	3.4
Dominican Republic	21.5	27.5	33.6	39.6	54	60	65	6.0	5.7	5.5	2.9	3.1	2.57	4.3
Ecuador	27.5	33.0	38.9	44.2	55	63	68	4.7	4.5	4.6	3.7	3.0	2.63	3.9
El Salvador	27.6	29.0	32.3	36.1	50	55	60	2.8	3.4	–	1.7	0.8	2.34	2.2
Nicaragua	28.0	34.0	39.3	45.7	53	55	58	4.1	4.5	–	4.1	1.9	2.99	3.5
Panama	35.4	42.4	48.2	53.5	54	58	61	4.3	4.5	2.9	3.2	3.4	2.40	3.4
Paraguay	28.1	28.7	29.4	30.0	49	56	63	2.9	3.1	3.8	4.7	3.4	2.61	3.4
Behind Urban Transition														
Costa Rica	29.9	31.3	36.6	43.0	47	50	54	4.2	5.0	3.1	–	4.6	3.08	4.0
Guatemala	24.0	29.9	35.2	41.6	38	39	41	5.2	3.0	0.7	3.0	6.7	2.69	3.6
Haiti	10.1	12.4	17.6	25.3	31	38	45	–	4.0	3.2	–	5.0	1.85	3.5
Honduras	17.3	22.2	29.0	35.2	41	48	56	2.9	4.2	3.6	–	4.5	3.09	3.7

Source: Own elaboration based on data from Harris (1975), ECLAC (1999), Cerrutti and Bertoncello (2003) and Latin American and the Caribbean Demographic Observatory (2009).

Table 3. Human Development Index (HDI), 1980–2011

	HDI Value														HDI Rank
Years	1980	1985	1990	1995	2000	2005	2006	2007	2008	2009	2010	2011			2011
Argentina	0.669	0.687	0.697	0.726	0.749	0.765	0.773	0.780	0.786	0.788	0.794	0.797			45
Bolivia	0.507	0.527	0.560	0.587	0.612	0.649	0.650	0.645	0.651	0.656	0.660	0.663			108
Brazil	0.549	0.575	0.600	0.634	0.665	0.692	0.695	0.700	0.705	0.708	0.715	0.718			84
Chile	0.630	0.654	0.698	0.722	0.749	0.779	0.780	0.789	0.796	0.798	0.802	0.805			44
Colombia	0.550	0.568	0.594	0.628	0.652	0.675	0.683	0.691	0.697	0.702	0.707	0.710			87
Costa Rica	0.614	0.626	0.656	0.684	0.703	0.723	0.729	0.735	0.737	0.738	0.742	0.744			69
Cuba	–	0.665	0.677	0.646	0.681	0.725	0.745	0.759	0.767	0.770	0.773	0.776			51
Dominican Republic	0.532	0.549	0.577	0.608	0.640	0.658	0.666	0.672	0.677	0.680	0.686	0.689			83
Ecuador	0.591	0.614	0.636	0.659	0.668	0.695	0.698	0.702	0.714	0.716	0.718	0.720			105
El Salvador	0.466	0.484	0.524	0.580	0.619	0.652	0.658	0.668	0.668	0.669	0.672	0.674			131
Guatemala	0.428	0.437	0.462	0.490	0.525	0.550	0.555	0.565	0.568	0.569	0.573	0.574			158
Haiti	0.332	0.374	0.397	0.404	0.421	0.429	0.433	0.443	0.445	0.449	0.449	0.454			121
Honduras	0.451	0.492	0.513	0.540	0.569	0.597	0.604	0.613	0.619	0.619	0.623	0.625			57
Mexico	0.593	0.629	0.649	0.674	0.718	0.741	0.748	0.755	0.761	0.762	0.767	0.770			129
Nicaragua	0.457	0.463	0.473	0.495	0.533	0.566	0.571	0.577	0.583	0.582	0.587	0.589			58
Panama	0.628	0.654	0.660	0.689	0.718	0.740	0.745	0.752	0.758	0.760	0.765	0.768			107
Paraguay	0.544	0.557	0.572	0.601	0.612	0.635	0.639	0.643	0.650	0.651	0.662	0.665			80
Peru	0.574	0.597	0.612	0.644	0.674	0.691	0.697	0.704	0.712	0.714	0.721	0.725			98
Uruguay	0.658	0.660	0.686	0.705	0.736	0.748	0.755	0.764	0.769	0.773	0.780	0.783			48
Venezuela	0.623	0.627	0.629	0.646	0.656	0.692	0.706	0.720	0.730	0.732	0.734	0.735			73
Very high human development	0.766	0.786	0.810	0.834	0.858	0.876	0.879	0.882	0.885	0.885	0.888	0.889			–
High human development	0.614	0.630	0.648	0.662	0.687	0.716	0.721	0.728	0.733	0.734	0.739	0.741			–
Medium human development	0.420	0.450	0.480	0.517	0.548	0.587	0.595	0.605	0.612	0.618	0.625	0.630			–
Low human development	0.316	0.334	0.347	0.363	0.383	0.422	0.430	0.437	0.443	0.448	0.453	0.456			–
Latin America and the Caribbean	0.582	0.604	0.624	0.650	0.680	0.703	0.708	0.717	0.723	0.725	0.731	0.734			–

Source: Own elaboration based on Human Development Index (HDI) value calculations based on data from UNDESA (2011), PNUD (2001) Barro and Lee (2010), UNESCO Institute for Statistics (2011), World Bank (2011) and IMF (2011).

References

Abreu, M. de (1988) *Evolução urbana do Rio de Janeiro*. Rio de Janeiro: Iplanrio, Zahar.

Adler, A. (2004) Chávez: mitad Perón, mitad Che Guevara. *El Nacional/Le Figaro*, 29 August, p. A-10.

Agache, D.A. (1932) *La remodelation d'une capitale*. Paris: Société Coopérative d'Architectes, 2 vols.

Aguirre, B. and Castillo, S. (2004) *De la 'gran aldea' a la ciudad de masas: el espacio público en Santiago de Chile, 1910–1929*. Santiago: Universidad Central.

Alberdi, J.B. (1852, 2008) *Bases y puntos de partida para la organización política de la República Argentina*. Buenos Aires: Losada.

Alegría, C. (1948, 1955) Prólogo, in *El mundo es ancho y ajeno*. Santiago: Ediciones Ercilla, pp. 7–19.

Allende, S. (2008) *Cinco discursos fundamentales*. Santiago: Editorial Aún Creemos en los Sueños.

Almandoz, A. (2000) *Ensayos de cultura urbana*. Caracas: Fundarte.

Almandoz, A. (2002–2009) *La ciudad en el imaginario venezolano*. Caracas: Fundación para la Cultura Urbana, 3 vols.

Almandoz, A. (2004a) Sobre el imaginario urbano de la Latinoamérica republicana, 1830–1950. *Cuadernos Hispanoamericanos*, **645**, pp. 7–21.

Almandoz, A. (2004b) The garden city in early twentieth-century Latin America. *Urban History*, **31**(3), pp. 437–452.

Almandoz, A. (2006a) *Urbanismo europeo en Caracas (1870–1940)*. Caracas: Fundación para la Cultura Urbana, Equinoccio, Universidad Simón Bolívar (USB).

Almandoz, A. (2006b) Urban planning and historiography in Latin America. *Progress in Planning*, **65**(2), pp. 81–123.

Almandoz, A. (2007) Modernización urbanística en América Latina. Luminarias extranjeras y cambios disciplinares, 1900-1960. *Iberoamericana*, **27**, pp. 59–80.

Almandoz, A. (2008a) Despegues sin madurez. Urbanización, industrialización y desarrollo en la Latinoamérica del siglo XX. *EURE. Revista Latinoamericana de Estudios Urbanos y Regionales*, **34**(102), pp. 61–76.

Almandoz, A. (2008b) *Entre libros de historia urbana. Para una historiografía de la ciudad y el urbanismo en América Latina*. Caracas: Equinoccio, Ediciones de la Universidad Simón Bolívar (USB).

Almandoz, A. (2008c) Urban history and cultural studies in Latin America, in Schneider, H.L. and Huber, L.M. (eds.) *Social Networks: Development, Evaluation and Influence*. New York: Nova Science Publishers, pp. 159–177.

Almandoz, A. (2009) Demandas políticas y reformas sociales en la masificación urbana latinoamericana, 1900–1930, in Aguiar, F., Lara, F. and Lara, N. (eds.) *Decidir en sociedad. Homenaje a Julia Barragán*. Caracas: Ediciones Chiryme-kp, pp. 329–343.

Almandoz, A. (ed.) (2010a) *Planning Latin America's Capital Cities, 1850–1950*. London: Routledge.

Almandoz, A. (2010b) Urbanization and urbanism in Latin America: from Haussmann to CIAM, in Almandoz, A. (ed.) *Planning Latin America's Capital Cities, 1850–1950*. London: Routledge, pp. 13–44.

Almandoz, A. (2010c) From urban to regional planning in Latin America, 1920–1950. *Planning Perspectives*, **25**(1), pp. 87–95.

Almandoz, A. (2010d) Entre Guerra Fría y Tercer Mundo. Urbanización y subdesarrollo en Latinoamérica, 1960–1980. *Argos*, **27**(53), pp. 193–217.

Almandoz, A. (2011) Immature take-offs: urbanization, industrialization and development in twentieth-century Latin America, in Harper, T.L. et al. (eds.) *Dialogues in Urban and Regional Planning*, Vol. 4. London: Routledge, pp. 205–222.

Almandoz, A. (2012) Introducción: Caracas, entre la ciudad guzmancista y la metrópoli revolucionaria, in Almandoz, A. (ed.) *Caracas, de la metrópoli súbita a la meca roja*. Quito: Organización Latinoamericana y del Caribe de Centros Históricos (Olacchi), pp. 9–25.

Almandoz, A. (2013a) *Modernización urbana en América Latina. De las grandes aldeas a las metrópolis masificadas*. Santiago: Instituto de Estudios Urbanos y Territoriales (IEUT), Pontificia Universidad Católica (PUC) de Chile.

Almandoz, A. (2013b) De Calibán a Próspero. Visiones urbanas de la modernidad nórdica entre la intelectualidad hispanoamericana, 1900–1945, in Rigotti, A.M and Pampinella, S. (eds.) *Entre puntos cardinales. Debates sobre una nueva arquitectura (1920–1950)*. Rosario: Prohistoria ediciones, pp. 299–321.

Almandoz, A. (2013c) Industrialización, urbanización y modernización sin desarrollo en la Latinoamérica del siglo XX, in Duque Franco, I. (ed.) *Historiografía y planificación urbana en América Latina*. Bogotá: Universidad Nacional de Colombia (UNC), Facultad de Ciencias Humanas, Departamento de Geografía, pp. 47–72.

Almandoz, A. (2013d) De las ciudades burguesas a las masificadas en Romero. Revisión conceptual e impacto historiográfico en América Latina, in Burucúa, J.E. et al. (eds.) *José Luis Romero. Vida histórica, ciudad y cultura*. Buenos Aires: Universidad Nacional de San Martín (UNSAM), pp. 199–220.

Amato, P. (1970) Elitism and settlement patterns in the Latin American city. *Journal of the American Institute of Planners*, **36**(2), pp. 96–105.

Anderson Imbert, E. (1976) *El realismo mágico y otros ensayos*. Caracas: Monte Ávila Editores.

Andrade, C.R.M. de (1998) Barry Parker, um arquiteto inglês na cidade de São Paulo. PhD dissertation, Universidade de São Paulo.

Anhaia Mello, L. de (1929) *Problemas de urbanismo*. São Paulo: Boletim do Instituto de Engenharia de São Paulo.

Arcaya, P.M. (1936) *The Gómez Regime in Venezuela and its Background*. Washington DC: no publisher.

Arias Lemos, F. (2008) *Le Corbusier en Bogotá: el proyecto del 'grand immeuble', 1950–1951*. Bogotá: Universidad Nacional de Colombia (UNC).

Aristiguieta Montero, R. (1879) *La administración Alcántara*. Caracas: Imprenta de vapor de 'La Opinión Nacional'.

Arráiz Lucca, R. (2007) *Venezuela: 1830 a nuestros días. Breve historia política*. Caracas: Editorial Alfa.

Arturo, J. (2002) Bogotá, in Ember, M. and Ember, C. (eds.) *Encyclopedia of Urban Cultures. Cities and Cultures around the World*. Danbury, CT: Grolier, Vol. I, pp. 389–396.

Ayala Mora, E. (2005) *Resumen de la historia del Ecuador*. Quito: Corporación Editora Nacional.

Aylwin, M. et al. (1990, 2008) *Chile en el siglo XX*. Santiago: Planeta.

Azuela, M. (1915, 1960) *Los de abajo. Novela de la revolución mexicana*. Lima: Ediciones Nuevo Mundo.

Baer, J.A. (1998) Buenos Aires: Housing Reform and the Decline of the Liberal State in Argentina, in Pineo, R. and Baer, J.A. (eds.) *Cities of Hope. People, Protests and Progress in Urbanizing Latin America, 1870–1930*. Boulder, CO: Westview Press, pp. 129–152.

Bähr, J. and Borsdorf, A. (2005) La ciudad latinoamericana. La construcción de un modelo. Vigencia y perspectivas. *Ur[b]es*, **2**(2), pp. 207–221.

Ballent, A. (2005) *Las huellas de la política. Vivienda, ciudad, peronismo en Buenos Aires, 1943–1955*. Buenos Aires: Universidad Nacional de Quilmes.

Barro, R. and Lee, J. (2010) *A New Data Set of Educational Attainment in the World, 1950–2010*. Available at: http://www.nber.org/papers/w15902.

Bastenier, M.A. (2012) El nieto del PRI. *El Nacional*, 8 July, p. I-12

Bataillon, C. and Rivière, H. (1973) *La Ciudad de México*, trans. Montemayor, C. and Anaya, J. México: Secretaría de Educación Pública.

Bell, P.L. (1922) *Venezuela. A Commercial and Industrial Handbook. With a Chapter on the Dutch West Indies*. Washington DC: Department of Commerce, Government Printing Office.

Benjamin, W. (1986) *Reflections. Essays, Aphorisms, Autobiographical Writings*, trans. Jephcott, E. New York: Schocken.

Berjman, S. (1998) *Plazas y parques de Buenos Aires: la obra de los paisajistas franceses. André, Courtois, Thays, Bouvard, Forestier, 1860–1930*. Buenos Aires: Gobierno de la Ciudad de Buenos Aires, Fondo de Cultura Económica (FCE).

Betancourt, R. (1958) *Posición y doctrina*. Caracas: Editorial Cordillera.

Beyhaut, G. and Beyhaut, H. (1985) *Historia universal Siglo XXI. América Latina. III. De la independencia a la segunda guerra mundial*, Vol. 23. México: Siglo Veintiuno Editores.

Blanco, A. (2006) *Razón y modernidad. Gino Germani y la sociología en la Argentina*. Buenos Aires: Siglo Veintiuno Editores.

Blanco, A.E. (1997) *Antología popular*. Caracas: Monte Ávila, Comisión Presidencial para el Centenario del Natalicio de Andrés Eloy Blanco.

Borja, J. (1997) Planeamiento estratégico y proyectos urbanos: nuevos territorios y nuevas economías, in *Planeamiento y gestión urbana estratégica en América Latina*. Santiago: Centro de las Naciones Unidas para el Desarrollo Regional (UNCRD), Corporación para el Desarrollo de Santiago, pp. 85–102.

Borja, J. (2007) Revolución y contrarrevolución en la ciudad global: las expectativas frustradas por la globalización de nuestras ciudades. *EURE. Revista Latinoamericana de Estudios Urbano Regionales*, **33**(100), pp. 35–50.

Bourguignon, F. (1998) Keynote Address: Inequality and Economic Growth, in Javed Burki, S. *et al.* (eds.) *Annual World Bank Conference on Development in Latin America and the Caribbean 1996. Poverty and Inequality*. Washington DC: The World Bank, pp. 3–6.

Bradford Burns, E. (1979) Cultures in conflict: the implications of modernization in nineteenth-century Latin America, in Bernhard, V. (ed.) *Elites, Masses and Modernization in Latin America, 1850–1930*. Austin, TX: University of Texas Press, pp. 11–77.

Bradford Burns, E. (1990). *La pobreza del progreso. América Latina en el siglo XIX*. México: Siglo Veintiuno Editores.

Brewer-Carías, A.R (1975) *Cambio político y reforma del Estado en Venezuela. Contribución al estudio del Estado democrático, social y de derecho*. Madrid: Editorial Tecnos.

Brunner, K. (1930) Problemas actuales de urbanización. *Anales de la Universidad de Chile*, **8**(1), pp. 11–40.

Brunner, K. (1939–1940) *Manual de Urbanismo*. Bogotá: Imprenta Municipal, 2 vols.

Brushwood, J.S. (1975, 1993) *La novela hispano-americana del siglo XX. Una vista panorámica*, trans. Williams, R.L. México: Fondo de Cultura Económica (FCE).

Buarque de Holanda, S. (1936, 2005) *Raízes do Brasil*. São Paulo: Companhia das Letras.

Bulnes, F. (1903, 1995) *Páginas escogidas*. México: Universidad Nacional Autónoma de México (UNAM).

Burgos, F. (1995) *Vertientes de la modernidad hispanoamericana*. Caracas: Monte Ávila Editores Latinoamericana.

Burke, P. (2001) Overture. The new history: its past and its future, in Burke, P. (ed.) *New Perspectives on Historical Writing*. Cambridge: Polity Press, pp. 1–24.

Burucúa, J.E. *et al.* (eds.) (2013) *José Luis Romero. Vida histórica, ciudad y cultura*. Buenos Aires: Universidad Nacional de San Martín (UNSAM).

Caballero, M. (1994) *Gómez, el tirano liberal*. Caracas: Monte Ávila Editores Latinoamericana.

Calderón, J. (2003) Los barrios marginales de Lima, 1961–2001. *Ciudad y Territorio. Estudios Territoriales*, **35**(136/137), pp. 375–389.

Campos, C.M. (2002) *Os rumos da cidade. Urbanismo e modernização em São Paulo*. São Paulo: Senac.

Candido, A. (1967, 2005) O significado de 'Raízes do Brasil', in Buarque de Holanda, S., *Raízes do Brasil*. São Paulo: Companhia das Letras, pp. 9–21.

Cané, M. (1883, 1942) *En viaje*. Buenos Aires: Editorial Molino.

Cardona, L. (2011) Venezuela subió un peldaño en índice de desarrollo humano. *El Nacional*, 3 November, p. III-3.

Cardoso, E. (1998) Latin America's External Finance: Old and New Uncertainties, in Javed Burki, S. et al. (eds.), *Annual World Bank Conference on Development in Latin America and the Caribbean 1996. Poverty and Inequality.* Washington DC: The World Bank, pp. 27–35.

Cardoso, F.H. and Faletto, E. (1969) *Dependencia y desarrollo en América Latina.* México: Siglo XXI.

Caride, H.E. (2002–2004) La ciudad representada. Metáforas, analogías y figuraciones en el urbanismo de Buenos Aires. *Anales del Instituto de Arte Americano e Investigaciones Estéticas 'Mario J. Buschiazzo'*, **37/38**, pp. 211–253.

Carl, G.E. (1980) *First Among Equals. Great Britain and Venezuela 1810–1910.* Syracuse, NY: Syracuse University.

Carmagnani, M. (2004) *El otro Occidente. América Latina desde la invasión europea hasta la globalización.* México: El Colegio de México, Fideicomiso Historia de las Américas, Fondo de Cultura Económica (FCE).

Carrera Damas, G. (1988) *Una nación llamada Venezuela. Proceso sociohistórico (1810–1974).* Caracas: Monte Ávila Editores.

Carrión, F. (1997) El regreso a la ciudad construida, in *Planeamiento y gestión urbana estratégica en América Latina.* Santiago: Centro de las Naciones Unidas para el Desarrollo Regional (UNCRD), Corporación para el Desarrollo de Santiago, pp. 175–187.

Castells, M. (ed.) (1973) *Imperialismo y urbanización en América Latina.* Barcelona: Gustavo Gili.

Castells, M. (1976) *La cuestión urbana*, trans. Oliván, I.C. de. México: Siglo Veintiuno Editores.

Castells, M. (1980) *Movimientos sociales urbanos*, trans. Romero, I. México: Siglo Veintiuno Editores.

Castro, C. (1902, 1962) Proclama de Castro ante el bloqueo extranjero, in *Documentos que hicieron historia. Siglo y medio de vida republicana 1810–1961.* Caracas: Presidencia de la República, 2 vols.

Castro, C. (1974) *Epistolario presidencial (1899–1908).* Caracas: Instituto de Estudios Hispanoamericanos, Universidad Central de Venezuela (UCV).

Caves, R.W. (ed.) (2005) *Encyclopedia of the City.* London: Routledge.

Cerrutti, M. and Bertoncello, R. (2003) *Urbanization and Internal Migration Patterns in Latin America.* Johannesburg: Centro de Estudios de Población Argentina.

Chion, M. and Ludeña, W. (2008) Lima's historic centre: old places shaping new social arrangements, in Irazábal, C. (ed.) *Ordinary Places, Extraordinary Events. Citizenship, Democracy and Public Space in Latin America.* London: Routledge, pp. 103–125.

Chiossone, T. (1989) *El decenio democrático inconcluso. 1935–1945.* Caracas: Ex-Libris.

Choay, F. (1983) Pensées sur la ville, arts de la ville, in Agulhon, M. (ed.) *Histoire de la France urbaine. La ville de l'âge industriel. Le cycle haussmannien.* Paris: Seuil, Vol. 4, pp. 158–271.

Clark, D. (2000) *Urban World/Global City.* London: Routledge.

Claverie, J-F. (2011) La descentralización: una voluntad de ahondar la democracia, in Quenan, C. and Velut, S. (eds.) *Los desafíos del desarrollo en América Latina. Dinámicas socioeconómicas y políticas públicas*. Paris: Institut des Amériques, Agence Française de Développement (AFP), pp.161–175.

Clichevsky, N. (1990) *Construcción y administración de la ciudad latinoamericana*. Buenos Aires: Instituto Internacional de Medio Ambiente y Desarrollo (IIED-América Latina), Grupo Editor Latinoamericano (GEL).

Clichevsky, N. (2003) Territorios en pugna: las villas de Buenos Aires. *Ciudad y Territorio. Estudios Territoriales*, **35**(136/137), pp. 347–374.

Collins, C.C. (2005) *Werner Hegemann and the Search for Universal Urbanism*. London: WW Norton & Company.

Collyns, D. (2014) Venezuela protest crackdown threatens region's democracy, warns Vargas Llosa. *The Guardian*, 10 April. Available at: http://www.theguardian.com/world/2014/apr/10/venezuela-protest-crackdown-threatens-democracy-latin-america-mario-vargas-llosa.

Comisión Nacional de Verdad y Reconciliación (1991) *Informe Rettig*. Available at: http://www.ddhh.gov.cl/ddhh_rettig.html.

Concha-Eastman, A. (2000) Violencia urbana en América Latina y el Caribe: dimensiones, explicaciones, acciones, in Rotker, S. (ed.) *Ciudadanías del miedo*. Caracas: Nueva Sociedad, Rutgers University, pp. 39–53.

Conferencias Internacionales Americanas, vol. 1: *1889–1936*. (1938) Washington DC: Dotación Carnegie para la Paz International.

Consalvi, S.A. (2011) John F. Kennedy, historias de medio siglo. *El Nacional*, 2 January, p. 5.

Contreras, C. (1939, 2003) La planificación de la Ciudad de México, 1918–1938, in Sánchez Ruiz, G. (ed.) *Planificación y Urbanismo visionarios de Carlos Contreras. Escritos de 1925 a 1935*. México: Universidad Nacional Autónoma de México (UNAM), Universidad Autónoma Metropolitana-Azcapotzalco, Universidad Autónoma de San Luis de Potosí, pp. 131–145.

Contreras, C. (2003) El Plano Regulador del Distrito Federal, in Sánchez Ruiz, G. (ed.) *Planificación y Urbanismo visionarios de Carlos Contreras. Escritos de 1925 a 1935*. México: Universidad Nacional Autónoma de México (UNAM), Universidad Autónoma Metropolitana-Azcapotzalco, Universidad Autónoma de San Luis de Potosí, pp. 85–129.

Correa, R. (2009) La política es esencial para cambiar el mundo. Entrevista a Michelle Bachelet. *El Nacional/El Mercurio*, 23 August, p. 4.

Cosío Villegas, D. (1973, 2005a) The modern span, in *A Compact History of Mexico* (1973), trans. Mattingly Urquidi, M. México: El Colegio de México, pp. 103–118.

Cosío Villegas, D. (1973, 2005b) The present, in *A Compact History of Mexico*, trans. Mattingly Urquidi, M. México: El Colegio de México, pp. 137–145.

Cosío-Zavala, M.E. (2011) Demografía, pobreza y desigualdades, in Quenan, C. and Velut, S. (eds.) *Los desafíos del desarrollo en América Latina. Dinámicas socioeconómicas y políticas públicas*. Paris: Institut des Amériques, Agence Française de Développement (AFP), pp. 83–110.

Crawford, W.R. (1944, 1961) *A Century of Latin American Thought*. Cambridge, MA: Harvard University Press.
Damazio, R. (nd) Uma reflexão decisiva sobre o homem cordial, in *Retratos do Brasil. Biblioteca Entre Livros*, **8**. São Paulo: Duetto, pp. 28–33.
Darío, R. (1912, 1991) *La vida de Rubén Darío escrita por él mismo*. Caracas: Biblioteca Ayacucho.
Darío, R. (1989) *El modernismo y otros ensayos*. Madrid: Alianza Editorial.
Dávila Boza, R. (1910) Pavimentación urbana, in *Trabajos del Cuarto Congreso Científico (1º Panamericano) celebrado en Santiago de Chile del 25 de diciembre de 1908 al 5 de enero de 1909*. Santiago: Imprenta, Litografía y Encuadernación 'Barcelona', 2 vols, pp. 494–502.
Davis, K. (1965, 1982) La urbanización de la población mundial, in *La ciudad*, trans. Gayá, G. Madrid: Scientific American, Alianza Editorial, pp. 11-36.
Davis, K. (1973) The evolution of Western industrial cities, in Davis, K. (ed.) *Cities. Their Origin, Growth and Human Impact: Readings from 'Scientific American'*. San Francisco, CA: W.H. Freeman, pp. 100–105.
de Almeida, M.C.F. (2002) *Tornar-se outro. O topos canibal na literatura brasileira*. São Paulo: Annablume.
de Andrade, O. (1981) *Obra escogida*. Caracas: Biblioteca Ayacucho.
de Andrade, O. (1990) *Pau-Brasil. Obras completas*. São Paulo: Editora Globo.
de Campos, H. (1981) Uma poética da radicalidade, in de Andrade, O., *Pau-Brasil. Obras completas*. São Paulo: Editora Globo, pp. 7–53.
de Castro, S. (2007) Prólogo, in Rosende, F. (ed.) *La Escuela de Chicago. Uma mirada histórica a 50 años del convenio Chicago/Universidad Católica. Ensayos en honor a Arnold C. Harberger*. Santiago: Facultad de Ciencias Económicas y Administrativas, Ediciones Universidad Católica de Chile, pp. 13–17.
de Certeau, M. (1975, 2002) *L'écriture de l'histoire*. Paris: Gallimard.
de Mattos, C.A (2010) *Globalización y metamorfosis urbana en América Latina*. Quito: Organización Latinoamericana y del Caribe de Centros Históricos (Olacchi), Municipio Metropolitano de Quito.
de Ramón, A. (2000) *Santiago de Chile (1541–1991). Historia de una sociedad urbana*. Santiago: Editorial Sudamericana.
de Ramón, A. (2006) *Historia de Chile. Desde la invasión incaica hasta nuestros días (1500–2000)*. Santiago: Catalonia.
de Solano, F. (ed.) (1978) *Estudios sobre la ciudad iberoamericana*. Madrid: Consejo Superior de Investigaciones Científicas (CSIC), Instituto Gonzalo Fernández de Oviedo.
del Pozo, J. (2002) *Historia de América Latina y del Caribe, 1825–2001*. Santiago: LOM Ediciones.
del Priore, M. and Venancio, R. (2010) *Uma breve história do Brasil*. São Paulo: Planeta.
Díaz Rodríguez, M. (1982) *Narrativa y ensayo*. Caracas: Biblioteca Ayacucho.
Diez, F. (2007) Buenos Aires: involuntary incentives to metropolitan dispersal. *Built Environment*, **33**(2), pp. 157–169.
Drakakis-Smith, D. (1990) *The Third World City*. London: Routledge.

Duque Franco, I. (2013) Trayectoria y perspectivas del planeamiento estratégico en las ciudades latinoamericanas, in Duque Franco, I. (ed.) *Historiografía y planificación urbana en América Latina*. Bogotá: Universidad Nacional de Colombia, Facultad de Ciencias Humanas, Departamento de Geografía, pp. 301–340.

Duverger, H. (1995) La insoportable solidez de lo que el viento se llevó. J.C.N. Forestier y la ciudad de La Habana. *DANA. Documentos de Arquitectura Nacional y Americana*, **37/38**, pp. 71–82.

Echeverría, E. (1839, 1977) *El Dogma socialista*, in *Utopismo socialista (1830–1893)*. Caracas: Biblioteca Ayacucho, pp. 89–130.

Echeverría, E. (1841, 1999) *La cautiva/ El matadero*. Buenos Aires: Emecé Editores.

Echeverría, E. (1871) *El matadro*. Buenos Aires: Imprenta Libreria de Mayo.

Economic Commision for Latin America and the Caribbean (ECLAC) (1963) *La urbanización en América Latina. Resultados de un trabajo sobre el terreno acerca de las condiciones de vida de un sector urbano*. Mar del Plata, Argentina: Cepal.

Economic Commission for Latin America and the Caribbean (ECLAC) (1979) *América Latina: las evaluaciones regionales de la estrategia internacional de desarrollo de los años setenta*. Santiago: Cuadernos de la Cepal.

Economic Commission for Latin America and the Caribbean (ECLAC) (1981) *El desarrollo de América Latina en los años ochenta*. Santiago: Naciones Unidas.

Economic Commission for Latin America and the Caribbean (ECLAC) (1999) *Demographic Bulletin No. 63, January 1999. Latin America: Total, Urban and Rural Population and Urban Percentage, by Quinquennium and Countries*. Available at: http://www.eclac.org/celade/publica/bol63/BD6311.html.

Edralin, J. (1997) Implementando planes de desarrollo económico en las ciudades: una perspectiva de gestión estratégica, in *Planeamiento y gestión urbana estratégica en América Latina*. Santiago: Centro de las Naciones Unidas para el Desarrollo Regional (UNCRD), Corporación para el Desarrollo de Santiago, pp. 47–61.

Edwards, J. (1973, 2006) *Persona non grata*. Santiago: Alfaguara.

Edwards, S. (1996) *Crisis and Reform in Latin America. From Despair to Hope*. Oxford: Oxford University Press.

Edwards, S. (2009) *Populismo o mercados. El dilema de América Latina*, trans. Correa, M.M. and Botero, P. Bogotá: Grupo Editorial Norma.

Edwards Bello, J. (1935, 2010) *La chica del Crillón*. Santiago: Editorial Universitaria.

Eyzaguirre, J. (1948, 2004) *Fisonomía histórica de Chile*. Santiago: Editorial Universitaria.

Feldman, S. (2005) *Planejamento e zoneamento. São Paulo 1947–1972*. São Paulo: Fapesp, Edusp.

Fernández, M. (1968) *Papeles de Recienvenido. Poemas, relatos, cuentos, miscelánea*. Buenos Aires: Centro Editor de América Latina.

Fernández López, M. (2008) Prólogo, in Alberdi, J.B. *Bases y puntos de partida para la organización política de la República Argentina*. Buenos Aires: Losada, pp. 7–27.

Ferrada, M. and Jiménez, C. (2007) La primera vivienda social en Valparaíso. Fines siglo XIX-inicios siglo XX, in Castillo, M. J. and Hidalgo, R. (eds.) *1906/2006. Cien años de política de vivienda en Chile*. Santiago: Universidad Nacional Andrés Bello, Pontificia

Universidad Católica de Chile (PUC), Universidad Central de Venezuela (UCV), pp. 29–49.
Figueroa Salas, J. (1995a) La ciudad lineal en Chile (1910–1930). *DANA. Documentos de Arquitectura Nacional y Americana*, **37/38**, pp. 64–70.
Figueroa Salas, J. (1995b) La recomposición de la forma urbana. K.H. Brunner 1932–1942. *DANA. Documentos de Arquitectura Nacional y Americana*, **37/38**, pp. 83–91.
Fossi, V. (1989) Desarrollo urbano y vivienda: la desordenada evolución hacia un país de metrópolis, in Naím, M. and Piñango, R. (eds.) *El caso Venezuela: una ilusión de armonía*. Caracas: Ediciones Instituto de Estudios Superiores de Administración (IESA), pp. 473–498.
Franco, J. (1967) *The Modern Culture of Latin America: Society and the Artist*. London: Pall Mall.
Frank, A.G. (1967, 1982) *Capitalismo y subdesarrollo en América Latina*. México: Siglo XXI.
Fraser, V. (2000) *Building the New World. Studies in Modern Architecture of Latin America 1930–1960*. London: Verso.
Frehse, F. (2002) São Paulo, in Ember, M. and C.R. (eds.) *Encyclopedia of Urban Cultures. Cities and Cultures around the World*. Danbury, CT: Grolier, Vol. IV, pp. 143–153.
Freyre, G. (1933, 2000) *Casa-grande e senzala*, in *Intérpretes do Brasil*. Rio de Janeiro: Editora Nova Aguilar.
Friedman, M. and Friedman, R.D. (1998) *Two Lucky People. Memoirs*. Chicago, IL: University of Chicago Press.
Friedmann, J. (1965) *Regional Development Policy: A Case Study of Venezuela*. Cambridge, MA: MIT Press.
García Calderón, F. (1912, 1979) *Las democracias latinas de América/La creación de un continente*. Caracas: Biblioteca Ayacucho.
García Calderón, F. (1913) *Latin America: its Rise and Progress*, trans. Miall, B. London: Fisher Unwin.
García Canclini, N. (1990) *Culturas híbridas. Estrategias para entrar y salir de la modernidad*. Buenos Aires: Editorial Sudamericana.
García Canclini, N. (2010) *Imaginarios urbanos*. Buenos Aires: Eudeba.
García-Guadilla, M.P. (2003) Territorialización de los conflictos sociopolíticos en una ciudad sitiada: *guetos* y feudos en Caracas. *Ciudad y Territorio. Estudios Territoriales*, **35**(136/137), pp. 421–440.
García-Guadilla, M.P. (2012) Caracas: de la colonia al socialismo del siglo XXI. Espacio, clase social y movimientos ciudadanos, in Almandoz, A. (ed.) *Caracas, de la metrópoli súbita a la meca roja*. Quito: Organización Latinoamericana y del Caribe de Centros Históricos (Olacchi), pp. 155–196.
GDF (Gobernación del Distrito Federal) (1939) Plan monumental de Caracas. *Revista del Concejo Municipal del Distrito Federal*, **1**, pp. 17–40.
Geisse, G. (1987) Tres momentos históricos en la ciudad hispanoamericana del siglo XIX, in Alomar, G. (ed.) *De Teotihuacán a Brasilia. Estudios de historia urbana iberoamericana y filipina*. Madrid: Instituto de Estudios de Administración Local (IEAL), pp. 397–433.
Gerard, P.-C. (1981) *El Caribe contemporáneo*. México: Siglo Veintiuno Editores.
Germani, G. (1969) *Sociología de la modernización*. Buenos Aires: Paidós.

Gil Fortoul, J. (1896) *El hombre y la historia. Ensayo de sociología venezolana*. Paris: Librería de Garnier Hermanos.

Giraldo, L.M. (2001) *Ciudades escritas. Literatura y ciudad en la narrativa colombiana*. Bogotá: Convenio Andrés Bello.

Glaab, C.N. and Brown, A.T. (1967) *A History of Urban America*. New York: Macmillan.

Goldstein, I.S. (nd) A invenção do mito da democracia racial, in *Retratos do Brasil. Biblioteca EntreLivros*, 8. São Paulo: Duetto, pp. 22–27.

Gomes, M.A. de F. (2005) Cultura urbanistica e contribução modernista. Brasil, anos 1930–1960. *Cadernos PPG-AU Faufba*. Urbanismo modernista. Brasil 1930–1960. Edição Especial, III, pp. 11–29.

Gomes, M.A. de F. and Huapaya, J.C. (2009) Diálogos modernistas com a paisagem: Sert e o Town Planning Associates na América do Sud, 1943–1951, in Gomes, M.A. de F. (ed.) *Urbanismo na América do Sul. Circulação de idéias e constituição do campo*. Salvador de Bahia: Edufba, pp. 149–173.

Gómez Carrillo, E. (1993) *La vida parisiense*. Caracas: Biblioteca Ayacucho.

González Casas, L. (1996) Modernity and the City. Caracas 1935–1958. PhD dissertation, Cornell University.

González Casas, L. (2002) Urbanismo y patrimonio. La conservación de los centros históricos, in *Premio Nacional de Investigación en Vivienda 2001*. Caracas: Consejo Nacional de la Vivienda (CONAVI), pp. 131–295.

González Téllez, S. (2005) *La ciudad venezolana. Una interpretación de su espacio y sentido de la convivencia nacional*. Caracas: Fundación para la Cultura Urbana.

Goodwin, P. (1943) *Brazil Builds: Architecture Old and New, 1652–1942/ Construção brasileira: arquitetura moderna e antiga 1642–1942*. New York: Museum of Modern Art.

Gorelik, A. (1999) *La grilla y el parque. Espacio público y cultura urbana en Buenos Aires, 1887–1936*. Buenos Aires: Universidad Nacional de Quilmes.

Gorelik, A. (2001) Mapas de identidad. La imaginación territorial en el ensayo de interpretación nacional: de Ezequiel Martínez Estrada a Bernardo Canal Feijóo. *Prismas. Revista de Historia Intelectual*, **5**, pp. 283–311.

Gorelik, A. (2005) *Das vanguardas a Brasília. Cultura urbana e arquitetura na América Latina*, trans. Pereira, M.A. Belo Horizonte: Editora UFMG.

Gourdon, H. (2011) El Estado en América Latina: democratización y gobernanza, in Quenan, C. and Velut, S. (eds.) *Los desafíos del desarrollo en América Latina. Dinámicas socioeconómicas y políticas públicas*. Paris: Institut des Amériques, Agence Française de Développement (AFP), pp. 111–142.

Griffin, C.C. (1961) *The National Period in the History of the New World. An Outline and Commentary*. México: Instituto Panamericano de Geografía e Historia.

Grimson, A. (2008) Prefacio, in Portes, R., Roberts, B. and Grimson, A. (eds.) *Ciudades latinoamericanas. Un análisis comparativo en el umbral del nuevo siglo*. Buenos Aires: Prometeo Libros, pp. 9–17.

Gross, P. (1991, nd) Santiago de Chile (1925–1990): planificación urbana y modelos políticos, in de Mattos, C. *et al.* (eds.) *Santiago en EURE. Huellas de una metamorfosis metropolitana 1970/2000*. Santiago: Instituto de Estudios Urbanos y Territoriales (IEUT), Pontificia Universidad Católica de Chile (PUC), pp. 129–169.

Grupo de Diarios de América (GDA) (2010) El tablero político se mueve en América Latina. *El Mercurio/El Nacional*, 5 June, p. I-10.

Grupo de Diarios de América (GDA) (2011) Panamá se transformó en el Singapur de América Latina. *El Mercurio/El Nacional*, 27 July, p. 8.

Guaregua, O. (2011) 90 millones de latinoamericanos y caribeños viven en la pobreza. *El Nacional*, 26 October, p. I-8.

Guerrero, L.B. (1978) *Modernismo y modernistas*. Caracas: Academia Nacional de la Historia.

Guevara, E. 'Che' (1960, 2009) *Guerrilla Warfare*. Melbourne: Ocean Press.

Gutiérrez, R. (1984) *Arquitectura y Urbanismo en Iberoamérica*. Madrid: Cátedra.

Gutiérrez, R. (2010) Buenos Aires, a great European city, in Almandoz, A. (ed.) *Planning Latin America's Capital Cities, 1850–1950*. London: Routledge, pp. 45–74.

Guzmán Blanco, A. (1876) *Mensajes presentados por el general Guzmán Blanco, como Presidente Provisional de los Estados Unidos de Venezuela, al Congreso de Plenipotenciarios en 1870, y como Presidente Constitucional al Cuerpo Legislativo en 1873, 74, 75 y 76*. Caracas: Imprenta de 'La Opinión Nacional' por Fausto Teodoro de Aldrey.

Guzmán Blanco, A. (1880) *Mensaje del general Guzmán Blanco al Congreso Constitucional*. Caracas: Imprenta de la 'Gaceta Oficial'.

Hall, P. (1974, 1992) *Urban and Regional Planning*. London: Routledge.

Halperin Donghi, T. (1967, 2005) *Historia contemporánea de América Latina*. Madrid: Alianza Editorial.

Hardoy, J.E. (ed.) (1975a) *Urbanization in Latin America. Approaches and Issues*. New York: Anchor Books.

Hardoy, J.E. (1975b) Two thousand years of Latin American urbanization, in Hardoy, J.E. (ed.) *Urbanization in Latin America. Approaches and Issues*. New York: Anchor Books, pp. 3–55.

Hardoy, J.E. (1988) Teorías y prácticas urbanísticas en Europa entre 1850 y 1930. Su traslado a América Latina, in Hardoy, J.E. and Morse, R.M. (eds.) *Repensando la ciudad de América Latina*. Buenos Aires: Grupo Editor Latinoamericano (GEL), pp. 97–126.

Hardoy, J.E. (1997) Las ciudades de América Latina a partir de 1900, in *La ciudad hispanoamericana. El sueño de un orden*. Madrid: Centro de Estudios Históricos de Obras Públicas y Urbanismo (Cehopu), Centro de Estudios y Experimentación de Obras Públicas (Cedex), Ministerio de Fomento, pp. 267–274.

Hardoy, J.E. and Satterthwaite, D. (1986) *Small and Intermediate Urban Centres: Their Role in Regional and National Development in the Third World*. London: Hodder & Stoughton.

Hardoy, J.E. and Schaedel, R.P. (eds.) (1975) *Las ciudades de América Latina y sus áreas de influencia a través de la historia*. Buenos Aires: Sociedad Interamericana de Planificación (SIAP).

Hardoy, J.E. and Tobar, C. (eds.) (1969) *La urbanización en América Latina*. Buenos Aires: Instituto Torcuato Di Tella.

Hardoy, J.E. et al. (1981) *El impacto de la urbanización en los centros históricos de América Latina*. Lima: PNUD, UNESCO.
Harouel, J.-L. (1981) *Histoire de l'Urbanisme*. Paris: Presses Universitaires de France (PUF).
Harris, W.D. Jr (1971) *The Growth of Latin American Cities*. Athens, OH: Ohio University Press.
Harth-terré, E. (1961) *Filosofía en el Urbanismo*. Lima: Editorial Tierra y Arte.
Harvey, D. (1973) *Social Justice and the City*. London: Edward Arnold.
Harvey, D. (1990) *The Condition of Postmodernity. An Enquiry into the Origins of Cultural Change*. Oxford: Blackwell.
Hauser, P.M. (ed.) (1967) *La urbanización en América Latina*. Buenos Aires: Solar, Hachette.
Haussmann, G.E.B. de (1890–1893, 1979) *Mémoires*. Paris: Guy Durier, 2 vols.
Hebbert, M. (2006) Town planning versus urbanismo. *Planning Perspectives*, **21**(3), pp. 233–251.
Herwig, H. (1986) *Germany's Vision of Empire in Venezuela, 1871–1914*. Princeton, NJ: Princeton University Press.
Hidalgo, R. (2005) *La vivienda social en Chile y la construcción del espacio urbano en el Santiago del siglo XX*. Santiago: Instituto de Geografía, Pontificia Universidad Católica de Chile (PUC), Centro de Investigaciones Diego Barros Arana.
Hidalgo, R. (2007) Cien años de política de vivienda social, cien años de expulsión de los pobres a la periferia de Santiago, in Castillo, M.J. and Hidalgo, R. (eds.) *1906/2006. Cien años de política de vivienda en Chile*. Santiago: Universidad Nacional Andrés Bello, Pontificia Universidad Católica de Chile (PUC), Universidad Central de Venezuela (UCV), pp. 51–63.
Hitchcock, H.-R. (1955) *Modern Architecture in Latin America since 1945*. New York: Museum of Modern Art.
Hofer, A. (2003) *Karl Brunner y el urbanismo europeo en América Latina*, trans. Ungar, L. and Martín, O. Bogotá: El Áncora Editores, Corporación La Candelaria.
Hommes, R. (1998) Welcoming address: poverty in Colombia, in Javed Burki, S. et al. (eds.) *Annual World Bank Conference on Development in Latin America and the Caribbean 1996. Poverty and Inequality*. Washington DC: The World Bank, pp. 10–12.
Hoshino, C. (1997) Introducción general al seminario 'Planeamiento y Gestión Urbana Estratégica en América Latina', in *Planeamiento y gestión urbana estratégica en América Latina*. Santiago: Centro de las Naciones Unidas para el Desarrollo Regional (UNCRD), Corporación para el Desarrollo de Santiago, pp. 37–44.
Huapaya Espinoza, J.C. (2009) A construção do Peru pelos peruanos: a experiência urbanistica em Lima, 1919–1963, in Gomes, M.A. de F. (ed.) *Urbanismo na América do Sul. Circulação de idéias e constituição do campo*. Salvador de Bahia: Edufba, pp. 203–230.
Hyde, T. (2012) *Constitutional Modernism. Architecture and Civil Society in Cuba, 1933–1959*. Minneapolis, MN: University of Minnesota Press.
International Monetary Fund (IMF) (2011) *World Economic Outlook, database*. Available at: http://www.imf.org/external/pubs/ft/weo/2011/01/weodata/index.aspx.

Irazábal, C. (2008) Citizenship, democracy and public space in Latin America, in Irazábal, C. (ed.) *Ordinary Places, Extraordinary Events. Citizenship, Democracy and Public Space in Latin America*. London: Routledge, pp. 11–34.

Irazábal, C. and Foley, J. (2008) Space, revolution and resistance: ordinary places and extraordinary events in Caracas, in Irazábal, C. (ed.) *Ordinary Places, Extraordinary Events. Citizenship, Democracy and Public Space in Latin America*. London: Routledge, pp. 144–169.

Javed Burki, S. (1998) Opening statement: dismantling the populist state, in Javed Burki, S. *et al.* (eds.) *Annual World Bank Conference on Development in Latin America and the Caribbean 1996. Poverty and Inequality*. Washington DC: World Bank, pp. 7–9.

Juárez, B. *et al.* (1859, 2007) Justificación de las Leyes de Reforma, in Juárez, B. *Antología*. México: Universidad Nacional Autónoma de México (UNAM), pp. 86–110.

Kaiser, S. (2008) The struggle for human territories: human right activists in Buenos Aires, in Irazábal, C. (ed.) *Ordinary Places, Extraordinary Events. Citizenship, Democracy and Public Space in Latin America*. London: Routledge, pp. 170–197.

Kaplan, M. (1972) La ciudad latinoamericana como factor de transmisión de control socioeconómico y político externo durante el período contemporáneo. *Boletín del Centro de Investigaciones Históricas y Estéticas*, **14**, pp. 90–124.

Kessel, C. (2001) *A vitrine e o espelho. O Rio de Janeiro de Carlos Sampaio*. Rio de Janeiro: Prefeitura da Cidade do Rio de Janeiro.

Kidd, B. (1898) *The Control of the Tropics*. London: Macmillan.

King, A.D. (1991) *Global Cities. Post-Imperialism and the Internationalization of London*. London: Routledge.

Knight, F.W. (1990) *The Caribbean. The Genesis of a Fragmented Nationalism*. Oxford: Oxford University Press.

Kostof, S. (1992) *The City Assembled. The Elements of Urban Form through History*. Boston, MA: Little Brown and Company.

Krauze, E. (2008) *El poder y el delirio*. Caracas: Editorial Alfa.

Krauze, E. (2012) México, la democracia imperfecta. *El Nacional*, 2 July, p. A-9.

Lamparelli, C.M. (1998) Louis-Joseph Lebret e a pesquisa urbano regional no Brasil. Crônicas tardias ou história prematura, in Padilha, N. (ed.) *Cidade e urbanismo. História, teorias e práticas*. Salvador de Bahia: Faufba, pp. 281–298.

Lanna, A. *et al.* (eds.) (2011) *São Paulo, os estrangeiros e a construção das cidades*. São Paulo: Alameda.

Larraín Bravo, R. (1909–1910) *La Higiene aplicada en las construcciones (alcantarillado, agua potable, saneamiento, calefacción, ventilación, etc.)*. Santiago: Imprenta Cervantes, 3 vols.

Latin American and the Caribbean Demographic Observatory (2009) *Urbanization Prospects*. Santiago: UN, ECLAC. Available at: http://www.eclac.cl/publicaciones/xml/8/38298/lcg2422P.pdf.

Lautier, B. (2011) Políticas de redistribución y de transferencias sociales, in Quenan, C. and Velut, S. (eds.) *Los desafíos del desarrollo en América Latina. Dinámicas socioeconómicas y políticas públicas*. Paris: Institut des Amériques, Agence Française de Développement (AFP), pp. 254–292.

Le Corbusier (C.E. Jeanneret) (1930) *Précisions sur un état présent de l'architecture et de l'urbanisme*. Paris: Les Éditions G. Crès & Cie.

Le Corbusier (1931, 1986) *Towards a New Architecture*. New York: Dover Publications.

Le Corbusier (1941, 1971) *La Charte d'Athènes* (1941). Paris: Éditions du Minuit.

Ledezma, P.F. (1993) Los últimos treinta años, in *Historia mínima de Venezuela*. Caracas: Fundación de los Trabajadores de Lagovén, pp. 185–202.

Leme, M.C. da S. (1999a) A formação do pensamento urbanístico no Brasil, 1865–1965, in Leme, M. C. da S. (ed.) *Urbanismo no Brasil, 1895–1965*. São Paulo: Fupam, Studio Nobel, pp. 20–38.

Leme, M.C. da S. (ed.) (1999b) *Urbanismo no Brasil, 1895–1965*. São Paulo: Fupam, Studio Nobel.

Leme, M.C. da S. (2003) Os desafios do urbanismo no Brasil: ensino e profissão, in Machado, D.B.P. et al. (eds.) *Urbanismo em Questão*. Rio de Janeiro: Prourb, Universidade Federal de Rio de Janeiro (UFRJ), CNPq, pp. 109–126.

Lewis, O. (1961) *The Children of Sánchez. Autobiography of a Mexican Family*. New York: Vintage Books.

Liernur, F. and Pschepiurca, P. (2008) *La red austral. Obras y proyectos de Le Corbusier y sus discípulos en la Argentina (1924–1965)*. Buenos Aires: Universidad Nacional de Quilmes/Prometeo 3010.

Liernur, F. and Silvestri, G. (1993) *El umbral de la metrópolis. Transformaciones técnicas y cultura en la modernización de Buenos Aires*. Buenos Aires: Sudamericana.

Lombardi, J. (1982) *Venezuela. The Search of Order, the Dream of Progress*. Oxford: Oxford University Press.

Lombardo, J.D. (1999) *Pensamiento urbanístico y desarrollo urbano en la Región Metropolitana de Buenos Aires*. Buenos Aires: Instituto del Conurbano, Universidad Nacional de General Sarmiento.

López, L. (1882, 1953) *La gran aldea*, in *Tres épocas de Buenos Aires*. Madrid: Aguilar, pp. 43–255.

López Villa, M. (1986) La arquitectura del '2 de Diciembre'. *Boletín del Centro de Investigaciones Históricas y Estéticas*, **27**, pp. 148–172.

López Villa, M. (1994) Gestión urbanística, revolución democrática y dictadura militar en Venezuela (1945–1958). *Urbana*, **14/15**, pp. 103–119.

Ludeña, W. (2011) Lima: transformaciones urbanas y reestructuración morfológica. Urbanismo, vivienda y centro histórico. Período 1990–2007, in de Mattos, C. and Ludeña, W. (eds.) *Lima-Santiago. Reestructuración y cambio metropolitano*. Santiago y Lima: Instituto de Estudios Urbanos y Territoriales (IEUT), Pontificia Universidad Católica de Chile (PUC), Centro de Investigación de la Arquitectura y la Ciudad, Pontificia Universidad Católica del Perú, pp. 69–106.

Luna, F. (1993, 2005) *Breve historia de los argentinos*. Buenos Aires: Planeta.

Lyons, J. and Magalhães, L. (2012) La desaceleración pone en duda el modelo de crecimiento brasileño. *El Nacional/Wall Street Journal of the Americas*, 12 July, p. I-9.

McLaughlin Green, C. (1968) *El crecimiento urbano de los Estados Unidos*, trans. Setaro, F. Buenos Aires: Ediciones Infinito.

Mármol, J. (1851–1855, 2000) *Amalia*. Madrid: Cátedra.

Martín-Barbero, J. (2010) Mediaciones urbanas y nuevos escenarios de comunicación, in Hernández, T. (ed.) *Ciudad, espacio público y cultura urbana. 25 conferencias de la Cátedra Permanente de Imágenes Urbanas*. Caracas: Fundación para la Cultura Urbana, pp. 23–39.

Martínez, T.E. (2004) El último Perón. *El Nacional*, 1 August, p. A-15.

Martínez, T.E. (2007) Isabel, la mejor discípula. *El Nacional*, 4 February, p. A-9.

Martínez Estrada, E. (1940, 1983) *La cabeza de Goliat. Microscopía de Buenos Aires*. Buenos Aires: Editorial Losada.

Martínez Olavarría, L. (1996) Problema de vivienda en Venezuela, in Lovera, A. (ed.) *Leopoldo Martínez Olavarría. Desarrollo urbano, vivienda y Estado*. Caracas: Fondo Editorial ALEMO, pp. 53–63.

Mattalia, S. (1995) Sueño y desilusión de la modernidad: imágenes de la ciudad en el fin de siglo latinoamericano, in González, B. *et al.* (eds.) *Esplendores y miserias del siglo XIX. Cultura y sociedad en América Latina*. Caracas: Monte Ávila Editores Latinoamericana, Equinoccio, Ediciones de la Universidad Simón Bolívar (USB), pp. 519–531.

Medina Febres, M. (1991) *Medo: caricaturas de lucha, 1936–1939*. Caracas: Presidencia de la República.

Mendoza, S. (ed.) (1980) *Así es Caracas*. Caracas: Editorial Ateneo de Caracas.

Meyer, L. (1973, 2005) Years of crisis, years of opportunity, in *A Compact History of Mexico*. trans. Mattingly Urquidi. M. México: El Colegio de México, pp. 147–158.

Molina, T. (2014) Venezuela es el segundo país más violento del mundo. *El Universal*, 11 April, p. 3–10.

Momentos clave de una era (2013) *El Nacional*, 7 March, pp. 6–7.

Montoya, J.W. (2006) *Cambio urbano y evolución discursiva en el análisis de la ciudad latinoamericana: de la dependencia a la globalización*. Bogotá: Universidad Nacional de Colombia (UNC).

Moraes, A.C.R. (2004) *Território e história no Brasil*. São Paulo: Annablume.

Morris, I.N. (1897) *With the Trade-Winds. A Jaunt in Venezuela and the West Indies*. New York: Putnams Sons.

Morse, R.M. (1971) Latin American cities in the 19th century: approaches and tentative generalizations, in Morse, R.M. *et al.* (eds.) *The Urban Development of Latin America 1750–1920*. Stanford, CA: Center for Latin American Studies, Stanford University, pp. 1–21.

Morse, R.M. (1973) *Las ciudades latinoamericanas*, 2 vols. Mexico: SEP.

Morse, R.M. (1975) El desarrollo de los sistemas urbanos en las Américas durante el siglo XIX, in Hardoy, J.E. and Schaedel, R.P. (eds.) *Las ciudades de América Latina y sus áreas de influencia a través de la historia*. Buenos Aires: Sociedad Interamericana de Planificación (SIAP), pp. 263–290.

Morse, R.M. (1978) Los intelectuales latinoamericanos y la ciudad (1860–1940), in Hardoy, J.E. *et al.* (eds.) *Ensayos histórico-sociales sobre la urbanización en América Latina*. Buenos Aires: Consejo Latinoamericano de Ciencias Sociales (CLACSO), Ediciones SIAP, pp. 91–112.

Morse, R.M. (1982) *El espejo de Próspero: un estudio de la dialéctica del Nuevo Mundo*, trans. Mastrangelo, S. México: Siglo Veintiuno Editores.

Mulhall, M.G. (1878) *The English in South America*. Buenos Aires: Standard Office.
Mumford, L. (1961) *The City in History. Its Origins, its Transformations, and its Prospects*. New York: Harcourt, Brace & World.
Munro, D. (1964) *Intervention and Dollar Diplomacy in the Caribbean 1900–1921*. Princeton, NJ: Princeton University Press.
Myrdal, G. (1957) *Economic Theory and Underdeveloped Areas*. London: Duckworth.
Naím, M. (2010) México, no; Brasil, si. *El Nacional*, 27 October, p. I-10.
Naím, M. (2013) Lo bueno, lo malo y lo feo. *El Nacional*, 13 March, p. I-10.
Needell, J. (1987) *A Tropical Belle Époque. Elite, Culture and Society in Turn-of-the-century Rio de Janeiro*. Cambridge: Cambridge University Press.
Negrón, M. (2001) *Ciudad y modernidad, 1936–2000. El rol del sistema de ciudades en la modernización de Venezuela*. Caracas: Instituto de Urbanismo, Comisión de Estudios de Postgrado, Facultad de Arquitectura y Urbanismo (FAU), Universidad Central de Venezuela (UCV).
Neruda, P. (1982) *Para nacer he nacido*. Barcelona: Seix Barral.
Novais, F.A. (1979) *Portugal e Brasil na crise do antigo sistema colonial (1777–1808)*. São Paulo: Editora Hucitec.
Núñez, E.B. (1943, 1986) *El hombre de la levita gris*. Caracas: Monte Ávila Editores.
Ocampo López, J. (1994, 2007) *Historia básica de Colombia*. Bogotá: Plaza & Janés.
Ochoa Vega, A. (1993) México. Formas arquitectónicas y ciudad, in Cortés, J.L. (ed.) *París-México. La primera modernidad arquitectónica*. México: Instituto Francés de América Latina (IFAL), Colegio de Arquitectos de México, Sociedad de Arquitectos Mexicanos (CAM-SAM), Universidad Autónoma Metropolitana-Xochimilco (UAM-X), pp. 89–92.
O'Donnell, G. (1982) *El estado burocrático-autoritario, 1966–1973*. Buenos Aires: Editorial de Belgrano.
Oficina Municipal de Planeamiento Urbano (OMPU) (1972) *Plan General Urbano de Caracas 1970–1990*. Caracas: OMPU.
O'Gorman, J. (1933, 2001) Lecture in *Pláticas sobre arquitectura. México, 1933*. México: Universidad Nacional Autónoma de México (UNAM), Universidad Autónoma Metropolitana-Azcapotzalco, pp. 53–67.
Pagden, A. (1995) *Lords of all the Worlds. Ideologies of Empire in Spain, Britain and France c.1500–c.1800*. New Haven, CT: Yale University Press.
Palma, G. (1978) Dependency: a formal theory of underdevelopment or a methodology for the analysis of concrete situations of underdevelopment. *World Development*, **7/8**, pp. 881–920.
Palou Egoaguirre, J. (2012) Un decaído México busca la fórmula para poder despertar de la siesta económica. *El Mercurio*, 29 June, p. A-10.
Paquette, C. (2011) Las políticas de inversión urbana, in Quenan, C. and Velut, S. (eds.) *Los desafíos del desarrollo en América Latina. Dinámicas socioeconómicas y políticas públicas*. Paris: Institut des Amériques, Agence Française de Développement (AFP), pp. 293–324.
Park, R.E. (1916, 1984) The city: suggestions for the investigation of human behavior

in the urban environment, in Park, R.E. and Burgess, E.W., *The City. Suggestions for Investigation of Human Behavior in the Urban Environment*. Chicago, IL: University of Chicago Press, pp. 1–46.

Park, R.E. and Burgess, E.W. (1925, 1984) *The City. Suggestions for Investigation of Human Behavior in the Urban Environment*. Chicago, IL: University of Chicago Press.

Parker, D.S. (1998) Civilizing the city of kings: hygiene and housing in Lima, Peru, in Pineo, R. and Baer, J.A. (eds.) *Cities of Hope. People, Protests and Progress in Urbanizing Latin America, 1870–1930*. Boulder, CO: Westview Press, pp.153–178.

Pavez, M.I. (1992) Precursores de la enseñanza del urbanismo en Chile. Período 1928–1953. *Revista de Arquitectura*, **3**, pp. 2–11.

Pavez, M.I. (2009–2010) Temprana modernidad del Urbanismo en Santiago de Chile: interacciones entre Jacques Lambert, Karl Brunner, Luis Muñoz y Roberto Humeres, in *Karl Brunner desde el Bicentenario*. Santiago: Facultad de Arquitectura y Urbanismo, Universidad de Chile, Embajada de Austria, pp. 12–25.

Paz, O. (1950, 1980) *El laberinto de la soledad*. México: Fondo de Cultura Económica (FCE).

Pereira, M. da S. (1995) Pensando a metrópole moderna: os planos de Agache e Le Corbusier para o Rio de Janeiro. *DANA. Documentos de Arquitectura Nacional y Americana*, **37/38**, pp. 97–105.

Pereira, M. da S. (2003) Notas sobre Urbanismo no Brasil: construções e crises de um campo disciplinar, in Machado, D.B.P. et al. (eds.) *Urbanismo em Questão*. Rio de Janeiro: Prourb, Universidade Federal de Rio de Janeiro (UFRJ), CNPq, pp. 55–83.

Pereira, M. da S. (2010) The time of the capitals: Rio de Janeiro and São Paulo: words, actors and plans, in Almandoz, A. (ed.) *Planning Latin America's Capital Cities, 1850–1950*. London: Routledge, pp. 75–108.

Pereira da Silva, M.L. (2012) Reflexões sobre a política habitacional na era Vargas, in Rezende, V (ed.) *Urbanismo na Era Vargas: a transformação das cidades brasileiras*. Niterói: Editora da UFF, Intertexto Editora, pp. 303–331.

Pérez Jiménez, M. (1955) *Cinco discursos del general Marcos Pérez Jiménez, Presidente de la República, pronunciados durante el año 1955 y obras realizadas por el Gobierno*. Caracas: Imprenta Nacional.

Pérez Oyarzun, F. (1991) Le Corbusier y Sudamérica en el viaje del 29, in Pérez Oyarzun, F. (ed.) *Le Corbusier y Sudamérica, viajes y proyectos*. Santiago: Escuela de Arquitectura, Pontificia Universidad Católica de Chile (PUC), pp. 15–41.

Pérez Oyarzun, F. and Rosas Vera, J. (2010) Cities within the city: urban and architectural transfers in Santiago de Chile, 1840–1940, in Almandoz, A. (ed.) *Planning Latin America's Capital Cities, 1850–1950*. London: Routledge, pp. 109–138.

Perroux, F. (1955) Note sur la notion de pôle de croissance. *Économie Appliquée*, **1/2**, pp. 307–320.

Picón Salas, M. (1953, 1991) *Los días de Cipriano Castro*. Caracas: Monte Ávila Editores.

Picón Salas, M. (1988) *Suma de Venezuela. Biblioteca Mariano Picón-Salas*, Vol. 2. Caracas: Monte Ávila Editores.

Picón Salas, M. (1996) *Europa-América. Biblioteca Mariano Picón-Salas*, Vol. 5. Caracas: Monte Ávila Editores Latinoamericana.

Pineo, R. and Baer, J.A. Urbanization, the working class and reform, in Pineo, R. and Baer J. A. (eds.) (1998a) *Cities of Hope. People, Protests and Progress in Urbanizing Latin America, 1870–1930*. Boulder, CO: Westview Press, pp. 258–274.

Pineo, R. and Baer J.A. (eds.) (1998b) *Cities of Hope. People, Protests and Progress in Urbanizing Latin America, 1870–1930*. Boulder, CO: Westview Press.

Piñera, S. (2011) El tercer muro. *El Nacional*, 18 January, p. I-8.

Pinheiro, E.P. (2002) *Europa, França e Bahia. Difusão e adaptação de modelos urbanos. (Paris, Rio e Salvador)*. Salvador: Edufba.

Pino Iturrieta, E. (1988) *Venezuela metida en cintura. 1900–1945*. Caracas: Cuadernos Lagovén.

Pino Iturrieta, E. (1993) Ideas sobre un pueblo inepto: la justificación del gomecismo, in Pino Iturrieta, E. (ed.) *Juan Vicente Gómez y su época*. Caracas: Monte Ávila Editores Latinoamericana, pp. 187–201.

Pinochet, Augusto (1980) *El día decisivo. 11 de septiembre de 1973*. Santiago: Editorial Andrés Bello.

Pinto Santa Cruz, A. (1962) *Chile, un caso de desarrollo frustrado*. Santiago: Editorial Universitaria.

Pírez, P. (2009) Introducción, in Pírez, P. (ed.) *Buenos Aires, la formación del presente*. Quito: Organización Latinoamericana y del Caribe de Centros Históricos (Olacchi), pp. 9–32.

Pizarro, E. (2000) Colombia: 'hacia un colapso institucional', in Rotker, S. (ed.) *Ciudadanías del miedo*. Caracas: Nueva Sociedad, Rutgers University, pp. 55–68.

Pocaterra, J.R. (1927, 1966) *Memorias de un venezolano de la decadencia*. Madrid: Edime, 4 vols.

Portes, A. and Roberts, B. (2008) Introducción. La ciudad bajo el libre mercado. La urbanización en América latina durante los años del experimento neoliberal, in Portes, R. et al. (eds.) *Ciudades latinoamericanas. Un análisis comparativo en el umbral del nuevo siglo*. Buenos Aires: Prometeo Libros, pp. 19–74.

Potter, R.E. and Lloyd-Evans, S. (1998) *The City in the Developing World*. London: Longman.

Prado, P. (1928, 2000) *Retrato do Brasil. Ensaio sobre a tristeza brasileira*, in *Intérpretes do Brasil*. Río de Janeiro: Editora Nova Aguilar.

Prado Júnior, C. (1968, 1999) *História e desenvolvimento. A contribuição da historiografia para a teoria e prática do desenvolvimento brasileiro*. São Paulo: Editora Brasiliense.

Prestes Maia, F. (1930) *Estudo de um plano de avenidas para a Cidade de São Paulo*. São Paulo: Melhoramentos.

Programa de las Naciones Unidas para El Desarrollo (PNUD) (2011) *Informe sobre desarrollo humano 2011. Sostenibilidad y equidad: un mejor futuro para todos*. New York: UN. Available at: http://hdr.undp.org/en/reports/global/hdr2011/download/.

Puga Borne, F. (1891) *Elementos de Hijiene*. Santiago: Imprenta Gutenberg, 2 vols.

Quenan, C. and Torija-Zane, E. (2011) Dinámicas económicas: tendencias y perspectivas, in Quenan, C. and Velut, S. (eds.) *Los desafíos del desarrollo en América Latina. Dinámicas socioeconómicas y políticas públicas*. Paris: Institut des Amériques, Agence Française de Développement (AFP), pp. 19–81.

Quenan, C., Velut, S. and Allou, S. (2011) Introducción. Las dinámicas económicas y sociales de América Latina: los grandes desafíos, in Quenan, C. and Velut, S. (eds.) *Los desafíos del desarrollo en América Latina. Dinámicas socioeconómicas y políticas públicas*. Paris: Institut des Amériques, Agence Française de Développement (AFP), pp. 11–17.

Quesada, F. (2001) *En el barrio Amón. Arquitectura, familia y sociabilidad del primer residencial de la élite urbana de San José, 1900-1935*. San José: Editorial de la Universidad de Costa Rica, Comisión Nacional de Conmemoraciones Históricas.

Quesada, F. (2007) *La modernización entre cafetales. San José, Costa Rica, 1880–1930*. Helsinki: Renvall Institute, University of Helsinki.

Quijano, A. (1977) *Dependencia, urbanización y cambio social en Latinoamérica*. Lima: Mosca Azul.

Quiroz Rothe, H. (2008) *Ciudades mexicanas del siglo XX*. México: Facultad de Arquitectura, Universidad Nacional Autónoma de México (UNAM).

Rama, A. (1984) *La ciudad letrada*. Hanover, NH: Ediciones del Norte.

Ramírez, J.F (2010) Teorías legitimadoras de la planificación urbana en Colombia 1950–2000. MPhil. dissertation working paper, Universidad Nacional de Colombia (UNC).

Ramón, G. (2010) The script of urban surgery: Lima, 1850–1914, in Almandoz, A. (ed.) *Planning Latin America's Capital Cities, 1850–1950*. London: Routledge, pp. 170–192.

Ramos, R. (1989) *Desencuentros de la modernidad en América Latina. Literatura y política en el siglo XIX*. México: Fondo de Cultura Económica (FCE).

Randle, P.H. (1968) *Qué es el Urbanismo*. Buenos Aires: Editorial Columba.

Randle, P.H. (1977) Introducción, in della Paolera, C.M., *Buenos Aires y sus problemas urbanos*. Buenos Aires: Oikos, pp. 11–20.

Rangel, C. (1976, 2005) *Del buen salvaje al buen revolucionario. Mitos y realidades de América Latina*. Caracas: Criteria.

Redfield, R. (1947, 1969) The Folk Society, in Sennett, R. (ed.) *Classic Essays on the Culture of Cities*. New York: Appleton-Century-Crofts, Meredith Corporation, pp. 180-205.

Reissman, L. (1964) *The Urban Process: Cities in Industrial Societies*. New York: The Free Press.

Remini, R.V. (2008) *A Short History of the United States. From the Arrival of Native American Tribes to the Obama Presidency*. New York: Harper Perennial.

Renan, E. (1878) *Caliban*. Paris: Calmann Lévy.

Reseña de la historia de los Estados Unidos (n/d) Servicio Informativo y Cultural de los Estados Unidos de América.

Rezende, V. (ed.) (2012) *Urbanismo na Era Vargas: a transformação das cidades brasileiras*. Niterói: Editora da UFF, Intertexto Editora.

Ribeiro, L.C.Q. (2003) Segregación, desigualdad y vivienda: la metrópolis de Río de Janeiro en los años 80 y 90. *Ciudad y Territorio. Estudios Territoriales*, **35**(136/137), pp. 295–314.

Rippy, J.F. (1944) *Latin America and the Industrial Age*. New York: Putnam's Sons.

Rippy, J.F. (1959) *British Investments in Latin America, 1822–1949. A Case Study in the Operations of Private Enterprise in Retarded Regions*. Minneapolis, MN: University of Minnesota Press.

Roberts, B. (1978) *Cities of Peasants. The Political Economy of Urbanization in the Third World*. London: Edward Arnold.

Roberts, B. and Portes, A. (2008) Conclusión. Enfrentando la ciudad del libre mercado. La acción colectiva urbana en América Latina, 1980–2000, in Portes, R. *et al.* (eds.) *Ciudades latinoamericanas. Un análisis comparativo en el umbral del nuevo siglo*. Buenos Aires: Prometeo Libros, pp. 509–556.

Rodó, J.E. (1900, 1912) *Ariel*. Valencia: E Sempere y Compañía, Editores.

Rodó, J.E. (1994) *Ciudadano de Roma*. Caracas: Biblioteca Ayacucho.

Rodríguez, J. (2010) Brasil, el gigante despertó. *El País/El Nacional*, 3 January, pp. 1–2.

Rodrigues Porto, A. (1992) *História urbanística da cidade de São Paulo (1554 a 1988)*. São Paulo: Carthago & Forte.

Rodwin, L. (1982) Ciudad Guayana, una ciudad nueva, in *La ciudad*. Madrid: Scientific American, Alianza Editorial, pp. 113–133.

Rofman, A.B. (1977) *Dependencia, estructura de poder y formación regional en América Latina*. México: Siglo Veintiuno Editores.

Romero, A. (1999) *Decadencia y crisis de la democracia*. Caracas: Editorial Panapo.

Romero, J.L. (1946, 2008) *Las ideas políticas en Argentina*. Buenos Aires: Fondo de Cultura Económica (FCE).

Romero, J.L. (1953, 2004) *La cultura occidental*. Buenos Aires: Siglo Veintiuno Editores.

Romero, J.L. (1976, 1984) *Latinoamérica, las ciudades y las ideas*. México: Siglo Veintiuno.

Romero, J.L. (1994, 2013) *A History of Argentina in the Twentieth Century*. University Park, PA. Pennsylvania State University Press.

Romero, J.L. (2002) *El obstinado rigor. Hacia una historia cultural de América Latina*. México: Centro Coordinador y Difusor de Estudios Latinoamericanos, Universidad Nacional Autónoma de México (UNAM).

Romero, L.A. (2007) Sectores populares, asociacionismo y política. Buenos Aires, 1912–1976, in Valenzuela Márquez, J. (ed.) *Historias urbanas. Homenaje a Armando de Ramón*. Santiago: Instituto de Historia, Ediciones Universidad Católica de Chile, pp. 291–311.

Rosas, F. (2010) *A Brief History of Peru*. Lima: Ediciones El Lector.

Rosende, F. (2007) Introduction, in Rosende, F. (ed.) *La Escuela de Chicago. Uma mirada histórica a 50 años del convenio Chicago/Universidad Católica. Ensayos en honor a Arnold C. Harberger*. Santiago: Facultad de Ciencias Económicas y Administrativas, Ediciones Universidad Católica de Chile, pp. 19–21.

Rostow, W.W. (1960, 1990) *The Stages of Economic Growth. A Non-Communist Manifesto*. Cambridge: Cambridge University Press.

Rotival, M. (1964) Planification et urbanisme. *Urbanisme*, **82/83**, pp. 42–45.

Rotker, S. (2000) Ciudades escritas por la violencia. (A modo de introducción), in Rotker, S. (ed.) *Ciudadanías del miedo*. Caracas: Nueva Sociedad, Rutgers University, pp. 7–22.

Rourke, T. (1936) *Tyrant of the Andes. The Life of Juan Vicente Gómez*. London: Michael Joseph.
Rowe, C. and Koetter, F. (1981) *Collage City*. Cambridge, MA: MIT Press.
Sabatini, F. and Salcedo, R. (2011) Understanding deep urban change. Patterns of residential segregation in Latin America, in Judd, D.R. and Simpson, D. (eds.) *The City Revisited. Urban Theory From Chicago, Los Angeles and New York*. Minneapolis, MN: University of Minnesota Press, pp. 332–355.
Sánchez Ruiz, G. (2003) El contexto que rodeó la propuesta de planificación del arquitecto Carlos Contreras, in Sánchez Ruiz, G. (ed.) *Planificación y Urbanismo visionarios de Carlos Contreras. Escritos de 1925 a 1935*. México: Universidad Nacional Autónoma de México (UNAM), Universidad Autónoma Metropolitana-Azcapotzalco, Universidad Autónoma de San Luis de Potosí, pp. 9–24.
Sánchez Ruiz, G. (2008) *Planeación moderna de ciudades*. México: Trillas.
Sanjuán, A.M. (2000) Democracia, ciudadanía y violencia en Venezuela, in Rotker, S. (ed.) *Ciudadanías del miedo*. Caracas: Nueva Sociedad, Rutgers University, pp. 81–93.
Sarmiento, D.F. (1845, 1985) *Facundo o civilización y barbarie*. Caracas: Biblioteca Ayacucho.
Sarmiento, D.F. (1845, 1991) *Recuerdos de provincia*. Caracas: Biblioteca Ayacucho.
Sarmiento, D.F. (1849) *De la educación popular*. Santiago: Imp. de Julio Belin y Cia.
Sassen, S. (2007) El reposicionamiento de las ciudades y regiones urbanas en una economía global: ampliando las opciones de políticas y gobernanza. *EURE. Revista Latinoamericana de Estudios Urbano Regionales*, **33**(100), pp. 9–34.
Savage, M. and Warde, A. (1993) *Urban Sociology, Capitalism and Modernity*. London: Macmillan.
Scarpaci, J.L. et al. (2002) *Havana. Two Faces of the Antillean Metropolis*. Chapel Hill, NC: University of North Carolina Press.
Schneeberger, C.A. (2003) *Minimanual compacto de história do Brasil. Teoría e prática*. São Paulo: Rideel.
Schumpeter, J. A. (1943, 2010) *Capitalism, Socialism and Democracy*. London: Routledge.
Scruggs, W.L. (1895) *The Venezuelan Question: British Aggressions in Venezuela, or the Monroe Doctrine on Trial*. Atlanta: Franklin Printing and Publishing Co.
Scruggs, W.L. (1900) *The Colombian and Venezuelan Republics with Notes on Other Parts of Central and South America*. Boston: Sampson, Marston & Low.
Segawa, H. (1995) 1911: Bouvard em São Paulo. *DANA. Documentos de Arquitectura Nacional y Americana*, **37/38**, pp. 31–35.
Segre, R. and Baroni, S. (1998) Cuba y La Habana. Historia, población y territorio. *Ciudad y Territorio. Estudios Territoriales*, **30**(116) pp. 351–379.
Semprún, J. (1918, 1983) El Norte y el Sur. Los Estados Unidos y la América Latina. Divagaciones sobre un tema de actualidad, in *Pensamiento político venezolano del siglo XIX*, Vol. 14: *La doctrina positivista*. Caracas: Congreso de la República, pp. 507–527.
Sierra, J. (1895, 2000) *Viajes. En tierra yankee. En la Europa latina*. México: Editorial Porrúa.
Sierra, J. (1939, 1990) *Prosas*. México: Universidad Nacional Autónoma de México (UNAM).

Silva, J.A. *De sobremesa* (1895, 1996). Madrid: Hiperión.
Silva Aristiguieta, A. (2001) *Breve historia de América Latina*. Caracas: Universidad Metropolitana.
Simmel, G. (1903, 1969) The metropolis and mental life, trans. Gerth, H.H., in Sennett, R. (ed.) *Classic Essays on the Culture of Cities*. New York: Appleton Century Crofts, pp. 47–60.
Sjoberg, G. (1965) *The Preindustrial City. Past and Present*. New York: The Free Press.
Sjoberg, G. (1973) The origin and evolution of cities, in Kingsley, D. (ed.) *Cities. Their Origin, Growth and Human Impact: Readings from 'Scientific American'*. San Francisco, CA: W.H. Freeman, pp. 19–27.
Sosa, R. (2000) Violencia y terror en la cultura política mexicana de fin de siglo, in Rotker, S. (ed.) *Ciudadanías del miedo*. Caracas: Nueva Sociedad, Rutgers University, pp. 69–80.
Spencer, H. (1864–1867) *The Principles of Biology*. London: Williams and Norgate.
Spengler, O. (1918, 1969) The Soul of the City, trans. Atkinson, C.F., in Sennett, R. (ed.) *Classic Essays on the Culture of Cities*. New York: Appleton Century Crofts, pp. 61–88.
Spengler, O. (1918–1922, 1998) *La decadencia de Occidente. Bosquejo de una morfología de la historia universal*, trans. García Morente, M. Madrid: Espasa-Calpe, 2 vols.
Stambouli, A. (2002) *La política extraviada. Una historia de Medina a Chávez*. Caracas: Fundación para la Cultura Urbana.
Stein, S.J. and Stein, B.H. (1970) *The Colonial Heritage of Latin America. Essays on Economic Dependence in Perspective*. Oxford: Oxford University Press.
Stieber, N. (1999) Microhistory of the modern city: urban space, its use and representation. *Journal of the Society of Architectural Historians*, **58**(3), pp. 382–391.
Stiglitz, J.E. (2003) *Globalization and Its Discontents*. New York: W.W. Norton.
Suárez Mayorga, A.M. (2006) *La ciudad de los elegidos. Crecimiento urbano, jerarquización social y poder político. Bogotá (1910–1950)*. Bogotá: Editora Guadalupe.
Subercaseaux, B. (1940, 2005) *Chile o una loca geografía*. Santiago: Editorial Universitaria.
Suchlicki, J. (1996, 2008) *Mexico. From Moctezuma to the Rise of the PAN*. Washington DC: Potomac Books.
Surel, Y. (2011) Las problemáticas de la acción pública, in Quenan, C. and Velut, S. (eds.) *Los desafíos del desarrollo en América Latina. Dinámicas socioeconómicas y políticas públicas*. Paris: Institut des Amériques, Agence Française de Développement (AFP), pp. 143–160.
Sutcliffe, A. (1981) *Towards the Planned City: Germany, Britain, the United States and France, 1780–1914*. Oxford: Blackwell.
Sutcliffe, A. (ed.) (1984) *Metropolis, 1890–1940*. London: Mansell.
Taffet, J.F. (2007) *Foreign Aid as Foreign Policy. The Alliance for Progress in Latin America*. New York: Routledge.
Tamayo, S. and Cruz-Guzmán, X. (2008) Political appropriation of public space: extraordinary events in the Zócalo of Mexico City, in Irazábal, C. (ed.) *Ordinary Places, Extraordinary Events. Citizenship, Democracy and Public Space in Latin America*. London: Routledge, pp. 35–58.

Tartarini, J.D. (1995) La visita de Werner Hegemann a la Argentina en 1931. *DANA. Documentos de Arquitectura Nacional y Americana*, **37/38**, pp. 54–63.
Taschner, S.P. (2003) Brasil y sus favelas. *Ciudad y Territorio. Estudios Territoriales*, **35**(136/137), pp. 315–333.
Taylor, N. (1998) *Urban Planning Theory since 1945*. London: Sage.
Tedesco, I. (2004) *Urdimbre estética, social e ideológica del indigenismo en América Latina*. Caracas: Universidad Pedagógica Experimental Libertador (UPEL).
Téllez, A.S. (1993) *La ciudad deseada*. Caracas: Fundarte, Ateneo de Caracas.
Téllez, G. (1988) *Cuellar, Serrano, Gómez. Arquitectura 1933–1983*. Bogotá: Fondo Editorial Escala.
Tenorio, M. (2000) L'idéal de la modernité: Mexico 1910: le rêve du dictateur, in Monnet, J. (ed.) *L'urbanisme dans les Amériques. Modèles de ville et modèles de société*. Paris: Éditions Karthala, pp. 61–89.
Tenreiro, O. (1995) Conversación con el General (R) Marcos Pérez Jiménez, en su residencia en Madrid, el día 5 de febrero de 1995. *Ciudad*, **1**, pp. 7–33.
Thatcher, M. (1993) *The Downing Street Years*. New York: Harper Collins.
Thatcher, M. (1995) *The Path to Power*. London: Harper Collins.
Tomas, F. (1993) México. 1920-1949: la primera modernidad arquitectónica, in Cortés, J.L. (ed.) *París-México. La primera modernidad arquitectónica*. México: Instituto Francés de América Latina (IFAL), Colegio de Arquitectos de México, Sociedad de Arquitectos Mexicanos (CAM-SAM), Universidad Autónoma Metropolitana-Xochimilco (UAM-X), pp. 61–88.
Tönnies, F. (1887, 1965) *Gemeinschaft* and *Gesellschaft*, trans. Loomis, C.P., in Parsons, T. (ed.) *Theories of Society. Foundations of Modern Sociological Theory*, Vol. 1. New York: The Free Press, pp. 191–201.
Torres, A.T. (2010) *La herencia de la tribu. Del mito de la Independencia a la Revolución Bolivariana*. Caracas: Editorial Alfa.
Touraine, A. (1999) *Comment sortir du libéralisme?* Paris: Fayard.
Tsiomis, Y. (1998) 1936, Le Corbusier fala, desenha, projeta, in Tsiomis, Y. (ed.) *Le Corbusier. Rio de Janeiro: 1929, 1936*. Rio de Janeiro: Secretaria Municipal de Urbanismo, Centro de Arquitetura e Urbanismo do Rio de Janeiro, pp. 32–40.
Ugarte, M. (1911) *El porvenir de la América Latina*. Valencia: E Sempere y Compañía Editores.
UNESCO Institute for Statistics (2011) *Data Centre*. Available at: http://stats.uis.unesco.org/unesco/tableviewer/document.aspx?ReportId=143.
United Nations Centre for Human Settlements (Habitat) (1996) *An Urbanizing World. Global Report on Human Settlements*. Oxford: Oxford University Press.
United Nations Department of Economic and Social Affairs (UNDESA) (2011) *The World Economic Situation and Prospects (WESP)*. Available at: http://www.un.org/en/development/desa/index.html.
United Nations Office on Drugs and Crime (UNODOC) (2011) *Global Study on Homicide, 2011. Trends/Context/Data*. Available at: http://www.unodc.org/documents/data-and-analysis/statistics/Homicide/Globa_study_on_homicide_2011_web.pdf.
Urban, F. (2012) *Tower and Slab. Histories of Global Mass Housing*. London: Routledge.

Uslar Pietri, A. (1979a) *Fantasmas de dos mundos*. Barcelona: Seix Barral.
Uslar Pietri, A. (1979b) América y la revolución, in *Ensayos venezolanos*. Caracas: Editorial Ateneo de Caracas, pp. 135–154.
Vainer, C. (2000) Pátria, empresa e mercadoria. Notas sobre a estratégia discursiva do Planejamento Estratégico Urbano, in Arantes, O. *et al*. (eds.) *A cidade do pensamento único. Desmanchando consensos*. Petrópolis: Editora Vozes, pp. 75–103.
Valdés, A. and Wiens, T. (1998) Rural Poverty in Latin America and the Caribbean, in Javed Burki, S. *et al*. (eds.) *Annual World Bank Conference on Development in Latin America and the Caribbean 1996. Poverty and Inequality*. Washington DC: World Bank, pp. 107–124.
Valenzuela, L. (2007) La Caja de Habitación Popular: el rostro cambiante de la vivienda en Chile, 1936-1952, in Castillo, M.J. and Hidalgo, R. (eds.) *1906/2006. Cien años de política de vivienda en Chile*. Santiago: Universidad Nacional Andrés Bello, Pontificia Universidad Católica de Chile (PUC), Universidad Central de Venezuela (UCV), pp. 65–84.
Valenzuela-Aguilera, A. (2014) *Urbanistas y visionarios. La planeación urbana de la Ciudad de Mexico en la primera mitad del siglo XX*. Mexico: Conaculta & Miguel Ángel Porrúa Editores.
Vallenilla Lanz, L. (1919, 1961) *Cesarismo democrático. Estudios sobre las bases sociológicas de la constitución efectiva de Venezuela*. Caracas: Tipografía Garrido.
Vargas Llosa, M. (2009) *Sables y utopías. Visiones de América Latina*. Bogotá: Aguilar.
Vargas Vila, J.M. (1913) *Los césares de la decadencia*. Paris: Librería América.
Vasconcelos, J. (1925, 2007) *La raza cósmica*. México: Editorial Porrúa.
Vasconcelos, J. (1935, 2003) *Ulises criollo*. México: Editorial Porrúa.
Vaz, L.F. (2002) *Modernidade e moradia. Habitação coletiva no Rio de Janeiro. Séculos XIX e XX*. Rio de Janeiro: 7 Letras, Faperj.
Vaz, L. F. and Jacques, P.B. (2003) Pequeña historia de las *Favelas* de Río de Janeiro. *Ciudad y Territorio. Estudios Territoriales*, **35**(136/137), pp. 259–272.
Vaz, L.F. and Jacques, P.B. (2006) Contemporary urban spectacularisation, in Monclus, J. and Guardia, M. (eds.) *Culture, Urbanism and Planning*. Aldershot: Ashgate, pp. 241–253.
Vicuña Mackenna, B. (1872) *La transformación de Santiago*. Santiago: Imprenta de la Librería del Mercurio.
Villalobos, S. (1979, 2010) *Breve historia de Chile*. Santiago: Editorial Universitaria.
Villoria-Siegert, N. and Almandoz, A. (2002) Transferring the neighborhood unit to Caracas: examples of foreign influence in Venezuela. *Critical Planning*, **9**, pp. 89–100.
Violich, F. (1944) *Cities of Latin America. Housing and Planning to the South*. New York: Reinhold Publishing Corporation.
Violich, F. (1975) Caracas: focus of the new Venezuela, in Wentworth Elredge, H. (ed.) *World Capitals. Toward Guided Urbanization*. New York: Doubleday, pp. 246–292.
Weiner, M. (1966) *Modernization*. Chicago, IL: University of Chicago Press.
Whitaker, A. (1948) *The United States and South America. The Northern Republics*. Cambridge, MA: Harvard University Press.
Williamson, E. (1992) *The Penguin History of Latin America*. Harmondsworth: Penguin.

Wilson, C.M. (1942, 1972) *Ambassadors in White. The Story of American Tropical Medicine*. New York: Kennikat Press.

Wirth, L. (1938, 1969) Urbanism as a way of life, in Sennett, R. (ed.) *Classic Essays on the Culture of Cities*. New York: Appleton-Century-Crofts, pp. 143–164.

Woodward, E.L. (1962, 1984) *Historia de Inglaterra*, trans. Gallego, E. Madrid: Alianza Editorial.

World Bank (1993) *Latin America and the Caribbean. A Decade after the Debt Crisis*. Washington, DC: Latin America and the Caribbean Regional Office.

World Bank (2006) *World Development Report 2007. Development and the Next Generation*. Washington DC: World Bank.

World Bank (2011) *World Development Indicators database*. Available at: http://data.worldbank.org/indicator. Accessed 20 January 2012.

Zumeta, C. (1899) *El continente enfermo*. New York: no publisher.

Zumeta, C. (1907, 1983) 'Oh, Miss Liberty', in *Pensamiento político venezolano del siglo XIX*, Vol. 14: *La doctrina positivista*. Caracas: Congreso de la República, pp. 149–150.

Index

Note: Figures are indicated by italic page numbers, Tables by emboldened numbers, and notes by suffix 'n[]' (e.g "38n[8,9]" means "page 38, notes 8 and 9")

Abercrombie, Patrick 134
absolute poverty 157, 162n[5]
academicism to functional modernism 99–105
acronyms and initials [listed] 189–190
Adams, Thomas 86n[29]
Agache, Donat-Alfred 82, 83, 107
agricultural labour productivity 97
Aguirre Cerda, Pedro 93, 109n[4]
Alberdi, Juan Bautista 18, 24–25, 25, 26–27, 28, 31, 38n[8,9]
Albers, Josef 102
Alegría, Ciro 76–77
Alemán, Miguel 90, 101
Alessandri Palma, Arturo 53, 67, 68, 93
Alessandri Rodríguez, Jorge 117
Alfaro, Eloy 50
Alfonsín, Raúl 142
Allende, Salvador 117–118, 121, 139, 145
Alliance for Progress (AFP) 11, 112–113, 116
   critiques 113
   Punta del Este Charter 113, 119
Almandoz, A., cited 12nn[5,6], 37n[1], 38nn[3,4], 62nn[1,12], 85nn[1,18], 86n[26], 109nn[1,5], 136n[1], 137n[26]
Altamirano Talavera, Luis 67
Alvear, Torcuato de 35
Amaral, Tarsila do 76
americanismo 76
Andean Pact 124, 147
Andrade, Mario de 76

Andrade, Oswald de 76
Anglo-American protectorates 43
Anhaia Mello, Luíz de 79, 80, 107
anti-globalization 164, 165, 171, 185
Arango, Josè Doroteo *see* Villa, Pancho
Arbenz, Jacobo 110, 111
Arcaya, Pedro Manuel 51
architectural modernism 99–105
Argentina
   1837 generation 18, 21, 30
   'alluvial era' of growth 52
   Civil Radical Union [UCR] 52, 68
   corralito [freezing of bank deposits, 2001] 171
   currency devaluation 142, 171
   external debt 142, 171
   Falklands War [1982] 142, 145
   foreign-aided plans 81, 82, 83, 84
   foreign investment [late-1950s] 116
   housing 61
   Human Development Index 184, 185, **208**
   human rights violations 141–142
   immigrants 31, 32, 61
   'Infamous Decade' [1930s] 68–69
   Menem's presidency 142, 151–152
   Perón's 'New Argentina' 91
   political and social reforms 52, 70
   population 31–32, **204**
   privatization programme [1990s] 151, 152
   regional planning 134
   unemployment levels 152, 171
   urban population **204**, **207**
   urbanism courses [early-1930s] 80
   see also Buenos Aires
Arguedas, José María 75, 76
Ariel [Rodó, 1900] 43
arielismo 9, 11, 42–43, 44, 64, 66

arielistas 8, 17, 64
Aristiguieta Montero, R. 33
Arlt, Roberto 74, 85n[20]
'aspirational constitutions' 166, 188n[2]
Asturias, Miguel Ángel 76, 85n[5], 137n[19]
Athens Charter 101, 102
Atlantic seaboard, relative prosperity 15
Ávila Camacho, Manuel 90, 188n[9]
Aylwin, Patricio 148
Azuela, Mariano 49

Bachelet, Michelle 181–182
Balmaceda, José Manuel 27, 53, 60
Barbosa, Rui 50
Barco, Virgilio 149
Barrientos, René 120
Bartholomew, Harland 81
Basadre, Jorge 86n[25]
Batista, Fulgencio 88, 102, 111
Batlle y Ordóñez, José 53, 67, 70
Bay of Pigs [Bahía de Cochinos] 'invasion' [1961] 112, 113
Beauvoir, Simone de 122
Bell, Purl Lord 64
Bella Época/Belle-Époque period 46, 47, 56
Belo Horizonte [Brazil] 15
Benjamin, Walter 47
Bernard, Émile 56
Betancourt, Rómulo 70, 111, 116, 117, 135
Betancur, Belisario 148
Beyhaut, Gustavo 9
Beyhaut, Helène 9
Bilbao, Francisco 27
Bioy Casares, Adolfo 76
Blanco, Andrés Eloy 85n[19]
Blanco Fombona, Rufino 62n[7]
Blest Gana, Alberto 27
Boari, Adamo 56
Bogotá
    Brunner's plans 84
    bus rapid transit system 160
    city centre [1975] *125*
    Le Corbusier's proposals 102
    population 16, 54, 71, 125
Bogotá Act [1948] 111, 113
Bogotazo violence [Colombia, 1948] 94–95

Bolívar, Simón 14
Bolivarian Revolution 170–171, 185, 186
    reaction to 186–187
Bolivia 120, 121, 124, 165, 186, 187, **204, 207, 208**
Borges, Jorge Luis 76
Borja, Jordi 159
Bosch, Juan 113
bourgeois cities 11, 46–47
    growth [in early-20th century] 54
Bouvard, Joseph Antoine 57
Bowen, Herbert Wolcott 41
Brady, Nicholas 147
Brady Plan(s) 147, 150, 151
Brasilia 92–93, 103, 104–105, *106*
    critique 105, 107
Brazil
    Cardoso's presidency 171–172
    coffee production 28–29
    Collor's impeachment [1992] 150
    colonization of 14
    conservative–liberal conflict 29
    constitution [1988] 166
    Estado Novo (New State) 69, 91–92
    functional modernism 103–105
    housing 56, 61, 62, 174
    Human Development Index **208**
    immigration 28, 50
    imperial era 27–29
    independence 28
    Kubitschek's government 92–93
    Lula's presidencies 172, 183–184
    military juntas [1960s–1970s] 115
    Old Republic 50, 69
    Olympic Games [2016] 184
    Plan Real [1994] 150
    postcolonial changes 14
    privatization programme [1990s] 149–150, 171
    railways 25, 28
    regional planning 107–108, 133
    São Paulo–Minas Gerais hegemony 50, 69
    social programmes [1990s] 173
    urban population **204, 207**
    urbanism courses [early-1930s] 79
    Vargas's governments 69, 91–92
    Workers' Party (PT) 172, 184
    see also Brasilia; Rio de Janeiro; São Paulo

BRICS members 184
Britain, predominance [1850s to 1900s] 22–23
British investments 15, 16, 42
Brito, Saturnino de 60
Brunner, Karl 72, 78, 84, 102, 106, 107
  Manual de Urbanismo 84, 106
Buarque de Holanda, Sergio 29, 77
Büchi, Hernán 148
Buenos Aires 17
  9 de Julio Avenue 71, 72
  conventillos [tenements] 36
  critique [1850s] 19
  della Paolera's master plan 79–80
  Florida Street 32
  foreign-aided plans 81, 82, 83
  French influence 23
  garden suburbs 59
  Hausmannesque works 34, 35
  housing 61
  Le Corbusier's proposals 83, 101
  Mayo Avenue 54
  population 16, 54, 71, 125
  regional planning 134
  sociological description 77
Bulnes, Francisco 47, 48, 49, 62n[11]
Burchard, Martin 58
Burgess, Ernest W. 12n[2], 108
Burke, Peter 5
Burucúa, J.E. 13n[9]
bus rapid transit (BRT) systems 160, 176
Bush, George 154
Bush, George W. 180

Cabrera, Lydia 86n[24]
Caldera, Rafael 117, 143, 154, 169
Calderón, Felipe 183
'Caliban' 42–43, 64, 180
Caliban [Renan, 1887] 44
Calles, Plutarco Elías 66, 67
Calvino, Italo 122
Câmara, Hélder 121
Cámpora, Héctor 141
Cancún [economic] North–South summit [1981] 146, 151
Cané, Miguel 15, 18
capitalism, criticism of 166, 180, 185
capitalist-led modernization, inequalities caused by 2–3

Caracas
  Centro Simón Bolívar 73
  foreign-aided plans 82–83
  garden suburbs 58
  Hausmannesque works 34, 35
  housing projects 102, *103*, 132
  hygiene reforms 60
  metro system *155*, 156
  'parochial plans' 160
  population 16, 54
  relocation programmes 132
  Sabana Grande [High Street, c. 1960] *128*
  shantytowns *129*, 132
  trams 57
Cárdenas, Cuauhtémoc 150
Cárdenas, Lázaro 66, 67, 88, 90, 100
Cardoso, Fernando Henrique 127, 150, 171, 183, 184
Carmagnani, Marcelo 25, 37n[2]
Carpentier, Alejo 75, 76, 77, 86n[23], 137n[19]
Carranza, Venustiano 49, 66
Cartagena de Indias [Colombia], Central Street *159*
Carvajal, Carlos 57
Castells, Manuel 3
Castelo Branco, Humberto 115
Castro, Cipriano 41, 50, 180
  Roosevelt's attitude to 41
Castro, Fidel 111, 122, *123*, 136n[5]
Catholic Church, and social developments in Latin America 120–121
caudillismo 18, 20, 30
Cavallo, Domingo 151, 152, 171
Central American Common Market (CACM) 147
central districts, elites' move away from 56, 71
centralized planning 132–136
Cerdá, Ildefonso 59
Chávez, Hugo 153, 165, 166, 169–170, 172, 173, 179, 180, 185, 186, 188n[4]
Chicago 17
'Chicago Boys' 140, 187
Chicago School of sociology 73
Chile
  19th-century reforms 26–27

Index • 237

agrarian reform [1960s] 117
Allende's government 117–118
Bachelet's presidencies 181–182
Communist Party 110
Concertación 148, 182
conservative–liberal combination 26
constitution [1833] 26
constitution [1925] 67–68
Corporation of Promotion of Production (CORFO) 93, 134
Defence of Democracy Act [1948] 110
Gini coefficient 182
housing programmes 61, 174
Human Development Index 182, **208**
human rights violations 140
immigration 27
neoliberal reforms 148, 181–182
Pinochet regime 139–140
Popular Front 93, 118
Popular Unity (UP) party 117, 118
'Portales era' 26–27, 139
public investment 182
regional planning 133–134
social reforms [1900s] 53
unemployment levels 140, 148
urban planning courses [late-1920s] 78
urban population **204, 207**
see also Santiago de Chile
Chimbote [Peru], TPA's project 100
China, as commodity export market 181, 184
Choay, Françoise 81
Christian revolutionary nationalism 121
CIA operations 111, 121
CIAM *see* Congrès Internationaux d'Architecture Moderne
Cienfuegos, Camilo 111
City Beautiful movement 81
civilization–barbarism conflict 17–21
    capital versus province 19–20
    federation versus unitarianism 20–21
Cleveland, Grover 40
Clichevsky, Nora 7
Clinton, William ['Bill'] 150, 168
Cold War 110, 144, 145
Collor de Mello, Fernando 149–150

Colombia
    agrarian reform [1930s–1950s] 94
    Bogotazo political violence 94–95
    conservative–liberal conflict 94
    constitution [1991] 149, 161, 168
    constitutional reform [1936] 94
    Gaviria's administration 149, 168
    gran revolcón 149, 168
    guerrilla groups 94, 95, 114, 169, 176
    Human Development Index **208**
    loss of Panama 63
    National Front governments 114
    neoliberal reforms 168, 186
    Popular National Alliance 114
    regional planning 133
    urban population **204, 207**
    US aid 168–169
    US investments 63
    see also Bogotá
Colosio, Luis Donaldo 167
'Colossus of the North' [USA] 39–42, 63, 180
commodities exports [2000s] 181
'compact' colonial city 188n[7]
Comte, Auguste 24, 51
Conditional Cash Transfer Programmes (CCTP) 173
Congrès Internationaux d'Architecture Moderne (CIAM) principles 83, 100–101, 103–104, 108
Coni, Emilio 37
conservative–liberal conflict 29, 94
constitutions 165–166
    'aspirational constitutions' 166, 188n[2]
    Brazil 166
    Chile 26, 67–68
    Colombia 149, 161, 168
    Mexico 29, 49, 66
    Peru 154, 166
    presidential-driven constitutions 165–166
    'protective constitutions' 166, 188n[2]
    Venezuela 70, 165–166
Contadora Group 145
Contreras Elizondo, Carlos 78, 80, 81, 107, 108
The Control of the Tropics [Kidd, 1898] 43

conventillos [tenements] 36, 61, 127
Corbusian modernism 83–84, 100–101
corporatism 66, 90, 91–92
Cortázar, Julio 137n[19]
Costa, Lúcio 73, 79, 99, 103, 105, 107
Costa Rica 55, 71, **204**, **207**, **208**
Cravotto, Mauricio 80
'creative destruction' 163, 188n[1]
Cremonesi, Ignazio 57
'Creole Haussmanns' 35
creole urban planners 80
Cristiani, Alfredo 187
Cruz, Oswaldo 37
Cuba
  agrarian reform 112
  Batista's dictatorship 88, 102, 111
  Human Development Index **208**
  independence 40, 64
  National Institute for Agrarian Reform (INRA) 111, 112
  urban population **205**, **207**
  US export/import embargo 112
  see also Havana
Cuba guerrillas 111, 122–123
Cuban Revolution [1959] 11, 111–112
  critiques 121–122
  effect on other countries 116
Cuevas Pietrasanta, José Luis 78
Currie, Lauchlin 133

dameros [checkerboards], Haussmannization of 34–36
'Dance of the Millions'[Colombia] 63, 168
D'Annunzio, Gabriele 45
Darío, Rubén 42, 43, 44, 46, 85n[4]
Darwin, Charles 38n[5]
Daudet, Alphonse 45
Dávila Boza, Ricardo 60
Davis, Kingsley 2, 3, 96
de Castro, Sergio 140
de Certeau, Michel 5–6
de la Madrid, Miguel 150
de Mattos, Carlos A. 4
de Ramón, Armando 26, 118
de Solano, Francisco 7
debt crisis [1980s] 140, 141, 142, 143, 144
decentralization processes 161, 166
del Pozo, José 9

Delgado Chalbaud, Carlos 70
della Paolera, Carlos *see* Paolera, Carlos della
demographic changes 16, 54, 70–71, 98
  and economic growth 87
dependency theory 3, 7, 16, 17, 115, 126–127
'developing countries' 89
development, and modernization 2, 89–90
developmentalism 88, 89
  Lula's approach 172
  Marxist response 127
Díaz, Porfirio 30, 47
Díaz Ordaz, Gustavo 113
Díaz Rodríguez, Manuel 46
Dilthey, Wilhelm 77
Dollar Diplomacy 40
Domínguez, Cipriano 73
Dominican Republic 64, 88, 111, 113, **205**, **207**, **208**
Dos Santos, Theotonio 127
Doyère, Emilio 57
'drive to maturity', factors affecting 89, 90
drug trafficking
  US-aided programme to fight 168, 177
  violence associated with 177
dual societies, factors affecting 98–99
Duhalde, Eduardo 171
Duras, Marguerite 122
Dutra, Gaspar 92

Echeverría, Esteban 17, 18, 20, 21–22
Echeverría, Luis 114, 143, 145
École Française d'Urbanisme (EFU) 81–83, 108
Economic Commission for Latin America and the Caribbean (ECLAC) 6, 88–89
  conception of development 88, 97, 109n[3]
  report(s) 157
economic growth
  and demographic transition 87
  mid-20th century 87
  stages [Rostow's model] 2, 11, 87, 89–90
economic nationalism 88

Ecuador 14, 50, 124, 165, 186, 187, **205, 207, 208**
Edwards, Jorge 121–122
Edwards Bello, Joaquín 75, 85n[21]
Egaña, Mariano 26
Eisenhower, Dwight D. 111
El Salvador 145, 176, 177, 187, **205, 207, 208**
embellishment of central areas 55–57
Escobar, Pablo 168
Estrada Cabrera, Manuel 51, 66
European influences, 19th century 21–24
exports, compared with East Asia 138
external debt
    Argentina 142, 152
    Colombia 148–149
    Latin America [as whole] 139, 141, 181
    Mexico 144
    Venezuela 143
Eyzaguirre, Jaime 27

Faletto, Enzo 127
Falklands War [1982] 142, 145
fascism, in Venezuela 51
Fasileau-Duplantier, Amon 57
favelas [Brazil's slums] 56, 129, 131, 132
federation 20
    versus unitarianism 21
Fernández, Macedonio 74, 76
Ferrari Hardoy, Jorge 101
Figueiredo, João Batista 141
Forestier, Jean-Claude Nicholas 81, 83
Fox, Vicente 173, 182
'fragmented' metropolis 177, 188n[7]
France, Anatole 45
Franco, Itamar 150
Franco, Jean 11, 44, 75–76
Frank, André Gunder 3, 127
Frank, Waldo 76
Frankfurt School of sociology 77
Fraser, Valerie 104, 105
Frei Montalva, Eduardo 113, 117, 130
French-oriented culture 23–24
Freyre, Gilberto 29, 77, 107
Friedman, Milton 139–140
Friedmann, John 135
Frondizi, Arturo 116
Frontin, André Paulo de 56

Fuentes, Carlos 122, 137n[19]
Fujimori, Alberto 154, 165, 179
functional modernism 99–105
Furtado, Celso 115, 127

Gache, Samuel 37
Gaitán, Jorge Eliécer 94, 114
Gallegos, Rómulo 70
Galtieri, Leopoldo 142
Gálvez, Manuel 62n[7], 85n[8]
García, Alan 154, 180
García Calderón, Francisco 8, 9, 24, 64
García Canclini, Néstor 8, 13n[10]
García Márquez, Gabriel 137n[19]
García Moreno, Gabriel 38n[6]
garden cities/suburbs 58–59, 82
Garnier, Charles 56
Garrastazu Médici, Emílio 115, 140
gated communities 177–178
Gaviria, César 149, 168
Gayol, Roberto 60
Geddes, Patrick 80, 107, 108
Geisel, Ernesto 140
General Agreement on Tariffs and Trade (GATT) 150, 151
Germani, Gino 3, 97–98
ghettoes 131
Gil Fortoul, José 21, 24, 51
Gini coefficient 1, 137n[25]
    in various countries 137n[25], 182, 187
global financial crisis [2008] 181
globalization
    architectural vocabulary of 178
    factors affecting 4, 176–177
    peripheral 161–162
    reactions against 164, 165, 171, 185
'Golden Calf' 43, 64
Gómez, Juan Vicente 51, 62, 66, 69
Gómez, Laureano 94
Gómez Carrillo, Enrique 45, 62n[9]
González Videla, Gabriel 110
'Good Neighbour' policy 3, 64, 65–66
Gorelik, Adrián 85n[17]
Goulart, João 113, 115, 172
Gran Colombia, disintegration of 14
Gran Venezuela [1970s] 117, 142, 143, 152
'Great Turnabout' [1830] 16–17
Greater London Plan 134

Gropius, Walter 102
Guatemala 51, 66, 110, 111, 176, **205, 207, 208**
Guerrero, Vicente 29
guerrilla fighters, idealization of 121, 122
guerrilla warfare
  Colombia 94, 95
  Cuba 111
  Mexico 167
Guevara, Ernesto ['Che'] 110, 111, 115, 119, 120, 121, 122
Guillén, Nicolás 86n[24]
Guillén Vicente, Rafael Sebastián *see* Marcos
Guimarães, Ulysses 141
Güiraldes, Ricardo 86n[23]
Guzmán, Nicomedes 85n[21]
Guzmán Blanco, Antonio 33, 35

Habsburg, Maximilian of 30
Haiti **205, 207, 208**
Halperin Donghi, Tulio 9
Harberger, Arnold 140
Hardoy, Jorge Enrique 6, 7, 12n[7], 15, 59
Harris, Walter D. 6, 129
Harvey, David 6, 128
Hauser, Philip M. 3, 6, 96–97
Haussmann, George E., Baron 34, 36, 83
Haussmannization 34–36
Havana
  CIAM-inspired master plan [1957] 102
  garden suburbs 58–59
  population 16, 54
Haya de la Torre, Victor 70
Hegemann, Werner 79, 84
Hénard, Eugène 81, 82, 83
Henríquez Ureña, Pedro 65, 67
heritage considerations 158
Herrera, Felipe 113
Herrera Campins, Luis 143
high-rise office complexes 178
Hirschman, Albert 88
historic centres, regeneration of 158, 174
Hitchcock, Henry-Russell 99
Homestead Act [USA, 1862] 17
Hommes, Rudolf 168

Honduras 177, 187, 188n[10], **205, 207, 208**
housing 61–62, 131–132
housing deficit, governmental responses 131–132, 174–175
Howard, Ebenezer 59
Huerta, Victoriano 49, 64
Huidobro, Vicente 76
Humala, Ollanta 186–187
Human Development Index (HDI), for various countries 182, 183, 184, 185, **208**
hygiene concerns 36–37, 56
  see also sanitary reforms
hyperinflation 141, 142, 149, 151

Ibáñez del Campo, Carlos 67, 68, 78
Iberian America 9
iconic buildings 72–73
Illía, Arturo 116
immigration, 19th century 27, 28, 31, 32
imperialism, criticism of 118, 119, 166, 185
import substitution industrialization (ISI) policy 3, 54, 87, 92, 112
  attempts to move to intermediate manufacture 125
  constraints on 123–124, 126
  effect on agricultural labour productivity 97
  end of 'easy' phase 88, 109n[2]
  and Venezuela 95, 116, 135, 137n[13]
incomplete reforms 166–172
indigenous urban planners 80
industrialization
  failure of 123–127
  urbanization affected by 3, 4, 97
informal economy 176
informal settlements *see* shantytowns
Ingeniero, José 86n[25]
initials and acronyms [listed] 189–190
Inter-American Conferences 60, 111
Inter-American Development Bank (IADB) 111
International Congresses of Americanists (ICA) 6–7
International Housing and Town Planning Congresses (IHTPC) 108

International Monetary Fund (IMF) 146, 147, 163, 173
inter-urban migration 155–156
investment rate [2000s] 181
ISI *see* import substitution industrialization (ISI)
Iturbide, Augustín 29

Jaussely, Léon 81–82, 83
Jecquier, Émile 57
Johnson, Lyndon B. 113
"Juan Bimba" [Joe Bloggs] 70, 74, 75, 85n[19]
Juárez, Benito 25, 29–30
Justo, Agustín Pedro 68

Kaplan, M. 127
Kennedy, John F. 11, 112, 113
Keynes, John Maynard 145
Keyserling, Hermann 76
Kidd, Benjamin 43
Kirchner, Cristina Fernández de 184–185
Kirchner, Néstor 171, 179
Kissinger, Henry 121
Krauze, Enrique 183
Kubitschek, Juscelino 87, 90, 92, 105, 107, 113, 115
Kurchan, Juan 101

La Plata [Argentina] 15
Lagos, Ricardo 180
Lambert, Jacques 82
land expropriation [in Chile & Cuba] 112, 117, 118
land seizures, by squatters 130
land use planning 133–136
    compared with spatial planning 160
    compared with strategic planning 158–159
Lanusse, Alejandro 141
Larraín Bravo, Ricardo 61
Lastarria, José Victorino 27
Latin America
    industrialization and urbanization compared with USA 16–17
    meaning of term 8–10
    population 15, 70, 172
Lawrence, D.H. 76
Le Corbusier 79, 82, 83, 83–84, 101, 102, 103, 104, 105
Le Play, Frédéric 108
Lebret, Joseph 108
Leguía, Augusto 51, 69
Leo XIII, Pope 61
Leoni, Raúl 117
Lerdo de Tejada, Miguel 29
Lesseps, Ferdinand de 63
Lewis, Oscar 127, 128
Liberation Theology 121
Liceaga, Eduardo 60
Lima
    housing deficit 131–132
    Plaza Mayor 179
    population 16, 54, 125
Lima Barreto, Alfonso de 62n[7]
Limantour, José 47–48
Linear City [*Ciudad Lineal*] 57
literary movements 44–45, 76–77
Lleras Camargo, Alberto 94, 114
Lleras Restrepo, Carlos 114
Lloyd-Evans, S. 2, 4, 12n[3]
López, Lucio 34
López Contreras, Eleazar 70
López Mateos, Adolfo 113
López Obrador, Andrés Manuel 182
López Portillo, José 144, 145
López Pumarejo, Alfonso 94
'lost decade' 139, 144, 158
Lugo, Fernando 187
Lugones, Leopoldo 62n[7], 85n[8]
Lula da Silva, Luiz Inácio 141, 166, 172, 179, 180, 183–184
Lusinchi, Jaime 143
Lynch, Benito 86n[23]

McGovern, George 136n[8]
Machado, Gerardo 69, 81
Machado de Assis, Joaquim 45
McKinley, William 43, 63
Madero, Francisco 49
Maduro, Nicolás 186
Maine battleship, sinking in Havana Harbour 40
Manual de Urbanismo [Brunner, 1939–1940] 84, 106
"Marcos" [Sub-commander] 167
marginal settlements 128–129, 174
    causes and manifestations 129–131
    see also shantytowns

Mariátegui, José Carlos 85n[10]
Marín, Pedro Antonio *see* Marulanda, Manuel
Mármol, José 18, 19, 20
Martí, José 46, 62n[8]
Martin-Barbero, J. 13n[10]
Martínez de Hoz, José Alfredo 142
Martínez Estrada, Ezquiel 77, 78
Martínez Inclán, Pedro 80, 102
Martínez Olivarría,Leopoldo 80
Marulanda, Manuel 169
masificación [overcrowding] 70, 71, 85n[14], 98
mass metropolises 70–74
Maupassant, Guy de 45
Maximilian of Habsburg 30
Mazzini, Giuseppe 18
Medellín [Colombia]
  cableway *175*, 176
  drugs cartel 168
Medina Angarita, Isías 70, 102
Medina Febres, Mariano 74, *75*
Menem, Carlos Saúl 142, 151, 152, 171
Meneses, Guillermo 74
MERCOSUR 147, 151, 186
metro systems 156, 176
metropolitan fervour 46–47
metropolitan population, mid-20th century 87
Mexican Revolution [1910] 48, 49
  drugs-related violence 177
  reformist phase 66–67, 90
Mexico
  1960s–1970s 113–114
  admittance to OECD and NAFTA 150, 151, 167, 182
  Chiapas Indians' insurgency 167
  conservative–liberal balance 29
  Constitution [1857] 29
  Constitution [1917] 49, 66
  corporate state 90
  currency devaluation 114, 143, 144, 167
  educational reforms 67
  effect of oil crisis [1973] 114
  housing programmes 174
  Human Development Index 183, **208**
  independence 29
  National Action Party (PAN) 182, 183
  National Solidarity Program (PRONASOL) 167
  petroleum and gas reserves 144
  porfiriato [1884–1911] 30, 47, 48, 167
  post-Revolution recuperation 49
  railways 25, 30
  regional planning 108, 133
  Revolutionary Institutional Party (PRI) 113, 150, 151, 167, 182, 183
  secularization reforms 29–30, 66
  social programmes [1990s] 173
  social reforms [1930s] 67, 90
  'Tequila crisis' [1994] 151, 167
  territorial losses to USA 29
  urban planning courses [late-1920s] 78
  urban population **205, 207**
Mexico City
  academic urbanism to functional modernism 100–101
  Ciudad Universitaria (University City) 101
  Contreras's plan 81
  Corbusian modernism 100–101
  embellishment of central areas 56
  garden suburbs 58, 59
  housing 175
  hygiene reforms 60
  Meyer's influence 100
  population 16, 54, 71, 87, 125
  tenant strikes 61
  Tlatelolco massacre [1968] 113
  vecindades [tenements] 127, 128
Meyer, Hans Emil ['Hannes'] 100
micro-historical approach 5
Minas Gerais [Brazil] 50, 69
Mirbeau, Octave 45
Mistral, Gabriela 67
Mitre, Bartolomé 18, 30
Mitterrand, François 145
modernismo (modernism) 45–46, 76
  international interest in 99
modernization
  and development 2, 89–90
  factors affecting 1–4
modernization-urbanization relationship 1–2, 89
  micro-historical approach 5

panoramic view 4, 6, 10
modus vivendi [with Britain & USA] 23, 40, 41, 172
Monroe, James 39
Monroe Doctrine 39, 42, 63
Montesquieu, Charles de Secondat, Baron de 188n[2]
Montevideo 31, 38n[8], 60, 82
Montigny, Grandjean de 28
Montt, Manuel 26
Moraes, Antonio Carlos Robert 1, 4
Moral, Enrique del 100
Morales, Juan Evo 166, 180
Morris, Ira Nelson 42
Morse, Richard 6, 7, 11, 12n[7]
Moses, Robert 102
motorways, privatization of 176
Mujica, José 180
Mulhall, Michael G. 15, 22, 23
Mumford, Lewis 8
muralismo (muralist movement) 76
Myrdal, Gunnar 2, 3, 88

nationalism 166
nationalization of private enterprises 67, 91, 115, 117, 118, 143, 165, 170, 185
nativismo 76
Navarro Wolff, Antonio 149
neighbourhood unit concept 102
neoliberalism 12, 146, 150, 171, 186–187
  effects 174–175
  reaction against 164–165, 180
neo-populism 164–165
Neruda, Pablo 110
Neutra, Richard 102
new left [2000s] 179–180
new liberal culture [2000s] 180
newcomers to cities 74–75
Nicaragua 64, 145, 176, 186, 187, **206, 207, 208**
Niemeyer, Oscar 99, 103, 105
Nixon, Richard 111, 145
'noble savage' myth 122
Noel, Carlos Martín 86n[28]
Non-Aligned Movement 91, 115, 120, 145
Noriega, Manuel 145
North American Free Trade Agreement (NAFTA), Mexico as member 150, 151, 167, 182
Nothmann, Victor 58

Obregón, Álvaro 66
Ocampo, Silvina 86n[23]
Ocampo, Victoria 76
O'Gorman, Juan 99
O'Higgins, Bernardo 26
oil crisis [1973], effects 114, 138, 144
Old World versus USA 64–65
Olmsted, Frederick Law 59
One-Thousand-Year War [1899–1902] 63
Onganía, Juan Carlos 116, 121
ordenamiento territorial [land use planning] 133–136
  compared with spatial planning 160
  compared with strategic planning 158–159
Organization of American States (OAS) 88, 111
Organization for Economic Cooperation and Development (OECD), Mexico as member 150, 151, 167, 182
Orozco, José Clemente 67, 76
Orrego, Antenor 85n[10]
Ortiz, Fernando 86n[24]
Ospina Pérez, Mariano 94
Otero Silva, Miguel 74
outward-oriented model of growth 16

Padilla, Heberto 122
Panama 63, 85n[2], 145, 187, **206, 207, 208**
Panama Canal 40, 63, 145, 187
Panama City 71, 84, 158
Pani, Mario 100
panoramic history 4, 6, 10
Paolera, Carlos della 79, 80, *80*, 84, 107, 134
Paraguay 121, 186, 187, **206, 207, 208**
  wars against 32, 38n[7]
Pardo Bazán, Emilia 45
Paris
  as archetype 24, 46, 64
  Great Exhibition [1900] 46–47, 57
Park, R.E. 12n[2], 73–74

Parker, Barry 59
Parsons, Talcott 89
'participative democracy' [Venezuela] 170
Party of Mexican Revolution 67, 90
Pasolini, Pier Paolo 122
Pastrana, Andrés 168
Paz, Octavio 29, 30, 48, 49
Pedro I 28, 38n[7]
Pedro II 28
Peña Nieto, Enrique 183, 188n[9]
Pereira de Sousa, Washington Luís 69
Pereira Passos, Francisco 35, 56, 83
Pérez, Carlos Andrés ['CAP'] 143, 145, 152, 154, 169
Pérez Galdós, Benito 45
Pérez Jiménez, Marcos 88, 95–96, 102, 111, 116, 132, 135, 137n[13], 188n[4]
peripheral globalization 161–162
Perón, Eva [Evita] Duarte de 91
Perón, Isabel Martínez de 141
Perón, Juan Domingo 88, 90–91, 116, 141, 145, 165, 171
Perroux, François 108, 135
Perry, Clarence 102
Peru
    constitution [1993] 154, 166
    economic reforms 154, 187
    Fujimori's presidency 154
    Humala's administration 186–187
    Human Development Index **208**
    Leguía's regime 51, 69
    Shining Path guerrillas 154, 176
    urban population **206, 207**
    Velasco Alvarado's dictatorship 121, 132, 145
    see also Lima
Philippines, independence 64
Picón Salas, Mariano 63, 66, 70
Piñera, Sebastián 182
Pinochet Ugarte, Augusto 139, 148, 166, 167
Plan Colombia [against drug trafficking] 168, 177
Plan of San Luis [1910] 49
planificación/planejamento 106
Pocaterra, José Rafael 70
Poëte, Marcel 86n[30]
'polarized' city 188n[7]
Pombal, Marquis of 22
poor population's peripheral location 128–129
    causes and manifestations 129–131
    see also shantytowns
Popular Front [Chile] 93
population density
    Caracas 132
    Latin America 15
populism 88, 90–91, 92, 93, 96, 165, 180, 182
    problems arising 139, 185–186
    resurfacing of 12, 164–165
Portales, Diego 26, 139
positivism 24, 51, 77
postcolonial changes 14–17
Potter, R.E. 2, 4, 12n[3]
poverty
    in 1960s/1970s 126
    in 1980s/1990s 157–158, 167, 182
    in 2000s 171, 182, 183, 185, 186, 187
    culture of 127–128
    factors affecting 128, 173
    urban 126, 128, 158
poverty-alleviation programmes 173
Prado, Paulo 14
Prado Júnior, Antônio 82
Prebisch, Raúl 68, 88, 109n[3], 113
Prestes, Luis Carlos 69
Prestes Maia, Francisco 79, 80, 81, 107
private satellite towns 178
privatization programmes 149–150, 151, 152, 171, 176
Prost, Henri 82
'protective constitutions' 166, 188n[2]
public spaces 178–179
    'extraordinary events' in 165, 179
public transport
    bus rapid transit systems 160, 176
    metro systems 156, 176
Puerto Rico, independence 64
Puga Borne, Federico 37
Punta del Este Charter 113, 119
Puntofijo Pact [Venezuela, 1958] 117, 143, 153, 154, 188n[4]
push–pull effect 3, 97

Quadros, Jânio 115

Quevedo, Miguel Ángel 60
Quijano, Aníbal 3, 127
Quiroga, Horacio 86n[23]
Quito [Ecuador], Rocafuerte Street *159*

Radiant City 101
railways
 Latin America 25, 28, 30
 USA 17
Rama, Ángel 11, 45, 74
Ramos, Julio 46, 62n[8]
Rangel, Carlos 122
Ravard, Rafael Alfonzo 135
Rawson, Guillermo 37
Razetti, Luis 53, 60
Reagan, Ronald 144, 145
regional planning 106–108
 in Brazil 107–108
 in Mexico 108
Regional Planning Association of America (RPAA) 107
regional poles of development 133, 135–136
Reissman, Leonard 2, 96
Renan, Ernest 44, 62n[5]
research and development (R&D) budget 181
residential sprawl 57–59
Resnais, Alain 122
Rettig Report 162n[1]
'revolution of expectations' 98–99
Reyes, Alfonso 65
Rio de Janeiro
 Central Avenue 56
 Central Railway Station *28*
 Cidade dos Motores (City of Engines) 100, 104, *105*
 elites' move from central districts 56
 embellishment of central areas 56
 foreign-aided plans 82, 83
 functional modernism 103–104, *104*
 garden suburbs 59
 housing 56, 61, 62
 International Exhibition [1922] 56
 Pereira Passos's schemes 35
 population 16, 28, 54, 87
 relocation programmes 132
 trams 57
 as venue for Portuguese court [1808–1822] 28
Rivas Mercado, Antonio 56
River Plate cities 31
Rivera, Diego 67, 76
road construction [in central areas] 71–72
Roberts, Bryan 7, 128
Roca, Julio 32, 52
Roca–Runciman Treaty [1933] 68
Rockefeller Foundation 85n[3]
Rodó, José Enrique 43–44, 65, 85n[4]
Rodrigues Alves, Francisco 35, 56
Rodríguez, Gumersindo 143
Rodríguez de Francia, José Gaspar 38n[6]
Rodwin, Lloyd 135, 136
Rojas, Ricardo 85n[8]
Rojas Pinilla, Gustavo 94, 102, 114
Romero, José Luis 7–8, 11, 12n[8], 20, 34, 47, 52, 85n[14], 98
Romero, Luis Alberto 185
Roosevelt, Franklin D. 3, 64, 65, 88
Roosevelt, Theodore 17, 40, 41, 43, 63
Roosevelt's Corollary 40, 41–42
Rosario [Argentina] 71
Rosas, Juan Manuel de 18, 20, 21, 25, 38n[7]
Ross Santa María, Gustavo 68
Rostow, Walt Whitman 2, 11, 87, 89–90, 112, 136n[7], 138
Rotival, Maurice 82, 102, 107
Rourke, Thomas 51
Rousseau, Jean-Jacques 122, 188n[2]
Rousseff, Dilma 180, 184
Rúa, Fernando de la 165
Rulfo, Juan 122
rural depopulation [1950s–1970s] 97
rural–urban migration
 causes 71, 131
 and urban poverty 126
 urbanization affected by 3, 54, 71, 97, 155

Sáenz Peña, Roque 52, 67, 70
Saint Simon, Claude Henri 18
Salinas de Gortari, Carlos 150, 167
Salvador de Bahia [Brazil] 28, 60, 79, 108, 174
Sampaio, Carlos 56, 62

Sampaio, Theodoro 60
Samper, Ernesto 168
San José de Costa Rica 55, 57–58, 71
Sandino, Augusto César 64
sanitary reforms 37, 59–61
Santiago de Chile
    Brunner's proposals 72, 84
    city centre [*c.* 1980] *126*
    Costanera Center 178
    embellishment of central areas 57
    ENTEL Tower *156*
    Hausmannesque works 34, 35, *35*
    housing projects 61, 175
    hygiene reforms 60
    metro system 156
    Plan Regulador Intercomunal 133–134
    population 16, 54, 71
    'Problems of Urbanization' conference [1959] 96–97
    rail link with Valparaíso 27
    Santiago Centro building *157*
    shantytown in *130*
    trams 57
    urbanization 125
Santos, Eduardo 94
Santos, Juan Manuel 186
São Paulo
    Bouvard's proposals 57
    control of rents 61
    foreign immigrants 50
    functional modernism 103
    garden cities/suburbs 58, 59
    Jardim America 59
    Light [tram] Station *55*
    metro system 156
    population 54, 87
    Prestes Maia's proposal 8, 79
    trams 57
São Paulo–Minas Gerais hegemony 50, 69
Saravia, Aparicio 52
Sarmiento, Domingo Faustino 18, 19, 20, 23, 30, 31
Sarney, José 141
Sartre, Jean-Paul 122
Satterthwite, David 7
Savage, M. 2
Schade Pohlenz, Alberto 78
Schaedel, Richard 6, 12n[7]
Schlesinger, Arthur 136n[8]

Schmidt, Robert 107
School of Dependence 3, 7, 17, 126–127, 128
    [former] theorist 150, 171
    see also dependency theory
Schumpeter, Joseph 182, 188n[1]
Scipio the African 51
Scruggs, William L. 39, 42
Second-Empire Paris, as archetype 24
'sectorial' city 188n[7]
segregation model 178
Semprún, Jesús 64, 65
Sert, Josep Lluís 99, 102, 105
Seven Years War [1756–1763] 22
shantytowns/squatter settlements 56, 73, 94, 97, 128–129
    causes and manifestations 129–131
    preventive medical care 174
Sierra, Justo 39, 40, 41, 48, 62n[10]
Silva Aristiguieta, A. 10, 13n[11]
Silva, José Asunción 45
Simmel, Georg 77
Siqueiros, David Alfaro 67, 76, *101*
Sitte, Camillo 57, 78, 84
Sjoberg, Gideon 1, 12n[1]
slavery, abolition of 22, 26, 50
social differentiation 73–74
social sciences 77–78
Solano López, Francisco 38n[7]
Somoza dynasty [Nicaragua] 145
Sordo Madaleno, Juan 100
Soria, Alberto 46
Soria, Arturo 57
Southern Cone countries
    bureaucratic–authoritarian regimes 139
    economic growth [mid-20th century] 87
Spain, loss of Latin American territories 65
Spanish–American war [1898] 40, 42
Spencer, Herbert 24, 38n[5], 62n[5], 77
Spengler, Oswald 76, 77
squatter settlements *see* shantytowns
Städtebau representatives 84
    see also Brunner; Hegemann; Sitte; Wagner
Stalinism 122

Standard Oil 85n[3], 91
Statue of Liberty [New York harbour] 44
Stieber, Nancy 5, 6
Stiglitz, Joseph E. 163, 164
Stroessner, Alfredo 121
structural functionalism 89
Stübben, Joseph 81
Subercaseaux, Benjamín 77, 78

Taine, Hippolyte 62n[5]
Téllez, A.S. 13n[10]
tenements 36, 61, 127, 128

Tennessee Valley Authority (TVA) 108
'Tequila crisis [1994] 151, 167
  economic impact 167, 169
territorial restructuring 161
Thatcher, Margaret, Baroness 138, 144, 145–146, 146, 151, 154
Theory of Dependence 3, 7, 17, 115, 126–127
  see also dependency theory; School of Dependence
Third Position [in Argentina] 91
'Third World priests' 121
Third World urbanization 3–4
Tisserand, L.M. 9
Tobar, Carlos 7
Tönnies, Ferdinand 1, 12n[2]
Torres González, Juan José 121
Torres Restrepo, Camilo 121
Torrijos, Omar 145
Touraine, Alain 165
town planning *see* urban planning
Town Planning Associates (TPA) 10, 99–100, 102, *105*
transport infrastructure 160, 176
Treaty of Paris 22
Trujillo, Rafael Leónidas 88, 111
Turbay, Gabriel 94
Turner, Frederick Jackson 17

Ugarte, Manuel 23–24, 64, 85n[4]
under-industrialization 97, 98
unemployment levels 140, 148, 157, 171
UNESCO Cultural Heritage of Humanity, Latin American centres 158
United Fruit Company 63, 112

urban cultural history 5–6
urban planning
  academic and professional breakthroughs 78–80
  Corbusian modernism 83–84
  École Française d'Urbanisme tradition 81–83
  by foreign advisers 81–84
  by indigenous/creole planners 80–81
  Städtebau approach 84
urban population
  listed for various countries **204–207**
  mid-19th century 15–16
  mid-20th century 87, **204–207**
urban poverty 126, 128, 158
urban regeneration 158–160, 174
urban renewal projects 72–73
urban sprawl 57–59
urbanismo 78–85
  replaced by *planificación/planejamento* 106
urbanization
  effects of industrialization 3, 4, 97
  percentage(s) 87, 155, **204–206**
Uribe, Álvaro 186
Uriburu, José Félix 68
Uruguay 52–53, 54, 71, 87, 98, 139, 147, 180, **206**, **207**, **208**
  see also Montevideo
USA
  industrialization and urbanization compared with Latin America 16–17
  interventions in Latin America 39–42, 43, 64
  investments 63
  military interventions 64, 112, 145
  Plan Colombia 168, 177
  shift in attitudes towards 180
  as symbol of democracy 65
Uslar Pietri, Arturo 70, 76, 137n[22]

'Vaccine Revolt' [Rio de Janeiro] 37
Valencia, Guillermo León 114
Vallejo, César 76
Vallenilla Lanz, Laureano 51, 64
Valparaíso [Chile] 26, 27
Vargas, Getúlio 69, 77, 88, 91–92, 132, 149, 165, 172

Vargas Llosa, Mario 122, 137n[19], 148, 151, 154, 166, 180, 183, 186
Vargas Vila, José María 33, 41
Vasconcelos, José 48, 49, 65, 67, 76, 86n[22]
Vázquez, Tabaré 18
vecindades [tenement buildings] 127, 128
Velasco Alvarado, Juan 121, 132, 145
Venezuela
   19th century 32–34
   agrarian reform [1960] 117
   Betancourt's government 116–117
   Black Friday [1983] 143, 152
   Caldera's presidencies 117, 154, 169
   Caracazo riots [1989] 152–153
   Carlos Andrés Pérez's governments 143, 152–154
   Chávez's Bolivarian Revolution 170–171, 185, 186
   Ciudad Guayana project 133, 135–136
   Comisión Nacional de Urbanismo (CNU) 102, 103
   constitution [1947] 70
   constitutional changes [1990s] 161, 165–166
   coups [1992] 153–154
   currency devaluation 143
   Gómez's dictatorship 51–52, 69
   Guzmán's presidencies 33
   homicide rate 177, 188n[10]
   housing shortage [1970] 132
   Human Development Index 185, **208**
   Institute of High Studies on Management (IESA) 152
   loan payments suspended [1900s] 41
   New National Ideal (NIN) doctrine 95, 102
   Pérez Jiménez's dictatorship 88, 95–96, 102, 111
   Puntofijo Pact [1958] 117, 143, 153, 154, 188n[4]
   republics 169, 170, 188n[4]
   revolution [1899] 50
   short-lived democracy [1930s–1940s] 69–70
   social programmes [1990s] 173–174
   urban population **206, 207**
   see also Caracas
Vicuña Mackenna, Benjamín 35
Videla, Jorge 142
Vietnam War 113, 120
"Villa, Pancho" 47, 49
Villa-Lobos, Heitor 77
Villanueva, Carlos Raúl 72, 99, 102, 132
violence in Latin America 176–177
Violich, Francis 102–103

Wagner, Otto 84
Warchavchik, Gregori 103
Warde, A. 2
Washington Consensus 12, 147, 163, 164, 166, 168
welfare states, transition towards 66–70
Weltstädte [world city] 77
'white coffee' policy [Brazil] 50, 69
Wiener, Paul Lester 99, 104, 105
Wilde, Oscar 45
Williamson, Edwin 9, 109n[2]
Wilson, Woodrow 64, 65
World Bank 146, 147, 163, 164
   recommendations [1990s] 164, 173
   reports [quoted] 138, 146–147
World War I, causes and opportunities 65

yellow fever vaccination 37
Young Argentina Association/Generation 18, 21
   Dogma manifesto 18, 21
Yrigoyen, Hipólito 52, 68

Zapata, Emiliano 47, 49
Zedillo, Ernesto 167
Zelaya, Manuel 187
Zumeta, César 43, 44